Excellent English 1
Language Skills for Success

Susannah MacKay
Kristin D. Sherman

Jan Forstrom
Marta Pitt
Shirley Velasco

Teacher's Edition by Kristin D. Sherman

Excellent English 1, Teacher's Edition

Published by McGraw-Hill ESL/ELT, a business unit of The McGraw-Hill Companies, Inc.
1221 Avenue of the Americas, New York, NY 10020. Copyright © 2008 by The McGraw-Hill
Companies, Inc. All rights reserved. No part of this publication may be reproduced or distributed
in any form or by any means, or stored in a database or retrieval system, without the prior written
consent of The McGraw-Hill Companies, Inc., including, but not limited to, in any network or other
electronic storage or transmission, or broadcast for distance learning.

ISBN 13: 978-0-07-719763-6
ISBN 10: 0-07-719763-1
1 2 3 4 5 6 7 8 9 10 VHN 11 10 09

Editorial director: Erik Gundersen
Series editor: Nancy Jordan
Developmental editor: Charlotte Sturdy
Project manager: Kristin Swanson
Cover designer: Witz End Design
Interior designer: NETS
Compositor: NETS

Cover photo:
  Hand: Getty
  Vet: Corbis
  Family with sold sign: Corbis
  Chef: Corbis
  Architect: Corbis
  Pix in Hand: MMH

Contents

Welcome to the Teacher's Edition

The Excellent English Teacher's Edition provides support to teachers using the Excellent English Student Book. Each unit of the Teacher's Edition begins with a list of the unit's lesson titles, the objective(s) for each lesson, the reading and writing strategies, and the Academic and Community Connection activities. Hundreds of additional activities are suggested throughout the Teacher's Edition to expand the use of the target grammar, vocabulary, and life skills in the Student Book.

The Excellent English Teacher's Edition offers clear, step-by-step procedures for each lesson. Seasoned teachers can use the instructions as a quick refresher, while newer teachers, or substitute teachers, can use the instructions as a helpful guide for conducting the Student Book activities in the classroom.

THE TEACHER'S EDITION PROVIDES:

- Step-by-step procedural notes for each Excellent English Student Book activity.
- Over 200 Expansion Activities that offer creative life-skill tasks tied to the activities in each unit, including the Big Picture scenes.
- Warm-up Activities designed to activate background knowledge before each lesson.
- "Big Picture" Expansion Activities that focus on listening, vocabulary, conversation, reading, and writing.
- Worksheets for corresponding Big Picture Expansion Activities.
- Grammar Chart Activities that allow students to practice and explore the material presented in the grammar charts.
- Culture, Grammar, Pronunciation, and Literacy Notes.
- Literacy Development Activities for literacy students.
- Academic Connection Activities that promote academic skills.
- Community Connection Activities that encourage students to become more aware of, and interact more with, their communities.
- Two-page achievement tests for each unit that assess listening, grammar, reading, and vocabulary skills. Listening passages for the tests are provided on the Instructor's Student Book Audio CD.
- Listening scripts for all audio program materials.
- Answer keys for the Student Book, Workbook, and Tests.

Program Overview

Excellent English: Language Skills for Success equips students with the grammar and skills they need to access community resources, while developing the foundation for long-term career and academic success.

Excellent English is a four-level, grammar-based series for English learners featuring a *Grammar Picture Dictionary* approach to vocabulary building and grammar acquisition. An accessible and predictable sequence of lessons in each unit systematically builds language and math skills around life-skill topics. *Excellent English* is tightly correlated to all of the major standards for adult instruction.

What has led the *Excellent English* team to develop this new series? The program responds to the large and growing need for a new generation of adult materials that provides a more academic alternative to existing publications. *Excellent English* is a natural response to the higher level of aspirations of today's adult learners. Stronger reading and writing skills, greater technological proficiency, and a deeper appreciation for today's global economy—increasingly, prospective employees across virtually all industries must exhibit these skill sets to be successful. Interviews with a wide range of administrators, instructors, and students underscore the need for new materials that more quickly prepare students for the vocational and academic challenges they must meet to be successful.

The Complete Excellent English Program

- The **Student Book** features 12 16-page units that integrate listening, speaking, reading, writing, grammar, math, and pronunciation skills with life-skill topics, critical thinking activities, and civics concepts.

- The **Student Book with Audio Highlights** provides students with audio recordings of all of the Grammar Picture Dictionary pages and conversation models in the Student Book.

- The **Workbook with Audio CD** is an essential companion to the Student Book. It provides:

  - Supplementary practice activities correlated to the Student Book.

  - Application lessons that carry vital, standards-based learning objectives through its *Family*

Connection, *Community Connection*, *Career Connection*, and *Technology and You* lessons.

  - Practice tests that encourage students to assess their skills in a low-stakes environment, complete with listening tasks from the Workbook CD.

- The **Teacher's Edition with Tests** provides:

  - Step-by-step procedural notes for each Student Book activity.

  - Expansion Activities for the Student Book, many of which offer creative tasks tied to the "Big Picture" scenes in each unit, including photocopiable worksheets.

  - Culture, Grammar, Vocabulary and Pronunciation Notes.

  - Two-page written test for each unit.

  - Audio scripts for audio program materials.

  - Answer keys for Student Book, Workbook, and Tests.

- The **Interactive Multimedia Program** incorporates and extends the learning goals of the Student Book by integrating language, literacy, and numeracy skill building with multimedia practice on the computer. A flexible set of activities correlated to each unit builds vocabulary, listening, reading, writing, and test–taking skills.

- The **Color Overhead Transparencies** encourage instructors to present new vocabulary and grammar in fun and meaningful ways. This component provides a full color overhead transparency for each of the "Big Picture" scenes, as well as transparencies of the grammar charts in each unit.

- The **Big Picture PowerPoint® CD-ROM** includes the "Big Picture" scenes for all four Student Books. Instructors can use this CD-ROM to project the scenes from a laptop through an LCD or data projector in class.

- The **Audio CDs** and **Audiocassettes** contain recordings for all listening activities in the Student Book. Listening passages for the unit test are provided on a separate Assessment CD or Cassette.

- The **EZ Test® CD-ROM Test Generator** provides a databank of assessment items from which instructors can create customized tests within minutes. The EZ Test assessment materials are also available online at www.eztestonline.com.

Student Book Overview

Consult the *Welcome to Excellent English* guide on pages xiv–xix of the Student Book. This guide offers instructors and administrators a visual tour of one Student Book unit.

Excellent English is designed to maximize accessibility and flexibility. Each unit contains the following sequence of eight two-page lessons that develop vocabulary and build language, grammar, and math skills around life-skill topics:

- Lesson 1: Grammar and Vocabulary (1)
- Lesson 2: Grammar Practice Plus
- Lesson 3: Listening and Conversation
- Lesson 4: Grammar and Vocabulary (2)
- Lesson 5: Grammar Practice Plus
- Lesson 6: Apply Your Knowledge
- Lesson 7: Reading and Writing
- Lesson 8: Career Connection and Check Your Progress

Each lesson in *Excellent English* is designed as a two-page spread. Lessons 1 and 4 introduce new grammar points and vocabulary sets that allow students to practice the grammar in controlled and meaningful ways. Lessons 2 and 5—the Grammar Practice Plus lessons—provide more open-ended opportunities for students to use their new language productively. Lesson 3 allows students to hear a variety of listening inputs and to use their new language skills in conversation. Lesson 6 provides an opportunity for students to integrate all their language skills in a real-life application. In Lesson 7, students develop the more academic skills of reading and writing through explicit teaching of academic strategies and exposure to multiple text types and writing tasks. Each unit ends with Lesson 8, an exciting capstone that offers both *Career Connection*—a compelling "photo story" episode underscoring the vocational objectives of the series—and *Check Your Progress*—a self-evaluation task.

Each lesson addresses a key adult standard, and these standards are indicated in the scope and sequence and in the footer at the bottom of the left-hand page in each lesson.

SPECIAL FEATURES IN EACH STUDENT BOOK UNIT

- **Grammar Picture Dictionary**. Lessons 1 and 4 introduce students to vocabulary and grammar through a picture dictionary approach. This context-rich approach allows students to acquire grammatical structures as they build vocabulary.

- **Grammar Charts**. Also in Lessons 1 and 4, new grammar points are presented in clear paradigms, providing easy reference for students and instructors alike.

- **"Grammar Professor" Notes**. Additional information related to key grammar points is provided at point of use through the "Grammar Professor" feature. A cheerful, red-haired character appears next to each of these additional grammar points, calling students' attention to learning points in an inviting and memorable way.

- **Math**. Learning basic math skills is critically important for success in school, on the job, and at home. As such, national and state standards for adult education mandate instruction in basic math skills. In each unit, a Math box is dedicated to helping students develop the functional numeracy skills they need for success with basic math.

- **Pronunciation**. This special feature has two major goals: (1) helping students hear and produce specific sounds, words, and minimal pairs of words so they become better listeners and speakers; and (2) addressing issues of stress, rhythm, and intonation so that the students' spoken English becomes more comprehensible.

- ***What About You?*** Throughout each unit of the Student Book, students are encouraged to apply new language to their own lives through personalization activities.

- **"Big Picture" Scenes**. Lesson 2 in each unit introduces a "Big Picture" scene. This scene serves as a springboard to a variety of activities provided in the Student Book, Teacher's Edition, Color Overhead Transparencies package and the "Big Picture" PowerPoint CD-ROM. In the Student Book, the "Big Picture" scene features key vocabulary and serves as a prompt for language activities that practice the grammar points of the unit. The scene features characters with distinct personalities for students to enjoy, respond to, and talk about.

- **Career-themed "Photo-Story."** Each unit ends with a compelling "photo story" episode. These four-panel scenes feature chapters in the life of an adult working to take the next step in his or her professional future. In Book 1, we follow Isabel as she identifies the next step she'd like to take in her career and works to get the education and training she needs to move ahead. The engaging photo-story format provides students with role models as they pursue their own career and academic goals.

CIVICS CONCEPTS

Many institutions focus direct attention on the importance on civics instruction for English language learners. Civics instruction encourages students to become active and informed community members. The Teacher's Edition includes multiple *Community Connection* activities in each unit. These activities encourage learners to become more active and informed members of their communities.

ACADEMIC SKILL DEVELOPMENT

Many adult programs recognize the need to help students develop important academic skills that will facilitate lifelong learning. The *Excellent English* Student Book addresses this need through explicit teaching of reading and writing strategies, explicit presentation and practice of grammar, and academic notes in the Teacher's Edition. The Teacher's Edition also includes multiple *Academic Connection* activities in each unit. These activities encourage learners to become more successful in an academic environment.

CASAS, SCANS, EFF, AND OTHER STANDARDS

Instructors and administrators benchmark student progress against national and/or state standards for adult instruction. With this in mind, *Excellent English* carefully integrates instructional elements from a wide range of standards including CASAS, SCANS, EFF, TABE CLAS-E, the Florida Adult ESOL Syllabi, and the Los Angeles Unified School District Course Outlines. Unit-by-unit correlations of some of these standards appear in the Scope and Sequence on pages xv–xix. Other correlations appear in the Teacher's Edition. Here is a brief overview of our approach to meeting the key national and state standards:

- **CASAS**. Many U.S. states, including California, tie funding for adult education programs to students performance on the Comprehensive Adult Student Assessment System (CASAS). The CASAS (www.casas.org) competencies identify more than 30 essential skills that adults need in order to succeed in the classroom, workplace, and community. *Excellent English* comprehensively integrates all of the CASAS Life Skill Competencies throughout the four levels of the series.

- **SCANS**. Developed by the United States Department of Labor, SCANS is an acronym for the Secretary's Commission on Achieving Necessary Skills (wdr.doleta.gov/SCANS/). SCANS competencies are workplace skills that help people compete more effectively in today's global economy. A variety of SCANS competencies is threaded throughout the activities in each unit of *Excellent English*. The incorporation of these competencies recognizes both the intrinsic importance of teaching workplace skills and the fact that many adult students are already working members of their communities.

- **EFF**. Equipped For the Future (EFF) is a set of standards for adult literacy and lifelong learning, developed by The National Institute for Literacy (www.nifl.gov). The organizing principle of EFF is that adults assume responsibilities in three major areas of life: as workers, as parents, and as citizens. These three areas of focus are called "role maps" in the EFF documentation. Each *Excellent English* unit addresses all three of the EFF role maps in the Student Book or Workbook.

- **Florida Adult ESOL Syllabi** provide the curriculum frameworks for all six levels of instruction: Foundations, Low Beginning, High Beginning, Low Intermediate, High Intermediate, and Advanced. The syllabi were developed by the State of Florida as a guide to include the following areas of adult literacy standards: workplace, communication (listen, speak, read, and write), technology, interpersonal communication, health and nutrition, government and community resources, consumer education, family and parenting, concepts of time and money, safety and security, and language development (grammar and pronunciation). *Excellent English* Level 1 incorporates into its instruction the vast majority of standards at the Low Beginning level.

- **TABE Complete Language Assessment System— English (CLAS-E)** has been developed by CTB/McGraw-Hill and provides administrators and teachers with accurate, reliable evaluations of adult students' English language skills. TABE CLAS-E measures students' reading, listening, writing, and speaking skills at all English proficiency levels and also assesses critically important grammar standards. TABE CLAS-E scores are linked to TABE 9 and 10, providing a battery of assessment tools that offer seamless transition from English language to adult basic education assessment.

- **Los Angeles Unified School District (LAUSD) Course Outlines.** LAUSD Competency-Based Education (CBE) Course Outlines were developed to guide teachers in lesson planning and to inform students about what they will be able to do after successful completion of their course. The CBE course outlines focus on acquiring skills in listening, speaking, reading and writing in the context of everyday life. *Excellent English* addresses all four language skills in the contexts of home, community and work, appropriately targeting Beginning Low adult ESL students.

TECHNOLOGY

Technology plays an increasingly important role in our lives as students, workers, family members and citizens.

Every unit in the Workbook includes a two-page lesson titled "Technology and You" that focuses on some aspect of technology in our everyday lives.

Administrators and instructors are encouraged to incorporate interactive tasks from the *Excellent English* Multimedia Program into classroom and/or lab use, as this package includes hours of meaningful technology-based practice of all key Student Book objectives.

The EZ Test® CD-ROM Test Generator—and its online version, available at www.eztestonline.com—allow instructors to easily create customized tests from a digital databank of assessment items.

NUMBER OF HOURS OF INSTRUCTION

The *Excellent English* program has been designed to accommodate the needs of adult classes with 80-180 hours of classroom instruction. Here are three recommended ways in which various components in the **Excellent English** program can be combined to meet student and instructor needs:

- **80-100 hours**. Instructors are encouraged to work through all of the Student Book materials. The Color Overhead Transparencies can be used to introduce and/or review materials in each unit. Instructors should also look to the Teacher's Edition for teaching suggestions and testing materials as necessary. *Time per unit: 8-10 hours.*

- **100-140 hours**. In addition to working through all of the Student Book materials, instructors are encouraged to incorporate the Workbook and the interactive multimedia activities for supplementary practice. *Time per unit: 10-14 hours.*

- **140-180 hours**. Instructors and students working in an intensive instructional setting can take advantage of the wealth of expansion activities threaded through the Teacher's Edition to supplement the Student Book, Workbook, and interactive multimedia materials. *Time per unit: 14-18 hours.*

Teaching Strategies

Approaches to Teaching Grammar

Some students may come from educational settings where English was taught almost exclusively through grammar and vocabulary. Other students may have acquired English through a more communicative approach. *Excellent English* is a grammar-based program that allows students from all backgrounds to feel comfortable as they acquire grammar, along with their other language skills, through *discovery*, *presentation*, *practice* and *production*.

1. DISCOVERY

- **Guided discovery.** Inductive approaches to teaching grammar encourage students to notice how grammar works in practice and figure out the rule for themselves. In *Excellent English,* students have the opportunity to see and hear the grammar structures in context as new vocabulary is presented in the Grammar Picture Dictionary. Students always begin their exposure to a new grammar point with a noticing activity, which focuses students' attention on form and function. Instructors can guide students through the rule discovery process by eliciting ideas about the rules that govern each structure. Many students may prefer that instructors begin with a presentation of the rules. Learners can be encouraged to glean rules on their own by asking questions (e.g., *When do we use an* s *on the end of the verb? With which pronouns?*). Guiding students through focused questioning can facilitate awareness-based understanding of grammar. When students contribute their own ideas, they can become more confident and independent learners.

2. PRESENTATION AND PRACTICE

- **Confirming rules.** Instructors can continue to reinforce grammar awareness through the more deductive approach provided by the grammar charts, which were designed to be clear and easily comprehensible. Teachers should make sure students understand how to navigate the charts in each unit of *Excellent English* and elicit reasons for the way the charts are formatted, making sure students understand that the focus structure is in a different color and the different parts of the sentence are in different columns. The charts can be used as the basis for expansion activities (suggested in the Teacher's Edition) or as a reference point for activities instructors create themselves.

- **Error correction.** When using a grammar-based approach to language learning, there is often a temptation to focus on error correction. However, research suggests that students must go through an interlanguage period, a stage in which their new language will not be perfect, but rather will reflect the transition the learner is going through. A learner may become insecure with too great of a focus on accuracy, and be reluctant to take risks that would allow him or her to become more fluent. *Excellent English* is structured so that students move from very controlled practice of new structures and vocabulary, through more open-ended practice, to more personalized production. Accuracy should be the focus in the very controlled activities, such as fill-in-the-blank, and correction should be immediate and constructive. Grammar should be acquired through productive activities that ask students to use the targeted structures in a meaningful way. When students are using grammar in communicative activities, correction should be limited, or simply noted, and feedback given after the task is completed.

- **Repetition.** Language acquisition, including grammar acquisition, is facilitated through exposure to appropriate input. Research suggests that grammar acquisition is more effective when it is accompanied by vocabulary instruction. Each unit of *Excellent English* allows students to hear, see, and repeat new words and structures numerous times. Students may need more frequent repetition drills to reinforce pronunciation and word order. One way to do this is to say sentences and have the class repeat chorally. Instructors can also use the "Big Picture" transparency to introduce or review grammar points, along with collocational vocabulary.

3. PRODUCTION

- **Communicative tasks.** Grammar should be practiced in the context of communicative tasks. Once students have practiced the structure through controlled activities, they should be encouraged to apply the target structure in more open-ended productive tasks. Later lessons in each unit of *Excellent English* require students to integrate language skills, including grammar, to complete higher–level activities such as role playing and group projects.

Author and educator David Nunan suggests simple teaching strategies for helping students learn and retain new information:

- Emphasize inductive over deductive approaches
- Keep the work load manageable
- Recycle information
- Begin to move learners from doing reproductive activities to being creative with the language
- Personalize grammar and language
- Encourage learners to see grammar as a process

These considerations, along with sound materials for teaching English, help foster an environment for language learning success. (For more information, see *Practical English Language Teaching: Grammar* by David Nunan (McGraw-Hill).)

Approaches to Teaching Workplace and Vocational ESL

Excellent English has many features that make it an ideal text for use in workplace/VESL classrooms. The reading and writing activities, the vocabulary, the *Career Connection* dialogs, and the technology in the Workbook especially prepare students to learn and understand new work-related terms and scenarios with confidence. These activities, combined with an instructor's guidance on personalizing the vocabulary and workplace situations, will engage students and help them learn and master the content they need most. The students will become productive and satisfied employees, managers, and employers.

When customizing *Excellent English* for use in your Workplace ESL class, consider the following suggestions:

- **Personalize the vocabulary.** Encourage learners to keep a vocabulary notebook for the words and terms found in the Student Book, for words that they hear in everyday life, and for words and phrases they hear and see on the job. Invite students to bring in questions about terms and words, then practice using the new vocabulary in sentences and in conversations. In addition, encourage students to bring in realia they see in everyday life and at their places of work. Have students practice reading and understanding all of the information in their surroundings.

- **Personalize the dialogs.** Communication is a very important skill for workplace success and safety. If there are key industries or employers in your area, use the model dialogs in the Student Book as jumping off points for conversations that might occur in certain industries or sectors.

- **Discuss common and specific work issues.** The *Career Connection* photo story at the end of each unit provides a springboard for discussion in a Workplace ESL class. The characters are in positive workplace environments and are effectively using resources to do well in their jobs and careers. Use these stories to encourage students to talk about situations they have experienced or want to experience.

- **Use all of the components of *Excellent English*.** In addition to the solid curriculum in the Student Book, it is ideal to have students use the Workbook to further strengthen their skills. The Workbook includes application lessons that carry vital, standards-based learning objectives through its *Family Connection, Community Connections, Career Connection,* and *Technology Connections* lessons.

The *Excellent English* series equips students with the grammar and skills they need to access community resources, while developing the foundation for long-term career and academic success.

Additional Resources

REFERENCE TITLES AVAILABLE FROM MCGRAW–HILL:

- **Teaching Adult ESL**, Betsy Parrish
- **Practical English Language Teaching: Grammar**, David Nunan

WEBSITES FOR GRAMMAR:

- http://www.ohiou.edu/esl/english/grammar/activities.html
- http://iteslj.org/links/ESL/Grammar_and_English_Usage/
- http://www.eslcafe.com/search/Grammar/
- http://www2.gsu.edu/~wwwesl/egw/eslgract.htm
- http://w2.byuh.edu/academics/languagecenter/CNN-N/CNN-N.html

WEBSITE FOR VESL/CAREER RESOURCES

- http://eff.cls.utk.edu/fundamentals/role_map_worker.htm

Assessment

The *Excellent English* program offer instructors, students, and administrators the following wealth of resources for monitoring and assessing student progress and achievement:

- **Standardized Testing Formats.** *Excellent English* is comprehensively correlated to the CASAS competencies and all of the other major national and state standards for adult learning. Students have the opportunity to practice the types of skills that will help them succeed on the CASAS tests.

- **End–of–Unit Tests.** The *Excellent English* Teacher's Edition includes end-of-unit tests. These paper-and-pencil tests help students demonstrate how well they have learned the instructional content of the unit. Each unit test includes five CASAS-style listening comprehension questions, five reading comprehension questions, five writing questions and 10 grammar questions. Practice with these question types will help prepare students who may want to enroll in academic classes.

- **Performance-based Assessment.** *Excellent English* provides several ways to measure students' performance on productive tasks, including the *Writing* tasks in Lesson 7 of each Student Book unit. In addition, the Teacher's Edition suggests writing and speaking prompts that instructors can use for performance-based assessment. These prompts derive from the Big Picture scene in each unit and provide rich visual input as the basis for the speaking and writing tasks asked of the students.

- **Portfolio Assessment.** A portfolio is a collection of student work that can be used to show progress. Examples of work that the instructor or the student may submit in the portfolio include writing samples, speaking rubrics, audiotapes, videotapes, or projects.

- **Self-assessment.** Self-assessment is an important part of the overall assessment picture, as it promotes students' involvement and commitment to the learning process. When encouraged to assess themselves, students take more control of their learning and are better able to connect the instructional content with their own goals. The Student Books include *Check Your Progress* activities at the end of each unit, which allow students to assess their knowledge of vocabulary and grammar. Students can chart their mastery of the key language lessons in the unit, and use this information to set new learning goals.

- **Other Linguistic and Non-linguistic Outcomes.** Traditional testing often does not account for the progress made by adult learners with limited educational experience or low literacy levels. Such learners tend to take longer and make smaller language gains, so the gains they make in other areas are often more significant. These gains may be in areas such as self-esteem, goal clarification, learning skills, and access to employment, community involvement, and further academic studies. The SCANS and EFF standards identify areas of student growth that are not necessarily language–based. *Excellent English* is correlated with both SCANS and EFF standards. Every unit in the Student Book and/or Workbook contains a lesson that focuses on the EFF roles of worker, family member, and community member. Like the Student Book, the Workbook includes activities that may provide documentation that can be added to a student portfolio.

- **EZ Test® CD-ROM Test Generator and EZ Test Online.** In addition to the reproducible unit tests found in the Teacher's Edition of *Excellent English*, instructors can use the EZ Test® CD-ROM Test Generator to easily create customized, paper-based tests from a digital databank of assessment items. Instructors can select question items from book-specific test banks and also augment these items with their own questions. Multiple versions of any test can be created so instructors can give different versions of the same test to different sections of students, or use these different versions within the same classroom. Answers keys are also automatically created. In addition, instructors can access *Excellent English* assessment materials through EZ Test Online (www.eztestonline.com). After registering for this testing service, instructors can create and deliver tests online and export their tests for use with course management systems such as Blackboard or save them for future use.

  EZ Test supports the use of following question types:
  - True or False
  - Yes or No
  - Multiple Choice
  - Fill in the Blank
  - Matching
  - Short Answer
  - Essay

Create EZ Tests for each Unit of Excellent English

Choose the questions.

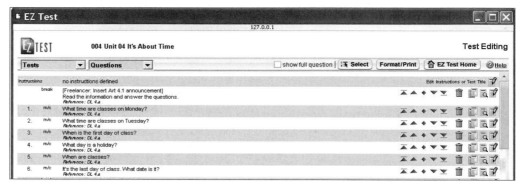

Preview the test.

Print the test!

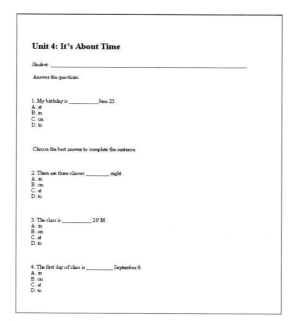

About the Authors

Kristin Sherman has 15 years of teaching experience in both credit and non-credit ESL programs. She has taught general ESL as well as classes focusing on workplace skills and literacy. In academic ESL programs, Kristin has taught in all skill areas and at all levels of proficiency. She has authored many ESL publications, including student books, teacher's editions, workbooks, and assessment tools. Her favorite project was the creation of a reading and writing workbook with her ESL students at the Mecklenburg County Jail in North Carolina.

Susannah MacKay has taught and served as a teacher trainer in community adult programs, community colleges, and secondary schools. Susannah especially enjoys her work developing materials for English instruction and has experience as both a writer and an editor of student books, teacher's editions, online learning components, and assessment tools. She has contributed to projects at all levels and in all skill areas, though she particularly enjoys literacy, reading, writing, and grammar. One of Susannah's most gratifying projects was piloting and launching a materials project for community-supported instruction centers across the Atlanta, Georgia metropolitan area.

Shirley Velasco is currently the principal for Miami Beach Adult and Community Education Center in Miami Beach, FL. She has been involved in education for over 28 years, and created a large adult ESOL program based on a curriculum developed to implement state and national standards. An author and consultant for several McGraw-Hill ESOL programs, she holds a Bachelor's degree from Barry University and a Master's degree in Educational Leadership from Nova Southeastern University.

CONSULTANTS:

Jan Forstrom is the EL Civics Coordinator at San Diego Community College District Continuing Education. She was recently elected to the California State CATESOL board and currently serves as assistant chair for adult–level ESL. She holds a Bachelor's degree in French and Education from Trinity College in Illinois and has 25 years' experience teaching adult ESL classes at a variety of levels. Jan is a frequent conference presenter at regional, state and national conferences on topics related to EL Civics and assessment. Jan co-authored *Contemporary English Book 2, Revised Edition* (McGraw-Hill 2002).

Marta Pitt is the ESOL, ABE, and GED Department Chair at Lindsey Hopkins Technical Education Center in Miami, Florida. She has been a classroom French and ESOL instructor and Department Chair for the past 32 years. Marta is fluent in Spanish, French, and Italian.

Student Book Scope and Sequence

Unit	Grammar	Vocabulary	Listening/ Speaking/ Pronunciation	Reading	Writing
Pre-Unit *page 2*	• Parts of speech (nouns, verbs, adjectives) • Pronouns	• Alphabet • Greetings • Numbers	• Follow classroom directions • Spell your name aloud	• Read sentences about school	• Write the names of your classmates
1 **All About You** *page 6*	• Simple present of *be*: Statements • Singular and plural nouns • Irregular plural nouns • Contractions • *a/an*	• Personal information • Countries • Occupations • Addresses	• Tell where people are from • Introduce yourself • Talk in a small group • Discuss occupations • Ask for and give personal information • **Pronunciation**: *Teens* vs. *ty's* (*fourteen* vs. *forty*) / Stress in numbers	• Read personal information forms • Read a personal letter • Identify capital letters in names	• Write about occupations • Complete forms • Write your name and address on an envelope • Use capital letters with: first names, streets, cities, the first letter of a sentence and salutations
2 **People** *page 22*	• *Yes/No* questions with simple present of *be* • Possessive adjectives • Possessives of nouns • Subject pronouns	• Personal characteristics • Physical appearance • Family members	• Describe physical appearance • Identify family members • Interpret a chart • Take and leave phone messages • **Pronunciation**: *Is he* vs. *Is she*	• Read about a family • Transcribe and read messages • Read a personal story • Use pictures to think about text	• Write about your family • Make a list to get ideas for writing
3 **At School** *page 38*	• *There is/There are* • Prepositions of location • Questions with *How Many*	• Classroom objects • Classroom furniture • School supplies • Library facilities • Directions and signs	• Tell about classroom objects • Name school supplies • Ask about library facilities • Listen to a phone conversation • Describe locations at school • Ask for and give directions at school • **Pronunciation**: Stress in compound nouns	• Examine a map of a school • Read a sign • Collect information from a website • Take notes on a diagram	• Complete a sign with information • Use correct punctuation • Capitalize the first letter of a sentence • Use periods or question marks
4 **It's About Time!** *page 54*	• *It's* with weather • Information questions (*What time, When*) with simple present of *be* • Prepositions of time (review)	• Weather words • Temperatures • Seasons • Months • Times • U.S. holidays • Ordinal numbers	• Describe weather and seasons • Listen to a weather report • Ask about and tell the time • Discuss holidays at work • **Pronunciation**: Ordinal numbers	• Read a pie chart • Read and understand a school calendar • Understand and write an email message • Locate important details before you read	• Write the time • Make a school calendar • Write about the weather

Civics/Lifeskills	Math	Critical Thinking	Correlations		
			CASAS Life Skill Competencies	SCANS Competencies	EFF Content Standards
• Follow directions	• Learn numbers 1-20	• Name the letters of the alphabet • Recognize numbers from 1-20	**1:** 0.1.1 **1:** 0.1.4 **1:** 0.1.5 **1:** 6.0.1	• Interpret and communicate information	• Listen actively • Speak so others can understand
• Address envelopes • Learn about community workers • Complete a school registration form • Read information from a Social Security card and employee badge	• Understand and pronounce numbers • Complete personal forms using numbers • Recognize patterns in forms	• Analyze information • Practice small talk • Relate to jobs	**1:** 0.2.1 **2:** 0.1.2 **3:** 0.1.4 **4:** 4.1.8 **5:** 0.1.2 **6:** 0.2.2 **7:** 0.2.3	• Acquire and evaluate information • Interpret and communicate information • Work with cultural diversity	• Convey ideas in writing • Resolve conflict and negotiate • Use math to solve problems and communicate • Learn through research
• Give and take a phone message • Have conversations at work	• Interpret a height chart • Say telephone numbers	• Describe yourself • List your ideas about a story • Compose a message • Review a telephone message	**1:** 0.1.2 **2:** 0.1.2, 0.1.4 **3:** 2.7.6 **4:** 0.1.4 **5:** 0.1.4, 6.6.1 **6:** 2.1.7, 2.1.8 **7:** 0.1.2, 0.2.4	• Understand systems • Apply technology to task • Participate as a member of a team	• Read with understanding • Convey ideas in writing • Cooperate with others • Reflect and evaluate
• Use library resources • Locate school facilities • Read a map to find places in a school	• Use multiplication to answer questions about classroom items • Locate room numbers in a building • Read enrollment and school statistics	• Identify classroom objects • Locate school facilities • Find your way around campus	**2:** 6.1.3 **3:** 2.1.8, 2.5.6 **4:** 2.2.1 **5:** 2.5.5 **6:** 2.5.4	• Organize and maintain information • Monitor and correct performance	• Speak so others can understand • Listen actively • Cooperate with others • Take responsibility for learning
• Communicate information about the weather • Listen to a weather report • Read a school schedule • Practice a conversation about school holidays	• Read a pie chart about the weather • Understand Celsius and Fahrenheit temperatures • Ask about and tell the time • Interpret a school calendar • Ordinal numbers Write dates	• Predict tomorrow's weather • Assess today's weather • Examine calendars • Compose schedules	**1:** 2.3.3, 5.7.3 **2:** 2.3.3 **3:** 1.1.5 **4:** 2.3.1 **5:** 2.3.2, 2.7.1 **6:** 2.5.5, 2.7.1 **7:** 0.2.3	• Interpret and communicate information • Understand systems	• Convey ideas in writing • Observe critically • Learn through research • Use information technology and communications

Unit	Grammar	Vocabulary	Listening/ Speaking/ Pronunciation	Reading	Writing
5 **In the Community** *page 70*	• Prepositions of location, Part 2 • Imperatives	• Places in the community • Direction words • Traffic signs	• Ask and answer questions about locations in the community • Give directions to places in the community • Discuss educational opportunities • **Pronunciation**: Sentence stress on important words	• Interpret a map • Understand traffic signs • Read a brochure • Look for headlines before you read	• Write directions to a place in the community • Write about a place in your city • Give details when you write
6 **Shopping** *page 86*	• Present Continuous statements • *How Much* questions with simple present of *be* • Demonstratives: *This/That/These/ Those*	• Clothing items • Colors • Clothing sizes • U.S. coins and bills • Prices	• Ask and answer questions about clothing • Describe clothing colors and sizes • Ask about prices • Listen to conversations about prices • Listen to an advertisement • **Pronunciation**: *t* in *isn't, aren't*	• Understand a consumer article • Use the words under pictures to learn information	• Create a shopping list for clothes • Write a personal check • Use quotes in writing • Make a budget
7 **Daily Routines** *page 102*	• Simple present statements • Adverbs of frequency *Yes/No* questions in the simple present	• Daily activities • Days of the week • Times of day	• Listen and report about people's daily routines • Talk about schedules • Discuss your daily routine • **Pronunciation**: *Does he/Does she*	• Interpret a work schedule • Scan for important information • Read an article about parenting • Look for numbers to learn important information	• Write a Saturday schedule • Write about your daily routine • Use *first, next, then,* and *last* to put activities in order
8 **Let's Eat!** *page 118*	• Count and non-count nouns • Simple present with *need* and *want* • Information questions (*where, when,* and *what*) with simple present • Connecting words (*and, but*)	• Foods • Food groups • Container words • Measure words • Weights • Menu sections	• Talk about your favorite foods • Talk about food prices at the supermarket • Order food from a menu • Ask for and give locations in a store • Make plans at work • **Pronunciation**: /I/ vs. /i/ (*it* vs. *eat*)	• Read and understand a menu • Read about foods in other countries • Notice connecting words (*and, but*)	• Write about foods and drinks you buy • Write about your eating habits • Write amounts of weights and measures • Use a Venn diagram to compare foods • Use *and* and *but* to connect sentences

Civics/Lifeskills	Math	Critical Thinking	Correlations		
			CASAS Life Skill Competencies	SCANS Competencies	EFF Content Standards
• Describe people and places in the community • Follow directions to places around town	• Calculate distance using a map	• Memorize traffic signs • Recall directions • Report an accident	1: 2.2.1 2: 2.5.1, 2.6.2 3: 2.5.3, 2.6.1 4: 2.2.1 5: 2.2.1, 2.2.2 6: 2.2.5 7: 2.5.1	• Teach others • Exercise leadership • Work with cultural diversity • Apply technology to task	• Read with understanding • Listen actively • Guide others • Use information technology and communications
• Choose the correct clothes for an occasion • Shop for clothes and accessories	• Identify U.S. coins and bills • Ask about prices • Write the price of items • Interpret a receipt • Write a personal check • Make a budget	• Select clothing styles • Evaluate quality • Choose size • Compare prices	1: 0.1.2 2: 0.1.2 3: 1.3.7, 1.3.9 4: 1.1.6 5: 1.2.1, 1.6.4 6: 1.2.1, 1.8.1 7: 1.2.1	• Allocate money • Acquire and evaluate information • Negotiate	• Read with understanding • Observe critically • Advocate and influence • Use math to solve problems and communicate
• Plan by scheduling • Calculate your pay according to your work schedule	• Use time for daily schedule • Compute hourly wages	• Apply job routines • Choose a schedule • Distinguish family and job routines • Answer questions about a pay stub	1: 0.2.4 2: 2.3.1, 2.3.2 3: 2.3.1 4: 0.2.1 5: 0.2.4 6: 4.2.1, 4.4.3 7: 0.2.4	• Allocate time • Allocate material and facility resources • Interpret and communicate information • Participate as a member of a team	• Listen actively • Solve problems and make decisions • Plan • Use math to solve problems and communicate
• Practice grocery shopping • Read and order from a menu • Prepare food for a business meeting	• Listen and write about food prices • Compare prices at the grocery store • Use weights and measurements in recipes	• Interpret unfamiliar foods • Calculate your share of lunch • Experiment with new menu items • Test a recipe • Judge quality and price of food	1: 1.3.8 2: 1.2.1, 1.3.8 3: 1.2.1, 1.3.8 4: 0.1.2 5: 0.1.2, 1.1.1 6: 1.2.2, 1.3.8 7: 2.7.2, 2.7.3	• Allocate time • Allocate material and facility resources • Organize and maintain information	• Speak so others can understand • Guide others • Take responsibility for learning • Reflect and evaluate

Unit	Grammar	Vocabulary	Listening/ Speaking/ Pronunciation	Reading	Writing
9 **Skills and Work** *page 134*	• Past tense statements • Regular past tense verbs • Irregular past tense verbs • *Can* for ability	• Job skills • Occupations • Parts of a pay stubs • Job advertisement abbreviations • Job application headings	• Talk about your abilities • Listen to descriptions of other people's jobs • Listen to a job interview • Practice job interviews • **Pronunciation**: *Can* vs. *can't*	• Read about jobs • Read a pay stub • Interpret job ads, understand the abbreviations • Use headings to find information	• Write about your abilities • Write about job skills • Fill out a job application • Edit important documents and forms
10 **Taking a Trip** *page 150*	• Simple past of *be*: Statements • Questions with the simple past of *be* • Adjectives	• Transportation (forms of) • Adjectives to describe travel • Travel problems • Recreation locations	• Talk about a trip • Talk about a bus schedule • Apologize for being late • Answer questions about yourself • Listen to an advertisement • Talk about advertisements • **Pronunciation**: Interjections	• Examine a bus schedule • Read an email • Read about a weather emergency • Use context to understand meaning	• Write about a vacation • Edit your writing for correct verb forms
11 **Health Matters** *page 166*	• *Should* for advice • Simple present of *have*	• Health problems • Parts of the body • Remedies • Health habits	• Describe people's feelings • Listen to telephone messages • Call in sick to work • Talk about health problems and remedies • Describe health problems to a doctor • **Pronunciation**: *Should/shouldn't*	• Read an appointment and an insurance card • Read about healthy habits • Use pictures to guess the meaning of new words	• Write a conversation you just heard • Write about health problems and remedies • Write advice for health problems • Indent a paragraph
12 **Planning Ahead** *page 182*	• *Be going to* for future: Statements • Object Pronouns • Questions with *Be Going To*	• Life milestones • Furniture appliances • Rooms of a house • Household repairs and improvements	• Talk about your future plans • Communicate with a landlord • Extend an invitation • **Pronunciation**: *Gonna* (for *going to*)	• Read and understand housing ads • Read about the three steps to change • Look at a title before reading a passage	• Write a to–do list • Write sentences about your plans • Use examples to make your writing interesting

Appendices

Civics/Lifeskills	Math	Critical Thinking	Correlations		
			CASAS Life Skill Competencies	SCANS Competencies	EFF Content Standards
• Read job ads • Complete a job application • Participate in an interview	• Interpret a pay stub • Read hourly pay	• Write a resume • Operate productively • Express employment related goals	**1:** 4.1.8 **2:** 4.1.8 **3:** 4.1.6 **4:** 4.6.4, 4.6.5 **5:** 4.2.1, 4.6.5 **6:** 4.1.3, 4.1.5 **7:** 4.1.2	• Allocate human resources • Serve clients or customers • Negotiate • Improve and design systems	• Speak so others can understand • Cooperate with others • Resolve conflict and negotiate • Reflect and evaluate
• Read an email • Interpret train schedules • Read vacation ads	• Understand a bus schedule • Understand a train schedule • Calculate travel times and cost using public transit	• Prepare according to train schedule • Arrange for emergencies • Compare fares • Schedule a vacation	**1:** 2.2.3 **2:** 0.1.2 **3:** 2.1.7, 4.6.4 **4:** 0.1.3, 0.2.4 **5:** 2.2.4 **6:** 0.2.1, 1.2.1 **7:** 2.3.3	• Allocate time • Allocate material and facility resources • Teach others • Improve and design systems	• Resolve conflict and negotiate • Solve problems and make decisions • Take responsibility for learning • Learn through research
• Read medicine labels • Complete a patient information form • Read appointment and insurance cards • Visit the doctor	• Understand time on an appointment card • Understand an insurance card	• Recognize symptoms • Classify diseases • Define good health habits	**1:** 3.1.1 **2:** 0.1.2, 3.1.1 **3:** 2.1.7, 2.1.8 **4:** 3.1.3 **5:** 1.4.1, 1.5.2 **6:** 1.4.2 **7:** 3.5.2, 3.5.5	• Allocate money • Organize and maintains information	• Observe critically • Guide others • Advocate and influence • Solve problems and make decisions
• Read housing ads • Plan for the future • Find housing in the community	• Interpret a calendar • Interpret a timeline • Add, subtract and divide numbers	• Discuss a rental lease • Explain timelines • Develop a floor plan	**1:** 0.1.2 **2:** 0.1.6, 7.1.4 **3:** 7.2.7 **4:** 1.4.1, 1.5.2 **5:** 1.4.1, 7.4.3 **6:** 1.4.2 **7:** 7.1.2, 7.1.4	• Allocate money • Acquire and evaluate information • Exercise leadership	• Advocate and influence • Solve problems and make decisions • Plan • Use information technology and communications

PRE-UNIT: Letters and Numbers

OBJECTIVE

Understand and say letters, numbers, and classroom directions

VOCABULARY

the alphabet	directions
numbers 1–20, 30, 40, 50, 60, 70, 80, 90, 100	listen
	open your book
	raise your hand
a noun: a book, a school, a teacher	read
	sit down
a pronoun: I, you, he she, it, we, you, they	stand up
	take out a pen
a verb: read, study, talk	turn to page 15
an adjective: happy, sad, tall	write your name

GRAMMAR

Parts of speech

COMPETENCIES

Spell names
Follow directions in class

WARM-UP ACTIVITY: Say your name

- Write *Hello. My name is* _____ on the board.
- Gesture to yourself and say your name (e.g., *Hello. My name is* _____.).
- Go around the class and have students say their names.

🎧 **1 LISTEN** and repeat the letters.

- Have students open their books and look at the letters.
- Play the CD or say the alphabet. Have students look at the letters and repeat.
- Play the CD again and have students point to the letters.

EXPANSION ACTIVITY: Point

- Copy the alphabet on the board.
- Have a volunteer come to the board. Say several letters in random order and have the students point to the letters on the board.
- Repeat with other students until students seem to be very familiar with the alphabet.

🎧 **2 LISTEN** and repeat the numbers.

- Have students open their books and look at the numbers.
- Play the CD or say the numbers. Have students look at the numbers and repeat.
- Play the CD again and have students point to the numbers.

EXPANSION ACTIVITY: Number recognition

- Write 20 numbers between 1 and 100 on the board in random order.
- Call on students and point to a number and elicit its name.

🎧 **3 LISTEN** and read.

- Direct students' attention to the picture. Point out or elicit that the women are meeting each other.
- Play the CD or say the conversation and have students follow along silently.
- Play the CD again and have students repeat.

4 TALK to four classmates. Write their names.

- Model the activity with a more advanced student. Have the students read A's lines, but use their own name. Respond with your own name and how to spell it. Switch roles.
- Call on students and ask them to spell their names.
- Have students talk to four classmates and write their names.

Classroom Directions

5 GRAMMAR PICTURE DICTIONARY. Listen and read.

- Direct students' attention to the pictures.
- Play the CD or read the directions and have students follow along silently.
- Play the CD again and have students repeat.
- Say the directions in random order and have students point.

6 TALK. Read the sentences to a partner. Your partner does the actions.

- Model the activity with a more advanced student. Take turns giving and following directions.
- Put students in pairs to take turns giving and following directions.

Grammar: Parts of Speech

1 LISTEN and repeat.

- Direct students' attention to the grammar picture charts.
- Play the CD and have students repeat. Make sure students understand the three different types of words presented: nouns as people, places, or things; verbs as actions; and adjectives as describing nouns. If necessary, demonstrate the words.

Pronouns

- Direct students' attention to the pronoun picture charts.
- Point to each pronoun and illustrate it by pointing to people in the class.

2 LISTEN and repeat the sentences.

- Direct students' attention to the chart of sentences.
- Play the CD and have students repeat.
- Put students in pairs to take turns reading the sentences aloud.

UNIT 1 All About You

Unit Overview

LESSON	OBJECTIVES	STUDENT BOOK	WORKBOOK
1 Grammar and Vocabulary 1	Make statements with *be* Give personal information	p. 6	p. 6
2 Grammar Practice Plus	Make statements with *be* Tell where people are from	p. 8	p. 7
3 Listening and Conversation	Introduce yourself Understand and pronounce numbers	p. 10	p. 8
4 Grammar and Vocabulary 2	Talk about occupations Use singular and plural nouns	p. 12	p. 10
5 Grammar Practice Plus	Use irregular plural nouns Talk about occupations and countries	p. 14	p. 11
6 Apply Your Knowledge	Ask for and give personal information Complete personal forms	p. 16	p. 12
7 Reading and Writing	Read a personal letter Address an envelope	p. 18	p. 14
• Career Connection	Identify forms of identification for employment	p. 20	p. 16
• Check Your Progress	Monitor progress	p. 21	p. 18

Reading/Writing Strategies

- Scan for names
- Use capital letters

Connection Activities

LESSON	TYPE	SKILL DEVELOPMENT
1	Community	Write names
2	Community	Locate places on a map
3	Academic	Identify capital cities
4	Community	Identify jobs and locations
6	Community	Get forms

WORKSHEET #/FOCUS	TITLE	TEACHER'S EDITION
1 Grammar	Using Singular and Plural Nouns	p. 246
2 Writing	Letters	p. 247

LESSON 1: Grammar and Vocabulary

OBJECTIVES

Make statements with *be*
Give personal information

VOCABULARY

address	single
email address	students
first name	teachers
last name	telephone number
married	zip code

GRAMMAR

Affirmative statements with *be*

COMPETENCIES

Identify first and last names, state name of
  self and others
Identify simple addresses

WARM-UP ACTIVITY: **Give your personal information**

- Write the words from this lesson on the board.
- Tell and write your personal information on the board. Gesture to yourself as you say your first and last name. Say you are a teacher.

🎧 ❶ GRAMMAR PICTURE DICTIONARY. Listen and repeat.

- Have students open their books and look at the pictures. Ask: *What do you see?* Write all the words the students know on the board.
- Have students look at the pictures and listen while you say the sentences or play the CD. Have students repeat in the pause.
- Call on students. Say a word or phrase from Activity 1 (e.g., *first name*). Elicit the information from the student.

EXPANSION ACTIVITY: **Beanbag toss**

- Model the activity. Call on a student and toss a ball or beanbag. Say one of the new words (e.g., *address*). After the student has caught the beanbag, elicit the information for the student.
- Continue until everyone has had a chance to participate. For more advanced classes, you may want to have students call on their classmates, taking turns saying words and eliciting opposites.

❷ NOTICE THE GRAMMAR. Look at Activity 1. Circle *am*, *is*, and *are*.

- Have students read the sentences and circle *am*, *is* and *are*.

ANSWER KEY

1. My first name (is) Diana. My last name (is) Montego.
2. My address (is) 351 East 4th Street, Washington, D.C.
3. My zip code (is) 20021.
4. My telephone number (is) (202) 555-4376.
5. My email address (is) dmontego27@college.edu.
6. I (am) single.
7. We (are) students.
8. Mr. and Mrs. Green (are) my teachers.
9. They (are) married.

EXPANSION ACTIVITY: Replace the word

- Give students two minutes to review the sentences.
- Have students close their books.
- Write the sentences on the board, but leave out all forms of the verb *be*.
- Elicit the missing words from the students.
- Have students open their books and confirm their answers.

GRAMMAR CHART: Affirmative Statements with *Be*

- Direct students' attention to the chart.
- Go over the information on the chart, including the usage note. You may want to read each sentence, pausing to have students repeat.
- Go over the contractions. Make sure students understand they are short forms, but mean the same thing as the long forms.

CHART EXPANSION ACTIVITY: Contractions

- Say each subject pronoun and make sure students understand what it refers to.
- Say each subject pronoun again and elicit the appropriate form of *be*.
- Say long forms (e.g., *She is*) and elicit the contraction (*She's*).

❸ **WRITE.** Complete the sentences. Use *am*, *is*, or *are*.

- Direct students' attention to the form. Make sure students know that Sam is giving his personal information.
- Go over the directions. Say *My name* and pause. Elicit *am*, *is* or *are*. Point out that *is* is written on the line.
- Have students complete the sentences with *am*, *is* or *are*.

- Put students in pairs to compare answers.
- Go over the answers with the class.

EXPANSION ACTIVITY: Read the form

- Direct students' attention to the form.
- Elicit other information (e.g., *first name*, *last name*, *city*, *zip code*).

❹ **WHAT ABOUT YOU?** Complete the sentences about you.

- Model the activity. Write the sentences starters on the board. Say your information and write it on the board to complete the sentences.
- Point to the students and have them complete the sentences.
- Walk around to monitor the activity and provide help as needed.
- Go over the information in the speech bubble.
- Put students in pairs to share their information, using the speech bubble as a model.
- Call on students to tell the class about themselves.

COMMUNITY CONNECTION: Write the name

- For an out-of-class assignment, have students find out and write the name, country of origin, and profession of one other person, not in their family.
- Call on students and elicit the name and its spelling.

LESSON 2: Grammar Practice Plus

OBJECTIVES

Make statements with *be*
Tell where people are from

VOCABULARY

China	Mexico
Colombia	Somalia
Cuba	the United States
Korea	

GRAMMAR

Negative statements with *be*

COMPETENCIES

Identify country of origin

WARM-UP ACTIVITY: Countries

- Bring in a map of the world.
- Write *I am from* _____ on the board.
- Point to yourself and say *I am from* _____ (the name of your country).
- Point to a more advanced student and ask *country*? Elicit the sentence with the appropriate completion.
- Go around the room eliciting the students' countries. It is not important that they know all the countries yet, just that they identify their own.

GRAMMAR CHART: Negative Statements with *Be*

- Go over the information in the chart. You may want to say each sentence and have students repeat. Go over the negative contractions.

CHART EXPANSION ACTIVITY: Fill it in

- If you have a pocket chart (available in teaching supply stores), write the following on strips: *I, You, He, She, it, We, You, They, am, are, is, not, from the United States*. Set the strips in the chart to create sentences with the negative forms of *be* missing.
- If you don't have a pocket chart, write all the subject pronouns on the board, leave a space and then write *from the United States*.
- Give students a couple of minutes to study the chart in their books.
- Call volunteers to the board to complete the sentences with the appropriate form of *be* and *not*. Have the class correct the sentences if necessary.

❶ WRITE. Complete the sentences. Use *am not*, *is not*, or *are not*.

- Go over the directions and the example.
- Have students write the negative forms of *be* on the lines to complete the sentences.
- Put students in pairs to compare answers.
- Go over the answers with the class.
- Optional: have students redo the activity using contractions.

ANSWER KEY

1. is not; **2.** are not; **3.** is not; **4.** are not;
5. are not; **6.** am not; **7.** is not; **8.** are not

EXPANSION ACTIVITY: Beanbag toss

- Review the guidelines for this activity (from Lesson 1).
- Call on a student, toss the beanbag, and say the first sentence of one of the items in Activity 1. Elicit the negative sentence.
- Continue until everyone has had a chance to participate. For more advanced classes, you may want to have students call on their classmates, taking turns saying words and eliciting opposites.

2 WHAT ABOUT YOU? Complete the chart. Use the words in the box.

- Go over the directions and the example.
- Go over the words in the box.
- Have students fill in the chart with words and phrases that describe them.
- Put students in pairs to say what they are and are not.
- Call on students to say one sentence with *I am* and one with *I'm not*.

EXPANSION ACTIVITY: *Yes/No* cards

- Distribute two index cards to every student.
- Have students write *yes* on one card and *no* on the other.
- Say a sentence (e.g., *I'm single.*). Have students hold up the *yes* card if they are single and the *no* card if they are not single.
- Continue with other sentences.

LITERACY DEVELOPMENT NOTE

Literacy students may have trouble seeing the apostrophe as a punctuation mark rather than a letter. You may want literacy students to copy the contractions into their notebooks to practice making apostrophes.

3 LISTEN and repeat.

- Direct students' attention to the Big Picture or put the transparency for Unit 1 on the overhead projector (OHP).
- Play the CD or read the sentences from the script and have students repeat.

4 LISTEN AGAIN and number.

- Play the CD or read the sentences from the script. Stop after the country and point out or elicit which country was said. Have students write 1 in the circle next to that country.
- Continue to play the CD or read the country names from the script. Have students write the number next to the picture.
- Put students in pairs to compare answers. Play the CD again if necessary.
- Go over the answers with the class.

LISTENING SCRIPT AND ANSWER KEY
Lesson 2, Activity 3
TCD1, 9
Listen and repeat.

1. Somalia	4. Colombia
2. the United States	5. China
3. Mexico	6. Cuba

5 TALK. Look at the picture. What countries are the people from?

- Go over the directions and the example sentences in the box.
- Call on students and start a sentence about a person in the picture (e.g., *Luz is from . . .*). Elicit the country name.
- With more advanced students, ask *Who is from Somalia?* Elicit the name (*Habiba*). Continue asking questions about the other countries.

6 WRITE. Complete the sentences.
Use *is, isn't, are,* or *aren't.*

- Go over the directions and the example.
- Have students complete the sentences.
- Put students in pairs to compare sentences.
- Go over the sentences with the class.

ANSWER KEY

1. is; 2. aren't; 3. are; 4. is; 5. isn't

COMMUNITY CONNECTION:
On the map

- Have students find their own countries on a world map.
- Have students find their city and state on a map of the United States.

LESSON 3: Listening and Conversation

OBJECTIVES

Introduce yourself
Understand and pronounce numbers

COMPETENCIES

Identify first and last names,
   state name of self and others
Use greetings
Identify country of origin

WARM-UP ACTIVITY: Numbers in your life

- Write three numbers that figure in your life (e.g., four numbers from your address, five numbers from your zip code, the three numbers of your area code). Tell students what each number represents.
- Have students write three numbers from their lives.
- Put students in pairs to say their numbers and the meaning.
- Elicit examples and write them on the board.

1 PRONUNCIATION: Stress in Numbers

A LISTEN and repeat.

- Review numbers from the Pre-Unit if necessary.
- Play the CD or read the numbers and have students repeat. Point out that the circle over the syllable indicates the syllable that is said with the most stress.

PRONUNCIATION NOTE

Point out that the *t* in the middle of each word is also pronounced differently. In all the *teen* words, the *t* sounds like a *t*. In the *–ty* words, the *t* sounds like a *d*.

B LISTEN and circle the word you hear.

- Go over the directions.
- Play the CD and stop after the first item, or read the first number from the script. Elicit the number. Point out that 13 is circled.
- Remind students to listen for the different stress patterns.
- Play the CD and have students circle the answer.
- Go over the answers with the class.

LISTENING SCRIPT AND ANSWER KEY
Lesson 3, Activity B

TCD1, 11
SCD, 4

Listen and circle the word you hear.

1. 13	3. 50	5. 70
2. 90	4. 116	6. 4010

C TALK. Work with a partner. Circle the word your partner says.

- Write the pairs of numbers on the board.
- Model the activity with a more advanced student. Call the student to the board. Say one of each pair of numbers and have the student circle it on the board. Erase the circles and switch roles.
- Put students in pairs to take turns saying and circling the numbers.

D LISTEN and circle the correct letter.

- Go over the directions. Tell students to circle the letter near the address or phone number they hear.
- Play the CD and stop after the first item, or read the first item from the script below. Point out that C is circled.
- Continue to play the CD or read the other items. Have students circle the correct answer.

- Put students in pairs to compare answers. If necessary, play the CD again.
- Go over the answers with the class.

LISTENING SCRIPT
Lesson 3, Activity 1
TCD1, 12

Listen and circle.

1. My address is 1540 Broad Street.
2. My phone number is (305) 555-1723.
3. My school is at 6013 Market Street.

ANSWER KEY

1. C; 2. A; 3. A

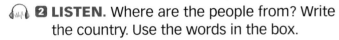 **2 LISTEN.** Where are the people from? Write the country. Use the words in the box.

- Direct students' attention to the photos. Point to each and say the name.
- Go over the directions.
- Play the CD and stop after the first conversation or read the first conversation from the script below. Elicit that Mary is from Colombia. Point out that Colombia is written on the line.
- Play the rest of the CD or read the other conversations. Have students write the country.
- Go over the answers with the class.

LISTENING SCRIPT
Lesson 3, Activity 2
TCD1, 13

Listen. Where are the people from? Write the country. Use the words in the box.

1. *A:* Hi, Mary. Where are you from?
   B: I'm from Colombia.
2. *A:* What is your name, please?
   B: Roberto Ruiz.
   A: What country are you from?
   B: Mexico
3. *A:* This is Han. She's from Korea.
   B: Hello, Han.

ANSWER KEY

1. Colombia; 2. Mexico; 3. Korea

EXPANSION ACTIVITY:
Conversation match

- Photocopy the lines from the conversations in Activity 3. Make enough copies so each pair of students has a set. Cut the conversations up so that each line is on a separate strip of paper. Mix the strips up.
- Put students in pairs. Give each pair a set of strips.
- Have students recreate the conversations.
- Go over their recreated conversations. Have students practice the conversations in pairs.

 3 LISTEN and read.

- Direct students' attention to the picture and ask *Who do you see?*
- Play the CD or read the conversation and have students follow along silently.
- Play the CD again and have students repeat.
- Put students in pairs to practice the conversation. Then have students switch roles.

EXPANSION ACTIVITY: Choral reading

- Divide the class in half. Cue one side to read Kevin's lines and the other side to read Claire's lines. Read with both sides to keep them together.
- Repeat several times, then have the two sides switch roles.

4 WHAT ABOUT YOU? Talk to six classmates. Complete the chart.

- Copy the chart on the board.
- Go over the directions and the example conversation.

- Model the activity. Introduce yourself. Elicit the name and country from the student. Remind the student to follow the model in the speech bubbles.
- Have students stand and walk around the room to talk to classmates and complete the chart.
- When students are finished, call on students to tell the class about someone on their charts (e.g., *Lena is from Russia.*).

5 GAME. Work in a small group. Play the game.

- Direct students' attention to the pictures. Go over what each person says.
- Model the activity with two students. Have the students say where they are from, then say where all three of you are from (e.g., *I'm from the United States, Lena is from Russia, Tien is from Vietnam.*).
- Put students in small groups to play the game.
- Walk around the room to monitor the activity and provide help as needed.

> **ACADEMIC CONNECTION: Write the capitals**
>
> - Explain what a capital city is and give examples (e.g., *Washington is the capital of the United States. Paris is the capital of France.*).
> - For an out-of-class assignment, have students look at a world map and write the capital cities for all of the countries mentioned in Activity 5.

LESSON 4: Grammar and Vocabulary

OBJECTIVES

Talk about occupations
Use singular and plural nouns

VOCABULARY

actor/actress	nurse
construction worker	office assistant
cook	police officer
dentist	salesclerk
doctor	server
firefighter	taxi driver
housekeeper	waiter

GRAMMAR

Singular and plural nouns
Articles *a/an*

COMPETENCIES

Use singular and plural nouns
Identify common occupations
Use articles *a* and *an*

WARM-UP ACTIVITY: Jobs and occupations

- Write *job* and *occupation* on the board.
- Say *I am a teacher. Teacher is my job or occupation.*
- Elicit student jobs or occupations if they know them.

🎧 ❶ GRAMMAR PICTURE DICTIONARY.
Listen and repeat.

- Have students look at the picture. Ask: *Who do you see?*
- Point to each person, say the job and have students repeat.
- Play the CD or say the sentences and have students repeat.
- Say the words in random order and have the students point to the pictures.

EXPANSION ACTIVITY: Say and point

- Put students in pairs.
- Have students take turns saying the jobs in random order and having their partners point.

❷ **NOTICE THE GRAMMAR.** Look at Activity 1. Underline *a* and *an*. Circle the words that end in *s*.

- Have students underline a and *an*. Elicit that the words ending in *s* do not have the articles *a* or *an*.
- Write the phrases with *a* and *an* on the board (*a doctor, a police officer, a dentist, an office assistant, a housekeeper, a cook, an actor, a salesclerk, a nurse*).
- Have students circle words ending in *s*, except for the word *is*.
- Elicit the words and write them on the board (*taxi drivers, servers, construction workers*).

ANSWER KEY

1. She is a doctor.	7. They are servers.
2. He is a police officer.	8. He is a cook.
3. He is a dentist.	9. He is an actor.
4. He is an office assistant.	10. She is a salesclerk.
5. She is a housekeeper.	11. They are construction workers.
6. They are taxi drivers.	12. He is a nurse.

GRAMMAR CHART: Singular and Plural Nouns

- Go over the information in the chart, including the usage notes.
- Make sure students understand what vowels and consonants are.
- Students need to understand that plural nouns represent two or more and that we use *are* with these nouns.
- Singular nouns are always only one thing. They must have an article before them, and they use *am*, *is*, or *are* depending on the subject.
- Point out that we usually add *s* to singular nouns to make them plural, but sometimes we spell the plural form differently.

CHART EXPANSION ACTIVITY: Consonant or vowel?

- Write all the letters of the alphabet on the board.
- Point to letters in random order and say them. Elicit if the letter is a consonant or a vowel.

❸ WRITE. Complete the sentences. Use *a* or *an*.

- Direct students' attention to the picture. Point out that we sometimes use the word *actress* for a female actor.
- Go over the example.
- Have students write *a* or *an* before each noun.
- Put students in pairs to compare answers.
- Go over the answers with the class.

ANSWER KEY

1. a; 2. an; 3. a; 4. a; 5. an

EXPANSION ACTIVITY: Other words

- Write other nouns students know on the board: *address, telephone number, email address, name, country, zip code, student, teacher, occupation, job.*
- Have students write *a* or *an* before each noun.
- Put students in pairs to compare answers.
- Go over the answers with the class.

ANSWER KEY

an address, a telephone number, an email address, a name, a country, a zip code, a student, a teacher, an occupation, a job

❹ CIRCLE the correct words.

- Go over the directions and the example.
- Have students circle the correct word in each sentence.
- Put students in pairs to compare answers.
- Call on students to read the sentences aloud to check their answers.

ANSWER KEY

1. a teacher; 2. cooks; 3. housekeepers;
4. a doctor; 5. police officers; 6. a salesclerk

CULTURE NOTE

- Point out that in the United States, it is acceptable to say you are a student if you do not have another occupation.
- Point out that people who do not have a job outside the home are sometimes called *homemakers*. This is the word they write on forms when it asks for *occupation*.

5 WHAT ABOUT YOU? Talk to a partner about *your* occupation.

- Go over the directions and the example.
- Model the activity with a more advanced student. Ask about his or her occupation and say yours, following the conversation mode.
- Put students in pairs to talk about their occupations.
- Call on students to tell the class about their partners' occupations.

COMMUNITY CONNECTION:
Where do they work?

- Write two headings on the board: *place* and *occupation/job.*
- Under *place*, write the name of your school. Under *occupation/job*, elicit or point out jobs that are at your school (*teacher*, *office assistant*), and write them on the board.
- As an out-of-class assignment, have students write down the names of two or three places they go to or pass each week and the occupations of people who they think work there.
- Elicit the places and jobs from the students.

LESSON 5: Grammar Practice Plus

OBJECTIVES

Use irregular plural nouns
Talk about occupations and countries

VOCABULARY

child/children   person/people
man/men   woman/women

GRAMMAR

Singular and plural nouns
Irregular plurals

COMPETENCIES

Talk about jobs

WARM-UP ACTIVITY: Man or woman?

- Introduce the words *man* and *woman*. Point to different people in the class and elicit if the person is a man or woman.
- Point to the people in the Grammar Picture Dictionary in Lesson 4 and elicit *man* or *woman*. Make sure students see that we use *he* for a man and *she* for a woman.

🎧 **1 LISTEN** and repeat.

- Direct students' attention to the pictures and words.
- Play the CD and have students repeat.

PRONUNCIATION NOTE

Make sure students hear and say the different sounds in *woman* vs. *women*. Point out that while the second vowel changes in spelling, the first vowel changes in sound.

EXPANSION ACTIVITY: Beanbag toss

- Call on a student, toss a ball or beanbag and say the singular form of a word (e.g., *woman*). Elicit the plural form (*women*).
- Continue with other students and singular nouns. Use nouns with both regular and irregular plural forms.

2 WHAT ABOUT YOU? Write the number.

- Go over the directions and have students look around the classroom.
- Have students write the correct numbers.
- Put students in pairs to compare answers.
- Go over the answers with the class.

3 WRITE. Complete the sentences about people in Diana's English class.

- Explain the chart's organization.
- Elicit the first occupation (*construction worker*) and ask how many men in Diana's English class are construction workers (*two*). Point out that in number 1, *men* has been written on the line to complete the sentence correctly.
- Make sure students understand what all the illustrations mean. Point out that sometimes students will write *man/men*, *woman/women*, and sometimes they will write the singular or plural form of the occupation.
- Have students complete the sentences by writing nouns on the lines.
- Put students in pairs to compare answers.
- Go over the answers with the class.

ANSWER KEY

1. men; 2. woman; 3. women; 4. cooks;
5. doctors; 6. people or students

CULTURE/CIVICS NOTE

Some of your students may come from cultures where it is rare to see women or men in certain professions. Point out that in the United States, men and women can do most if not all occupations.

EXPANSION ACTIVITY: Tally and write

- Copy the chart from Activity 3 on the board.
- Write all the occupations of students in your class in the first column.
- For each occupation, have students raise their hands if they have that occupation.
- Make tally marks in the columns for men and women.
- Have students write sentences about the results.

❹ **TALK** about the picture.

- Go over the directions and the example.
- Say different nouns for people and occupations and elicit the number students see in the picture.

BIG PICTURE CONVERSATION/ VOCABULARY EXPANSION ACTIVITY: *Is/isn't, are/aren't*

- Have students look at the Big Picture in their books, or put the transparency for Unit 1 on the OHP.
- Model the activity. Say a name from the picture and an occupation (*Harold, construction worker*). Elicit or say a sentence with those two nouns (*Harold isn't a police officer*.).
- Continue with other names and occupations. Include two or more people in some of your examples.

BIG PICTURE GRAMMAR EXPANSION ACTIVITY: **Using Singular and Plural Nouns**

- Photocopy and distribute Worksheet 1: Using Singular and Plural Nouns.
- Have students look at the picture on page 15 of Lesson 5 in their books.
- Go over the directions and the example.
- Have students complete the worksheet with the appropriate nouns.
- Go over the answers with the class.

WORKSHEET 1 ANSWER KEY

1. Two construction workers
2. Two nurses
3. Two police officers
4. One server
5. One cook
6. One taxi driver
7. Nine men
8. Three women
9. Three children
10. Fifteen people

5 LISTEN and write the country. Then look at the picture and complete the chart.

- Go over the directions.
- Play the CD and stop after the first sentence or read the first sentence from the script. Point out that Somalia is written in the chart. Point out that Musa is a man and a nurse and that those words are also written in the chart.
- Continue to play the CD or read the sentences. Have students complete the chart.
- Put students in pairs to compare answers.
- Go over the answers with the class.

LISTENING SCRIPT
Lesson 5, Activity 5

TCD1, 17

Listen and write the country. Then look at the picture and complete the chart.

1. Musa is from Somalia.
2. Luis is from Mexico.
3. Lily is from Vietnam.
4. Ivan is from Russia.

ANSWER KEY

Name	Country	Man or woman?	Job
Musa	Somalia	man	nurse
Luis	Mexico	man	server
Lily	Vietnam	woman	nurse
Ivan	Russia	man	taxi driver

6 WRITE. Choose a person from the picture. Write three sentences about the person.

- Go over the directions and the example sentences.
- Have students choose a person. Point out that they only know the countries for the people in the chart, but they could make up the countries for other people if they want to.

- Have students write three sentences about the person in the picture. Remind students to follow the examples.
- Put students in pairs to read their sentences aloud.
- Call on students and say a person's name. Elicit sentences about the person.

EXPANSION ACTIVITY: Team challenge

- Divide the class into two teams.
- Have each team write sentences about the people in the picture. Tell each team to write equal numbers of sentences with correct and incorrect information.
- Alternate calling on members of the two teams and have them read a sentence. Elicit *yes* or *no* from the other team.

LESSON 6: Apply Your Knowledge

OBJECTIVES

Ask for and give personal information
Complete personal forms

VOCABULARY

employee badge number	male
female	marital status
gender	Social Security number

COMPETENCIES

Fill out personal information forms
Answer questions about personal information
Identify gender and marital status
Distinguish among various personal information numbers

WARM-UP ACTIVITY: Personal documents

- Have students look in their purse or wallet for a card or document with personal information.
- Put students in pairs to talk about what type of information is on the document.
- Elicit the type of information and write it on the board.

❶ LISTEN. Complete the sentences.

- Direct students' attention to the photo. Point out that it is Anna Park and she is talking on the CD.
- Go over the directions and the example.
- Play the CD or read the script. Have students complete the sentences.
- Play the CD again and have students confirm their answers.
- Go over the answers with the class.

LISTENING SCRIPT
Lesson 6, Activity 1
TCD1, 18

Listen. Complete the sentences.

1. My name is Anna Park.
2. My telephone number is 512-555-7702.
3. My address is 70 Pine Street.
4. My zip code is 20026.
5. I'm single and I am a police officer.

ANSWER KEY

1. is Anna Park; **2.** is 512-555-7702; **3.** is 70 Pine Street; **4.** is 20026; **5.** single/a police officer

❷ WRITE. Complete the form.

- Direct students' attention to the box. Point out that gender means *man* or *woman*. On forms, we write *male* for man, and *female* for woman. Point out that *married* and *single* are words for *marital status*.
- Have students fill out the form for Anna Park, using the information from Activity 1.
- Copy the form on the board. Go over the answers.

ANSWER KEY

Reston Adult School

Name: __Anna_____ __Park_____
       First   Last

Address: __70 Pine Street_____

City: __Washington__ State: __DC__ Zip: __20026__

Telephone number (__512__) __555__ - __7702____

Marital Status ☐ Married   Gender ☐ Male
               ☑ Single   ☑ Female

Occupation: __police officer_____

EXPANSION ACTIVITY: What is?

- Write the words *What is her* _____ on the board.
- Point out that we ask about personal information with questions that begin *What is*.
- Elicit examples of types of information and write questions beginning with *What is her* (*first name*, *last name*, *address*, *city*, *zip code*, *telephone number*, *area code*, *marital status*, *gender*, *occupation*).
- Point out that *What's* is the contraction for *What is*.
- Put students in pairs to take turns asking and answering the questions on the board about the information in Activities 1 and 2.
- Call on students and ask the questions. Elicit the answers.

MATH: Recognize Patterns

- Direct students' attention to the pictures. Make sure students understand what the new phrases mean (*Social Security number*, *employee badge number*).
- Go over the example. Point out or elicit that the Social Security number (SSN) is *b*, because SSNs have a 3-2-4 pattern.
- Have students match the other examples to the type of information.
- Go over the answers with the class.

CULTURE/CIVICS NOTE

- Point out that zip codes must have five digits, but are often followed by a dash and four more digits. The additional information subdivides the zip code into smaller areas.
- In many parts of the country, you must dial the area code before the phone number, meaning that all phone numbers are 10 digits (3-3-4).

ANSWER KEY

1. b; 2. c; 3. e; 4. a; 5. d

❸ LISTEN and read.

- Direct students' attention to the picture. Ask questions: *Who do you see? Where are they?*
- Play the CD or read the conversation as students follow along silently.
- Ask comprehension questions: *What is Luz's last name? What is her address? What is her zip code? What is her telephone number? What is her occupation?*
- Play the CD again and have students repeat.
- Put students in pairs to take turns reading the parts of Luz and the office assistant.

❹ PRACTICE THE CONVERSATION with a partner. Ask and answer questions. Use the forms below.

- Go over the directions and the example question and answer.
- Model the activity with a more advanced student. Have the student play the role of Mark. Ask questions and cue the student to respond with Mark's information.
- Put students in pairs. Have students take turns asking and answering questions about the two forms. Have one student play Mark and the other play Wen, then switch roles.
- Walk around the room to monitor the activity and provide help as needed.
- Have pairs of students say the conversations in front of the class.

EXPANSION ACTIVITY: Your form

- Have students create a personal information form like the one on page 17, using their own information.
- Walk around to monitor the activity and provide help as needed.
- Put students in pairs to share their information.
- Tell students to keep the form for reference.

CULTURE/CIVICS NOTE

- Students may not want to share information with their classmates. Point out that they can give different information if they want (e.g., an address that is not their own).
- Point out that we must give accurate information on official forms.

COMMUNITY CONNECTION: Get a form

- As realia, bring in forms that ask for personal information (driver's license or learner's permit applications, rental applications, school registration forms, library card applications). Point out that government forms (e.g., W2, W4) can be found online.
- Elicit the type of information each form asks for.
- For an out-of-class assignment, have students find similar forms on their own and bring them in. Discuss as a group.

CULTURE/CIVICS NOTE

In the United States, many important forms can be found online. Some companies and agencies require that forms be submitted online as well.

LESSON 7: Reading and Writing

OBJECTIVES

Read a personal letter
Address an envelope

READING TIP

Look for capital letters to find names in a reading

WRITING TIP

Use capital letters in writing

COMPETENCIES

Address letters and envelopes
Identify proper names

WARM-UP ACTIVITY: Who do you write to?

- Bring in examples of mail. Ask students who they write to and who writes to them.
- Put students in pairs to talk about the people they write to.

Reading

❶ THINK ABOUT IT. What is a capital letter? When do we write a capital letter?

- Read the question. Elicit answers from students.

❷ BEFORE YOU READ. Look at the letter. Circle the names of people.

- Direct students' attention to the photo. Ask *Who is it?*
- Go over the tip in the box. Point out that names are easy to find because they begin with capital letters.
- Go over the directions. Point out that they are looking for and circling names. They do not have to read the letter yet. Remind students to circle only the names of people, not names of countries.
- Elicit the names they circled and write them on the board.

ANSWER KEY

Ms. Smith, Lena Parker, Brad

❸ READ THE LETTER. Underline the names of countries and cities.

- Go over the directions. Make sure students understand the concept of *to* and *from*. The letter is from Lena, and to Ms. Smith.
- Have students read the letter silently, or read the letter aloud to the class and have students repeat after each sentence.
- Have students underline the names of countries and cities.
- Elicit the answers from the class and write them on the board.

ANSWER KEY

Russia, United States, San Diego

❹ CIRCLE *yes* or *no*.

- Read the first sentence. Nod your head and ask *yes,* then shake your head and ask *no?* Elicit that the answer is *yes,* that Ms. Smith is a teacher. Point out that *yes* is circled.
- Have students read the sentences and circle *yes* or *no,* or read each sentence aloud and have students circle the answer.
- Put students in pairs to compare answers.
- Go over the answers with the class.

ANSWER KEY

1. yes; **2.** no; **3.** no; **4.** yes; **5.** no

5 WRITE. Look at the letter above. Write the words with a capital letter.

- Go over the directions and the example.
- Have students write other capitalized words from the letter on the lines.
- Put students in pairs to compare their lists.
- Elicit words from the students and write them on the board.

ANSWER KEY

Dear, Ms., Smith, I (5 times), English, My, Lena (2 times), Parker (2 times), Russia (2 times), In, United States, American, His, He, Brad, San Diego, It's, Thank

EXPANSION ACTIVITY: Literacy development—sentence strips

- Copy the sentences from the letter onto separate strips. Leave enough space between each word for word discrimination. The sentences need to be large enough to be read by all the students.
- Put the sentence strips on the board in the correct order. Read each sentence aloud and have students repeat. You may want to point to each word as you read.
- Take the sentences down and mix them up.
- Have volunteers come to the board and put the sentences in the correct order. Have the other students help.
- You may want to photocopy the sentences and cut them into strips so that each student or pair of students has a set to reassemble.

BIG PICTURE READING EXPANSION ACTIVITY: Letters

- Photocopy and distribute Worksheet 2: Letters
- Put the transparency for Unit 1 on the OHP or have students look at the Big Picture in their books.
- Go over the directions.
- Have students read the letters and write the name of the character.
- Put students in pairs to compare answers.
- Go over the answers with the class.

WORKSHEET 2 ANSWER KEY

1. Ivan; 2. Luis; 3. Lily

Writing

- Go over the writing tip in the box.
- Go over the rules for capital letters.
- Go over the titles in the chart and when they are used.

1 WRITE the sentences again. Use capital letters.

- Go over the directions and the example. Elicit why each letter in the new sentence is capitalized (e.g., *My*—first letter in a sentence, *Hector*—first name).
- Have students rewrite the sentences using uppercase letters where appropriate.
- Put students in pairs to compare sentences.
- Have volunteers write the sentences on the board.

ANSWER KEY

1. My name is Vera King. 2. I am from China.
3. We are from Miami, Florida. 4. He is in Mr. Green's class. 5. Dr. Johnson is from Canada.

2 WRITE your name and address on the envelope.

- Direct students' attention to the envelope. Go over the return address. Ask comprehension questions: *What is her address? What city? What zip code?*
- Go over the directions.
- Have students address the envelope to themselves. Remind students to use capital letters where appropriate.
- Walk around to monitor the activity and provide help as needed.

BIG PICTURE WRITING EXPANSION ACTIVITY: Five sentences

- Put the transparency for Unit 1 on the OHP or have students look at page 15 in their books.
- Have students write five sentences about different people in the picture. Remind students to use capital letters for names and to start a sentence.
- Have volunteers write sentences on the board.

Career Connection

OBJECTIVE

Identify form of identification for employment

COMPETENCIES

Read documents for employment

WARM-UP ACTIVITY: What is a boss?

- Ask *What is a boss?* Elicit answers.
- Elicit the names of bosses from students in the class.

🎧 **❶ READ** and listen. Then practice with a partner.

- Direct students' attention to the photos. Tell students this is a story about Isabel. Have students point to Isabel in the photos.
- Make sure students understand what a *boss* is.
- Play the CD and have students follow along silently.
- Play the CD again and have students repeat.
- Put students in pairs to take turns reading the roles of Isabel and her new boss.
- Ask: *What is the name of the new boss?*

❷ CHECK *yes* or *no*.

- Read the first sentence and elicit *yes* or *no.* Point out that *no* is checked.
- Have students read the sentences and check their answers, or read each sentence aloud and have students repeat and then check their answers.
- Go over the answers with the class.

ANSWER KEY

1. no; 2. yes; 3. no; 4. yes; 5. yes

CHECK YOUR PROGRESS!

- Have students circle the answers.
- Have students check whether each answer is right or wrong.
- Have students total their correct answers and fill in the chart.
- Have students create a learning plan and/or set learning goals.

ANSWER KEY

1. is; 2. am; 3. are; 4. a doctor; 5. teachers;
6. nurses; 7. phone number; 8. address;
9. single; 10. nurse; 11. cook; 12. housekeeper

Unit Overview

LESSON	OBJECTIVE	STUDENT BOOK	WORKBOOK
1 Grammar and Vocabulary 1	Ask and answer *yes/no* questions with *be* Describe personal characteristics	p. 22	p. 20
2 Grammar Practice Plus	Ask and answer *yes/no* questions with *be* Describe physical appearance	p. 24	p. 21
3 Listening and Conversation	Identify and describe people	p. 26	p. 22
4 Grammar and Vocabulary 2	Identify family members Use possessive adjectives	p. 28	p. 24
5 Grammar Practice Plus	Use possessives of nouns Interpret a chart	p. 30	p. 25
6 Apply Your Knowledge	Take and leave phone messages	p. 32	p. 26
7 Reading and Writing	Read a personal story Make a list to get ideas for writing	p. 34	p. 28
• Career Connection	Match personal characteristics to jobs	p. 36	p. 30
• Check Your Progress	Monitor progress	p. 37	p. 32

Reading/Writing Strategies

• Look at pictures as a pre-reading strategy   • Make lists as a pre-writing strategy

Connection Activities

LESSON	TYPE	SKILL DEVELOPMENT
1	Academic	Use a dictionary
2	Community	Use adjectives to describe a political figure
3	Academic	Tally and write about results
4	Community	Use the internet to do research
6	Community	Use the phone
8	Community	Listen for job qualities

WORKSHEET #/FOCUS	TITLE	TEACHER'S EDITION
3 Grammar	Adjectives; Posessive Forms	p. 248
4 Reading	Berta and Carl	p. 249

LESSON 1: Grammar and Vocabulary

OBJECTIVES

Ask and answer *yes/no* questions with *be*
Give personal information

VOCABULARY

funny	neat
hardworking	outgoing
lazy	serious
messy	shy

GRAMMAR

Yes/No questions with *be*
Short answers

COMPETENCIES

Use *be* in descriptions of people
Use *be* plus an adjective

WARM-UP ACTIVITY: What do you know?

- Put the transparency for Unit 2 on the overhead projector (OHP) or have students look at the Big Picture on page 25.
- Write the words from this lesson on the board.
- Elicit which words students know already.

🎧 ❶ GRAMMAR PICTURE DICTIONARY. Listen and repeat.

- Have students open their books and look at the pictures. Ask: *What do you see?* Write all the words the students know on the board.
- Have students look at the pictures and listen while you say the words or play the CD.
- Say the sentences or play the CD again and have students repeat.
- Call on students. Ask a question and elicit the answer.

- Put students in pairs, taking turns saying the questions in random order as the partner points to the picture.

EXPANSION ACTIVITY: Spell it

- If necessary, review the alphabet from the Pre-Unit.
- Model the activity. Say one of the words and then spell it (*messy, m, e, s, s, y*).
- Call on students and say a word. Have students spell it.
- For a challenge activity, give students two minutes to review the words.
- Have students close their books. Ask volunteers to spell the words. Or, put students in pairs. Have one student look at the words in the book and say them as the partner spells them.

EXPANSION ACTIVITY: Beanbag toss

- Model the activity. Call on a student and toss a ball or beanbag. Say one of the new words (e.g., *messy*). After the student has caught the beanbag, say *neat* and have the students repeat.
- Write the word *opposite* on the board. Point out that *messy* and *neat* are opposites.
- Call on a student, toss the beanbag, and say a word. Elicit the opposite.
- Continue until everyone has had a chance to participate. For more advanced classes, you may want to have students call on their classmates, taking turns saying words and eliciting opposites.

2 NOTICE THE GRAMMAR. Look at Activity 1. Underline *is* and *are.* Circle *isn't* and *aren't.*

• Have students read the sentences and underline *is* and *are.* Then have students circle *isn't* and *aren't.*

• Ask questions: *What words are first in the questions? When do we use* **is**? **was**? *When do we use* **isn't** *and* **aren't**?

ANSWER KEY

1. Is Drew **messy?**
Yes, he is.

2. Is Ian messy?
No, he isn't. He's **neat.**

3. Is Maya **hardworking?**
Yes, she is.

4. Is Susie hardworking?
No, she isn't. She's **lazy.**

5. Is Henry **funny?**
Yes, he is.

6. Is Dan funny?
No, he isn't. He's **serious.**

7. Is Miko **outgoing?**
Yes, she is.

8. Are Ken and Hiro outgoing?
No, they aren't. They're **shy.**

EXPANSION ACTIVITY: Replace the word

• Give students two minutes to review the sentences in Activity 1.

• Have students close their books.

• Write the sentences on the board, but leave out all forms of the verb *to be.*

• Elicit the missing words from the students.

• Have students open their books and confirm their answers.

GRAMMAR CHART: *Yes/No* **Questions with** *Be*

• Direct students' attention to the chart or project the transparency or CD.

• Go over the information on the chart. You may want to read the questions and answers, pausing to have students repeat.

• Go over the usage notes.

CHART EXPANSION ACTIVITY: Pair practice

• Cover the first column of the chart on the transparency. Elicit the form of *be.*

• Put students in pairs to take turns asking and answering the questions in the chart. Encourage students to answer the questions in both the affirmative and the negative.

3 CHECK. Look at page 22. Check the answers.

• Direct students' attention to page 22. Point to Susie. Read the first question: *Is Susie hard–working?* Elicit the answer. Point out that *No, she isn't* has been checked.

• Read each question and have students repeat.

• Have students put check marks next to the answer.

• Put students in pairs to check their answers.

• Go over the answers with the class.

• Put students in pairs to practice reading the questions and answers.

ANSWER KEY

1. No, she isn't. 2. No, he isn't. 3. No, she isn't.
4. Yes, he is. 5. Yes, they are.

EXPANSION ACTIVITY: Write sentences.

- Read the first question from Activity 3 aloud. Then write the beginning of a sentence on the board: *Susie is*. . . . Elicit the completion (*lazy*) and write it on the board to complete the sentence.
- Have students write sentences for each question in Activity 3 to correctly describe the people. For some classes with more beginning students, write the sentence starters on the board (e.g., *1. Susie is; 2. Greg is*).Headings on the board: nouns, verbs, adjectives.

EXPANSION ACTIVITY:
Question challenge

- With more advanced students, ask them to change one word in each question in Activity 3: either the name or the adjective to create new questions.
- Put students in pairs to take turns asking and answering their new questions.

4 WHAT ABOUT YOU? Answer the questions about you. Write *Yes, I am* or *No, I'm not.*

- Read the questions aloud and have students repeat.
- Call on students and ask the first question. Elicit the answers. Tell students to write the answer that is true for them.
- Have students write the answers to the other questions.
- Put students in pairs to take turns asking and answering the questions.
- Call on students and ask the questions.

EXPANSION ACTIVITY:
Meet your classmates

- Write the questions from Activity 4 on the board.
- Model the activity. Call on students to answer the first question. If a student answers *yes, I am,* write his or her name on the board next to the question.
- Have students stand and walk around the room to ask and answer the questions. Remind students to write down the names of classmates who answer *yes* to the questions.
- Continue until students have received at least one yes answer to every question.
- Call on students to tell the class about one of their classmates (e.g., *Yen-Ching is shy.*).

ACADEMIC CONNECTION:
Dictionary work

- Have students choose two words from the Grammar Picture Dictionary to look up and write other words that mean the same.

LESSON 2: Grammar Practice Plus

OBJECTIVES

Ask and answer *yes/no* questions with *be*
Describe physical appearance

VOCABULARY

handsome	short
heavy	tall
old	thin
pretty	young

GRAMMAR

Yes/No questions with *be*
Short answers

COMPETENCIES

Use *be* in descriptions of people
Use *be* plus an adjective
Use *yes/no* questions and answers

WARM-UP ACTIVITY: Opposites

- Write *Opposite Pairs* on the board.
- Elicit examples from Lesson 1 *(messy-neat),* and write them on the board.
- Tell students that some of the new words are also opposite pairs.
- Have students look at the new words and guess which ones are opposite pairs.

❶ WRITE. Complete the sentences. Use *is* or *are.*

- Go over the directions and the example.
- Have students write *is* or *are* on the lines to complete the sentences.
- Put students in pairs to compare answers.

LISTEN and repeat. Are your answers correct?

- Play the audio and have students repeat. Have students check their answers.

LISTENING SCRIPT
Lesson 2, Activity 1
TCD1, 22

Listen and repeat. Are your answers correct?

1. Nick is **tall.**	2. Ray is **short.**
3. Mike is **heavy.**	4. Liz is **thin.**
5. Sara is **old.**	6. Anna and Kelly are **young.**
7. Tina is **pretty.**	8. Don is **handsome.**

ANSWER KEY

1. is; 2. is; 3. is; 4. is; 5. is; 6. are; 7. is; 8. is

EXPANSION ACTIVITY: Beanbag toss

- Review the guidelines for this activity (from Lesson 1).
- Call on a student, toss the beanbag, and say a word. Elicit the opposite.
- Continue until everyone has had a chance to participate. For more advanced classes, you may want to have students call on their classmates, taking turns saying words and eliciting opposites.

EXPANSION ACTIVITY: Famous people

- Bring in photos of famous people from magazines or download them from the internet. Try to find examples of people who illustrate each new word in Activity 1.
- Model the activity. Point to one of the photos and say a sentence (e.g., *Tom Cruise is short.*).
- Put students in pairs to write sentences about famous people using the new adjectives. They may get ideas from the photos or think of their own ideas.
- Call on students to read their sentences to the class.

2 CIRCLE *Is* or *Are.* Then match the questions and answers.

- Write the first question on the board, including the blank line. Point to the first blank and elicit the verb (*Is*). Point out that *Is* is circled.
- Have students circle *Is* or *Are* for each question.
- With lower level classes, you may want to go over the completed questions first, before you have students match questions and answers. More advanced classes may be able to do both tasks independently.
- Have students match the answers to the questions.
- Go over the answers with the class.
- Put students in pairs to practice asking and answering the questions.

ANSWER KEY

1. Is/e; 2. Are/a; 3. Is/h; 4. Is/f; 5. Are/b;
6. Is/d; 7. Are/g; 8. Are/c

EXPANSION ACTIVITY: Line-ups

- In very large classes, call a group of students to the front of the class. In smaller classes, do the line-ups with all the students.
- Have students line up from tallest to shortest. Point to one side of the room and say *tall.* Point to the other side and say *short.* Students don't know the superlative form yet, so convey the task with gestures or by repositioning the students in the line.
- Have students line up from oldest to youngest.
- Point to one side of the room and say *messy,* point to the other side and say *neat.* Have students position themselves along the continuum according to where they think they are.
- Continue with other adjectives they have learned.

LITERACY DEVELOPMENT NOTE

Emerging literacy students may need additional practice with the vocabulary. You may want to suggest they write each new vocabulary word on a note card. Color-coding opposite pairs may help students remember the association. Students, especially literacy students, may find it helpful to draw pictures on the vocabulary cards.

3 TALK about the picture. Describe the people.

- Go over the directions.
- Direct students' attention to the Big Picture or put the transparency on the projector. Read the example sentence.
- Put students in pairs. Have students take turns describing people in the picture.
- Call on students. Point to different characters in the Big Picture and elicit sentences.

BIG PICTURE CONVERSATION/ VOCABULARY EXPANSION ACTIVITY: Who Am I?

- Have students look at the Big Picture or put the color overhead transparency for Unit 2 on the OHP.
- Model the activity. Say several sentences about a character in the picture (e.g., *I am young, I am pretty.*). Elicit the name (*Patricia*).
- Put students in pairs to practice describing and guessing characters. You may want to put students in small groups and assign each student a character to facilitate this activity.
- Call on students to say their sentences to the class and elicit the name from the other students.

 4 LISTEN. Look at the picture. Listen to the questions and check the answers.

- Go over the directions.
- Have students check the boxes for the answer as you say the questions or play the CD.
- Put students in pairs to compare answers.
- Say the questions or play the CD again so students can confirm.
- Go over the answers with the class.

LISTENING SCRIPT
Lesson 2, Activity 4
TCD1, 23

Listen. Look at the picture. Listen to the questions and check the answers.

1. Is Berta funny?
2. Is Sam hardworking?
3. Is Kay old?
4. Are Pam and Bob short?

ANSWER KEY

1. No, she isn't. 2. No, he isn't. 3. Yes, she is.
4. Yes, they are.

EXPANSION ACTIVITY: Dictation

- Have students write the questions from Activity 4 as you read the questions or play the CD. Repeat twice.
- Put students in pairs to compare sentences.
- Have volunteers write the questions on the board.

5 WRITE questions about the picture.

- Go over the directions and the example.
- Have students write questions.
- Go over the questions with the class.
- Put students in pairs to practice asking and answering the questions with their partners.

ANSWER KEY

1. Are Bob and Pam tall? 2. Is Chin old?
3. Is Gabby hardworking? 4. Answers will vary.

EXPANSION ACTIVITY: Question match

- Write each adjective on an index card and put in one pile. Write each character's name on an index card and put in another pile.
- Model the activity. Choose a card from each pile, and read the words aloud (*Berta, heavy*). Ask a question (*Is Berta heavy?*).
- Have students choose a card from each pile to make a question and ask a classmate.

COMMUNITY CONNECTION: Political figures

- Assign students an important political or civic person to research.
- Have students write three adjectives that describe the person.
- Call on students to share what they learned with their classmates.

LESSON 3: Listening and Conversation

OBJECTIVE

Identify and describe people

COMPETENCIES

Use *be* in descriptions of people
Use *be* plus an adjective
Use *yes/no* questions and answers

WARM-UP ACTIVITY: Famous people

- Elicit the names of famous movie and TV stars students know. Write the names on the board.
- Elicit descriptions from students.

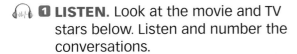 **1 LISTEN.** Look at the movie and TV stars below. Listen and number the conversations.

- Direct students' attention to the photos. Elicit the names of the actors and, if possible, movies they have been in. Elicit adjectives.
- Say the first conversation or play the CD. Stop after the first conversation and elicit who about the women are talking about (Jim Carrey). Point out that *1* is written in the box under Jim Carrey's picture.
- Say the conversations or play the CD and have students number the conversations in order.
- Have students compare answers in pairs.
- Go over the answers with the class.

 LISTENING SCRIPT
Lesson 3, Activity 1
TCD1, 24

Listen. Look at the movie stars below. Listen and number the conversations.

Conversation 1
Female 1: I think he's funny.
Female 2: Really?
Female 1: Uh-huh. He's thin too.

Conversation 2
Female 1: Wow. Look. She's tall.
Male 1: And pretty too.

Conversation 3
Male 1: She's pretty.
Male 2: Who? The heavy one or the thin one?
Male 1: The heavy one.

Conversation 4
Male: He isn't tall.
Female: But he's handsome.

GRAMMAR NOTE

You may want to point out or remind students about the meaning of *and*: that it can be used to join two adjectives (e.g., *He is tall. He is serious. = He is tall and serious.*).

ANSWER KEY

1. Jim Carrey; **2.** Uma Thurman; **3.** Queen Latifah; **4.** Antonio Banderas

CULTURE NOTES

- Jim Carrey is a comic actor who has been in such films as *The Cable Guy, Liar, Liar, Ace Ventura,* and *The Truman Show.*
- Uma Thurman is a model and has acted in movies including *Pulp Fiction.*
- Queen Latifah is a music star as well as an actor. She has been in *Chicago, Last Holiday,* and *Bringing Down the House.*
- Antonio Banderas is an actor from Spain who has been in the *Zorro* and *Spy Kids* movies.

LISTEN AGAIN. Write the missing adjective.

- Play the CD again and have students write the missing words. Point out that each line represents a letter in the word.
- Go over the answers with the class.

ANSWER KEY

1. funny; 2. pretty; 3. heavy; 4. handsome

 PRONUNCIATION: *Is he/Is she*

A. LISTEN to the questions.

- Play the CD or read the questions as students follow along silently.
- Play the CD or read the questions again and have students repeat.

 LISTENING SCRIPT
Lesson 3, Activity A

TCD1, 25
SCD, 9   Listen to the questions. Then listen again and repeat.

1. Is he tall?	2. Is she tall?
3. Is he hardworking?	4. Is she hardworking?
5. Is he from China?	6. Is she from China?

B. LISTEN to the questions. Circle the answer.

- Remind students to listen for the difference between *is he* and *is she.*
- Play the CD and have students circle the answer.
- Go over the answers with the class.

LISTENING SCRIPT
Lesson 3, Activity B

TCD1, 26
SCD, 10   Listen to the questions. Circle the answers.

1. Is he shy? 2. Is she messy? 3. Is she from Mexico? 4. Is he handsome? 5. Is he single? 6. Is she a police officer?

ANSWER KEY

1. Yes, he is. 2. No, she isn't. 3. No, she isn't.
4. Yes, she is. 5. No, he isn't. 6. Yes, she is.

BIG PICTURE LISTENING EXPANSION ACTIVITY: Chin or Gabby?

- Dictate the questions below.
  1. *Is he handsome?*
  2. *Is she pretty?*
  3. *Is he old?*
  4. *Is she short?*
- Put students in pairs to compare questions.
- Have students write *Chin* or *Gabby* next to each question, then answer the questions.

ANSWER KEY

1. No, he isn't. 2. Yes, she is. 3. Yes, he is.
4. No, she isn't.

2 LISTEN and read.

- Direct students' attention to the picture. Ask questions: *Who do you see?*

- Play the CD or read the conversation as students follow along silently.
- Play the CD or read the conversation again and have students repeat.
- Ask *Is Victor short?*

🎧 **3 PRACTICE THE CONVERSATION** with a partner.

- Go over the directions.
- Model the activity. Have a more advanced student read B's lines. Model how to substitute the different names and adjectives.
- Put students in pairs to practice the conversation, making the appropriate substitutions.
- Walk around to monitor the activity and provide help as needed.
- Call on students to say the conversation to the class.

4 WHAT ABOUT YOU? Walk around the room and talk to your classmates. Complete the chart.

- Copy the chart on the board.
- Go over the directions and the example conversation.
- Model the activity. Ask a student if he or she is outgoing. If the answer is *yes*, ask for the student's name and write it on the chart on the board.
- Have students stand and walk around the room to talk to classmates and complete the chart.
- When students are finished, call on students to tell the class about someone on their charts (e.g., *Lena is shy.*).

ACADEMIC CONNECTION:
Tally and write

- Erase the name you wrote on the chart on the board. Ask students to raise their hands if they can answer *yes* to your questions. Ask about each adjective in the chart (e.g., *Are you outgoing?*) and have students raise their hands.
- Tally the results in the chart or have a student tally the results.
- Have students write sentences about the results (e.g., *Five people are outgoing.*).

LESSON 4: Grammar and Vocabulary

OBJECTIVES

Identify family members
Use possessive adjectives

VOCABULARY

aunt	grandmother
brother	husband
cousin	mother
daughter	sister
father	son
grandfather	wife

GRAMMAR

Possessive adjectives

COMPETENCIES

Identify family members and their relationships
Use possessive adjectives

WARM-UP ACTIVITY: Describe a person

- Have students look at the people in the picture. Have students choose a person in the picture and write two adjectives.
- Call on students and elicit the adjectives. Have the class guess who it is.
- Ask students who they live with in their family.

🎧 ❶ GRAMMAR PICTURE DICTIONARY. Listen and repeat.

- Have students look at the picture. Ask: *Who do you see?*
- Point to each person, say the relationship word and have students repeat.
- Play the CD or say the sentences and have students repeat.
- Say the words in random order and have the students point to the pictures.

❷ NOTICE THE GRAMMAR. Look at Activity 1. Circle *her* and *their*.

- Have students circle *her* and *their*.
- Go over the answers with the class.

ANSWER KEY

Ann Wyatt is a doctor in San Jose, California. Roger is (her) **husband**.
John is Ann's father. Nancy is (her) **mother**. Nancy is John's wife.
Roger and Ann's **daughter** is Grace, and (their) **son** is Paul.
Paul and Grace's **grandfather** is John, and (their) **grandmother** is Nancy.
Adam is Roger's **brother**. Mira is Adam's **wife**.
Karen and Jenny are Ann's **sisters**.
Karen, Jenny, and Mira are Grace and Paul's **aunts**.
Adam and Greg are (their) **uncles**.
Dina and Cole are (their) **cousins**.

GRAMMAR CHART: Possessive Adjectives

- Go over the information in the chart.
- You may want to read the sample sentences in the chart and have students repeat.
- Demonstrate the meaning of possessive adjectives. Hold up your book and say *my book*. Hold up a student's book and say *his* or *her book*.

CHART EXPANSION ACTIVITY: Match possessives to subject

- Have students cover the subject pronoun column of the chart.
- Say possessive adjectives and elicit the subject pronoun.

3 WRITE. Complete the sentences. Use *my, your, his, her, our, your,* or *their.*

- Go over the directions and the example. Read *Ann has a sister.* Ask *Is Ann's sister a man or woman? He or she?* Elicit that the possessive adjective is *her.* Point out that *her* is written on the line.
- Have students complete the sentences with possessive adjectives. See the expansion activity below for a way to provide scaffolding for the activity.
- Put students in pairs to compare answers.
- Go over the answers with the class.

ANSWER KEY

1. Her; 2. Her; 3. His; 4. Their; 5. Her; 6. Their; 7. Our; 8. My

EXPANSION ACTIVITY: Family list

- Model the activity. Write *My family* on the board. Then write your family members on the board as you list them aloud (e.g., *a sister, two brothers, a father, a mother, three aunts*).
- Have students list their own family members.
- Put students in pairs to compare lists.

4 WHAT ABOUT YOU? Write about your family.

- Go over the directions and the example.
- Model the activity. Write sentences about your family.
- Have students write about their families.
- Put students in pairs to talk about their families.
- Call on students to tell the class about people in their families.

EXPANSION ACTIVITY: Family photos

- Have students bring in or draw pictures of their families.
- Put students in pairs to ask and answer questions about their partners' families (*Who is that? Is your brother tall?*).
- Call on students to tell the class about one of the people in their partners' families.

EXPANSION ACTIVITY: Category sort

- Explain the activity. You will call out a category of family member (e.g., *brothers*). Students should sort themselves into groups by the number that they have. For example, there should be a group of students with one brother, a group with two brothers, and so on.
- Call out a category and remind students to form groups by number. When students are sorted, call on a representative from each group to tell you the number. Repeat the number (e.g., *two brothers*) as you point to the group. Let students switch groups if they need to.
- Continue with other family members (*sisters, cousins, aunts, uncles, sons, daughters*). This activity should be as fast-paced as possible.

ACADEMIC CONNECTION: Online research

- Have students choose a famous American to research.
- As an out-of-class assignment, have students use a favorite search engine to conduct internet research on their chosen subject. Tell students to write down how many brothers and sisters and children the subject has.
- Call on students to tell the class what they found out.

LESSON 5: Grammar Practice Plus

OBJECTIVES

Use possessives of nouns and adjectives
Interpret a chart

GRAMMAR

Possessives of nouns

MATH/NUMERACY

Use height charts and measurements

COMPETENCIES

Use possessive forms of nouns
Describe family members
Recognize U.S. measurements

ANSWER KEY

1. Ted's; 2. Frank and Ella's; 3. Ted's; 4. Ella's;
5. Frank's; 6. Ted's and Kristin's

EXPANSION ACTIVITY: Matching pairs

- Put students in pairs.
- Distribute index cards. Have students write each adjective from pages 22 and 24 (e.g., *old*) on a card and each relationship name (e.g., *husband*) on a card.
- Model the activity. Choose a family member card and show the students (e.g., *sister*). Choose the matching adjective card and show the students (e.g., *shy*). Say a sentence (*My sister is shy.*).
- Have students work with their partner, taking turns matching cards and saying sentences.

EXPANSION ACTIVITY: Small group work

- Model the activity. Tell about two people in your family (e.g., *My sister is tall, My father is funny.*).
- Have the students write sentences about your information using the possessives of nouns.
- Have volunteers write sentences on the board (e.g., *The teacher's sister is tall, Ms. Hunter's father is funny.*).
- Put students in groups of three or four to take turns talking about the people in their families.
- Have students write sentences about their group members' families. (e.g., *Tam's mother is short.*).
- Have volunteers write sentences on the board.

WARM-UP ACTIVITY: What belongs to whom?

- Point to one or more people in the class. Elicit the names and the appropriate possessive adjective (e.g., *Maria/her chair; Mario/his desk*).

GRAMMAR CHART: Possessives of Nouns

- Go over the information in the chart, including the usage note. Make sure students see that we add *'s* to nouns to show possession or ownership.
- You may want to read the sample sentences in the chart and have students repeat.

1 WRITE. Look at the picture. Complete the sentences. Use possessives of nouns.

- Direct students' attention to the picture. Elicit the words for family members.
- Go over the example.
- Have students write the possessives of nouns on the lines. Remind students to add an *'s* to the names.
- Go over the answers with the class.

2 WRITE. Complete the sentences.

- Go over the information in the Grammar Professor note.
- Go over the directions and the example.
- Have students choose the correct word in parentheses and write it on the line.
- Go over the answers with the class.

ANSWER KEY

1. sisters; 2. brother's; 3. mother's;
4. grandmothers; 5. sisters; 6. children

3 WHAT ABOUT YOU? Write about your family in the chart.

- Go over the directions and the example in the chart.
- Have students complete the chart.
- Put students in pairs to talk about their families. Go over the example in the box.
- Call on students to tell the class about someone in their partner's family.

EXPANSION ACTIVITY: Challenge dictation

- Dictate three sentences to the class. Read each sentence three times (e.g., *My grandmother is old and short, My sister is outgoing and lazy, My daughter is young and shy.*).
- Have students compare sentences with a partner.
- Have volunteers write the sentences on the board.
- Put students in pairs. Have students dictate sentences in random order to their partners.
- Have students correct their partners' sentences.

BIG PICTURE GRAMMAR/VOCABULARY EXPANSION ACTIVITY: Using adjectives

- Each student or pair of students will need the adjective cards from the Matching Pairs expansion activity.
- Put the color transparency for Unit 2 on the OHP or have students look at the Big Picture in their books.
- Explain the activity: when you point to a character, the students should hold up a correct card.
- Model the activity. Point to Berta and signal to students to hold up an adjective card. Call on students to read their cards to the class.
- Continue pointing to other people and have students hold up appropriate cards. This is a fast-paced activity.

MATH: Height Charts

- Go over the information about measurement.
- Go over the abbreviations in the box.
- Direct students' attention to the chart and ask questions: *How many centimeters is 6 feet? How many feet and inches is 160 centimeters? Is 5 feet short for an American woman?*
- Go over the example.
- Have students answer the other questions.
- Go over the answers with the class.

CULTURE/CIVICS NOTE

Point out that this scale is for American men and women. Average height might be much shorter or much taller in other countries.

ANSWER KEY

1. 5 feet, 11 inches/tall; 2. 5 feet, 5 inches/short;
3. Answers will vary

BIG PICTURE GRAMMAR EXPANSION ACTIVITY: Adjectives; Possessive Forms

- Put the transparency for Unit 2 on the OHP or have students look at the Big Picture on page 25.
- Photocopy and distribute Worksheet 3— Adjectives; Possessive Forms.
- Go over the directions.
- Have students complete the worksheet and then compare answers with a partner.
- Go over the answers with the class.

WORKSHEET 3 ANSWER KEY

1. tall; 2. short; 3. young; 4. old; 5. pretty;
6. heavy; 7. lazy
1. Gabby's; 2. Carl's; 3. Pam's; 4. Pam's;
5. Bob's; 6. Chin's

LESSON 6: Apply Your Knowledge

OBJECTIVE

Take and leave phone messages

COMPETENCIES

Identify self and ask to speak to someone on the phone
Respond appropriately on the phone
Take written telephone messages

WARM-UP ACTIVITY: Role playing

- Call a student to the front of the room. Pretend to call the student on the phone. Elicit appropriate ways to answer the telephone and write them on the board.
- Have another volunteer come to the front. Pretend to call again and demonstrate how to introduce yourself and ask to speak to someone.
- Continue with other students and switch roles.

1 **READ** the message slips. Circle the family words.

- Go over the directions.
- Have students read the slips and circle the words for family members.
- Go over the answers with the class.

ANSWER KEY

A. uncle; B. cousin; C. brother

2 **LISTEN** to the conversation. Write the letter of the message slip.

- Play the CD and have students write the letter (A, B, or C) of the message they hear. Remind students to look at the three message slips.

LISTENING SCRIPT
Lesson 6, Activity 2
TCD1, 29

Listen to the conversation. Write the letter of the message.

(phone ringing)
A: Hello?
B: Hi. Is Lucy there?
A: No, she's not. She's at school. May I take a message?
B: Yes, please. This is her brother Jack. I'm here in Boston. Our parents are here too.
A: What's your phone number?
B: (617) 555-1903.

ANSWER KEY

C

LISTEN AGAIN. Circle *yes* or *no*.

- Go over the directions.
- Have students read the sentences.
- Say the conversation or play the CD and have students circle *yes* or *no*.
- Put students in pairs to compare answers.
- Go over the answers with the class.

ANSWER KEY

1. no; 2. yes; 3. no; 4. no

EXPANSION ACTIVITY: Write sentences

- Have students write two sentences about messages A and C, one of which is true and one of which is false.
- Put students in pairs to read their partners' sentences and say *yes* or *no*.

3 LISTEN to the message. Complete the message slip.

- Go over the directions.
- Direct students' attention to the message slip. Review where the information will go.
- Have students complete the message slip as you say the conversation or play the CD.

LISTENING SCRIPT
Lesson 6, Activity 3

TCD1, 30

Listen to the message. Complete the message slip.

> (phone ringing)
> A: Hello?
> B: Hello. Is Ben there?
> A: No, he's not. May I take a message?
> B: Yes, please. This is his aunt Ann.
> A: What's your phone number?
> B: I'm in New York. It's (212) 555-3064.

ANSWER KEY

To: Ben
From: Aunt Ann
Phone number: (212) 555-3064

4 LISTEN and read.

- Direct students' attention to the picture. Ask questions: *Who do you see? Where are they? What is that?* Elicit that two people are on the telephone and one is taking a message.
- Have students follow along and repeat as you say the conversation or play the CD.
- Ask comprehension questions: *Who is the phone call for? Who is on the phone? What is Julie's telephone number? Is Wendy there? Who is Julie?*
- Play the CD again and have students repeat.
- Put students in pairs to take turns reading the parts of Monica and Julie.

5 PRACTICE THE CONVERSATION with a partner.

- Go over the directions and the information.
- Model the activity with a student. Have the students read Monica's lines. Substitute the information in 1 (*This is her brother Tino.*).
- Put students in pairs. Have students take turns giving and taking messages using the information in Activity 5.
- Walk around the room to monitor the activity and provide help as needed.
- Have pairs of students say the conversations in front of the class.

6 TALK with a partner. Give and take telephone messages. Use the message slip below.

- Go over the directions and the example conversation.
- Have students choose someone they want to call.
- Put students in pairs to role play. Tell students they can use their own information or make it up.

EXPANSION ACTIVITY:
Answering machine

- Explain the activity. Tell students you are the telephone answering machine and you will read some recorded messages. Students should write the messages down.

- Read the following recorded messages or create your own. You may want to make a beep sound between each one to remind students that you are the message machine.

  This is _____. I'm not home. Please leave a message. [beep]

  Hi, _____. This is your student, Min. My phone number is 555-8776. [beep]

  Hello. My name is Ray Perez. I am in your English class. My telephone number is 555-0338.

  Hey, _____. This is your cousin, Ben. My number is 555-2249.

- Put students in pairs to compare messages.

- Call on students to read their messages to the class.

COMMUNITY CONNECTION:
Phone a friend

- For an out-of-class assignment, have students phone a friend, neighbor, or coworker who doesn't speak the first language of the student. If the person isn't home, the students should practice leaving a message. If the person is home, the student can practice giving his or her phone number over the telephone.

LESSON 7: Reading and Writing

OBJECTIVES

Read a personal story
Make a list to get ideas for writing

READING TIP

Use pictures to think about a reading

WRITING TIP

Make lists to get ideas for writing

COMPETENCIES

Write simple sentences on a familiar topic
Scan for specific information in simple reading
    material
Use *be* in descriptions of people

WARM-UP ACTIVITY: Personal characteristics

- Have two volunteers who are quite different come to the front of the room. Elicit characteristics for each and write them on the board. Point out that they are different.
- Have two volunteers who are more similar come to the front of the room. Elicit their characteristics. Point out that they are similar.

Reading

❶ THINK ABOUT IT. Are you similar to the people in your family?

- Explain the difference between *similar* and *different.* Use two students who look similar and have things in common to illustrate *similar.*
- Read the question. Elicit answers from students.

❷ BEFORE YOU READ. Look at the photo. What is the reading about? Check the answer.

- Go over the reading tip in the box.
- Go over the directions. Point out that they are just guessing; they do not have to read yet.
- Direct students' attention to the photo and ask: *Brothers?* Elicit that the answer is *no.* Point to the box and shake your head.
- Have students check what they think will be in the story.
- Elicit ideas from the class.

EXPANSION ACTIVITY: Two adjectives

- Have students list two adjectives for each person in the photo.
- Put students in pairs to compare ideas.
- Elicit ideas from the class and write them on the board.

❸ READ. Circle the adjectives.

- Have students read the paragraph, or read the paragraph aloud sentence by sentence and have students repeat.
- Have students circle the adjectives.
- Ask comprehension questions: *Who are the sisters? Who is a student? Who is a doctor? Who is hardworking?*
- Elicit the adjectives in the paragraph.

ANSWER KEY

Circle: tall, thin, hardworking, funny, different, messy, neat

❹ WRITE adjectives to describe Claire and Liz.

- Direct students' attention to the chart. Go over the example.
- Have students write other adjectives in the chart.
- Put students in pairs to compare ideas.

- Elicit ideas from the students and write the ideas on the board.

ANSWER KEY

Claire: not thin, tall, hardworking, funny, messy
Liz: tall, thin, hardworking, funny, neat

EXPANSION ACTIVITY: Literacy development—sentence strips

- Copy the sentences from the paragraph onto separate strips. Leave enough space between each word for word discrimination. The sentences need to be large enough to be read by all the students.
- Put the sentence strips on the board in the correct order. Read each sentence aloud and have students repeat. You may want to point to each word as you read.
- Take the sentences down and mix them up.
- Have volunteers come to the board and put the sentences in the correct order. Have the other students help.
- You may want to photocopy the sentences and cut them into strips so that each student or pair of students has a set to reassemble.

⑤ WRITE. Answer the questions.

- Read the first question. Elicit the answer. Point out that *No, she isn't* is written on the line.
- Have students answer the questions.
- Put students in pairs to compare answers.
- Go over the answers with the class.

ANSWER KEY

1. No, she isn't. 2. No, she isn't. 3. Yes, they are.
4. Yes, they are.

EXPANSION ACTIVITY: Write questions

- Have students write two more questions about the paragraph.
- Elicit the questions and write them on the board.
- Have students answer the questions.

BIG PICTURE READING EXPANSION ACTIVITY: Berta and Carl

- Photocopy and distribute Worksheet 4: Berta and Carl.
- Put the transparency for Unit 2 on the OHP or have students look at the Big Picture on page 25.
- Copy the diagram on the board.
- Go over the directions and the examples on the diagram. Make sure students understand the outer sections are either Berta or Carl, and the inner section is for both.
- Have students write adjectives and other information in the diagram. Remind students to use the visual information in the picture as well as the text.
- Put students in pairs to share their ideas.
- Elicit ideas from the students and write them on the board.

WORKSHEET 4 ANSWER KEY

Berta is: short, heavy, serious all the time, shy, likes soccer
Carl is: tall, thin, funny, out going, likes soccer, not serious in school
Berta and Carl are: Oscar's children, serious about soccer, messy

Writing

- Go over the writing tip in the box.
- Point out or elicit that making lists is a way of brainstorming or getting ideas before we write—that it helps us to begin the writing process.

❶ WRITE. In the chart, make a list of five adjectives that describe you. Now think of a family member. Write five adjectives that describe your family member.

- Review the adjectives in the box.
- Model the activity. Copy the chart on the board. Write your name in the left column and one of your relatives in the right.
- Tell the students about you and write five adjectives in the chart on the board. Then tell about a family member as you write adjectives in the appropriate place on the board.
- Have students complete the chart.
- Walk around to monitor the activity and provide help as needed.
- Put students in pairs to talk about their charts.

EXPANSION ACTIVITY: Venn diagrams

- Draw a Venn diagram with two overlapping circles on the board.
- Model the activity. Use the information from your chart in Activity 1 to complete the diagram. As you fill in the outer edges, say *different*. As you add details to the overlapping area, say *similar.*
- Have students complete the Venn diagrams about themselves and a family member. Encourage students to use the information in Activity 1 and to add information as needed.
- Put students in pairs to share their information.

---

❷ WRITE about you and your family member.

- Go over the directions.
- Have students complete the sentences with information about themselves and their family member. Remind students to use the information from Activity 1.
- Walk around to monitor the activity and provide help as needed.
- Put students in pairs to read their sentences.
- Call on students to read their sentences to the class.

EXPANSION ACTIVITY: Who is it?

- Have students rewrite all their sentences except for the first one on a separate sheet of paper.
- Collect the papers. Read a paragraph aloud to the class and elicit guesses as to who it is.
- Continue with other papers.
- In a variation, put students in small groups. Collect their papers and redistribute. Have students guess which group member wrote the paragraph.

BIG PICTURE WRITING EXPANSION ACTIVITY: Two characters

- Put the transparency for Unit 2 on the OHP or have students look at page 25 in their books.
- Have each student choose two characters or assign each student two characters from the Big Picture.
- Ask students to create a Venn diagram to compare their two characters.
- Put students in pairs to talk about their ideas.
- Have students write three to five sentences about the two characters.
- Ask volunteers to read sentences to the class.

Career Connection

OBJECTIVE
Match personal characteristics to jobs

COMPETENCIES
Recognize qualities for job promotions Begin to set education and employment goals

WARM-UP ACTIVITY: Jobs

- Ask who in the class has a job.
- Call on students who have jobs and ask if they are similar to or different from the people they work with.

🎧 **❶ READ AND LISTEN.** Then practice with a partner.

- Direct students' attention to the photos. Tell students this is the continuation of the story about Isabel. Have students point to Isabel in the photos.
- Play the CD and have students follow along silently.
- Play the CD again and have students repeat.
- Put students in pairs to take turns reading the roles of Isabel and her coworker.

❷ WRITE. List adjectives for Isabel and Laura.

- Write *Isabel* and *Laura* on the board. Elicit one adjective for each and write it.
- Have students list adjectives in their notebooks for Isabel and adjectives for her boss, Laura.
- Elicit answers and write them on the board.

ANSWER KEY
Isabel: hardworking, organized, friendly Laura: new, tall, pretty, hardworking, organized, friendly, good

❸ WHAT ABOUT YOU? List adjectives for you. Write a job or occupation for each adjective.

- Go over the directions and the example.
- Have students complete the chart.
- Put students in pairs to talk about their charts.
- Call on students and ask about their adjectives and jobs they could do.

COMMUNITY CONNECTION: Outside speaker

- Invite one or more outside speakers to come to the class and talk about their jobs and the qualities that help them in that job.
- Have students take notes. Elicit the jobs and qualities and write them on the board.

CHECK YOUR PROGRESS!

- Have students circle the answers.
- Have students check whether each answer is right or wrong.
- Have students total their correct answers and fill in the chart.
- Have students create a learning plan and/or set learning goals.

ANSWER KEY
1. Are; 2. Is; 3. Am; 4. sisters; 5. mother's; 6. brothers; 7. outgoing; 8. neat; 9. short; 10. aunt; 11. grandmother; 12. uncle

Unit Overview

LESSON	OBJECTIVE	STUDENT BOOK	WORKBOOK
1 Grammar and Vocabulary 1	Use *there is* and *there are* Identify classroom objects	p. 38	p. 34
2 Grammar Practice Plus	Identify school supplies Use multiplication	p. 40	p. 35
3 Listening and Conversation	Ask about library facilities	p. 42	p. 36
4 Grammar and Vocabulary 2	Use prepositions to locate places at school	p. 44	p. 38
5 Grammar Practice Plus	Read a map of a school Describe locations at school	p. 46	p. 39
6 Apply Your Knowledge	Ask for and give directions at school Read a sign	p. 48	p. 40
7 Reading and Writing	Read a website Use correct punctuation	p. 50	p. 42
• Career Connection	Identify locations in the workplace	p. 52	p. 44
• Check Your Progress	Monitor progress	p. 53	p. 46

Reading/Writing Strategies
Connection Activities

• Take notes using a diagram   • Use correct punctuation

LESSON	TYPE	SKILL DEVELOPMENT
1	Community	Describe one's home
2	Academic	Conduct a survey and report results
3	Academic	Research library offerings
4	Academic	Use compound words
5	Academic	Use a map
6	Community	Understand a building directory
6	Academic	List places in alphabetical or numerical order
8	Community	Describe a workplace

WORKSHEET #/FOCUS	TITLE	TEACHER'S EDITION
5 Grammar	In the Classroom	p. 250
6 Writing	Icons	p. 251
7 Reading, Writing	Our Classroom/Our School	p. 252

LESSON 1: Grammar and Vocabulary

OBJECTIVES

Use *there is* and *there are*
Identify classroom objects

VOCABULARY

board	desk
CDs	map
chair	pencil sharpener
clock	table
computer	trash can
copier	window

GRAMMAR

There is/There are

COMPETENCIES

Identify classroom objects

WARM-UP ACTIVITY

- Put the transparency for Unit 3 on the overhead projector (OHP) or have students look at the Big Picture on page 41.
- Elicit words the students know and write them on the board.

❶ GRAMMAR PICTURE DICTIONARY. Listen and repeat.

- Have students open their books and look at the pictures. Ask: *What do you see?* Write all the words the students know on the board.
- Have students look at the pictures and listen while you say the words or play the CD.
- Say the sentences or play the CD again and have students repeat.
- Say classroom objects in random order and have students point to the pictures.
- Have students look around classroom and point out objects they see.

EXPANSION ACTIVITY: Alphabetize

- Make sure students know what alphabetical order is. Point out or elicit that when words begin with the same initial letter, students must look at the second or third letter to alphabetize.
- Put students in pairs to write the bold-faced words from Activity 1 in alphabetical order.
- Have volunteers write the words on the board.

❷ NOTICE THE GRAMMAR. Look at Activity 1. Underline *There is* and *There are.* Circle the plural words (the words that end in -s).

- Have students read the sentences and underline *There is* and *There are.* Then have students circle the plural words.
- Ask questions: *When do we use* is? *When do we use* are?

ANSWER KEY

1. There is a map.
2. There is a clock.
3. There are many desks.
4. There is a table.
5. There is a computer.
6. There are three windows.
7. There is a pencil sharpener.
8. There is a trash can.
9. There are CDs.
10. There is a board.
11. There is a copier.
12. There are many chairs.

EXPANSION ACTIVITY: Replace the word

- Give students two minutes to review the sentences.
- Have students close their books.
- Write the sentences on the board, but leave out all forms of the verb *be*.
- Elicit the missing words from the students.
- Have students open their books and confirm their answers.

GRAMMAR CHART: *There is* and *There are*

- Direct students' attention to the chart.
- Go over the information on the chart. You may want to read the statements and the questions and answers, pausing to have students repeat.

CHART EXPANSION ACTIVITY: Form of *be*

- Cover the column with the verbs on the transparency. Elicit the form of *be.*
- Put students in pairs to take turns asking and answering the questions in the chart. Encourage students to answer the questions in both the affirmative and the negative.

3 WRITE. Look at the picture. Complete the sentences. Use *is, isn't, are,* or *aren't.*

- Direct students' attention to the picture. Ask questions: *Is there a map? Is there a table? Are there six students?*
- Read the first sentence and elicit *is* or *are.* Point out *is* is written on the line.
- Have students complete the sentences with the appropriate negative or affirmative form of *be.*
- Put students in pairs to compare answers.
- Go over the answers with the class.

EXPANSION ACTIVITY: Question challenge

- Change the first statement in Activity 3 to a question (*Is there one map?*). Elicit the answer (*Yes, there is.*).
- Have students rewrite the statements as questions.
- Put students in pairs to compare questions.
- Have students write the questions on the board.
- Have students take turns asking and answering the questions with their partners.

4 WHAT ABOUT YOU? Complete the sentences about *your* classroom.

- Go over the directions and the example.
- Model the activity. Point to an object in your classroom. Elicit its name (*table*). Elicit the completion (*There is _____ table.*).
- Have students complete the sentences. If necessary, identify the objects they should write about.
- Put students in pairs to read their sentences aloud.
- Call on students to read their sentences to the class.

EXPANSION ACTIVITY: *Yes/No* **cards**

- Distribute two index cards to each student. Have students write *yes* on one and *no* on the other.

- Say sentences about objects in your classroom (e.g., *There are two boards.*). Have students hold up the appropriate card. Keep the activity fast-paced.

EXPANSION ACTIVITY: Quick response

- Call on a student and say one of the vocabulary words (*desk*). Elicit a sentence beginning with *There is* or *There are* and the correct number in your classroom.

- Continue the activity until everyone has had a chance to participate.

COMMUNITY CONNECTION: At your home

- For homework, have students write three sentences using the vocabulary words about things in their homes.

LESSON 2: Grammar Practice Plus

OBJECTIVES

Identify school supplies
Use multiplication

VOCABULARY

bag	marker
backpack	notebook
book	pen
cell phone	pencil

GRAMMAR

There is and *there are* in statements and questions

COMPETENCIES

Use *there* is/*there* are in statements and questions
Identify classroom objects

MATH/NUMERACY

Multiplication questions with *how many*

WARM-UP ACTIVITY: Other things in the classroom

- With books closed, elicit the words students know for things in the classroom. Encourage students to include the words from Lesson 1, as well as other words they know.
- Write their ideas on the board.

1 WRITE words under the pictures. Use the words in the box.

- Go over the directions and the words in the box. Say each word and have students repeat.
- Point to the first picture and elicit the word (*pencil*). Point out *pencil* is written on the line and crossed out in the box.

- Have students write the words on the lines.
- Put students in pairs to compare answers.

 LISTEN and repeat. Are your answers correct?

- Play the audio and have students repeat. Have students check their answers.

LISTENING SCRIPT AND ANSWER KEY
Lesson 2, Activity 1

TCD1, 34

Listen and repeat. Are your answers correct?

1. pencil; 2. pen; 3. backpack; 4. marker;
5. cell phone; 6. bag; 7. book; 8. notebook

EXPANSION ACTIVITY: A *what?*

- This activity can help students practice clarification questions.
- Write on the board: *This is a* _____ and *A what?*
- Model the activity. Hold up a pencil, and say *This is a pencil.* Cue students to ask *A what?* And repeat *A pencil.*
- Call on a student and cue the student to hold up one of the objects from Activity 1 and say *This is a* _____. Ask *A what?* Elicit the name of the object again.
- Continue the activity with other students and objects.
- In a variation, put students in groups of three or four to take turns saying the name of an object.

LITERACY DEVELOPMENT NOTE

Point out or elicit that the words in the box in Activity 1 are in alphabetical order. Make sure students understand what that means.

LITERACY EXPANSION ACTIVITY: Spell it

- Call on students, say a word from Activity 1 and have students spell it. Literacy students can look at the book.
- Assign each student a word from Lessons 1 and 2 to write on an index card of piece of paper. Assist students to post the labels on the objects in the classroom.

2 WRITE. Look in your bag or backpack. Write the things you see.

- Copy the chart on the board.
- Model the activity. Open your bag or purse and pull out items. As you do, say what it is and write it on the board (*There is a cell phone, There are two pens.*).
- Have the students complete the chart. If they don't have a bag or backpack, have them use items in their pockets or pencil cases.
- Go over the example conversation.
- Put students in pairs to talk about what they have.

EXPANSION ACTIVITY: Venn diagram

- Draw a Venn diagram on the board. Write your name above one section and the name of a student above the other. Complete the diagram, writing the things that only you have in one outer section, the things only your student has in the other outer section, and the things you both have in the overlapping area in the center.
- Put students in pairs to complete a Venn diagram comparing and contrasting the items they have in their bags or backpacks.

MATH: Multiplication

- Go over the directions.

- Go over the example. Make sure students understand how multiplication works. If necessary give other examples ($3 \times 3 = 3 + 3 + 3$, $4 \times 5 = 5 + 5 + 5 + 5$).
- Have students write the equations.
- Put students in pairs to read the equations.
- Go over the answers with the class.

VOCABULARY NOTE

Write the words for each symbol on the board: $+$ plus, $=$ equals, $\times$ times. Remind students to say the words when they are reading the equations.

ANSWER KEY

1. $2 \times 2 = 4$; **2.** $3 \times 2 = 6$; **3.** $6 \times 20 = 120$

EXPANSION ACTIVITY: Math challenge

- Put students in pairs and have them each write a new math problem. Remind students to use the problems in the book as models.
- Have pairs exchange and solve problems.
- Call on students to read the problems and equations to the class or have them write them on the board for the rest of the class to solve.

---

3 TALK about the picture.

- Go over the directions and the example sentences.
- Direct students' attention to the picture.
- Call on students. Say an object and elicit a sentence beginning with *There is* or *There are*.

BIG PICTURE SPEAKING EXPANSION ACTIVITY: Team challenge

- Have students look at the Big Picture or put the color overhead transparency for Unit 3 on the OHP.
- Divide the class into two teams.
- Have each team write sentences about the picture, one correct and one incorrect. Suggest each pair of students write one correct and one incorrect sentence.
- Give students two minutes to study the picture. With books closed, alternate calling on members of each team to read a sentence. One member of the opposing team must say *yes* if the sentence is correct, *no* if it is incorrect.
- Optional: keep score on the board.

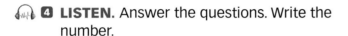 **❹ LISTEN.** Answer the questions. Write the number.

- Go over the directions.
- Have students look at the picture and write the number as you say the questions or play the CD. Make sure students understand that *how many* is asking about the number.
- Put students in pairs to compare answers.
- Say the questions or play the CD again so students can confirm.
- Go over the answers with the class.

 LISTENING SCRIPT
Lesson 2, Activity 4
TCD1, 35

Listen. Answer the questions. Write the number.

1. How many students are there?
2. How many desks are there?
3. How many notebooks are there?
4. How many maps are there?
5. How many markers are there?
6. How many books are there?
7. How many cell phones are there?
8. How many backpacks are there on the floor?

ANSWER KEY

1. 16; 2. 17; 3. 11; 4. 0; 5. 3; 6. 11; 7. 11; 8. 5

EXPANSION ACTIVITY: Dictation

- Have students write the questions from Activity 4 as you read the questions or play the CD. Repeat twice.
- Put students in pairs to compare sentences.
- Have volunteers write the questions on the board.

❺ TALK with a partner. Ask and answer questions about the things in the picture.

- Go over the directions and the examples. Point out that students can ask questions beginning with *Is there* or *Are there,* or *How many.*
- Put students in pairs to practice asking and answering the questions with their partners.

ACADEMIC CONNECTION: Survey

- Have students choose two items to ask their classmates about (e.g., *Is there a cell phone in your bag? How many pencils are in your backpack?*).
- Have students stand and walk around the class to ask each classmate about the two items. Remind students to tally the results.
- Call on students to share the results with the class (e.g., *There are nine cell phones.*). Write the information on the board (e.g., *cell phones—9*).

BIG PICTURE GRAMMAR EXPANSION ACTIVITY: In the Classroom

- Photocopy and distribute Worksheet 5: In the Classroom.
- Go over the directions and the example.
- Have students complete the worksheet and then compare answers with a partner.
- Go over the answers with the class.

WORKSHEET 5 ANSWER KEY

1. Yes, there are. 2. Yes, there is. 3. No, there aren't. 4. No, there isn't. 5. There is one teacher. 6. There are 8 bags. 7. There are 8 men. 8. There are 9 women.

LESSON 3: Listening and Conversation

OBJECTIVE

Ask about library facilities

VOCABULARY

books in Spanish	DVDs
computer classes	meeting room

COMPETENCIES

Ask about resources at a library

WARM-UP ACTIVITY: Say and point

- Say each of the new vocabulary words or phrases in random order and have students point to the pictures in their books.

 ❶ WRITE. Complete the questions with *Is there* or *Are there.*

- Write the first question on the board without the completion (_____ *a meeting room?*). Elicit the completion *Is there.* Point out that *Is there* is written on the line.
- Have students complete the questions with *Is there* or *Are there.*
- Play the CD or read the questions and have students repeat and check their answers.
- Have students compare answers in pairs.
- Go over the answers with the class.

LISTENING SCRIPT
Lesson 3, Activity 1

TCD1, 36

Listen and repeat. Are your answers correct?

1. Is there a meeting room?
2. Are there computer classes?
3. Are there DVDs?
4. Are there books in Spanish?

ANSWER KEY

1. Is there; **2.** Are there; **3.** Are there; **4.** Are there

 ❷ LISTEN and circle the letter.

- Direct students' attention to the pictures. Elicit the names of the objects.
- Play the CD or read the sentences as students circle the letter of the object they hear.
- Go over the answers with the class.

LISTENING SCRIPT
Lesson 3, Activity 2

TCD1, 37

Listen and circle the letter.

1. The DVDs are on the desk.
2. There is a copier in the meeting room.
3. My backpack is on the table.

ANSWER KEY

1. A; **2.** C; **3.** C

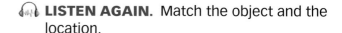 **LISTEN AGAIN.** Match the object and the location.

- Go over the directions.
- Play the CD again and have students match the location to the object.
- Go over the answers with the class.

ANSWER KEY

1. b; **2.** a; **3.** c

🎧 **3 LISTEN** and read.

- Direct students' attention to the picture and ask *What is in the picture?*
- Play the CD as students follow along silently.
- Play the CD again and have students repeat.
- Put students in pairs to practice the conversation.

EXPANSION ACTIVITY: Dictation and order

- With books closed, dictate the sentences from Activity 3 in random order. Have students write them. Say each sentence at least three times.
- Put students in pairs to put the conversation in order. Tell students to write *1* next to the first sentence in the conversation, and so on.
- Have students check the order in the book.

---

4 PRACTICE THE CONVERSATION with a partner.

- Direct students' attention to each picture and elicit the name of the object.
- Go over the directions.
- Model the activity. Have a more advanced student read A's lines. Model how to substitute a different object. Cue the student to respond with the correct number.
- Put students in pairs to practice the conversation, making the appropriate substitutions. Have students switch roles.
- Walk around to monitor the activity and provide help as needed.
- Call on students to say the conversation for each of the substitutions to the class.

5 TALK. Look at the website. Ask and answer questions with a partner.

- Direct students' attention to the website. Have students read the information silently, or read it aloud as students follow along.
- Go over the directions and the example conversation.
- Put students in pairs to ask and answer questions about the Midtown Library.
- Call on students and ask questions about the library.

COMMUNITY CONNECTION: Go online

- As an out-of-class or lab assignment, have students use a search engine and search for a library near your school or in their own neighborhoods.
- Ask students to write down five things the library offers.
- Call on students to share what they found out.

LESSON 4: Grammar and Vocabulary

OBJECTIVE

Use prepositions to locate places at school

VOCABULARY

elevator
lobby
office
public telephone
restroom

snack bar
stairs
vending machine
water fountain

GRAMMAR

Prepositions of location (*in, on, at*)

COMPETENCIES

Use prepositions of location
Talk about places at school

WARM-UP ACTIVITY: Icons

- Photocopy and distribute Worksheet 6: Icons
- Put students in pairs to identify what each icon means.
- Call on students and elicit their ideas. Write the words on the board. Point out that they don't need to know all the words at this point.
- Have literacy students copy the words on the sheet. Tell students to save the worksheet for later reference.

WORKSHEET 6 ANSWER KEY

1. information; 2. information; 3. parking;
4. telephone; 5. food/restaurant/snack bar;
6. stairs; 7. elevator; 8. men's restroom;
9. women's restroom

🎧 **❶ GRAMMAR PICTURE DICTIONARY.**
   Listen and repeat.

- Have students look at the picture. Ask: *What do you see?*
- Play the CD or say the sentences and have students repeat.
- Say the words in random order and have the students point to the pictures.

❷ NOTICE THE GRAMMAR. Read the sentences in Activity 1. Circle *in* and *on.*

- Have students circle *in* and *on.*
- Go over the answers with the class.

ANSWER KEY

1. The lobby is (on) the first floor.
2. The stairs are over there.
3. The elevator is (in) the lobby.
4. The water fountain is (in) the snack bar.
5. The snack bar is (in) the Harper building.
6. The vending machine is (in) the hall.
7. The restrooms are (on) the first floor.
8. The office is (on) the second floor.
9. The public telephones are (in) the office.

GRAMMAR CHART: Prepositions of Location

- Go over the information in the chart, including the usage notes.
- You may want to read the sample sentences in the chart and have students repeat.
- At this point, students are only going to learn about three prepositions of location. They will learn about other prepositions of place (e.g., *next to, between*) in Unit 4. At this level, students will learn a few prepositions of direction (*to, from*), but will not learn other prepositions (*with, for*).

CHART EXPANSION ACTIVITY: Beanbag toss

- Call on a student, toss the beanbag and say a place (e.g., *35 Main Street*). Elicit the preposition (*at*). Have the student toss the beanbag back.
- Continue the activity using all three prepositions on the chart until everyone has had a chance to participate.

3 WRITE. Complete the sentences. Use *in, on,* or *at.*

- Go over the directions and the example. Read *The water fountain is _____ the hall.* Elicit that the preposition we need is *in.* Point out that *in* is written on the line.
- Have students complete the sentences with prepositions.
- Put students in pairs to compare answers.
- Go over the answers with the class.

ANSWER KEY

1. in; **2.** on; **3.** on; **4.** in; **5.** in; **6.** at; **7.** in/at; **8.** at

EXPANSION ACTIVITY: Write *yes/no* questions

- Have students write *yes/no* questions for each sentence in Activity 3. Encourage students to change the information in some of the questions (e.g., *Is the water fountain in the snack bar?*).
- Put students in pairs to practice asking and answering the questions.
- Call on students and ask questions.

4 WHAT ABOUT YOU? Complete the sentences about your school. Use *in, on,* or *at.*

- Go over the directions.
- Read the first sentence starter and elicit the completion. Have students write the appropriate place on the line.
- Have students complete the other sentences.
- Put students in pairs to read their sentences.
- Call on students to tell the class the location of one thing at your school.

ACADEMIC CONNECTION: Compound words

- Point out that compound words are two words put together to refer to one thing.
- Write two headings on the board: *one–word compounds, two–word compounds.* Elicit an example of each and write the words under the headings (e.g., *restroom, water fountain*).
- Have students write the words from the unit under the appropriate headings. Encourage students to add three more compounds to their list to name things at your school (e.g., *copy machine, fax machine, whiteboard*).

LESSON 5: Grammar Practice Plus

OBJECTIVES
Read a map of a school
Describe locations at school

VOCABULARY	
computer lab	library
information desk	security office

GRAMMAR
Prepositions of location

PRONUNCIATION
Stress in compound nouns

COMPETENCIES
Use prepositions of location
Talk about places at school

WARM-UP ACTIVITY: Spell it

- Direct students' attention to the bold-faced words in Activity 1.
- Call on students, say a phrase and have students spell it. Less advanced students can look at the words as they spell. For added challenge, more advanced students can try to spell the words without looking.

❶ WRITE. Complete the sentences. Use the words in the box.

- Direct students' attention to the first picture. Elicit the preposition. Point out that *on* is written on the line.
- Have students write the prepositions.

🎧 LISTEN and repeat. Are your answers correct?

- Play the CD or read the sentences and have students repeat and confirm their answers.
- Go over the answers with the class.

LISTENING SCRIPT
Lesson 5, Activity 1

TCD1, 40

Listen and repeat. Are your answers correct?

1. The information desk is on the first floor.
2. The security office is at 521 Fifth Street.
3. The library is on Fifth Street.
4. The computer lab is in Room 102.

ANSWER KEY
1. information desk; **2.** security office;
3. library; **4.** computer lab

🎧 PRONUNCIATION: *Stress in Compound Nouns*

A. LISTEN and repeat.

- Go over the directions. Explain that when we stress a word, we say it a little louder and longer. (See following expansion activity for a way to illustrate stress.)
- Play the CD and stop after the first phrase, or read the first phrase. Elicit that *water* is stressed and *fountain* is not. Point out that *water* is circled.

B. CIRCLE the stressed word or word part.

- Play the rest of the CD and have students circle the stressed word. Elicit which words are stressed (all of the first words in the compounds).

C. TALK. Read the words to a partner.

- Put students in pairs to practice reading the compounds aloud with appropriate stress.
- Call on students and say a number. Have the student say the compound with appropriate stress. Correct if necessary.

LISTENING SCRIPT AND ANSWER KEY
Lesson 5

TCD1, 41
SCD, 17   Listen and repeat.

1. (water) fountain	7. (computer) lab
2. (back) pack	8. (pencil) sharpener
3. (snack) bar	9. (note) book
4. (cell) phone	10. (information) desk
5. (trash) can	11. (security) office
6. (rest) room	12. (vending) machine

EXPANSION ACTIVITY: Stress with rubber bands

- Give each student a rubber band. Say one of the words or phrases. For long syllables, stretch the rubber band wide between your thumb and forefinger as you say it, then bring your fingers together for shorter, unstressed syllables.
- Continue to say words and phrases and have students manipulate the rubber bands appropriately.

BIG PICTURE LISTENING EXPANSION ACTIVITY: Dictation

- Put the color transparency for Unit 3 on the OHP or have students look at the Big Picture in their books.
- Point to new compounds as you say the words and phrases at least three times. Have the students write the words (*whiteboard, computer table, classroom, skateboard, pencil case*). Dictate the spelling of unfamiliar words (e.g., s-*k-a-t-e-b-o-a-r-d*).
- Say the words and phrases again and have students circle the stressed word or word part.

2 MATCH. Look at the map. Match the questions and answers.

- Direct students' attention to the map of the school building. Make sure students understand that they are looking down at the layout of the first floor of Baker Building.
- Go over the directions.
- Read the first question. Elicit that the trash can is in the hall. Point out that *a* is written on the line in question 1.
- Have students match the questions and answers by writing the letters on the lines.
- Put students in pairs to compare answers.
- Go over the answers with the class.
- Have students take turns asking and answering the questions with their partners.

ANSWER KEY

1. a; 2. e; 3. b; 4. c; 5. d

EXPANSION ACTIVITY: Draw a map

- Have students draw the floor plan of your school or building.
- Have students label places they know on the floor plan.
- Put students in pairs to ask and answer questions about their floor plans.

❹ **GAME.** Think of a place or thing in your school. Say where it is. Your partner guesses.

- Go over the directions and the example.
- Model the activity. Say where something is and elicit the name of the thing.
- Put students in pairs to play the game.
- Call on students to say where something is and have the class guess what it is.

COMMUNITY CONNECTION: Campus maps

- As an out-of-class assignment, have students go online to get a map (or get one on campus) of your school or a college or university near you.
- Have students bring the printed copy to class.
- Put students in pairs to practice asking and answering questions about the map.

LESSON 6: Apply Your Knowledge

OBJECTIVES

Ask for and give directions at school
Read a sign

COMPETENCIES

Read a building directory
Read a map
Ask about locations

WARM-UP ACTIVITY: Building directories

- Brainstorm a list of places where students have seen building directories. Write the places on the board. Point out that students will learn about more places in Unit 5.

1 READ the sign. Write the places on the map.

- Direct students' attention to the sign. Ask *Where are signs like this?*
- Go over the directions.
- Have students read the sign. Ask questions: *Where is the library? Where is the snack bar?*
- Direct students' attention to the diagram of the building. Ask *Where is room 203?* Make sure students know it is to the right of room 202. Have students write *203* on the line next to *Room.*
- Have students read the sign and write the places on the diagram of the building.
- Go over the answers with the class.

ANSWER KEY

2nd floor	Room 201 (classroom)	Room 202 (classroom)	Room <u>203</u> <u>Library</u>	Main Hall Information Desk
1st floor	Room 101 <u>Security Office</u>	Room <u>102</u> <u>Computer Lab</u>	Room 103 <u>Snack Bar</u>	

 2 LISTEN. Write the location.

- Play the CD and have students write the location next to the object. Be sure they include the preposition.

LISTENING SCRIPT
Lesson 6, Activity 2
TCD1, 42

Listen. Write the location.

Welcome to Washington School and English class. The vending machines are in the snack bar. There are student books in the library. There are restrooms in the main hall.

ANSWER KEY

1. in the snack bar; **2.** in the library; **3.** in the main hall

EXPANSION ACTIVITY: Challenge dictation

- Play the CD and pause after each sentence so students can write what they hear. Play the CD as many times as necessary.
- Have volunteers write the sentences on the board.

3 LISTEN and read.

- Direct students' attention to the picture. Ask questions: *Who do you see? Where are they?* Elicit that two students are talking at school.
- Have students follow along and repeat as you say the conversation or play the CD.
- Ask comprehension questions: *Where is the snack bar? What floor is it on?*
- Play the CD again and have students repeat.
- Put students in pairs to take turns reading the parts of Tony and Ingrid.

GRAMMAR NOTE

Point out or elicit that *where's* is a contraction of *where is,* and *it's* is the contraction of *it is.*

4 PRACTICE THE CONVERSATION from Activity 3 with a partner. Ask about the places in the picture.

- Go over the directions and the information.
- Model the activity with a student. Have the students read Tony's lines. Cue the student to ask about one of the places in the picture (e.g., *computer lab*). Respond with the appropriate location (e.g., *It's in the Blake Building, on the second floor.*).
- Put students in pairs. Have students take turns asking for and giving locations.
- Walk around the room to monitor the activity and provide help as needed.
- Have pairs of students say the conversations in front of the class.
- Call on students and ask where things are.

5 WHAT ABOUT YOU? Complete the sign with information about your school.

- Go over the directions.
- Have students complete the sign.
- Put students in pairs to compare signs.
- Have students write the information on the board.

- Put students in pairs to practice asking and answering questions about places at school.

EXPANSION ACTIVITY: Welcome to our school

- Have students write an announcement like the one they heard in Activity 2 for your school. Remind students to use the information from the Challenge Dictation expansion and the information from their signs to write their own welcome announcement.
- Call on students to read their announcements to the class.

COMMUNITY CONNECTION: A building directory

- For an out-of-class assignment, have students find a building directory at your school or in a building they know about.
- Have students copy the information from the directory.
- Put students in pairs to ask and answer questions about the directories.

ACADEMIC CONNECTION: Alphabetical/ numerical order

- Have students rewrite their signs from Activity 5 in two ways: to list the places alphabetically, and to list the places by numerical order (according to room number).

LESSON 7: Reading and Writing

Read a website
Use correct punctuation

READING TIP

Take notes using a diagram

WRITING TIP

Begin a sentence with a capital letter.
Use a period or question mark at the end of a sentence.

COMPETENCIES

Read a school website
Take notes on a graphic organizer
Write sentences

WARM-UP ACTIVITY: Websites

Explain or elicit what a website is. If you have access to computers, pull up a website for your school or a school in your area.

Reading

❶ THINK ABOUT IT. What classes are there at your school?

• Read the question and elicit answers. Write student responses on the board.

❷ BEFORE YOU READ. Look at the website. What is the reading about? Check.

• Direct students' attention to the website. Elicit or point out what a website is.
• Go over the directions. Point out that they are just guessing, they do not have to read yet.
• Have students check what they think will be in the story.

• Elicit what students think the website is about and how they know.

ANSWER KEY

school

EXPANSION ACTIVITY: Two website topics

• Have students list two topics they can find on the website menu on the left.

❸ READ. Take notes on the diagram.

• Go over the tip in the box.
• Direct students' attention to the diagram. Point out or elicit that the details for each big idea are in the circles surrounding the bigger idea.
• Have students read the information, or read the paragraph aloud, sentence by sentence, and have students repeat.
• Have students take notes on the diagram as they read.
• Put students in pairs to compare notes.
• Copy the diagram on the board.
• Have volunteers add information to the diagram on the board.

ACADEMIC NOTE

Point out that graphic organizers such as this mind map diagram helps students to understand and remember information that they read.

ANSWER KEY

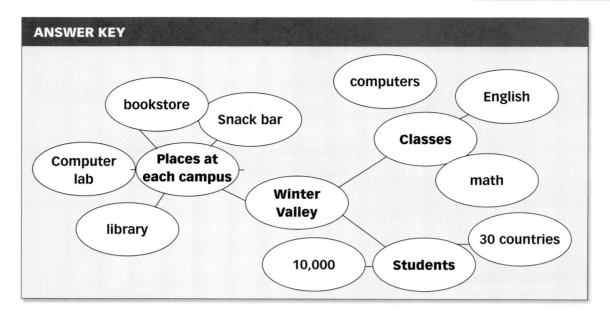

④ WRITE. Answer the questions.

- Go over the directions. Read each question aloud and have students repeat.
- Have students answer the questions.
- Put students in pairs to compare ideas.
- Go over the answers with the class.
- Put students in pairs to take turns asking and answering the questions.

ANSWER KEY

1. more than 150; 2. 10,000; 3. three

EXPANSION ACTIVITY: Literacy development—sentence strips

- Copy the sentences from the paragraph onto separate strips. Leave enough space between each word for word discrimination. The sentences need to be large enough to be read by all the students.
- Put the sentence strips on the board in the correct order. Read each sentence aloud and have students repeat. You may want to point to each word as you read.
- Take the sentences down and mix them up.
- Have volunteers come to the board and put the sentences in the correct order. Have the other students help.
- You may want to photocopy the sentences and cut them into strips so that each student or pair of students has a set to reassemble.

EXPANSION ACTIVITY: Write questions

- Have students write two more questions about the paragraph.
- Elicit the questions and write them on the board.
- Have students answer the questions.

BIG PICTURE READING EXPANSION ACTIVITY: Our Classroom/Our School

- Photocopy and distribute Worksheet 7: Our Classroom/Our School.
- Put the transparency for Unit 3 on the OHP or have students look at the Big Picture in their book.
- Have students read the information and answer the questions.
- Put students in pairs to share their ideas.
- Elicit ideas from the students and write them on the board.

WORKSHEET 7 ANSWER KEY

A: 16; 16; 1; 1
B: 1. There are three classrooms. 2. There are 48 students. 3. There are three teachers. 4. No, there isn't. 5. Yes, there are. 6. The vending machines are in the hall.

Writing

- Go over the writing tip in the box.

EXPANSION ACTIVITY: Notice the punctuation

- Have students circle all of the capital letters and periods in the reading on page 50.
- Put students in pairs to compare answers.

ACADEMIC NOTES

- At this point, students will not be focusing on most other aspects of punctuation. Point out that we use question marks instead of periods when we are asking a question.
- Remind students they can refer to Unit 2 to review the other rules of capitalization.

❶ **EDIT.** Add a period at the end of each sentence.

- Go over the directions and the example.
- Have students add periods to the ends of the sentences.
- Put students in pairs to read each other's sentences and make sure the periods are there.
- Call on students to read sentences aloud and say *period* at the end of each one.

ANSWER KEY

My school is in San Francisco. There is a library and a snack bar at my school. My classroom is on the first floor. There are 24 desks in my classroom. There is also a table. Two computers are on the table. There are 21 students in the class. Seven students are from Mexico, two are from Honduras, five are from Vietnam, four are from Russia, and three are from Somalia. There are books and notebooks for all the students.

EXPANSION ACTIVITY: *There is/There are*

- Write two headings on the board: *There is* and *There are.*
- Have students list the items in the paragraph that follow each heading.
- Put students in pairs to compare lists or go over as a group.

❷ **WRITE.** Answer the questions about your class. Use complete sentences.

- Go over the directions.
- Have students complete the sentences with information about your class.
- Walk around to monitor the activity and provide help as needed.
- Put students in pairs to read their sentences.
- Call on students to read their sentences to the class.

BIG PICTURE WRITING EXPANSION ACTIVITY—The classroom

- Put the transparency for Unit 3 on the OHP or have students look at the Big Picture in their books.
- Have each student write three sentences about the picture. Remind students to use capital letters and periods.
- Put students in pairs to read their sentences.

3 EDIT your work. Look at each sentence.

- Go over the directions.
- Have students read their sentences and check for capital letters and periods in each sentence.
- Put students in pairs to exchange and check the sentences.

ACADEMIC NOTE

Point out that checking work for accuracy and making necessary changes and corrections is an important skill for academic and professional settings.

Career Connection

OBJECTIVE

Identify locations in the workplace

WARM-UP ACTIVITY

- Draw a smiley face and a frowny face on the board. Point to something you like in the classroom and smile. Write the example under the smiley face. Do the same thing with something you don't really like and the frowny face.
- Have students write two things they like and two things they don't like about your classroom.
- Put students in pairs to compare ideas.

🎧 **❶ READ** and listen. Then practice with a partner.

- Direct students' attention to the photos. Tell students this is the continuation of the story about Isabel. Have students point to Isabel in the pictures.
- Play the CD and have students follow along silently.
- Play the CD again and have students repeat.
- Put students in pairs to take turns reading the roles of Isabel and her coworker.
- Ask: *What is a tour? What is good about the office? What is not good or bad?*

❷ WRITE. Look at Laura's office. What things are good? What things are bad? Complete the chart.

- Copy the chart on the board.
- Go over the directions. Make sure students understand *good* and *bad.*
- Have students write their ideas in the chart.
- Elicit answers and write them in the chart on the board.

❸ WHAT ABOUT YOU? What is in the perfect office for you? Talk to a partner.

- Go over the directions.
- Model the activity. Describe your perfect office.
- Put students in pairs to talk about their ideas.

EXPANSION ACTIVITY: Draw it

- Distribute large sheets of blank paper.
- Put students in pairs or small groups to design and draw a perfect office. Have students label the objects and places in the office.
- Call the groups to the front of the classroom to display and describe their perfect offices, or post the pictures around the room.

COMMUNITY CONNECTION: Workplaces you know

- As an out-of-class assignment, have students describe the good and bad things about a workplace they know. Or, have students interview a friend, coworker or neighbor about their workplace and write down the good and bad things.

CHECK YOUR PROGRESS!

- Have students circle the answers.
- Have students check whether each answer is right or wrong.
- Have students total their correct answers and fill in the chart.
- Have students create a learning plan and/or set learning goals.

ANSWER KEY

1. There are; 2. Are there; 3. No, there aren't.
4. on; 5. at; 6. in; 7. pens; 8. cell phone;
9. pencil; 10. library; 11. vending machines;
12. lobby

Unit Overview

LESSON	OBJECTIVE	STUDENT BOOK	WORKBOOK
1 Grammar and Vocabulary 1	Use *it's* to describe the weather	p. 54	p. 48
2 Grammar Practice Plus	Read a pie chart Describe weather and seasons	p. 56	p. 49
3 Listening and Conversation	Understand a weather report Understand Celsius and Fahrenheit temperatures	p. 58	p. 50
4 Grammar and Vocabulary 2	Ask about and tell the time Ask and answer information questions with *be*	p. 60	p. 52
5 Grammar Practice Plus	Identify U.S. holidays Review prepositions with time	p. 62	p. 53
6 Apply Your Knowledge	Interpret a school calendar	p. 64	p. 54
7 Reading and Writing	Understand and write an email message	p. 66	p. 56
• Career Connection	Identify holidays at work	p. 68	p. 58
• Check Your Progress	Monitor progress	p. 69	p. 60

Reading/Writing Strategies

• Scan for details   • Check punctuation in emails

Connection Activities

LESSON	TYPE	SKILL DEVELOPMENT
1	Academic	Use antonyms
2	Community	Research weather and seasons
3	Academic	Use conversion tables for the metric system
3	Academic	Report the weather
4	Community	Research community college classes
5	Academic	Research a holiday
6	Community	Identify dates on an academic calendar
7	Community	Set up an email account
8	Community	Identify federal holidays

WORKSHEET #/FOCUS	TITLE	TEACHER'S EDITION
8 Grammar, Literacy	Making Conversation	p. 253
9 Grammar	*It's* with Time and Weather	p. 254
10 Reading	Emails	p. 255

LESSON 1: Grammar and Vocabulary

OBJECTIVE

Use *it's* to describe the weather

VOCABULARY

clear	humid
cloudy	rainy
cold	snowy
cool	sunny
foggy	warm
hot	windy

GRAMMAR

It's with weather

COMPETENCIES

It's for weather
Weather conditions

WARM-UP ACTIVITY: Unit opener

- Put the transparency for Unit 4 on the overhead projector (OHP) or have students look at the Big Picture on page 57.
- Elicit words the students know and write them on the board.

❶ GRAMMAR PICTURE DICTIONARY. Listen and repeat.

- Have students open their books and look at the pictures. Ask: *What do you see?* Write all the words the students know on the board.
- Say the sentences or play the CD and have students repeat.
- Say the sentences in random order and have students point to the pictures.
- Put students in pairs and take turns saying the questions in random order as their partner points to the picture.

VOCABULARY NOTE

Point out that some weather adjectives are formed by adding a *–y* to a noun (*rain – rainy*). *Rain* and *snow* are also verbs. Students may want to write the word families in a vocabulary notebook.

EXPANSION ACTIVITY: Spell it

- Model the activity. Say one of the words and then spell it (*sunny, s-u-n-n-y*).
- Call on students and say a word. Have students spell it.
- For a challenge activity, give students two minutes to review the words.
- Have students close their books. Ask volunteers to spell the words. Or, put students in pairs. Have one student look at the words in the book and say them as the partner spells them.

EXPANSION ACTIVITY: Flashcards

- Distribute index cards to each student.
- Have students draw the weather word on one side of the card and write it on the other.
- Put students in pairs to review the vocabulary.

❷ NOTICE THE GRAMMAR. Look at Activity 1. Circle *It's.* Underline the weather words.

- Go over the directions. Make sure students understand what you mean by weather words (the bold-faced words in the sentences).
- Have students read the sentences and circle *It's,* and underline the weather words.

ANSWER KEY

1. (It's) hot.	7. (It's) cool.
2. (It's) sunny.	8. (It's) cloudy.
3. (It's) humid.	9. (It's) rainy.
4. (It's) warm.	10. (It's) cold.
5. (It's) clear.	11. (It's) windy.
6. (It's) foggy.	12. (It's) snowy.

EXPANSION ACTIVITY: Read by numbers

- Call on students and say a number. Have the student read the sentence.

GRAMMAR CHART: *It's* with Weather

- Direct students' attention to the chart.
- Go over the information in the chart, including the usage note. You may want to read the questions and answers, pausing to have students repeat.
- Point out or elicit that we can also say *It isn't* as the negative contraction.

❸ WRITE. Look at the pictures. Complete the sentences with weather words.

- Go over the directions.
- Direct students' attention to the first photo. Elicit weather words (*rainy, foggy, cool* or *cold*). Point out that *rainy* is written on the line.
- Have students complete the sentences with weather words.
- Put students in pairs to check their answers.
- Go over the answers with the class

ANSWER KEY

Answers may vary.
1. rainy; 2. foggy; 3. hot; 4. sunny; 5. sunny; 6. warm; 7. cold; 8. rainy

EXPANSION ACTIVITY:
Question challenge

- Direct students' attention to the first picture and ask *Is it rainy?* Elicit *Yes, it is.* Ask *Is it sunny?* Elicit *No, it's not.*
- Have students write three questions about each photo.
- Walk around the room to monitor the activity and provide help as needed.
- Put students in pairs to take turns asking and answering questions.
- Call on students and ask *yes/no* questions.

❹ WHAT ABOUT YOU? Talk to a partner. How's the weather today in your city?

- Go over the directions and the example.
- Read each question aloud and have students repeat.
- Put students in pairs to take turns asking and answering the questions.

ACADEMIC CONNECTION: Opposites

- Have students work with a partner to create pairs of opposites from the weather words in Activity 1.
- Have students check their ideas in a thesaurus or online thesaurus. Point out that opposites are usually called *antonyms* and may be abbreviated as *ant.*

ANSWER KEY

Warm/humid—cool; hot—cold; clear/sunny—cloudy/foggy/rainy

LESSON 2: Grammar Practice Plus

OBJECTIVES
Read a pie chart
Describe weather and seasons

VOCABULARY	
fall	July
spring	August
summer	September
winter	October
January	November
February	December
March	Bogotá
April	Chicago
May	London
June	Mexico City

GRAMMAR
It's with weather
In with seasons

WARM-UP ACTIVITY: Where's Chicago?

- Write *Chicago* on the board. If you have a map, have a student locate the city.
- Elicit everything students know about Chicago or can guess about it, and write the ideas on the board.

1 WRITE. Complete the sentences. Use the words in the box.

- Go over the directions and the example.
- Have students complete the sentences.
- Put students in pairs to compare answers.

🎧 **LISTEN** and repeat.

- Play the audio and have students repeat. Have students check their answers.

🎧 **LISTENING SCRIPT**
Lesson 2, Activity 1
TCD2, 3
Listen and repeat.

1. It's cool in the spring.
2. It's hot in the summer.
3. It's windy in the fall.
4. It's cold in the winter.

ANSWER KEY
1. cool; 2. hot; 3. windy; 4. cold

2 READ the pie charts about the weather in Chicago. Answer the questions.

- Go over the list of months. Say each month and have students repeat.
- Direct students' attention to the pie charts. Ask *What color is for sunny days? What color is for foggy days? What color is for snowy days?*
- Read the first question. Have students look at the pie chart for January and identify the section that indicates *snowy*. Ask *Is it snowy in January?* Elicit *Yes, it is.* Point out *Yes, it is* is written on the line. Ask *How many days are in January? How many days are snowy?* Make sure students see that about half the days are snowy.
- Read each question aloud and have students repeat.
- Have students answer the questions.
- Go over the answers with the class.
- Put students in pairs to take turns asking and answering the questions.

ANSWER KEY
1. Yes, it is. 2. No, it's not. 3. Yes, it is. 4. Yes, it is. 5. No, it's not. 6. Yes, it is.

EXPANSION ACTIVITY: It's not. . . .

- Have students write new sentences about Chicago's weather, using *It's not* and different weather words.
- Put students in pairs to read their sentences aloud.
- Have volunteers write their sentences on the board.

CULTURE/CIVICS NOTE

Point out or elicit that the seasons change around the third week of March, June, September and December. The day each season begins is usually marked on a calendar (around the 21st of the month).

ACADEMIC NOTE

Point out that being able to interpret charts and graphs is an important academic and reading skill. Make sure that students understand the pie chart shows the relationship of parts to the whole.

EXPANSION ACTIVITY: Alphabetical order

- Have students write the list of months in alphabetical order.

LITERACY DEVELOPMENT ACTIVITY: Order the months

- Distribute index cards. Have less advanced students write one month on each of the cards.
- Have students shuffle the cards then put the cards in chronological order.
- Have students sort the cards by season. Remind students that some months fall in more than one season.

❸ WHAT ABOUT YOU? Write about the weather in your city.

- Go over the directions.
- Have students complete the sentences with weather words to describe the weather in their native countries in the different months.
- Put students in pairs to read their sentences aloud.
- Call on students to read a sentence to the class.

❹ TALK about the pictures.

- Go over the directions.
- Direct students' attention to the big picture or put the transparency on the projector. Point to the woman in the first picture. Ask *Is it hot or cold?*
- Put students in pairs. Have students take turns describing the weather in each picture.
- Call on students. Point to different pictures and elicit sentences.

BIG PICTURE SPEAKING EXPANSION ACTIVITY: Where am I?

- Have students look at the Big Picture or put the color overhead transparency for Unit 4 on the OHP.
- Put students in pairs to write three sentences about each of the pictures.
- Call on students to say their sentences to the class and elicit the city from the other students.

❺ LISTEN. Number the people.

- Go over the directions.
- Have students number the pictures as you say the sentences or play the CD.
- Put students in pairs to compare answers.
- Say the questions or play the CD again so students can confirm.
- Go over the answers with the class.

LISTENING SCRIPT
Lesson 2, Activity 5

TCD2, 4

Listen. Number the pictures.

1. Elizabeth is a student in London. Right now, it's winter. It's cold and foggy.
2. Carlos is in Mexico City. It's winter, but it's warm and sunny.
3. Hong is in Chicago. It's winter. It's cold and windy.
4. Eduardo is in Bogotá. It's summer. It's hot and humid.

ANSWER KEY

1. lower right; 2. upper right; 3. upper left; 4. lower left

LISTEN AGAIN. Complete the sentence with a season.

- Go over the directions and the example.
- Play the CD and have the students write the season.
- Put students in pairs to check their answers.
- Go over the answers with the class.

ANSWER KEY

1. winter; 2. winter; 3. winter; 4. summer

CULTURE/CIVICS NOTE

- Point out or elicit that the first three cities are in the northern hemisphere. Bogotá is in the southern hemisphere, so it is in the opposite season as the cities in the northern hemisphere.
- Show on a map or globe.

EXPANSION ACTIVITY: Dictation

- Have students write the sentences from Activity 4 as you read the script or play the CD. Repeat twice.
- Put students in pairs to compare sentences.
- Have volunteers write the sentences on the board.

6 TALK to a partner. Ask about the weather in London, Mexico City, and Bogotá.

- Go over the directions and the example.
- Put students in pairs to ask and answer questions about the weather in the different cities.

COMMUNITY CONNECTION:
What season is it?

- Assign students a city to research.
- Have students go online to find out the weather and the season for the city today.
- Call on students to share their information with the class.
- Have students list the cities by hemisphere.

LESSON 3: Listening and Conversation

OBJECTIVES

Understand a weather report
Understand Celsius and Fahrenheit temperatures

COMPETENCIES

Temperature in Fahrenheit
Access weather information

WARM-UP ACTIVITY: Category sort

- Write different news and weather sources on the board (*network TV, cable TV, radio, internet, friends or family, newspaper, magazines*). Make sure students understand what each word means.
- Have students get into groups according to what they use the most for news and weather.

 1 LISTEN to the weather report. Look at the map and circle the correct picture.

- Direct students' attention to the weather map. Say the names of different cities and have students point to the cities on the map.
- Point to each of the weather icons next to each city and elicit what they mean.
- Read the weather report or play the CD and have students circle the appropriate weather icon.

LISTENING SCRIPT
Lesson 3, Activity 1

TCD2, 5

Listen to the weather report. Look at the map and circle the correct picture.

Here is a look at today's weather. In Miami, it's very sunny. It's hot. It's 98°. In New York, it's not hot. It's only 60°. It's cool, and it's rainy. In Boston, it's 30°. It's cold and snowy.

ANSWER KEY

Miami: sun; New York: raindrops; Boston: snowflakes

LISTEN AGAIN. Write the temperature.

- Play the CD again and have students write the temperature next to the city on the map.
- Have students compare answers in pairs.
- Go over the answers with the class.

ANSWER KEY

Miami: 98; New York: 60; Boston: 30

MATH: Temperatures
Match the temperatures in Celsius to the temperatures in Fahrenheit.

- Direct students' attention to the thermometers/temperature scales. Make sure they see the Fahrenheit scale on the left and the Celsius scale on the right.
- Point to the 11 on the Celsius scale and the 52 on the Fahrenheit scale. Students should see they are side by side.
- Have students match the temperatures.
- Go over the answers with the class.

ANSWER KEY

1. b; 2. d; 3. a; 4. c

BIG PICTURE LISTENING EXPANSION ACTIVITY: Four Temperatures

- Dictate the following sentences: *It's 20 degrees and snowy. It's 50 degrees and foggy. It's 80 degrees and humid. It's 60 degrees and sunny.*
- Put students in pairs to compare sentences.
- Have volunteers write the sentences on the board.
- Have students match the sentence to the picture.

ACADEMIC CONNECTION: Conversion tables

- Have students go online to find conversion tables for the metric system: Fahrenheit and Celsius, centimeters and feet, kilograms and pounds.

❷ LISTEN and read.

- Direct students' attention to the picture. Ask questions: *Who do you see?*
- Play the CD or read the conversation as students follow along silently.
- Play the CD or read the conversation again and have students repeat.
- Check comprehension: *Is it hot in Seattle? What's the weather in Rio?*
- Put students in pairs to practice the conversation.

❸ PRACTICE THE CONVERSATION with a partner.

- Go over the directions.
- Model the activity. Have a more advanced student read B's lines. Model how to make substitutions.
- Put students in pairs to practice the conversation, making the appropriate substitutions.

- Walk around to monitor the activity and provide help as needed.
- Call on students to say the conversation to the class.

EXPANSION ACTIVITY: LITERACY DEVELOPMENT—Sentence strips

- Photocopy Worksheet 8: Making Conversation. Make enough so that each pair of students has a set.
- Cut the strips along the dotted lines.
- Put students in pairs and give each pair a set of strips.
- Have students create conversations for the first three items in Activity 4, using the strips.
- Walk around to monitor the activity and provide help as needed.

❹ WRITE. Choose a city. Write a weather report. Read the report to your classmates.

- Go over the directions and the example in the picture.
- Have students complete the sentences in the speech bubble to write a weather report for a particular city. Suggest they use a city in Activity 1 if they need structure.
- Call on students to read their weather reports to the class.

COMMUNITY CONNECTION: Weather reports

- For an out-of-class assignment, have students find out the weather for the next class day for any city they choose.
- Have students write the weather report and deliver it to the class.

LESSON 4: Grammar and Vocabulary

OBJECTIVES

Ask about and tell time
Ask and answer information questions with *be*

VOCABULARY

at night	in the evening
in the afternoon	in the morning

GRAMMAR

What time and *when* questions with *be*

COMPETENCIES

Use *It's* with time
Analog and digital clocks

WARM-UP ACTIVITY: What time is it?

- Point to the clock in the room, or a wristwatch and ask *What time is it?*
- Elicit the answer and write it on the board in two forms, with numerals and with number words.

🎧 **❶ GRAMMAR PICTURE DICTIONARY.** Listen and repeat.

- Have students look at the pictures
- Play the CD or say the sentences and have students repeat.
- Say the times in random order and have the students point to the pictures.

❷ NOTICE THE GRAMMAR. Look at Activity 1. Circle *What time* and *When*. Underline *is*.

- Have students circle *What time* and *When.* Point out that these are question words. Have students underline *is* in the questions.
- Go over the answers with the class.

ANSWER KEY

(What time) is it?	(When) is your class?
1. It's two o'clock.	7. It's in the morning.
2. It's two oh five.	
3. It's two fifteen.	8. It's in the afternoon.
4. It's two–twenty.	
5. It's two–thirty.	9. It's in the evening.
6. It's two–forty-five.	10. It's at night.

VOCABULARY NOTE

- Students may ask about other ways to say the time. If so, point out that we also have expressions with *to/til* or *past* (10 to 12, a quarter til 2, 20 past 3, a quarter past 4).
- Explain that we use A.M. for the times between midnight and noon, and P.M. for the times between noon and midnight.
- Point out that we use *in* with the morning, afternoon, and evening, and we use *at* with night.
- Explain that someone can also ask *What is the time?*

EXPANSION ACTIVITY: Dictate and sort

- Dictate 10 times on the clock, including A.M. and P.M.
- Put students in pairs to check their answers and then sort the answers into the four categories: *in the morning, in the afternoon, in the evening, at night.*

GRAMMAR CHART: What Time and When Questions with *Be*

- Go over the information in the chart.
- You may want to read the sample sentences in the chart and have students repeat.

CHART EXPANSION ACTIVITY: Ask and answer

- Have students cover the answers.
- Ask the questions in the chart and elicit answers that are true for your students.

❸ WRITE. Put the questions in order. Then write the answers.

- Go over the directions and the examples. Make sure students understand how to create questions and answers using the prompts.
- Have students write the questions.
- Put students in pairs to compare questions.
- Go over the questions with the class.
- Have students write the answers.
- Go over the answers with the class.
- Put students in pairs to ask and answer the questions.

ANSWER KEY

1. When is Eva's birthday? It's in April.
2. What time is the test? It's at 10:30.
3. When is the first day of class? It's on September 3rd.
4. What time is the English class? It's at 4:00.
5. When are their birthdays? They're in May.

EXPANSION ACTIVITY: Practice

- Give students two minutes to study the questions and answers.
- With books closed, ask questions that follow the model in Activity 3 (e.g., *When is Jack's birthday?*). Elicit appropriate answers (e.g., *It's in May.*). Point out that students don't need to actually know the information. They can make it up, but an answer must be appropriate.

❹ WHAT ABOUT YOU? Write your answers.

- Go over the directions.
- Have students answer the questions.
- Put students in pairs to take turns asking and answering the questions.
- Call on students to tell the class when their birthdays are.

COMMUNITY CONNECTION: Community college

- As an out-of-class assignment, have students go online to find out when the community college classes begin the next term.

LESSON 5: Grammar Practice Plus

OBJECTIVES

Identify U.S. holidays
Review prepositions of time

VOCABULARY

Halloween	New Year's Day
Independence Day	Thanksgiving
Labor Day	Valentine's Day

GRAMMAR

Using prepositions of time

PRONUNCIATION/NUMERACY

Ordinal numbers

COMPETENCIES

Identify holidays
Use prepositions of time

WARM-UP ACTIVITY: Picture prompts

- Bring in pictures of items associated with holidays (or bring in the items). Examples might be: party hat, valentine, fireworks, flag, pencil, mask, pumpkin, black cat, turkey, pilgrim, fall leaves.
- With books closed, show each item and have students work in pairs to guess what holiday it is associated with.
- Elicit ideas and write them on the board.

❶ WRITE. Complete the conversations.

- Go over the directions and the example.
- Have students write just the months on the lines.
- Put students in pairs to compare answers.

- Play the CD and have students repeat and check their answers.
- Go over the answers with the class.

 LISTENING SCRIPT
Lesson 5, Activity 1
TCD2, 8

Listen and repeat. Are your answers correct?

1. When is New Year's Day? It's on January 1st.
2. When is Valentine's Day? It's on February 14th.
3. When is Independence Day? It's on July 4th.
4. When is Labor Day? It's in September.
5. When is Halloween? It's on October 31st.
6. When is Thanksgiving? It's in November.

ANSWER KEY

1. January; 2. February; 3. July; 4. September;
5. October; 6. November

EXPANSION ACTIVITY: Weather forecasts

- Put students in pairs.
- Have students work with their partners to write a weather forecast for each holiday in your city. Model the sentence structure if needed: *It's New Year's Day. The temperature is 24. It's cold and snowy.*
- Call on students to read a forecast for one of the holidays.

LITERACY DEVELOPMENT NOTES

- Literacy students may have trouble writing weather forecasts, even with a model on the board. You may want to use sentence strips to scaffold the weather forecast expansion activity.
- Point out that holidays are capitalized. This will help literacy students identify holiday words.

🎧 PRONUNCIATION: Ordinal Numbers

A LISTEN and repeat.

- Play the CD and have students repeat.

PRONUNCIATION NOTE

Many students have trouble with the *–th* sound. Encourage students to stick their tongue between their teeth to make the sound correctly.

B LISTEN to the sentences. Check the word you hear.

- Go over the directions.
- Play the CD and have students repeat.
- Go over the answers with the class.

LISTENING SCRIPT
Lesson 5, Activity B

TCD2, 10
SCD, 23

Listen to the sentences. Check the word you hear.

1. Today is December 15th.
2. There are 21 students.
3. I am 30 years old.
4. Independence Day is on July 4th.
5. I have 12 pencils.
6. It's April 9th.

ANSWER KEY

1. fifteenth; **2.** twenty-one; **3.** thirty; **4.** fourth; **5.** twelve; **6.** ninth

VOCABULARY NOTE

For most numbers, the ordinal number differs from the cardinal number only in the ending (*-th*). However, beginning students may be confused by the very different forms *first, second,* and *third.* Make sure students notice the patterns: *first, twenty-first, thirty-first,* and so on.

EXPANSION ACTIVITY: Challenge dictation

- Play the CD and have students write the sentences they hear.
- Have volunteers write the sentences on the board.

C TALK with a partner. Say one word from pair of words in B. Your partner listens and circles the word.

- Go over the directions.
- Model the activity. Say *fifteen* and ask students which word they should circle.
- Put students in pairs to take turns saying a word and circling the word they hear.

2 WRITE the words in the chart.

- Go over the directions and the words in the box.
- Go over the example.
- Have students write the words from the box in the correct places in the chart.
- Put students in pairs to compare answers.
- Go over the answers with the class.

ANSWER KEY

IN	ON	AT
2008	July 4th	9:15
summer	December 2nd	7:45
May	January 15th	
February		
winter		

EXPANSION ACTIVITY: Beanbag toss

- Call on a student, toss a beanbag and say a time expression (e.g., *August 5th*). Elicit the correct preposition before the time expression (on *August 5th*).
- Continue until everyone has had a chance to participate.

❸ WRITE. Complete the sentences. Use *in*, *on*, or *at*.

- Go over the directions and the example.
- Have students write the correct prepositions on the lines.
- Put students in pairs to read their sentences.
- Go over the answers with the class.

ANSWER KEY

1. at; 2. in; 3. on; 4. in; 5. in; 6. on; 7. at; 8. on

❹ TALK with three classmates. Complete the chart.

- Go over the directions and the example questions and answers.
- Put students in groups of four, or have students stand and walk around the room to talk to three classmates. Remind students to ask the three questions of each classmate and complete the chart.

GRAMMAR NOTE

You may want to point out that we often answer *wh-* questions with short answers. Point out that in the example questions for Activity 5, the short answers would be: *Colombia, June 19,* and *hot and humid.*

BIG PICTURE GRAMMAR EXPANSION: *It's* **with Time and Weather**

- Photocopy and distribute Worksheet 9: *It's* with Time and Weather.
- Put the transparency for Unit 4 on the OHP or have students look at the pictures in their books.
- Go over the directions.
- Have students complete the sentences.
- Go over the answers with the class.

WORKSHEET 9 ANSWER KEY

1. It is December 15th.
2. It is winter.
3. It is cold.
4. It is Chicago.
5. It is December 15th.
6. It is winter.
7. It is warm and sunny.
8. It is Mexico City.
9. It is December 15th.
10. It is summer.
11. It is hot and humid.
12. It is Bogotá.
13. It is December 15th.
14. It is winter.
15. It is cold and foggy.
16. It is London.

ACADEMIC CONNECTION: A holiday

- As an out-of-class assignment, have students go online or to the library to find out three facts about one of the holidays in Activity 1.
- Call on students to share what they learned with the class.

LESSON 6: Apply Your Knowledge

OBJECTIVE

Interpret a school calendar

COMPETENCIES

Understand school calendars and attendance

WARM-UP ACTIVITY: Holidays

- Bring in or photocopy a month or two from your school calendar. This can be a version from the school's website.
- Have groups of students see if they can identify dates for school or national holidays.

❶ READ the list of important school dates. Circle the dates with no classes.

- Go over the directions.
- Direct students' attention to the calendar and ask questions: *When is the first day of class? When is winter break? When is spring break?*
- Have students circle the dates with no class.
- Go over the answers with the class.

ANSWER KEY

September 4, October 16, November 23, December 16–18, December 18–January 3, March 12–16, May 27–29

❷ CIRCLE the correct letter.

- Go over the directions and the example.
- Have students answer the questions and then compare answers with a partner.
- Go over the answers with the class.

ANSWER KEY

1. A; 2. C; 3. B

EXPANSION ACTIVITY: Three questions

- Put students in pairs to write three questions about the calendar.
- Have each pair ask and answer questions with another pair of students.
- Call on students to read a question. Elicit the answer.

 ❸ LISTEN to the conversations. Complete the calendar.

- Direct students' attention to the picture and ask *Who is in the picture?*
- Direct students' attention to the calendar. Go over the directions.
- Play the CD and have students write the information on the calendar.
- Put students in pairs to compare answers.
- Go over the answers with the class.

LISTENING SCRIPT
Lesson 6, Activity 3

TCD2, 11–13   Listen to the conversations. Complete the calendar.

Conversation 1
A: Excuse me. When is the first day of class?
B: It's on August 31st.
A: And what time is class?
B: 10:00 A.M.
A: Okay. Thank you!

Conversation 2
A: Mr. Brown?
B: Yes?
A: What is the first holiday?
B: It's Labor Day. It's on September 4th.
A: Are there classes?
B: No, there aren't. There are no classes.

Conversation 3

A: Asheville Community School, can I help you?

B: Hi. I'm a new student. Is there a new student meeting?

A: Yes, on September 7th. At 7:00 P.M.

B: Thanks!

ANSWER KEY

August 31	First day of class 10 A.M. Teacher Mr. Brown
September 4	Labor Day, no class
September 7	New Student Meeting, 7 P.M., Room 410

🎧 **4 LISTEN** and read.

- Direct students' attention to the picture. Ask questions: *Who do you see? Where are they?*
- Have students follow along and repeat as you say the conversation or play the CD.
- Play the CD again and have students repeat.
- Put students in pairs to take turns reading the parts of the teacher and student.

5 PRACTICE THE CONVERSATION with a partner. Use the list of dates on page 64.

- Go over the directions and the information.
- Model the activity with a student. Have the students read the student's lines. Substitute the information.
- Put students in pairs. Have students take turns as student and teacher using the information in Activity 4.
- Walk around the room to monitor the activity and provide help as needed.
- Have pairs of students say the conversations in front of the class.

EXPANSION ACTIVITY: This year's calendar

- Bring in calendars for this year, or have students bring them in.
- Have students look up the dates for Labor Day and Thanksgiving Day. Have students notice what other holidays are marked on the calendar (President's Day, Martin Luther King Day, Memorial Day).

6 PUT IT TOGETHER. Work in a small group. Make a school calendar for a new school.

- Go over the directions.
- Direct students' attention to the notice. Ask questions: *What is the name of the school? When are classes? Who is the teacher? When is the first day of class? Is there class on Valentine's Day?*
- Put students in small groups. Have students make a school calendar in their notebooks or on a big piece of paper.
- Walk around the room to monitor the activity and provide help as needed.

COMMUNITY CONNECTION: K–12 schools

- As an out-of-class assignment, have students obtain a school calendar for their children's schools, or for the public K–12 schools in their neighborhoods. Tell students they can get one online, or from the school itself.
- Elicit important dates from the school calendars, including holidays and start and end dates.

LESSON 7: Reading and Writing

OBJECTIVE
Understand and write an email message

READING TIP
Look for important details before you read

WRITING TIP
Check punctuation in emails

COMPETENCIES
Use email

WARM-UP ACTIVITY: Do you use email?

- Put students in pairs to answer these questions: *Do you use email? How many times in a week? Who do you email?*
- Call on students to tell the class about their partner's email use.

Reading

❶ THINK ABOUT IT. Write an email address you know. Who is it for?

- Go over the directions.
- Have students write an email address they know. Write your email address on the board in case they don't know one.
- Elicit names of the people students have email addresses for.

❷ BEFORE YOU READ. Look at the email. Circle the words from the box.

- Go over the tip in the box.
- Go over the directions and the words in the box.
- Have students look at the email and circle the words from the box.

❸ READ the email. What season is it?

- Have students read the email, or read the email aloud sentence by sentence and have students repeat.
- Ask comprehension questions: *What season is it? Who is Joshua? Where are Joshua and Mike? What's the date?*

ANSWER KEY
Winter

❹ CIRCLE the correct letter.

- Read each question and have students repeat.
- Have students answer the questions.
- Go over the answers with the class.
- Put students in pairs to practice asking and answering the questions.

ANSWER KEY
1. A; 2. A; 3. C; 4. C

EXPANSION ACTIVITY: Literacy development—sentence strips

- Copy the sentences from the paragraph onto separate strips. Leave enough space between each word for word discrimination. The sentences need to be large enough to be read by all the students.
- Put the sentence strips on the board in the correct order. Read each sentence aloud and have students repeat. You may want to point to each word as you read.
- Take the sentences down and mix them up.
- Have volunteers come to the board and put the sentences in the correct order. Have the other students help.
- You may want to enlarge and photocopy the sentences from the email and cut them into strips so that each student or pair of students has a set to reassemble.

EXPANSION ACTIVITY: Write questions

- Have students write two more questions about the email.
- Elicit the questions and write them on the board.
- Have students answer the questions.

BIG PICTURE READING EXPANSION ACTIVITY: Emails

- Photocopy and distribute Worksheet 10: Emails.
- Put the transparency for Unit 4 on the OHP or have students look at the picture on page 57.
- Go over the directions. Have students write the name of the person who sent the email.
- Put students in pairs to share their ideas.
- Elicit ideas from the students and write them on the board.

WORKSHEET 10 ANSWER KEY

Circle: winter, cool, foggy, snowy, warm, humid, sunny, summer, cold, winter
From: Elizabeth, Eduardo

Writing

- Go over the writing tip in the box.

❶ MATCH. Look at the email on page 66. Match the information.

- Go over the directions and the example.
- Have students match the information.
- Put students in pairs to compare ideas.
- Go over the answers with the class.

ANSWER KEY

1. d; 2. c; 3. b; 4. e; 5. a

❷ WRITE. You're on vacation. You're going to write an email to a friend or family member. Write the information for *your* email.

- Go over the directions.
- Have students complete the chart. Point out that they can write anything they want in the subject line, but it is usually about the content of the email. Encourage students to use real emails if they have/know them.
- Put students in pairs to talk about the information in their charts.

❸ WRITE your email.

- Model the activity. Write an email on the board. Use imaginary information about where you might be during a vacation.
- Have students write the missing information on the lines to complete the email. Tell students they can make up the place, the season and the weather.
- Call on students to read their emails to the class.

BIG PICTURE WRITING EXPANSION
ACTIVITY: **Carlos or Hong?**

- Put the transparency for Unit 4 on the projector or have students look at page 57 in their books.
- Have students write an email as either Carlos or Hong. Remind students to describe the weather and the season.
- Put students in pairs to read their emails.

COMMUNITY CONNECTION:
Email accounts

- As an out-of-class or lab assignment, have students create email accounts or activate school email accounts if you have them. Suggest students use hotmail or gmail to set up accounts if they don't have access to one already. Remind students to write down their usernames and passwords in a secure place until they can remember them.
- Give students your email address.
- Have students email you and pretend they are in their native countries. Remind students to describe the weather and the season.

Career Connection

OBJECTIVE

Identify holidays at work

COMPETENCIES

Understand work holidays

WARM-UP ACTIVITY: A day off

- Explain or elicit what a day off is. Point out that when we have a day off, we don't go to school or work.
- Elicit the days your students have off each week.

🎧 **1 READ** and listen.

- Direct students' attention to the photos. Tell students this is the continuation of the story about Isabel. Have students point to Isabel in the photos.
- Play the CD and have students follow along silently.
- Play the CD again and have students repeat.
- Put students in pairs to take turns reading the roles of Isabel and her coworker.
- Ask: *What holiday is it?*

2 TALK. Answer the questions.

- Read each holiday and have students repeat.
- Put students in pairs to ask and answer the questions.
- Call on students and ask a question.

ANSWER KEY

1. Labor Day; 2. 9:15 A.M.; 3. at work;
4. There is no work today. It is a holiday.

3 WHAT ABOUT YOU? Are there holidays for your school or your job? Make a list. Then read your list to a partner.

- Go over the directions.
- Have students list holidays for school or for their jobs.
- Put students in pairs to talk about their lists.
- Call on students to tell the class about one holiday at school or work.

COMMUNITY CONNECTION: Federal Holidays

- As an out-of-class or lab assignment, have students go online and search for federal holidays in the United States.
- Have students write the holidays on a piece of paper.
- Elicit the holidays and write them on the board.

CHECK YOUR PROGRESS!

- Have students circle the answers.
- Have students check whether each answer is right or wrong.
- Have students total their correct answers and fill in the chart.
- Have students create a learning plan and/or set learning goals.

ANSWER KEY

1. rainy; 2. hot; 3. cold; 4. in; 5. at; 6. on;
7. What time; 8. When; 9. When; 10. January;
11. July; 12. November

UNIT 5 In the Community

Unit Overview

LESSON	OBJECTIVE	STUDENT BOOK	WORKBOOK
1 Grammar and Vocabulary 1	Use prepositions to locate places in the community	p. 70	p. 62
2 Grammar Practice Plus	Ask and answer questions about locations in the community	p. 72	p. 63
3 Listening and Conversation	Ask and tell about locations Use a map	p. 74	p. 64
4 Grammar and Vocabulary 2	Use imperatives to give directions	p. 76	p. 66
5 Grammar Practice Plus	Understand traffic signs	p. 78	p. 67
6 Apply Your Knowledge	Calculate distance using a map	p. 80	p. 68
7 Reading and Writing	Read a brochure Write using details	p. 82	p. 70
• Career Connection	Identify educational opportunities	p. 84	p. 72
• Check Your Progress	Monitor progress	p. 85	p. 74

Reading/Writing Strategies

- Scan headings prior to reading
- Provide details in writing

Connection Activities

LESSON	TYPE	SKILL DEVELOPMENT
1	Community	Identify places near school
2	Community	Identify and locate important places in the community
3	Community	Locate important information in a phone book
4	Community	Identify a traffic sign
6	Community	Give directions to a public place
8	Academic	Access educational opportunities online

WORKSHEET #/FOCUS	TITLE	TEACHER'S EDITION
11 Grammar	Where Is It?	p. 256
12 Reading	Places in the Community	p. 257

LESSON 1: Grammar and Vocabulary

OBJECTIVE

Use prepositions to locate places in the community.

VOCABULARY

apartment building	house
bank	library
drugstore	post office
gas station	supermarket
hospital	

GRAMMAR

Prepositions of location

COMPETENCIES

Use prepositions
Identify places in the community

WARM-UP ACTIVITY: What do you know?

- Have students look at the pictures in Activity 1. Elicit the words students know for places in the community.
- Write the words on the board.

🎧 ❶ GRAMMAR PICTURE DICTIONARY. Listen and repeat.

- Say the sentences or play the CD and have students repeat.
- Say the names of places and have students point to the picture.
- Put students in pairs and have them take turns saying the places in random order as their partner points to the picture.

EXPANSION ACTIVITY: Alphabetical order

- Have students work in pairs and write the places in alphabetical order.
- Have volunteers write the words on the board in order.

❷ NOTICE THE GRAMMAR. Look at Activity 1. Underline the places. Circle the prepositions.

- Go over the directions. Make sure students know what prepositions are. Remind students that *in, at,* and *on* in Unit 3 were prepositions. If necessary, cue students that the prepositions follow the verb *be.*
- Have students read the sentences and underline the places and circle the prepositions.

ANSWER KEY

1. The bank is across from the school.
2. The supermarket is next to the bank.
3. The drugstore is next to the supermarket.
4. The houses are behind the school.
5. The apartment building is next to the bank.
6. The library is next to the school.
7. The hospital is across from the drugstore.
8. The post office is between the school and the hospital.
9. The gas station is in front of the supermarket.

EXPANSION ACTIVITY: Scrambled letters

- Give students two minutes to review the new vocabulary.
- Have students close their books.
- Write the following sets of letters on the board: *rbyialr, lspoitah, sna attigos.*
- Have students unscramble the letters to write words.
- Have students open their books and confirm their answers.

ANSWER KEY

library, hospital, gas station

GRAMMAR CHART: Prepositions of Location

- Direct students' attention to the chart.
- Go over the information on the chart. You may want to read the sentences, pausing to have students repeat.
- Go over the usage note.

CHART EXPANSION ACTIVITY: Who's next to you?

- Model the activity. Point to a student and say the name of the other students around him or her (e.g., *Tran is next to Ming. Tran is between Ming and Ricardo. Tran is in front of Nadia. Tran is behind Bernice.*).
- Call on students and ask questions: *Who is next to you? Who are you between? Who is in front of you? Who is behind you?*

EXPANSION ACTIVITY: Where's the teacher?

- Ask questions about people and objects in the room: *Where's the teacher? Where's the clock? Where's Hector? Where's the pencil sharpener?*
- To make the activity more challenging, ask the question and give the preposition that the student must use in answering.

3 WRITE. Look at the picture. Write the correct preposition.

- Go over the directions and the example.
- Have students complete the sentences with the correct prepositions.

ANSWER KEY

1. next to; **2.** between; **3.** next to; **4.** behind
5. between

COMMUNITY CONNECTION: What's next to the school?

- As an out-of-class assignment, have students notice what is *next to, across from* and behind your school.
- Have students write sentences about the school using *next to, between, across, behind, from* and *in front of.*
- Put students in pairs to compare sentences.
- Have volunteers write sentences on the board.

4 WHAT ABOUT YOU? Write sentences about you. Use prepositions and your classmates' names.

- Go over the directions and examples.
- Have students complete the sentences with the correct prepositions and names.
- Call on students and have them tell you where they are sitting.

LESSON 2: Grammar Practice Plus

OBJECTIVE
Ask and answer questions about locations in the community.

VOCABULARY
community center	movie theater
fire station	police station
hotel	restaurant

GRAMMAR
Prepositions of location

COMPETENCIES
Use prepositions
Identify places in the community

WARM-UP ACTIVITY: Match the object to the place

- Draw iconic pictures on the board to represent the places in Activity 1 (e.g., a plate, knife and fork, a screen with a face on it, a police car with flashing light, flames or a ladder truck, a basketball net, a bed).
- Have students guess what the places are for each picture.

🎧 **1 LISTEN** and repeat.

- Say the words or play the CD and have students repeat.
- Say the names of places and have students point to the picture.
- Put students in pairs and take turns saying the places in random order as their partner points to the picture.

2 WRITE. Match the occupations and the workplaces. Write words from the box in the chart.

- Go over the directions. If necessary, review the occupations/jobs from Unit 1.
- Go over the words in the box and the example.
- Have students write the words from the box in the appropriate places in the chart.
- Put students in pairs to compare ideas.
- Go over the answers with the class.

ANSWER KEY
Occupations	Workplaces
1. police officer	police station
2. sales clerk	supermarket
3. server	restaurant
4. doctor	hospital
5. housekeeper	hotel

EXPANSION ACTIVITY: One more

- Put students in pairs to list one more job for each workplace.
- Call on students to share their ideas. Write the ideas on the board.
- Have students write any new words from the board in their vocabulary notebooks.

LITERACY DEVELOPMENT NOTE

Literacy students may have difficulty recognizing separate words. Have students write the place names in two lists: *One–word places* and *two–word places.*

3 WHAT ABOUT YOU? Choose a place in your city. Complete the sentences.

- Go over the directions and the example.
- Have students choose a place they know. Remind students to look at the new words in Lessons 1 and 2 for ideas.
- Have students complete the sentences.
- Put students in pairs to read their sentences aloud.
- Call on students to read their sentences to the class.

4 TALK about the picture.

- Go over the directions.
- Direct students' attention to the Big Picture or put the transparency on the OHP. Point to the doctors and read the sentence.
- Put students in pairs. Have students take turns describing people and places in the picture.
- Call on students. Point to different people or places in the Big Picture and elicit sentences.

BIG PICTURE CONVERSATION/ VOCABULARY EXPANSION ACTIVITY: On the Phone

- Have students look at the Big Picture or put the color overhead transparency for Unit 5 on the OHP.
- Model the activity. Pretend you are one of the people in the picture and you are talking on your cell phone. Say where you are (e.g., *I'm in front of the hospital. I'm with Doctor Han*.). Have students point to the person who is on the cell phone.
- Put students in pairs to practice describing and guessing who is on the phone.

5 LISTEN. Number the places in the picture.

- Go over the directions.
- Have students write the words for places as you say the sentences or play the CD.
- Put students in pairs to compare answers.
- Say the questions or play the CD again so students can confirm.
- Go over the answers with the class.

LISTENING SCRIPT
Lesson 2, Activity 5

TCD2, 18

Listen. Number the places in the picture.

1. The hospital is next to the apartment building.
2. The bank is between the drugstore and the post office.
3. The fire station is across from the apartment building.
4. The supermarket is between the community center and the movie theater.

ANSWER KEY

hospital: 1; bank: 2; fire station: 3; supermarket: 4

EXPANSION ACTIVITY: Dictation

- Have students write the sentences from Activity 5 as you read them or play the CD. Repeat twice.
- Put students in pairs to compare sentences.
- Have volunteers write the sentences on the board.

6 TALK with a partner. Ask about the places.

- Go over the directions and the example conversation.
- Put students in pairs to practice asking and answering the questions with their partners.

COMMUNITY CONNECTION: Important places in your community

- Assign students an important place or building in your community. Include places such as libraries, community colleges, museums, city hall, courthouses. Make sure students understand what each place is.
- Have students look up the address for the assigned place.
- Bring in a map and have students find their place on the map.
- Have students point to their place and describe where it is.

LESSON 3: Listening and Conversation

OBJECTIVES

Ask and tell about locations
Use a map

COMPETENCIES

Ask for, give, clarify directions

WARM-UP ACTIVITY: Where is it?

- Direct students' attention to each picture and elicit what it is.
- Call on students and elicit a sentence about the picture (*The post office is next to the bank.*).

 1 LISTEN. Circle the correct letter.

- Say the conversations or play the CD and have students circle the letter.
- Have students compare answers in pairs.
- Go over the answers with the class.

LISTENING SCRIPT
Lesson 3, Activity 1
TCD2, 19

Listen. Circle the correct letter.

1. *A:* Where's the post office?
   B: It's next to the bank.
2. *A:* Where's the hospital?
   B: It's across from the fire station.
3. *A:* Where is the school?
   B: It's between the library and the apartment building.

ANSWER KEY

1. B; 2. A; 3. C

EXPANSION ACTIVITY: Write the question

- Have students look at their answers and rewrite the conversations from memory.
- Play the CD and have students correct the conversations.

 2 LISTEN. Write the places on the map.

- Go over the directions.
- Play the CD or say the first conversation. Elicit that *bank* should be written across from the post office in square 4.
- Play the rest of the CD or read the other conversations. Have students write the places on the map.
- Put students in pairs to compare maps.
- Play the CD again so students can check their answers.

LISTENING SCRIPT
Lesson 3, Activity 2
TCD2, 20

Listen. Write the places on the map.

1. *A:* Where's the supermarket?
   B: It's across from the post office.
2. *A:* Where is the community center?
   B: It's next to the supermarket.
3. *A:* Where's the fire station?
   B: It's next to the community center.
4. *A:* Where's the bank?
   B: It's across from the fire station.
5. *A:* Where's the movie theater?
   B: It's between the post office and the bank.

ANSWER KEY

post office	movie theater	bank
supermarket	community center	fire station

🎧 **3 LISTEN** and read.

- Direct students' attention to the picture. Ask questions: *Who do you see?*
- Play the CD or read the conversation as students follow along silently.
- Play the CD or read the conversation again and have students repeat.
- Ask *Where is the school? Where is the post office?*

EXPANSION ACTIVITY: 24 cards

- Write the words from the conversation on index cards, one word to a card.
- Shuffle and give each student one card.
- Have students walk around the room, saying the word to put themselves in order of the conversation.
- Have students say their words in order to recreate the conversation. Encourage students to use appropriate speed and intonation, even with their single words.

4 PRACTICE THE CONVERSATION with a partner.

- Go over the directions.
- Model the activity. Have a more advanced student read A's lines. Model how to substitute a different name and preposition of location.
- Put students in pairs to practice the conversation, making the appropriate substitutions.
- Walk around to monitor the activity and provide help as needed.
- Call on students to say the conversation to the class.

5 WHAT ABOUT YOU? Talk to a partner about the places in the box.

- Go over the directions and the example conversation. Make sure students know what *favorite* means.

- Model the activity. Cue the student to ask you about a favorite place. Answer with the correct information.
- Put students in pairs to take turns asking and answering questions about their favorite places.
- Call on students and ask them about a place.

COMMUNITY CONNECTION: Phone books

- As an out-of-class assignment, have students look up their favorite supermarket, movie theater, restaurant and drugstore in the phone book to find the address and telephone number.
- Have students write the information in their notebooks.
- Elicit the address and phone number for one place the students looked up.

LESSON 4: Grammar and Vocabulary

OBJECTIVE
Use imperatives to give directions

VOCABULARY	
cross	right
enter	start
go	stop
left	straight
make	turn
park	U-turn

GRAMMAR
Imperatives

COMPETENCIES
Use imperatives

WARM-UP ACTIVITY: Classroom instructions

- Review classroom instructions with students (from the Pre-Unit, page 3).
- Say and write several instructions (*Stand up. Go to the board.*) and have students demonstrate them.
- Circle the verbs in the classroom instructions that you have written on the board.

🎧 ❶ GRAMMAR PICTURE DICTIONARY.
   Listen and repeat.

- Have students look at the pictures.
- Play the CD or say the sentences and have students repeat.
- Say the sentences in random order and have the students name the picture number.

❷ NOTICE THE GRAMMAR. Look at Activity 1. Circle the verbs.

- Have students circle the verbs.
- Go over the answers with the class.

ANSWER KEY
How do I get to your apartment?
1. (Start) on Main Street.
2. (Turn) left on 1st Avenue.
3. (Turn) right on Broadway.
4. (Go) straight on Broadway.
5. (Don't stop) in front of the apartment building.
6. (Make) a U-turn.
7. (Park) next to the police station.
8. (Cross) the street.
9. (Enter) the building and (go) to the third floor.

GRAMMAR CHART: Imperatives

- Go over the information in the chart, including the usage note.
- You may want to read the sample sentences in the chart and have students repeat.
- Point out that there is a subject in imperatives (*you*), but we don't say it. The subject is understood.
- Point out that the verb form doesn't change in imperatives.

Unit 5　97

CHART EXPANSION ACTIVITY: Signs

- Draw arrows on different pieces of paper. Draw the same arrows again, only put a red circle and bar across the arrow.

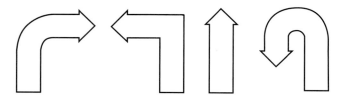

- Hold up the sign and elicit the imperative (e.g., *Turn left, Don't make a U-turn*).

3 WRITE. Complete the sentences. Use the words in the box.

- Go over the directions, the words in the box, and the example.
- Have students complete the sentences with the verbs from the box.
- Put students in pairs to compare answers.
- Go over the answers with the class.

ANSWER KEY

1. Start; 2. Turn; 3. Go; 4. Stop; 5. Park

EXPANSION ACTIVITY: Total physical response (TPR)

- If your classroom is not already arranged in rows, have your students arrange the desks that way.
- Ask a volunteer to come to the front of the room. Place the student at the head of an aisle, between two rows of desks. Have a student give an imperative (e.g., *Go straight.*). Have another student give the next direction (*Turn left.*).
- Continue with other students and other directions until everyone has given a command.
- If necessary, model the activity first by giving a few commands.

COMMUNITY CONNECTION: Traffic sign

- As an out-of-class assignment, have students copy one traffic sign they see.
- As the warm-up to the next lesson, have students display their sign in class. Elicit the imperative.

LESSON 5: Grammar Practice Plus

OBJECTIVE
Understand traffic signs

GRAMMAR
Using Imperatives

PRONUNCIATION
Sentence stress

COMPETENCIES
Understanding traffic signs Give directions

WARM-UP ACTIVITY: Road signs

- With books closed, ask students *What signs do you see on the roads?* Elicit ideas and write them on the board.

🎧 **1 LISTEN** and repeat.

- Direct students' attention to the signs and elicit the ones they know.
- Play the CD and have students repeat.
- Say the signs in random order and have students point.
- Put students in pairs to take turns saying the signs and pointing.

BIG PICTURE READING EXPANSION ACTIVITY: Signs

- Put the transparency for Unit 5 on the OHP.
- Have students identify any street signs (*Stop*).
- Ask students if they could put any other signs from page 78 on the Big Picture, and if so, where.
- Answers and discussions will vary.

2 WRITE. Look at the signs. Complete the sentences.

- Go over the directions and the example.
- Have students write the words on the line to complete the sentences.
- Put students in pairs to compare answers.
- Go over the answers with the class.

ANSWER KEY
1. Don't turn right; 2. one-way; 3. Don't enter; 4. Stop; 5. Don't park

PRONUNCIATION: Sentence stress
A. LISTEN to the sentences. Underline the stressed word or words.

- Go over the directions and the example. Remind students that when we stress a word, we say it louder and longer. Point out that in this case, we stress words that are important in understanding the directions.
- Play the CD and have students underline the stressed words.
- Elicit the underlined words from students.

LISTENING SCRIPT AND ANSWER KEY
Lesson 5, Activity A

TCD2, 24
SCD, 28

Listen to the sentences. Underline the stressed word or words.

1. Turn <u>right</u> on <u>2nd</u> Avenue.
2. <u>Stop</u> in front of the <u>store</u>.
3. Go <u>straight</u> on Oak Lane.
4. <u>Cross</u> the street.
5. <u>Park</u> next to the <u>police station</u>.
6. Turn <u>left</u> on <u>Johnson</u> Road.

B. LISTEN AGAIN and repeat. Then practice with a partner.

- Go over the directions.
- Play the CD and have students repeat.
- Put students in pairs to take turns saying the sentences with the appropriate stress.
- Call on students to say a sentence. Correct the stress pattern if necessary.

3 LISTEN to the directions. Number the sentences in the correct order.

- Go over the directions.
- Play the CD and stop after the first sentence. Point out that *1* is written on the line next to *Turn left on 6th Avenue.*
- Play the rest of the CD and have students write the number next to the direction.
- Have students match the sentences to the signs.
- Put students in pairs to listen again and write in the missing words.
- Go over the answers with the class.

LISTENING SCRIPT
Lesson 5, Activity 3

TCD2, 26

Listen to the directions. Number the sentences in the correct order.

Go straight on Broadway. Then . . .
1. Turn left on 6th Avenue. Don't turn right.
2. Don't go on 4th Avenue. It's a one-way street.
3. Do not enter on Sherman Drive.
4. Stop at E Street in front of the apartment building.
5. Don't park on the street. Go behind the apartment building.

ANSWER KEY

2. 1. 4. 3. 5.

4 READ the directions. Look at the map. Circle the incorrect words in the directions.

- Go over the directions. Make sure students see they are trying to follow the dotted line and get to the bus stop.
- Go over the example.
- Have students look at the map and circle the incorrect words in each sentence.
- Put students in pairs to compare answers.
- Have students rewrite the directions with the correct information.
- Have volunteers write the sentences on the board.

ANSWER KEY

1. Go straight on (Main Street).
2. Turn (right) on 5th Avenue.
3. (Don't) cross Johnson Road.
4. Turn (left).
5. Stop in front of the (bank).

CORRECTED:

1. Go straight on Baker Street.
2. Turn left on 5th Avenue.
3. Cross Johnson Road.
4. Turn right.
5. Stop in front of the drugstore.

BIG PICTURE GRAMMAR EXPANSION ACTIVITY: Where Is It?

- Photocopy and distribute Worksheet 11: Where Is It?
- Go over the directions and the example.
- Have students complete the worksheet and then compare answers with a partner.
- Go over the answers with the class.

WORKSHEET 11 ANSWER KEY

1. A. right; B. Go; C. on the right
2. A. Enter; B. right; C. on the left
3. A. Exit the school. B. Turn left. C. Go one block. D. Cross the street.

LESSON 6: Apply Your Knowledge

OBJECTIVE

Calculate distance using a map

MATH

Calculate distance (in blocks)

COMPETENCIES

Read maps
Calculate distance
Ask for, give and clarify directions
Use *from* and *to*

WARM-UP ACTIVITY: Online maps

- Ask students if they have ever seen or used an online map service.
- Bring in a download of a map and directions to and from a local place in your city.

❶ READ. Look at the map. Circle the street names.

- Direct students' attention to the map and ask questions: *What streets are there? What places do you see? What is the address of the police station?*
- Go over the directions.
- Have students circle the street names on the map.
- Elicit the names of streets and write them on the board.

ANSWER KEY

Main Street, Oak Lane, Princeton Street,
1st Street–10th Street

❷ LISTEN. Complete the sentences.

- Direct students' attention to the handwritten directions.

- Go over the directions.
- Play the CD and stop after the first sentence. Point out that *Turn right* is written on the line.
- Play the rest of the CD and have students complete the sentences.
- Put students in pairs to compare answers.
- Play the CD again.
- Go over the answers with the class.

LISTENING SCRIPT
Lesson 6, Activity 2
TCD2, 27

Listen. Complete the sentences.

1. Turn right on Princeton Street.
2. Go straight for two blocks.
3. Cross at 1st Street.
4. Turn left on 5th Street.
5. Park on the street in front of the house.

ANSWER KEY

1. Turn right; 2. straight; 3. Cross; 4. Turn left;
5. Park/house

EXPANSION ACTIVITY: Return trip

- Have students write directions to go from the house back to the starting point.
- Put students in pairs to read the directions.
- Have a volunteer read the directions to class.

MATH: Calculating Distance

A. Look at the map above. Calculate the distances.

- Read the sentence about blocks.
- Direct students' attention to the map.
- Go over the directions.
- Have students write the number of blocks.

CULTURE/CIVICS NOTE

In cities, towns and some suburbs, streets are laid out often in a grid pattern. This means that people can use *block* to talk about location (*The store is one block from the school.*) and distance (*The library is two blocks away.*).

B. TALK with a partner about your answers.

- Go over the directions and the example.
- Put students in pairs to talk about their answers.
- Go over the answers with the class.

ANSWER KEY

1. 4; 2. 4; 3. 2; 4. 4

EXPANSION ACTIVITY: Around your school

- Have students draw a map for the area around your school. Encourage students to make the map large enough to include several blocks in every direction.
- Have students add all the places they can remember.
- Put students in small groups to ask and answer questions about their maps. Remind students to ask about distance in blocks.

3 LISTEN and read.

- Direct students' attention to the picture. Ask questions: *Who do you see? Where are they?*
- Have students follow along silently as you say the conversation or play the CD.
- Ask comprehension questions: *Where is the hotel? What is it next to? How many blocks away is it?*
- Play the CD again and have students repeat.
- Put students in pairs to take turns reading the parts.

4 PRACTICE THE CONVERSATION with a partner. Look at the map on page 80. Give

directions from the Community Center to each place.

- Go over the directions and the information.
- Model the activity with a student. Have the students read A's lines. Cue the student to ask about the drugstore. Model how to substitute the appropriate information.
- Have pairs of students take turns giving directions. Monitor the activity as needed.

EXPANSION ACTIVITY: You are here

- Give students a single starting point on the map in Activity 1.
- Have individual students choose one place on the map and write directions from the starting point to that place.
- Call on students to read their directions. Have the class guess the end place.

5 WRITE. Look at the map on page 80. Choose two places. Draw a line from one place to the other place. Then write directions.

- Go over the directions. Have students choose a starting and ending place.
- Have students write the directions.
- Put students in pairs to take turns reading directions and guessing where the directions take them.
- Call on students to read their directions to the class. Elicit the place.

COMMUNITY CONNECTION: Give directions to a public place

- For an out-of-class assignment, have students use the map from the Community Connection in Lesson 2 to write directions from one public place to another. You may want to print multiple copies and have students work in pairs to write the directions.
- Have students exchange directions and find the two places on the map.

LESSON 7: Reading and Writing

OBJECTIVES

Read a brochure
Write using details

READING TIP

Use headings to find information

WRITING TIP

Take notes to help organize your writing

COMPETENCIES

Read a brochure
Use a phone directory

Reading

WARM-UP ACTIVITY: Brochures

Bring in one or more brochures or flyers for some place in your community. Show it to the class and ask what it is and what kind of information they think it might have. Write the ideas on the board.

1 THINK ABOUT IT. What public places are there in your community? Check the places.

- Go over the directions.
- Have students check the places in their communities or neighborhoods.
- Elicit the places students checked.

2 BEFORE YOU READ. What public places are there in Madison? Look at the brochure. Make a list.

- Go over the reading tip in the box. Make sure students understand what headings are.
- Go over the directions.

- Direct students' attention to the brochure.
- Have students write the places in Madison.
- Elicit the places.

ANSWER KEY

Community center, police station, fire station, hospital

3 READ the brochure. Underline the words for streets and places in the community.

- Have students read the brochure silently, or read the brochure aloud sentence by sentence and have students repeat.
- Have students underline the words for streets and places.
- Ask comprehension questions: *Where is the community center? What are the hours? How many fire trucks are there? When is the emergency room open?*

ANSWER KEY

Community Center: Main Street; next to the hospital
Police Station: Main Street
Fire Station: next to the police station; Main Street
Hospital: across from fire and police stations

4 MATCH the place to the information.

- Direct students' attention to the chart. Go over the example.
- Have students write other adjectives in the chart.
- Put students in pairs to compare ideas.
- Elicit ideas from the students and write the ideas on the board.

EXPANSION ACTIVITY: Literacy development—sentences strips

- Copy the sentences from the brochure onto separate strips. Leave enough space between each word for word discrimination. The sentences need to be large enough to be read by all the students.
- Put the sentence strips on the board in the correct order. Read each sentence aloud and have students repeat.
- Take the sentences down and mix them up.
- Have volunteers come to the board and put the sentences in the correct order.
- You may want to photocopy the sentences from the brochure and cut them into strips so that each student or pair of students has a set to reassemble.

BIG PICTURE READING EXPANSION ACTIVITY: Places in the Community

- Photocopy and distribute Worksheet 12: Places in the Community.
- Put the transparency for Unit 5 on the OHP or have students look at the Big Picture in their books.
- Put students in pairs to share their ideas.
- Write ideas on the board.

Writing

1 WRITE the name of a store or other place in your city.

- Have students write the name of a place they know in your city or town.

2 WRITE notes about the place.

- Go over the writing tip in the box. Point out that details often answer questions that begin with *what, where, when, who* and so on.
- Have students write the information on the lines. Encourage students to look in a phone book, online, or at a map to find information.
- Put students in pairs to share their ideas.

3 WRITE about the place in your city.

- Have students complete the sentences with information about a place in your city.
- Walk around to monitor the activity and provide help as needed.
- Put students in pairs to read their sentences.
- Call on students to read their sentences.

EXPANSION ACTIVITY: Places in the community

- Give each student an index card.
- Have students rewrite their sentences from Activity 3 on their index cards.
- Collect the cards and read each aloud.
- Optional: omit the place name and have students guess what place it is.
- Post a map of your city on a wall in the classroom. Post the index cards on or near the map. If you don't have a map, keep the index cards in a file for student reference.

BIG PICTURE WRITING EXPANSION ACTIVITY: Describe a place

- Have students look at the Big Picture.
- Have each student choose a place.
- Ask students to write ideas such as the street, location, and other details.
- Have students follow the model in Activity 3 to write about a place.
- Ask volunteers to read their sentences.

Career Connection

OBJECTIVE

Identify educational opportunities

COMPETENCIES

Ask for details

WARM-UP ACTIVITY: Classes

Put students in pairs or small groups to list places where they can take classes of any kind. Elicit the ideas and write them on the board.

❶ READ and listen.

- Direct students' attention to the photos. Tell students this is the continuation of the story about Isabel. Have students point to Isabel in the photos.
- Play the CD and have students follow along silently.
- Play the CD again and have students repeat.
- Put students in pairs to take turns reading the roles of Isabel and her coworker.
- Ask: *What is Isabel getting information about?*

❷ TALK. Answer the questions.

- Read each question aloud and have students repeat.
- Have students answer the questions in writing first. Then put students in pairs to ask and answer the questions.
- Call on students and ask questions.

ANSWER KEY

1. the corner of Main Street and 10th Avenue;
2. medical classes; 3. five blocks; 4. happy

❸ WHAT ABOUT YOU? Answer the questions about your school.

- Go over the directions and the questions.
- Have students answer the questions.
- Elicit answers from the class.

ACADEMIC CONNECTION: Other programs

- If your school has a website, show students how to access it. You may also want to provide website addresses for other schools or educational programs in your community.
- Have students choose a subject or program they are interested in. It can be career-oriented or for personal development and interest.
- Have students find a place that offers classes in their area of interest.

CHECK YOUR PROGRESS!

- Have students circle the answers.
- Have students check whether each answer is right or wrong.
- Have students total their correct answers and fill in the chart.
- Have students create a learning plan and/or set learning goals.

ANSWER KEY

1. in front of	7. Turn
2. between	8. Park
3. next to	9. Stop
4. hospital	10. straight
5. restaurant	11. turn
6. supermarket	12. U-turn.

UNIT 6 Shopping

Unit Overview

LESSON	OBJECTIVE	STUDENT BOOK	WORKBOOK
1 Grammar and Vocabulary 1	Use present continuous to talk about shopping	p. 86	p. 72
2 Grammar Practice Plus	Identify clothing items	p. 88	p. 73
3 Listening and Conversation	Describe clothing colors and sizes	p. 90	p. 74
4 Grammar and Vocabulary 2	Identify U.S. coins and bills Use *How much* to ask about prices	p. 92	p. 76
5 Grammar Practice Plus	Use demonstratives to identify clothing Interpret a receipt	p. 94	p. 77
6 Apply Your Knowledge	Understand a clothing advertisement Write a personal check	p. 96	p. 78
7 Reading and Writing	Understand a consumer article Use quotes in writing	p. 98	p. 80
• Career Connection	Make a budget	p. 100	p. 82
• Check Your Progress	Monitor progress	p. 101	p. 84

Reading/Writing Strategies • Read captions • Use quotes

Connection Activities

LESSON	TYPE	SKILL DEVELOPMENT
1	Academic	Create a vocabulary notebook
2	Community	Observe people in a public place
3	Academic	Research appropriate job interview attire
3	Community	Use the Yellow Pages
4	Academic/Community	Research important facts about a president
6	Academic	Take notes while listening
6	Community	Research online banking options
8	Academic	Research online budget worksheets

WORKSHEET #/FOCUS	TITLE	TEACHER'S EDITION
13 Grammar	What Are They Doing?	p. 258
14 Reading	Match the Quotes	p. 259

LESSON 1: Grammar and Vocabulary

OBJECTIVE

Use present continuous to talk about shopping

VOCABULARY

backpack	shop
buy	talk
carry	try on
help	wait
look (for)	work

GRAMMAR

Present Continuous

COMPETENCIES

Use present continuous

WARM-UP ACTIVITY: Unit opener

- Put the transparency for Unit 6 on the overhead projector (OHP) or have students look at the Big Picture on page 89.
- Elicit words the students know and write them on the board.

◯ **❶ GRAMMAR PICTURE DICTIONARY.** Listen and repeat.

- Have students open their books and look at the pictures.
- Say the sentences or play the CD and have students repeat.
- Say the sentences in random order and have students say the picture number.
- Put students in pairs and take turns saying the sentences in random order as their partner points to the picture.
- Call on students and say a number. Elicit the sentence.

EXPANSION ACTIVITY: Spell the verb

- Write *buying* on the board. Elicit the base form of the verb (*buy*).
- Have students write the base form of all the verbs in Activity 1.
- Have volunteers write the words on the board.

VOCABULARY NOTE

Make sure students see that *looking* is followed by *for,* and *trying* is followed by *on.* Students will not learn about phrasal verbs at this level, but they should notice the two parts of these verbs.

❷ NOTICE THE GRAMMAR. Look at Activity 1. Underline *is* and *are.* Circle the verbs + *-ing.*

- Have students read the sentences and underline *is* and *are.* Then have students circle the main verbs.
- Ask questions: *What is she buying in number 1? What are the girls doing in number 6? In what number are people carrying bags?*

ANSWER KEY

1. She is (buying) a dress.
2. He is (looking) for a book.
3. She is (shopping) with her children.
4. They are (working) at the cash register.
5. The sales clerk is (helping) the customer.
6. The girls are (talking.)
7. She is (trying) on a jacket.
8. They are (carrying) bags.
9. He is (waiting) in line.

PRONUNCIATION NOTE

- Point out that the *–ing* sound is made by closing the back of the throat. We don't really pronounce the *g*.
- Point out that when people speak quickly, they sometimes drop the *g* sound altogether (e.g., *lookin'*).

EXPANSION ACTIVITY: Replace the word

- Give students two minutes to review the sentences.
- Have students close their books.
- Write the sentences on the board, leaving out the form of *be,* and putting the main verb in parentheses as a prompt (*She _____ (buy) a dress.*).
- Elicit the missing words from the students.
- Have students open their books and confirm their answers.

GRAMMAR CHART: Present Continuous

- Direct students' attention to the chart or project the transparency or CD.
- Go over the information on the chart. You may want to read the sentences, pausing to have students repeat.
- Point out that we often use contractions with the affirmative statements as well (e.g., *She's shopping, We're waiting, I'm talking, You're reading*).
- Point out that we follow spelling rules in adding *–ing* to a verb. Or, write the rules on the board:
  1. one-syllable words ending in consonant-vowel-consonant (e.g., *stop/stopping*)—double the final consonant before adding *–ing.*
  2. words ending in a silent *–e* (e.g., *take/taking*)—drop the *e,* then add *–ing.*
  3. words that end in *ie* (*tie/tying*)—change the *ie* to *y,* then add *–ing.*

CHART EXPANSION ACTIVITY: Question form

- Write the *yes/no* question forms on the board. Students don't need to be able to from questions at this point, but they can recognize questions and respond.
- Ask questions about people in the class: *Is Maria wearing pants? Are Luis and Tam reading their books?*

❸ WRITE. Complete the sentences. Use the present progressive (affirmative or negative).

- Have students write the correct form of the verb.
- Put students in pairs to check their answers.

ANSWER KEY

1. is buying; 2. isn't buying; 3. is shopping;
4. aren't waiting; 5. am not talking; 6. is carrying;
7. are looking for; 8. are working

EXPANSION ACTIVITY: Rewrite

- Write the first sentence on the board. Then rewrite it in the negative.
- Have students rewrite the sentences, making affirmative sentences negative and negative sentences affirmative.
- Write the sentences on the board.

❹ WHAT ABOUT YOU? Look around your classroom. Write a sentence for each verb.

- Have students write sentences using the verbs in the present continuous. Encourage students to use both singular and plural subjects and to write about themselves.
- Put students in pairs to read their sentences.

ACADEMIC CONNECTION: Vocabulary notebooks

- Have students list all the verbs they have learned so far in a vocabulary notebook.
- Have students write the *–ing* form next to the base form of the verb.

LESSON 2: Grammar Practice Plus

OBJECTIVE

Identify clothing items

VOCABULARY

black	purple
blue	red
brown	shirt
dress	shoes
green	shorts
hat	skirt
jacket	white
orange	yellow
pants	

GRAMMAR

Present continuous

COMPETENCIES

Use present continuous
Identify colors
Identify clothing

COMPETENCIES

Use *be* in descriptions of people
Use *be* plus an adjective

WARM-UP ACTIVITY: List by color

- Show examples of different colors.
- Put students in pairs or small groups to list everything in the classroom by color.
- Give students three minutes to list as many things as they can.
- Ask questions: *How many red things did you list? How many blue things?*
- Write the colors on the board. Elicit the names of things that color and write them on the board, or have students write the things on the board.

① **WRITE** the colors. Use the words in the box.

- Say each word in the box and have students repeat.
- Go over the directions and the example.
- Have students write the colors on the lines to complete the sentences.
- Put students in pairs to compare answers.

 LISTEN and repeat. Are your answers correct?

- Play the audio and have students repeat. Have students check their answers.

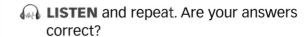 **LISTENING SCRIPT**
Lesson 2, Activity 1
TCD2, 31

Listen and repeat. Are your answers correct?

1. Anita is wearing a white dress and a green hat.
2. Matt is wearing orange shorts and a yellow jacket.
3. Larisa is wearing a red shirt and a blue skirt.
4. Marco is wearing brown pants and black shoes.

ANSWER KEY

1. white/green; 2. orange/yellow; 3. red/blue; 4. brown/black

EXPANSION ACTIVITY: Word unscramble

- With books closed, write the following letter combinations on the board: *dre, kbcla, uble, wollye.*
- Tell students the letters are the scrambled letters for four colors.
- Have students unscramble the letters to write the four colors (*red, black, blue, yellow*).

2 WRITE. What are your classmates wearing? Write three clothing words in the chart. Then count the number of each color.

- Go over the directions and the example. Make sure students understand how to make tally marks in the appropriate columns.
- Have students complete the chart.
- Put students in small groups to talk about their charts.
- Call on students to tell the class about one clothing item and color (e.g., *Four people are wearing white shirts.*).

CULTURE NOTE

- You may want to point out that we associate some colors with certain occasions. For example, brides often wear white, and people usually wear black or other dark colors to a funeral.
- Ask students about what colors are associated with certain occasions or feelings in their cultures.

EXPANSION ACTIVITY: Bar Graphs

- Model how to make a bar graph, using the example in the chart.

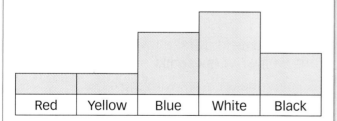

Red	Yellow	Blue	White	Black

- Have students create a bar graph for one row of their charts.
- Put students in pairs to compare charts.

3 GAME. Write about a person in your class. Don't write the person's name. Read your sentences to three classmates. Your classmates guess the student.

- Go over the directions and the example.
- Have students write a description, including at least three things.
- Put students in groups of three to take turns reading their descriptions and guessing.
- Call on students to read their descriptions to the class. Elicit the name of the person.

4 TALK about the picture.

- Direct students' attention to the Big Picture.
- Go over the directions and the example.
- Call on students and ask questions about the characters in the picture.

BIG PICTURE SPEAKING EXPANSION ACTIVITY: Who am I?

- Have students look at the Big Picture or put the color overhead transparency for Unit 6 on the OHP.
- Model the activity. Say several sentences about a character in the picture (e.g., *I am young. I am wearing red pants.*). Elicit the name (*Brad*).
- Put students in pairs to practice describing and guessing characters. You may want to put students in small groups and assign each student a character to facilitate this activity.
- Call on students to say their sentences to the class and elicit the name from the other students.

---

5 LISTEN. Complete the sentences.

- Go over the directions and the example.
- Have students write words to complete the sentences.
- Put students in pairs to compare answers.
- Say the questions or play the CD again so students can confirm.
- Go over the answers with the class.

**LISTENING SCRIPT
Lesson 2, Activity 5**

TCD2, 32

Listen. Complete the sentences.

1. Brad is wearing red pants.
2. Marta is wearing a purple shirt.
3. Clara is buying white shoes.
4. Ali is waiting for his wife.
5. Paula is helping Marta.
6. Oscar is carrying four bags.

ANSWER KEY

1. pants; 2. shirt; 3. shoes; 4. waiting; 5. helping; 6. carrying

BIG PICTURE GRAMMAR EXPANSION ACTIVITY: What Are They Doing?

- Photocopy and distribute Worksheet 13: What Are They Doing?
- Put the transparency for Unit 6 on the OHP or have students look at the Big Picture on page 89.
- Have students complete the worksheet.
- Put students in pairs to share their ideas.
- Go over the answers with the class.

WORKSHEET 13 ANSWER KEY

1. c; 2. b; 3. e; 4. a; 5. d; 6. Lydia is carrying two bags. 7. Lara is looking at Brad's red pants. 8. Elena is buying a hat.

6 WRITE. Find the people in the picture. Write their names on the picture.

- Go over the directions.
- Have students write the names from Activity 5 on the picture.
- Put students in pairs to compare ideas.
- Put the transparency for Unit 6 on the OHP. Point to the people and elicit the name.

7 CHECK the answers.

- Go over the directions and the example conversation.
- Read each question aloud and have students repeat.

ANSWER KEY

1. No, he isn't. 2. No, he isn't. 3. No, she isn't. 4. Yes, she is.

TALK. Ask and answer the questions with a partner.

- Put students in pairs to take turns asking and answering the questions.
- Go over the answers with the class.

EXPANSION ACTIVITY: Question game

- Model the activity. Think of someone in the class. Elicit questions from the students (*Is the person female? Is she wearing jeans? Is she behind Yuri?*). Tell students they must ask five questions before they can guess a name, and that each new question must be asked by a different student.

- Have a student come to the front of the class and think of someone, eliciting questions.

- Continue until everyone has asked at least one question.

**COMMUNITY CONNECTION:
Observation in a public place**

- As an out-of-class assignment, have students go to a public place and write sentences about what people are doing. Encourage students to choose public places such as the ones they learned about in Unit 5.

- Have students read sentences to the class.

LESSON 3: Listening and Conversation

OBJECTIVE
Identify clothing sizes

VOCABULARY	
extra large	medium
extra small	small
large	

COMPETENCIES
Identify clothing sizes

WARM-UP ACTIVITY: **Same and different**

- Direct students' attention to the pictures in Activity 1.
- Ask students to identify what is the same and what is different in each set of pictures.

❶ LISTEN. Circle the correct letter.

- Go over the directions.
- Say the conversations or play the CD and have students circle the letter.
- Have students compare answers in pairs.
- Go over the answers with the class.

LISTENING SCRIPT
Lesson 3, Activity 1
TCD2, 33

Listen. Circle the correct letter.

1. A: Hello. Can I help you?
   B: Yes, I'm looking for pants.
   A: What color?
   B: Brown.
   A: Okay. The brown pants are over there.
   B: Thank you!
2. A: Hello. Can I help you?
   B: Yes, I'm looking for a black skirt.
   A: What size?
   B: Small.
   A: Okay. There are black skirts over there.
   B: Thanks!
3. A: Hello. Can I help you?
   B: Yes, I'm looking for a jacket. A purple jacket.
   A: What size?
   B: Medium.
   A: Okay. The jackets are over there.
   B: Thank you!

ANSWER KEY
1. A; 2. B; 3. C

PRONUNCIATION: *Isn't* and *Aren't*

A. LISTEN to the sentences. Listen for the *t* in *isn't* and *aren't*.

- Play the CD or read the sentences as students follow along silently.
- Play the CD or read the sentences again and have students repeat.

PRONUNCIATION NOTE

Point out that when we say an affirmative and a negative sentence together, as in Activity A, we tend to stress the negative (*isn't*) and/or the different information (*large/small*).

B. LISTEN to the sentences. Circle *is* or *isn't, are* or *aren't.*

- Remind students to listen for the negative contractions.
- Play the CD and have students circle the answer.
- Go over the answers with the class.

LISTENING SCRIPT
Lesson 3, Activity B

TCD2, 35
SCD, 33

Listen to the sentences. Circle *is* or *isn't, are* or *aren't.*

1. Oscar isn't buying brown pants.
2. Sara and Maria are looking for a black skirt.
3. Mark isn't trying on a blue jacket.
4. They aren't looking for a red shirt.

ANSWER KEY

1. isn't; 2. are; 3. isn't; 4. aren't

C. TALK. Read the sentences in B to your partner.

- Go over the directions.
- Put students in pairs to read the sentences aloud.

EXPANSION ACTIVITY: Pair work

- Put students in pairs to take turns saying one of the sentences in Activity B (either affirmative or negative) as their partners point to the word they hear.

2 LISTEN and read.

- Direct students' attention to the picture. Ask questions: *Who do you see? Where are they?*
- Play the CD or read the conversation as students follow along silently.
- Play the CD or read the conversation again and have students repeat.
- Ask *What is the woman looking for? What color does she want? What size is she looking for?*
- Put students in pairs to practice the conversation. Have students switch roles.

GRAMMAR NOTE

Point out that we sometimes ask short questions such as *What color? What size?*

CULTURE NOTES

- Your students may be interested in shopping behavior in the United States. Explain that we often use the expression *I'm just looking* if we don't want help, or if we don't plan to buy anything.
- Point out that we don't usually bargain over prices. The stores set prices and that is what the customer pays. The only exception is if something is damaged, then the customer might ask if the price can be reduced.

3 PRACTICE THE CONVERSATION with a partner.

- Go over the directions.
- Model the activity. Have a more advanced student read A's lines. Model how to substitute different clothing items, colors and sizes.
- Put students in pairs to practice the conversation, making the appropriate substitutions.
- Walk around to monitor the activity and provide help as needed.
- Call on students to say the conversation to the class.

EXPANSION ACTIVITY: Garage sale

- Bring in, or have students bring in old clothes.
- Set the clothes on tables as they might be at a garage sale. Explain that people often sell things they don't want at garage sales.
- Put students in pairs to practice asking for and answering questions about clothing items at your "garage sale."

4 WRITE. You are shopping for clothes. Make a list of clothes you are looking for. Write the colors and sizes.

- Copy the chart on the board.
- Go over the directions.
- Model the activity. Tell the students what you are going to wear to a New Year's Eve party. Write your ideas on the chart on the board.
- Have students complete the chart.
- When students are finished, put students in pairs to practice asking a salesperson for the clothes on their lists. Remind students to use the conversation in Activity 3 as a model.

CULTURE/CIVICS NOTE

Students may be confused by our sizing system. Point out that children's sizes often correspond roughly to age, teenaged girls' sizes are odd numbers (1, 3, 5, 7), adult women are by even numbers (2, 4, 6, 8), and men by S, M, L or by inches.

ACADEMIC CONNECTION: Job interview clothes

- As an out-of-class assignment, have students do research on the internet to find out about the kind of clothing they should wear to a job interview in the United States. It's okay if they do their research in their first language, but they need to present it to the class in English.

COMMUNITY CONNECTION: Yellow Pages

- Explain or elicit what the Yellow Pages are and how we use them.
- As an out-of-class assignment, have students look up three places that sell clothing they need for themselves or their families.

LESSON 4: Grammar and Vocabulary

OBJECTIVE

Identify U.S. coins and bills
Use *how much* to ask about prices

VOCABULARY

a dime	a penny
a dollar	a quarter
five dollars	ten dollars
a nickel	twenty dollars

GRAMMAR

Questions with *how much*

COMPETENCIES

Identify coins and bills
Ask for and give prices

NUMERACY

Identify coins and bills

WARM-UP ACTIVITY: What's in your pockets?

- Have students look in their pockets or bags for loose change and put it on their desks.
- Ask students how much money they have. If they don't know how to count it yet, have students keep the money out until after Activity 1.

🎧 **❶ GRAMMAR PICTURE DICTIONARY.**
   Listen and repeat. How much is it?

- Direct students' attention to the pictures.
- Play the CD or say the sentences and have students repeat.

- Say the words and phrases in random order and have the students point to the pictures.

CULTURE NOTE

Point out that the faces of presidents are usually on coins and bills: a penny, Lincoln; a nickel, Jefferson; a dime, Franklin Roosevelt; a quarter, George Washington.

❷ NOTICE THE GRAMMAR. Look at Activity 1. Circle *How much.* Underline *is* and *are.*

- Have students circle *How much* and underline *is* and *are.* Go over the answers with the class.

ANSWER KEY

9. (How much) is the pen? It's a dollar–fifty.
10. (How much) are the hats? They're five–forty.
11. (How much) are the sweaters? They're twenty-two fifty.
12. (How much) is the backpack? It's fifteen seventy-five.

GRAMMAR CHART: *How Much* Questions with *Be*

- Go over the information in the chart, including the usage note.
- You may want to read the sample sentences in the chart and have students repeat.
- Make sure students see that they use *they* with plural subjects and *it* with singular subjects.
- Point out or elicit that we usually use contractions to give the price (*It's, They're*).

CHART EXPANSION ACTIVITY: Questions
Put students in pairs to practice asking and answering the questions in the chart. You may also want to write additional items and prices on the board. Call on students and ask questions. Elicit appropriate answers

3 WRITE the amounts.

- Go over the directions.
- Direct students' attention to the first picture. Go over the example, counting the coins.
- Have students answer the questions.
- Put students in pairs to compare answers.
- Go over the answers with the class.

ANSWER KEY

1. $0.62; 2. $0.16; 3. $0.37; 4. $0.54

4 WRITE. Complete the questions. Use *is* or *are.* Then answer the questions.

- Direct students' attention to the pictures and elicit what the items are.
- Go over the directions.
- Have students complete the questions and then write answers using *is* or *are.*
- Put students in pairs to compare answers and practice the conversations in Activity 4.
- Go over the answers with the class.

ANSWER KEY

1. is/It's $15.75. 2. are/They're $29.99.
3. are/They're $24.99. 4. is/It's 12.50.

EXPANSION ACTIVITY: Make change

- For each item in Activity 4, tell the class the amount of money you are giving the salesclerk. For example, in 1, say you are giving $20. Have students calculate how much change you should get back.
- Put students in pairs to compare answers.
- Elicit answers from the class.

ACADEMIC/COMMUNITY CONNECTION: Presidents

- Put students in small groups.
- Assign each group a president found on one of the coins or bills.
- Have students research the president and write down three important things about the president.
- Have students share information with their groups.
- Call on students to tell the class about the president they researched.

LESSON 5: Grammar Practice Plus

<table>
<tr><td>**OBJECTIVES**</td></tr>
<tr><td>Use demonstratives to identify clothing
Interpret a receipt</td></tr>
</table>

<table>
<tr><td>**GRAMMAR**</td></tr>
<tr><td>Demonstratives: *this, that, these, those*</td></tr>
</table>

<table>
<tr><td>**MATH/NUMERACY**</td></tr>
<tr><td>Writing money</td></tr>
</table>

<table>
<tr><td>**COMPETENCIES**</td></tr>
<tr><td>Demonstratives: *this, that, these, those*
Ask for and give prices
Read receipts</td></tr>
</table>

WARM-UP: This pencil, that book

- Pick up a pencil, hold it close to you and say *This pencil is my pencil.* Point to a student's pencil at a distance away and say *That pencil is your pencil.* Do the same thing with two pencils and *these* and *those.*
- Call on students to use demonstratives with classroom objects.
- Ask questions with demonstratives: *What is this? What is that?*

❶ WRITE. Complete the sentences. Use the words in the box.

- Direct students' attention to the pictures. Make sure they understand that *this* is used with close singular nouns, *that* with singular nouns at a distance, *these* with close plural nouns, and *those* with plural nouns at a distance.
- Have students write the prices.
- Play the CD and have students repeat and check their answers.
- Go over the answers with the class.

LISTENING SCRIPT
Lesson 5, Activity 1

TCD2, 38

Listen and repeat. Are your answers correct?

<table>
<tr><td>1. This shirt is $7.00.</td></tr>
<tr><td>2. That skirt is $25.00.</td></tr>
<tr><td>3. These jackets are $50.00.</td></tr>
<tr><td>4. Those hats are $32.00.</td></tr>
</table>

<table>
<tr><td>**ANSWER KEY**</td></tr>
<tr><td>1. This; 2. That; 3. These; 4. Those</td></tr>
</table>

❷ CIRCLE the correct word.

- Go over the directions.
- Direct students' attention to the picture.
- Go over the answers with the class.

<table>
<tr><td>**ANSWER KEY**</td></tr>
<tr><td>1. These; 2. That; 3. This; 4. This; 5. These</td></tr>
</table>

BIG PICTURE LISTENING EXPANSION ACTIVITY: Who is talking?

- Put the transparency for Unit 6 on the OHP or have students look at the Big Picture in their books.
- Dictate the following sentences. Say each sentence at least three times.
  These bags are heavy.
  This skirt is pretty.
  How much are these shoes?
- Put students in pairs to compare sentences.
- Have volunteers write the sentences on the board.
- Have students write the name of the person who is speaking next to the sentence.

ANSWER KEY

These bags are heavy. (Oscar)
This skirt is pretty. (Marta)
How much are these shoes? (Clara)

EXPANSION ACTIVITY: Garage sale items

- Get out the clothes from the garage sale Expansion Activity in Lesson 3. Distribute the clothing around the room.
- Put students in pairs. Have students walk around the room asking and answering questions about the prices of different items. Remind students to use demonstratives.

MATH: Money

A. WRITE. Complete the chart.

- Direct students' attention to the chart and elicit another way to write the amount ($0.25).

- Have students complete the chart.
- Go over the answers with the class.

ANSWER KEY

1	25¢	$0.25	twenty-five cents
2	84¢	$0.84	eighty-four cents
3	55¢	$0.55	fifty-five cents
4	19¢	$0.19	nineteen cents

CULTURE/CIVICS NOTES

- Point out that prices in stores are usually in the form preceded by the dollar sign.
- Point out that we need to be able to write out the amounts in words because that is how we write checks.
- Explain that although we need to write the numbers as words and in the long form on checks, we usually say them in a shorter way (e.g., *five-sixty-five*).

B. WRITE the words.

- Go over the directions and the example.
- Have students write the words.
- Have volunteers write the words on the board.

ANSWER KEY

1. five dollars and sixty-five cents
2. two dollars and seventy-four cents
3. eighteen dollars and twelve cents
4. forty-two dollars and thirty-one cents

EXPANSION ACTIVITY: Price dictation

- Dictate several prices to students. Have students write the prices in numerals and then in words.

3 TALK with a partner. Student A, look at the picture below. Student B, look at page 198. Point to the pictures and talk with your partner. Write the prices of the clothes.

- Go over the directions and the example.
- Model the activity with a more advanced student.
- Put students in pairs. Designate one partner as A, the other as B. Have students look at the appropriate pages.
- Walk around the room to monitor the activity and provide help as needed.

GAME. Now describe a clothing item to your partner. Your partner guesses the item.

- Go over the directions and the example for the game.
- Model the activity. Describe something in the picture and elicit guesses.
- Have students play the game in pairs.

4 LISTEN to the conversations. Correct the prices.

- Go over the directions.
- Direct students' attention to the receipts and ask questions: *How much is the dress at Clothes Corner? How much is the skirt?* Explain what *total* means.
- Play the CD and have students correct the prices.
- Put students in pairs to compare receipts.
- Elicit the corrections from the class.

LISTENING SCRIPT
Lesson 5, Activity 4

TCD2, 39–41

Listen to the conversations. Correct the prices.

1. *A:* Excuse me. How much is this shirt?
   B: That shirt is $7.00.
   A: There is a problem with my receipt. The total is wrong.
   B: Oh, okay. Your new total is $59.00.
   A: Thanks!

2. *A:* Hi! Please help me.
   B: What is the problem?
   A: There is a problem with my receipt. How much are these pants?
   B: Those pants are $29.
   A: Not $32?
   B: No… Oh, I'm sorry. Your new total is $51.00.
   A: Thank you.

3. *A:* Excuse me. There is a problem with my receipt. How much are these shoes?
   B: They're $35.00.
   A: The total is wrong.
   B: I'm sorry. Your new total is $76.00.
   A: Thanks.

ANSWER KEY

1. Change $8.00 to $7.00, change $60.00 to $59.00
2. Change $32.00 to $29.00, change $54.00 to $51.00
3. Change $40.00 to $35.00, change $81.00 to $76.00

EXPANSION ACTIVITY: Reading receipts

- Bring in receipts.
- Put students in pairs and give each pair at least one receipt.
- Have students list the information they can find on the receipt.
- Elicit the ideas and write them on the board (*place, address, time, date, items, prices, totals, tax*).

LESSON 6: Apply Your Knowledge

WARM-UP ACTIVITY: Real advertisements

- Bring in ads from the newspaper or mailers, or have students bring them in.
- Ask students what information they can find in the ads. Write their ideas on the board.
- Save the ads for additional practice in this lesson.

❶ READ the advertisement. Circle the sale prices.

- Go over the directions.
- Have students read the ads and circle the sale prices.
- Go over the answers with the class.

ANSWER KEY

$29, $19, $40, $7
$12, $15, $35, $22

❷ LISTEN to the radio ad. Circle the clothes you hear about in the ad.

- Play the CD and have students circle the clothing items they hear about.

LISTENING SCRIPT
Lesson 6, Activity 2

TCD2, 42

Listen to the radio ad. Circle the clothes you hear about in the ad.

A: This week, come to Clothes Corner! All our clothes are ON SALE! Shirts, pants, dresses! Shoes, too!
B: How much are the pants?
A: Black pants are on sale! $29!
B: How much are dresses?
A: There are purple and blue dresses. They're $40!
C: How much are shoes?
A: Brown shoes! Only $35!
D: How much are shirts?
A: Children's shirts, all colors, are $7! Don't miss this sale! Come to Clothes Corner today!

ANSWER KEY

pants, dresses, shoes, children's shirts

ACADEMIC CONNECTION: Take notes

- Play the CD for Activity 2 again and have students take notes on the items that are on sale. Have students write item details and prices. Play the CD as many times as necessary.
- Put students in pairs to compare notes.
- Elicit the information they noted and write it on the board (e.g., *shirts, all colors, $7*).

❸ WRITE. Look at the ad above. Write a shopping list with five things from Clothes Corner for you or a person in your family.

- Direct students' attention to the picture and ask: *What is the person doing?*
- Go over the directions.

- Have students write five things on their lists.
- Put students in pairs to talk about their lists.

🎧 **4 LISTEN** and read.

- Direct students' attention to the picture. Ask questions: *Who do you see? Where are they?*
- Have students follow along and repeat as you say the conversation or play the CD.
- Ask comprehension questions: *What is the customer looking for? Are they on sale? How much are they?*
- Play the CD again and have students repeat.
- Put students in pairs to take turns reading the conversation.

EXPANSION ACTIVITY:
Conversation cards

- Write each word from the conversation on a separate card. Shuffle the cards.
- Have students study the conversation.
- Give each student one card.
- Have students stand and walk around the room, recreating the conversation by putting themselves in order by their cards.

---

5 PRACTICE THE CONVERSATION with a partner. Use your shopping list from Activity 3 on page 96.

- Go over the directions and the example.
- Model the activity with a student. Ask about something else in the advertisement in Activity 1.
- Put students in pairs. Have students take turns playing the role of customer and salesclerk. Remind students to ask about the items on their lists they created in Activity 3.
- Walk around the room to monitor the activity and provide help as needed.
- Have pairs of students say the conversations in front of the class.

6 WRITE. Use your shopping list. Write a receipt. Then write a check to Clothes Corner.

- Direct students' attention to the check and ask questions: *Who is the check to? How much is it for? Who is writing the check?*
- Model the activity. On the board, write a receipt for some items you would like to buy. Write the total. Then write a check on the board for the total.
- Have students write receipts for their shopping items, and then write a check for the total.

7 TALK. Tell a partner about the new clothes you are buying.

- Put students in pairs to talk about what they are buying.

COMMUNITY CONNECTION:
Online bill pay

- Explain or elicit that people can pay for purchases and bills in several ways; check, cash, credit card, debit card, and money order. Many banks also offer online bill paying.
- Have students find out if their bank or a bank in your area offers online banking and bill paying options.
- Elicit the names of banks that offer the services and how customers can use this option.

LESSON 7: Reading and Writing

OBJECTIVES

Understand a consumer article
Use quotes in writing

READING TIP

Use the words under pictures to learn information

WRITING TIP

Use quotes to add more information

COMPETENCIES

Read an article on consumer related topics
Understand and use quotes

WARM-UP ACTIVITY: Clothing sources

- Put students in pairs to talk about their favorite stores for clothing, school supplies, and food. Elicit ideas and write them on the board.

Reading

❶ THINK ABOUT IT. Where can you buy clothes in your city?

- Go over the directions and the question.
- Put students in pairs or talk as a group to brainstorm a list of clothing stores.
- Elicit ideas and write them on the board.

❷ BEFORE YOU READ. Look at the sentences under the pictures in the article below. What are the names of the people in the pictures?

- Go over the reading tip in the box.
- Go over the directions.
- Have students look at the captions and find the names.
- Elicit the names from the class.

ANSWER KEY

Mary, Joe, Tina

EXPANSION ACTIVITY: Write a caption

- Bring in photos or pictures of people from magazines or newspapers.
- Have students look at the captions again and identify the types of information in captions (people's names, ages, other identifying information, quotes).
- Give each student a photo.
- Have students write captions for their photos, using the present continuous tense.
- Call on students to display the photo and read the caption to the class.

❸ READ the newspaper article. Underline the sentences in quotation marks (" ").

- Have students read the paragraph, or read the paragraph aloud sentence by sentence and have students repeat.
- Have students underline the quotes.
- Ask comprehension questions: *What time of year is it? What do parents look for? What do young people want?*
- Elicit the quotes.

ANSWER KEY

"The service is very good. The salesclerks are friendly and helpful."
"The prices are excellent!"
"I am looking for my school clothes at COOL Clothes. There's a great selection—there are a lot of good colors and many sizes."

4 WRITE. Complete the chart.

- Direct students' attention to the chart. Go over the example.
- Have students complete the chart.
- Put students in pairs to compare ideas.
- Go over the answers with the class.

ANSWER KEY

	Shopper Name	Store Name	What is good?
1.	Mary	Clothes Mart	service
2.	Joe	Value Clothes	prices
3.	Tina	Cool Clothes	colors, selection

EXPANSION ACTIVITY: Literacy development—sentence strips

- Copy the sentences from the article onto separate strips. Leave enough space between each word for word discrimination. The sentences need to be large enough to be read by all the students.
- Put the sentence strips on the board in the correct order. Read each sentence aloud and have students repeat. You may want to point to each word as you read.
- Take the sentences down and mix them up.
- Have volunteers come to the board and put the sentences in the correct order. Have the other students help.

BIG PICTURE READING EXPANSION ACTIVITY: Match the Quotes

- Photocopy and distribute Worksheet 14: Match the Quotes.
- Put the transparency for Unit 6 on the OHP or have students look at the Big Picture on page 89.
- Go over the directions. Make sure students understand both the *said* and *asks* form.
- Have students complete the worksheet.
- Put students in pairs to share their ideas.
- Go over the answers with the class.

WORKSHEET 14 ANSWER KEY

1. Lydia; 2. Paula; 3. Brad; 4. Ali; 5. Clara;
6. Marta
1. Lydia says, "The children's shoes are on the second floor."
2. Paula asks, "Can I help you with those skirts?"
3. Brad says, "I like these red pants."
4. Ali says, "I'm tired."
5. Clara says, "The shoe colors are great. I really like the white ones."
6. Marta says, "These black shirts are a good price."

Writing

1 WRITE the sentences as quotes.

- Go over the writing tip in the box.
- Go over the directions and the example.
- Have students rewrite the sentences using quotation marks.
- Put students in pairs to compare sentences.
- Have volunteers write the sentences on the board.

GRAMMAR NOTE

Point out that we use open quotes before we begin the quoted material, and close quotes at the end. Punctuation (commas, periods, question marks) goes inside the quotation marks. If the quote comes at the end of the sentence, we use ending punctuation. If it comes before the speech tag (e.g., *"These prices are good," says Mary*), we use a comma inside the quote, before the tag.

ANSWER KEY

1. Pedro says, "I'm shopping at Tall-Mart. The prices are really good!"
2. Alicia says, "I'm looking for clothes for school at Low Price Village."
3. Paul says, "My friend and I are buying our shoes at Skater's World."
4. James says, "I'm at Amazing Apparel. The service is excellent here."
5. Musa says, "I'm a nurse. I'm shopping for nurse clothes at Neat Nurses."

EXPANSION ACTIVITY: Pair interviews

- Write three questions on the board: *Where do you shop? What is good about that store? What is important to you?*
- Put students in pairs to ask and answer the questions. Tell students to write down exactly what their partners say.
- Have students write at least one sentence using quotes from their partners.
- Call on students to read their sentences to the class.

2 WRITE. Look at the article on page 98. Then complete the article below. Tell where each person is shopping: *Clothes Mart, Value Clothes,* or *Cool Clothes.* Write a quote for each person.

- Have students look at the pictures.
- Instruct students to write captions that might go with pictures.

ANSWER KEY

Answers may vary.

BIG PICTURE WRITING EXPANSION ACTIVITY: Three quotes

- Put the transparency for Unit 6 on the OHP or have students look at the Big Picture in their books.
- Have each student choose a character or assign each student a character from the Big Picture.
- Have students write three sentences that the character might say. Remind students to use quotes.
- Ask volunteers to read sentences to the class.

Career Connection

WARM-UP ACTIVITY: Expenses

Ask *What do you spend money on or buy every week?* Elicit ideas and write them on the board.

🎧 **❶ READ** and listen.

- Direct students' attention to the pictures. Tell students this is the continuation of the story about Isabel. Have students point to Isabel in the pictures.
- Play the CD and have students follow along silently.
- Play the CD again and have students repeat.
- Put students in pairs to take turns reading the roles of Isabel and her coworker.
- Ask: *What does Isabel pay for every month?*

❷ WRITE. Answer the questions.

- Go over the directions.
- Direct students' attention to the list of expenses.
- Read each question aloud and have students repeat.
- Have students answer the questions.
- Put students in pairs to compare answers.
- Go over the answers with the students.

ANSWER KEY
1. A course catalog; 2. $75; 3. $300; 4. $650

❸ WHAT ABOUT YOU? Write a list of your expenses each month.

- Go over the directions.
- Brainstorm a list of expenses with the class and write their ideas on the board.
- Have students list their expenses.
- Put students in pairs to talk about their expenses. Explain that they don't have to say what they spend on each thing—they can say what they want to.
- Call on students to tell about one expense.

COMMUNITY CONNECTION: Internet research

- Explain that we often talk about our monthly expenses as a monthly budget.
- Have students use a favorite search engine and use the words "monthly budget."
- Have students print out a monthly budget worksheet that they find online.

CHECK YOUR PROGRESS!

- Have students circle the answers.
- Have students check whether each answer is right or wrong.
- Have students total their correct answers and fill in the chart.
- Have students create a learning plan and/or set learning goals.

ANSWER KEY
1. is waiting; 2. are talking; 3. is working; 4. pants; 5. a dress; 6. a dress; 7. are; 8. is; 9. are; 10. $30.00; 11. $25.95; 12. twelve dollars and ninety-five cents

Unit Overview

LESSON	OBJECTIVE	STUDENT BOOK	WORKBOOK
1 Grammar and Vocabulary 1	Use simple present tense to talk about daily routines	p. 102	p. 86
2 Grammar Practice Plus	Use adverbs of frequency to talk about routines	p. 104	p. 87
3 Listening and Conversation	Talk about schedules	p. 106	p. 88
4 Grammar and Vocabulary 2	Ask and answer *yes/no* questions in the simple present tense	p. 108	p. 90
5 Grammar Practice Plus	Talk about weekly activities	p. 110	p. 91
6 Apply Your Knowledge	Interpret a work schedule Compute hourly wages	p. 112	p. 92
7 Reading and Writing	Scan for important information Use sequence words to describe daily activities	p. 114	p. 94
• Career Connection	Plan for continuing education	p. 116	p. 96
• Check Your Progress	Monitor progress	p. 117	p. 98

Reading/Writing Strategies

• Scan for numbers prior to and after reading. • Use sequencing words when you write.

Connection Activities

LESSON	TYPE	SKILL DEVELOPMENT
1	Community	Interview a person for information
2	Academic	Listen for frequency expressions
4	Community	Interview a person for information
5	Academic	Create a study schedule
6	Community	Interview a person for information
7	Community	Scan for numbers in a newspaper
8	Academic	Research information on class times

WORKSHEET #/FOCUS	TITLE	TEACHER'S EDITION
15 Grammar	*Yes/No* Questions	p. 260
16 Reading	What's Next?	p. 261

LESSON 1: Grammar and Vocabulary

OBJECTIVE

Use simple present tense to talk about
  daily routines

VOCABULARY

brush teeth	get up
cook dinner	go to bed
do homework	read a book
eat breakfast	take a shower
get dressed	

GRAMMAR

Simple present tense statements

COMPETENCIES

Use simple present
Daily activities
Personal grooming

WARM-UP ACTIVITY: Unit opener

- Put the transparency for Unit 7 on the overhead projector (OHP) or have students look at the Big Picture on page 105.
- Elicit words the students know and write them on the board.

🎧 ❶ GRAMMAR PICTURE DICTIONARY. Listen and repeat.

- Have students open their books and look at the pictures. Ask *What do you see?*
- Say the sentences or play the CD and have students repeat.
- Say the sentences in random order and have students point to the picture.
- Call on students and say a number. Have the students read the sentence.

EXPANSION ACTIVITY: Mime

- Model the activity. Say one of the phrases (e.g., *brush teeth*) and mime it.
- Call on students and say a word. Have students mime it.
- Call students to the front of the room. Whisper one of the phrases and have the student mime it. Elicit guesses from the class.

❷ **NOTICE THE GRAMMAR.** Look at Activity 1. Circle the verbs that end in *s.* Underline the subjects in these sentences.

- Go over the directions.
- Have students circle the verbs ending in *s* and underline the subjects.
- Go over the answers with the class.

ANSWER KEY

1. Jim (gets) up at 7:00.
2. Then he (takes) a shower.
3. He (gets) dressed at 7:15.
4. They eat breakfast at 7:45.
5. Jim (brushes) his teeth at 8:30.
6. Abby (does) homework in the afternoon.
7. Jim (cooks) dinner.
8. Karen (reads) books at night.
9. Abby and Amy go to bed at 8:00.

EXPANSION ACTIVITY: What time do you _____?

- Elicit the time expressions in Activity 1.
- Read the first sentence in Activity 1.
- Model the activity. Say the first sentence but substitute *your* information (e.g., *I get up at 6:30.*).
- Put students in pairs to talk about when they do each activity.
- Call on students to tell the class about when they do one of the activities.

GRAMMAR CHART: Simple Present Tense Statements

- Direct students' attention to the chart or project the transparency or CD.
- Go over the information on the chart and the usage note. You may want to read the sentences, pausing to have students repeat.
- If students ask about *it*, point out that *it* is followed by a verb ending in *s*, just like *he* and *she*.
- Point out the *s* endings for the third person singular in affirmative statements.

PRONUNCIATION NOTE

Point out that the *s* ending can have either a *z* or an *s* sound. It has an *s* sound after unvoiced consonant sounds (*c, f, k, p, t*) and a *z* sound after the voiced consonant and vowel sounds.

CHART EXPANSION ACTIVITY: Pronunciation of *s* endings

- Write three headings on the board: *sounds like s, sounds like z, sounds like iz*.
- Have students copy the headings in their notebooks.
- Say the verbs from Activity 1 that end in *s*. Have students write the verbs under the correct headings.
- Have students practice pronouncing verbs again under each heading.

❸ CIRCLE the correct form of the verb.

- Go over the directions.
- Have students circle the correct form of the verb.
- Put students in pairs to compare answers.
- Go over the answers with the class.

ANSWER KEY

1. gets up; 2. don't cook; 3. doesn't eat; 4. does; 5. don't read

❹ WRITE. Complete the sentences with the correct form of the verb.

- Go over the directions and the example.
- Have students complete the sentences.
- Put students in pairs to compare answers.
- Go over the answers with the class.

ANSWER KEY

1. read; 2. doesn't cook; 3. eat; 4. don't sleep; 5. takes

5 **WHAT ABOUT YOU?** Talk with a partner. What do you do _____?

* Have students work in pairs to find out what their activities are at different times of the day.

EXPANSION ACTIVITY: Find someone who

* Write the following phrases on the board: *gets up at 6 A.M., works five days a week, brushes his/her teeth three times a day, goes to bed after midnight, cooks dinner.*
* Have students stand and walk around the room to find someone who does each of the things listed.

COMMUNITY CONNECTION: Interview

* As an out-of-class assignment, have students talk to a friend, neighbor or coworker to find out what times they do the activities in Activity 1.
* Have students write three sentences about the person they talked to.
* Call on students to read their sentences to the class.

LESSON 2: Grammar Practice Plus

OBJECTIVE

Use adverbs of frequency to talk about routines

VOCABULARY

always	sometimes
Friday	Sunday
Monday	Thursday
never	Tuesday
often	usually
Saturday	Wednesday

GRAMMAR

Simple present
Adverbs of frequency

COMPETENCIES

Use simple present
Daily activities
Days of the week
Adverbs of frequency

WARM-UP ACTIVITY: Abbreviations

- Write the abbreviations for the days of the week on the board.
- Have students write the long forms next to each abbreviation.
- Have literacy students write each day of the week on a separate index card, shuffle, and sort them.

🎧 ❶ LISTEN and repeat.

- Go over the directions.
- Play the CD and have students repeat.
- Make sure students understand that *usually* is between 50% and 100% of the time.

EXPANSION ACTIVITY: Category sort

- Explain the activity. You will say a sentence (e.g., *I eat breakfast at 7 A.M.*) and students should walk around and talk to each other and then stand with the students who would use the same adverb of frequency with that statement (e.g., *never*).
- Have students stand. Say an activity with a time (*I cook dinner.*). Cue students to talk to each other and stand with people who use the same adverb. Elicit a sentence from a member of each group, using an adverb of frequency.
- Continue with other statements. Keep the activity fast-paced.

❷ WRITE. Look at Miguel's schedule. Complete the sentences.

- Direct students' attention to the schedule. Ask questions: *What time does Miguel eat breakfast? When does he work on Monday? What does he do at 7:30 in the morning?*
- Go over the example.
- Have students write adverbs of frequency on the lines.
- Go over the answers with the class.
- Put students in pairs to practice asking and answering the questions.

GRAMMAR NOTE

Point out that the adverb of frequency goes before the verb.

ANSWER KEY

1. always; 2. usually; 3. sometimes;
4. sometimes; 5. sometimes; 6. always

LITERACY DEVELOPMENT NOTE

Emerging literacy students may need additional practice with the vocabulary. You may want to suggest they write each new vocabulary word on an index card. It might be helpful for students to practice making sentences with their activity and adverb of frequency cards.

3 WHAT ABOUT YOU? Complete the sentences about you.

- Go over the directions.
- Have students complete the sentences using adverbs of frequency.
- Put students in pairs to read their sentences.
- Call on students to read their sentences to the class.

4 TALK about the picture. Describe the family's daily activities.

- Go over the directions.
- Direct students' attention to the Big Picture or put the transparency on the OHP.
- Put students in pairs. Have students take turns describing the activities of the people in the picture.
- Call on students. Point to different characters in the Big Picture and elicit sentences about the activities.

5 LISTEN. Write the people's names on the picture.

- Go over the directions.
- Have students say the names as you say the questions or play the CD.
- Put students in pairs to compare answers.
- Say the questions or play the CD again so students can confirm.
- Go over the answers with the class.

LISTENING SCRIPT
Lesson 2, Activity 5

TCD2, 47

Listen. Write the people's names on the picture.

At 9:00 on Saturday mornings . . .

1. Luz usually takes a shower.
2. Roberto often cooks breakfast.
3. Miguel always brushes his teeth.
4. Rosa usually gets dressed.
5. Jose and Mariela sometimes read books.

BIG PICTURE CONVERSATION/ VOCABULARY EXPANSION ACTIVITY: Who Am I?

- Have students look at the Big Picture or put the color overhead transparency for Unit 7 on the OHP.
- Model the activity. Say several sentences about a character in the picture (e.g., *I am young, I am pretty, I get dressed at nine.*). Elicit the name (*Rosa*).
- Put students in pairs to practice describing and guessing characters. You may want to put students in small groups and assign each student a character to facilitate this activity.
- Call on students to say their sentences to the class and elicit the name from the other students.

6 WRITE sentences about the family's Saturday morning activities.

- Go over the directions and the example.
- Have students write sentences.
- Put students in pairs to compare sentences.
- Call on students to read their sentences to the class.

ANSWER KEY (Answers may vary.)

1. Luz usually takes a shower.
2. Roberto often cooks breakfast.
3. Miguel always brushes his teeth.
4. Rosa never gets dressed.
5. Jose and Mariela sometimes read/play with toys.

7 WHAT ABOUT YOU? Talk to a partner. What do you do on Saturdays?

- Go over the directions and the example.
- Model the activity. Describe what you do using adverbs of frequency.
- Put students in pairs to talk about what they do on Saturdays.
- Call on students to tell the class about one thing their partners do on Saturdays.

ACADEMIC CONNECTION: Other frequency expressions

- Have students write down other frequency expressions they hear over the next few days.
- Elicit the examples and write them on the board (e.g., *rarely, once in a while, now and then, every day, on Mondays*).

LESSON 3: Listening and Conversation

OBJECTIVE

Talk about schedules

COMPETENCIES

Use simple present
Daily activities
Days of the week
Adverbs of frequency

EXPANSION ACTIVITY: Write the adverb

- Have students listen to the CD again and write the adverb of frequency they hear.
- Have students write a new sentence for each adverb.
- Put students in pairs to read their sentences.
- Call on students to read their sentences to the class.

WARM-UP ACTIVITY: Write a story

- Direct students' attention to the pictures in Activity 1.
- Have students create a story using at least five of the pictures.
- Put students in pairs to read their stories.
- Call on students to read sentences to the class.

 ❶ LISTEN. Circle the correct letter.

- Say the sentences or play the CD and have students circle the letter.
- Have students compare answers in pairs.
- Go over the answers with the class.

LISTENING SCRIPT
Lesson 3, Activity 1

TCD2, 48

Listen. Circle the correct letter.

1. Bella always gets up at 7:00 on Wednesdays.
2. Hector often cooks dinner at 7:00.
3. Elisa usually eats breakfast at 10:00 on Saturdays.

ANSWER KEY

1. B; 2. A; 3. C

 ❷ LISTEN. Lisa is talking about her schedule. Number the pictures in order.

- Go over the directions.
- Play the CD and have students write a number 1–4 under each picture to show the order of Lisa's schedule.
- Put students in pairs to compare answers.
- Go over the answers with the class.

 LISTENING SCRIPT
Lesson 3, Activity 2

TCD2, 49

Listen. Lisa is talking about her schedule. Number the pictures in order.

Lisa: Hi, Elena!
Elena: Oh hi, Lisa. How are you?
Lisa: I'm tired...
Elena: Why?
Lisa: I'm doing a lot right now....
Elena: Like what?
Lisa: Well, I always get up at 6:00 and shower. After my shower, I eat breakfast with my family, and then I work all day ... I often work eight or ten hours. At night, I usually cook dinner or help my children. I sometimes read. I go to bed at 11:00.

ANSWER KEY

2, 4, 3, 1

🎧 **LISTEN AGAIN.** Match.

- Go over the directions and the example.
- Play the CD and have students draw a line to match the adverb to the activity.
- Go over the answers with the class.

ANSWER KEY

1. c; 2. b; 3. a

🎧 **3 LISTEN** and read.

- Direct students' attention to the picture. Ask questions: *Who do you see? Where are they?*
- Play the CD or read the conversation as students follow along silently.
- Play the CD or read the conversation again and have students repeat.
- Ask: *What time is it? What is he doing?*
- Put students in pairs to practice reading the conversation. Have students switch roles.

4 PRACTICE THE CONVERSATION with a partner.

- Go over the directions.
- Model the activity. Have a more advanced student read A's lines. Model how to substitute a different activity and time.
- Put students in pairs to practice the conversation, making the appropriate substitutions.
- Walk around to monitor the activity and provide help as needed.
- Call on students to say the conversation to the class.

5 GAME. Work in a small group. Say an activity you do and when you do the activity. Listen to your classmates, then say their activities.

- Go over the directions and the examples.
- Put students in small groups to practice saying everyone's activities.
- Call on students to tell the class about the people in their groups.

BIG PICTURE LISTENING EXPANSION ACTIVITY: A schedule

- Put the transparency for Unit 7 on the OHP or have students look at the Big Picture in their books.
- Dictate three sentences: *I usually get up at 7:00 on Saturdays. I often go for a walk at 7:30. At 8:30, I always start to cook breakfast.* Repeat each sentence three times.
- Put students in pairs to compare sentences.
- Have volunteers write the sentences on the board.
- Elicit the name of the person (*Roberto*).

LESSON 4: Grammar and Vocabulary

OBJECTIVE

Ask and answer yes/no questions in the simple present tense

VOCABULARY

call family	study
drive to work	take a class
go to school	walk to school
play soccer	watch television
ride the bus	

GRAMMAR

Yes/no questions in the simple present tense
Short answers

PRONUNCIATION

Does he versus does she

COMPETENCIES

Yes/no questions with the simple present
Short answers

WARM-UP ACTIVITY: *Yes/no* cards

- Distribute two index cards to each student. Have students write *yes* on one card, and *no* on the other.
- Ask *yes/no* questions about their activities in the simple present (e.g., *Do you go to school at night?*) and have students hold up the appropriate card.
- Keep the activity moving quickly. It doesn't matter that they don't know the form yet; this will get students used to the form receptively.

🎧 **❶ GRAMMAR PICTURE DICTIONARY.** Listen and repeat.

- Have students look at the pictures. Ask *What do you see?*

- Play the CD or say the sentences and have students repeat.
- Say the new vocabulary in random order and have the students point to the pictures.

❷ NOTICE THE GRAMMAR. Read the questions. Circle *Do* or *Does*. Underline the subject.

- Go over the directions and the example.
- Have students circle *Do* or *Does* and underline the subject.
- Go over the answers with the class.

ANSWER KEY

1. A: (Does) he go to school at night?
   B: Yes, he does.
2. A: (Does) she take a class on Mondays?
   B: No, she doesn't.
3. A: (Does) he study in the morning?
   B: No, he doesn't.
4. A: (Does) she walk to school with a friend?
   B: No, she doesn't.
5. A: (Does) he drive to work every day?
   B: Yes, he does.
6. A: (Do) they ride the bus?
   B: Yes, they do.
7. A: (Does) she call her family at night?
   B: Yes, she does.
8. A: (Does) he watch television at night?
   B: Yes, he does.
9. A: (Do) they play soccer on Saturdays?
   B: Yes, they do.

GRAMMAR CHART: *Yes/No* Questions in the Simple Present Tense

- Go over the information in the chart, including the usage note.
- You may want to read the sample sentences in the chart and have students repeat.
- If students ask, point out that questions with *it* are formed in the same way as questions with *he* and *she.*

• Point out or elicit that the verb form that follows the subject in question form is always the simple form—it does not end in *s*.

CHART EXPANSION ACTIVITY: Statement to question

• Say simple statements in the present tense (*You go to class at 9 A.M., They study English at night.*).

• Call on students and elicit the *yes/no* questions.

EXPANSION ACTIVITY: Change questions

• Have students rewrite the questions in Activity 1 so that the subject is *you* (*Do you go to school at night?*).

• Have students write the questions with *you* on the board.

• Put students in pairs to practice asking and answering the questions.

• Ask students questions.

3 CIRCLE the correct words.

• Go over the directions and the example.

• Have students circle the correct form.

• Put students in pairs to compare answers.

• Go over the answers with the class.

ANSWER KEY

1. Do; 2. do; 3. Do; 4. do

EXPANSION ACTIVITY: Partner practice

• Model the activity with a more advanced student. Practice the conversation in Activity 3. Substitute your own name, work information and school schedule.

• Walk around the room to monitor the activity and provide help as needed.

• Call on students to practice the conversation in front of the class.

4 WHAT ABOUT YOU? Put the words in order to make questions. Then check the right answer for *you*.

• Go over the directions and the example.

• Have students write the questions.

• Go over the questions with the class.

• Have students answer the questions about themselves.

• Put students in pairs to ask and answer the questions.

ANSWER KEY

1. Do you work on Mondays? 2. Do you play soccer with your friends? 3. Does your family eat dinner together? 4. Do you ride the bus?

COMMUNITY CONNECTION: Interview

• As an out-of-class assignment, have students ask a friend, neighbor or coworker the questions in Activity 4.

• Have students write the information from the interview as statements.

• Have students share what they found out with the class.

LESSON 5: Grammar Practice Plus

OBJECTIVE

Talk about weekly activities

VOCABULARY

arrive	leave
come home	take a break

GRAMMAR

Yes/no questions with the simple present tense
Short answers

COMPETENCIES

Yes/no questions with the simple present tense
Short answers

WARM-UP ACTIVITY: Schedules

• Write your schedule on the board saying when you arrive at school, when you take a break, when you leave work, and when you come home. Tell the class your schedule. Ask the class about their schedules.

❶ WRITE. Answer the questions.

• Direct students' attention to the pictures. Ask *Where are they?*
• Go over the directions and the example.
• Have students look at the pictures and answer the questions.
• Play the CD and have students listen, repeat, and check their answers.
• Put students in pairs to ask and answer the questions.
• Go over the answers with the class.

LISTENING SCRIPT
Lesson 5, Activity 1

TCD2, 52

Listen and repeat. Are your answers correct?

1. *A:* Does Rosa arrive at 9:00 a.m.?
   B: Yes, she does.
2. *A:* Does Alicia take a break at 12:15 p.m.?
   B: No, she doesn't.
3. *A:* Do they leave work at 5:00 p.m.?
   B: No, they don't.
4. *A:* Does she come home at 7:00 p.m.?
   B: Yes, she does.

ANSWER KEY

1. Yes, she does. **2.** No, she doesn't. **3.** No, they don't. **4.** Yes, she does.

EXPANSION ACTIVITY: Your story

• Have students write their own sentences using the verbs *arrive, take a break, leave* and *come home,* to describe their schedules at school or work.
• Put students in pairs to read their sentences.
• Call on students to tell the class about their partners' schedule.

❷ WRITE. Complete the conversations. Use *do* or *does* and the verb.

• Go over the directions and the example.
• Have students complete the conversations.
• Put students in pairs to compare answers.
• Go over the answers with the class.
• Have students practice the conversations with their partners.

PRONUNCIATION: *Does he/Does she*

 A LISTEN and repeat.

- Go over the directions.
- Play the CD and have students repeat.

B LISTEN. Circle *he* or *she*.

- Go over the directions and the example.
- Play the CD and have students circle *he* or *she*.
- Go over the answers with the class.

LISTENING SCRIPT
Lesson 5, Activity B

TCD2, 54

Listen. Circle *he* or *she*.

1. Does she drive a car?
2. Does he go to school?
3. Does she work on Saturdays?
4. Does he ride the bus?

ANSWER KEY

1. she; 2. he; 3. she; 4. he

EXPANSION ACTIVITY: Luis or Luisa

- Make sure students understand that Luis is a male name and Luisa is a female name.
- Put students in pairs.
- Have students ask the questions in Activity B, using either *he* or *she*. Have their partners answer *Luis?* Or *Luisa?* to confirm that they heard the correct pronoun, and then give an answer.

3 LISTEN. What time does Kristin do each activity? Write the times in the chart.

- Go over the directions and the example.
- Play the CD and have students write the times.
- Put students in pairs to compare answers.
- Go over the answers with the class.

 LISTENING SCRIPT
Lesson 5, Activity 3

TCD2, 55

Listen. What time does Kristin do each activity? Write the times in the chart.

A: Hi, Kristin. How are you?
B: Pretty good, thanks, Mike. I'm very busy these days, though.
A: Oh, really?
B: Yes, I have a new job. I'm a salesclerk at Shoe World. I arrive at work every morning at 8:00 and I leave at 6:00.
A: Huh, that's a long day. Do you take a break?
B: Yes, I take a lunch break at 1:00.
A: That's good.
B: And I take a class in the evening.
A: Really? Do you eat dinner?
B: Yes, I go home and eat dinner at 7:00. My class is at 8:00.
A: You *are* busy.

ANSWER KEY

Activity	Time
1. arrive at work	8:00 A.M.
2. leave work	6:00 P.M.
3. eat dinner	7:00 P.M.
4. take a class	8:00 P.M.

④ WRITE the answers.

- Go over the directions.
- Have students answer the questions.
- Go over the answers with the class.
- Put students in pairs to practice asking and answering the questions.

ANSWER KEY

1. No, she doesn't. She arrives at 8 A.M.; **2.** No, she doesn't. She leaves at 6 P.M.; **3.** Yes, she does. She eats dinner at 7 P.M.; **4.** Yes, she does. She takes a class at 8 P.M.

⑤ WHAT ABOUT YOU? Complete the question with a word from the box. Ask the question to six classmates.

- Go over the directions and the example conversation.
- Have students write one activity on the line.
- Have students stand and walk around the room to ask the question of six classmates. Remind students to write the time if the student answers *yes.*
- Call on students to tell the class about a classmate's answer.

BIG PICTURE GRAMMAR EXPANSION ACTIVITY: *Yes/No* **Questions**

- Photocopy and distribute Worksheet 15: *Yes/No* Questions.
- Put the transparency for Unit 7 on the OHP or have students look at the Big Picture in their books.
- Go over the directions and the example.
- Have students complete the worksheet and then compare answers with a partner.
- Go over the answers with the class.

WORKSHEET 15 ANSWER KEY

1. Yes, he does. **2.** No, she doesn't. **3.** No, they don't. **4.** No, they don't. **5.** Yes, she does. **6.** Yes, he does. **7.** No, they don't. **8.** Yes, she does.

ACADEMIC CONNECTION: Study schedules

- Put students in small groups to discuss the ideal number of hours they should spend studying English or doing homework each week.
- Have students write a weekly schedule for their study time. Remind students to make the schedule doable. For example, it might be better to do 30 minutes a day on the bus than to try to study four hours straight on Sunday.
- Have students share their study schedule in their small groups.
- At the end of a week, ask students how well they did following their schedules.

LESSON 6: Apply Your Knowledge

OBJECTIVES

Interpret a work schedule
Compute hourly wages

MATH

Hourly wages

COMPETENCIES

Understand work schedules

WARM-UP ACTIVITY: Work schedules

- Ask students if they work.
- Elicit examples of work schedules. Or, have students do a lineup of least to most number of hours of work. Go down the line and find out how many hours everyone works per week.

❶ TALK with a partner. When do the people work?

- Go over the Professor note.
- Go over the directions and the example conversation.
- Put students in pairs to ask and answer questions about the work schedule.
- Call on students and ask questions: *When does John work? Who works on Monday morning?*

❷ LISTEN to the conversations. Write the names on the work schedule above.

- Point out that the schedule is not complete.
- Play the CD, more than once if necessary, and have students write the names on the schedule.
- Put students in pairs to compare answers.
- Go over the answers with the class.

LISTENING SCRIPT
Lesson 6, Activity 2

TCD2, 56

Listen to the conversations. Write the names on the work schedule above.

1. *A:* Do you work, Bima?
   B: Yes, I do. I work Monday, Tuesday, and Wednesday.
2. *A:* You work a lot, Tony.
   B: Not really. Only Monday, Wednesday, and Friday.
3. *A:* Hong, do you work on Thursday?
   B: Yes, I do. I work on Tuesday, Wednesday, and Thursday.
4. *A:* John, you work too much.
   B: You're right. I work on Tuesday, Thursday, Friday, and Saturday.

ANSWER KEY

Wednesday: Tony, 11–3; Thursday: Hong, 9–1; Saturday: John, 9–6

EXPANSION ACTIVITY: Ask questions

- Have students write three *yes/no* questions about the schedule.
- Put students in pairs to take turns asking and answering their questions.
- Call on students and have them ask their questions of a classmate.

MATH: Hourly Wages

- Read the information.
- Go over the math.
- Look at the work schedule in Activity 1. Complete the chart.
- Have students count the hours each person worked and write it in the column *number of hours.*

- Have students compute the total money earned in one week.
- Go over the answers with the class.

ANSWER KEY

Name	Number of hours		Hourly wage		Total money in one week
Bima	10	×	$8.00	=	$80.00
Hong	10	×	$8.00	=	$80.00
John	22	×	$8.00	=	$176.00

EXPANSION ACTIVITY: Word problems

- Write a word problem on the board that involves number of hours and hourly wage (e.g., *Luz works 40 hours a week. She makes $7.00 an hour. How much does she make a week?*).
- Have students compute the amount.
- Have students write a word problem.
- Put students in pairs to exchange and solve the problem.

CULTURE/CIVICS NOTES

- Students who work may get paid in different ways. Point out that some workers get paid by the hour, whereas others get paid a salary, even if they work more or fewer hours than 40 hours a week.
- Explain that there is a federal minimum wage, which is increased by Congress when necessary.

3 LISTEN and read.

- Direct students' attention to the picture. Ask questions: *Who do you see? Where are they?*
- Have students follow along as you play the CD.
- Play the CD again and have students repeat.

- Ask comprehension questions: *What is the problem? What is on Wednesday?*
- Put students in pairs to take turns reading the conversation.

4 PRACTICE THE CONVERSATION with a partner.

- Go over the directions and the information.
- Model the activity with a student. Have the students read A's lines. Substitute the information in Activity 1 (*My soccer game/ Friday night/Tony*). Cue the student to ask about Tony.
- Put students in pairs to practice the conversation. Monitor as needed.
- Have pairs of students say the conversations in front of the class.

5 WHAT ABOUT YOU? Work in a group of three students. You and your classmates work together at a restaurant. Think about your schedule this Saturday. Choose a work time for each student. Write the names next to the work times.

- Go over the directions and the example conversation.
- Put students in groups of three.
- Have students complete the schedule.
- Call on students and ask who will work when.

COMMUNITY CONNECTION: Interview

- Write questions on the board: *What is your usual work schedule? How many hours a week do you work? Do you spend time with your friends and family in the evening and on weekends?*
- As an out-of-class assignment, have students interview a coworker, friend, or family member and record the answers.
- Call on students to tell the class about the person they interviewed.

LESSON 7: Reading and Writing

OBJECTIVES

Scan for important information
Use sequence words to describe daily activities

READING TIP

Look for numbers before and after you read to learn important information

WRITING TIP

Use *first, next, then* and *last* to put activities in order

COMPETENCIES

Use chronological connectors

WARM-UP ACTIVITY: Things to read

- Ask students *What do you read every day or every week?* Elicit ideas and write them on the board. Point out that students read different types of information in this class.

Reading

1 THINK ABOUT IT. Write words to describe a good father.

- Go over the directions.
- Brainstorm with the class a list of adjectives to describe people and write them on the board. You may want to introduce some.
- Have students write words to describe a good father. Suggest students write sentences about what a good father does.
- Put students in pairs to share ideas.
- Call on students to share their ideas with the class.

2 BEFORE YOU READ. Look at the article. Circle three numbers.

- Go over the reading tip in the box. Point out that this is a good skill for answering questions on tests, and finding specific information such as dates and amounts.
- Go over the directions.
- Have students look for and circle three numbers in the reading. Remind students they should not read, just look quickly.
- Elicit numbers from the class.

ANSWER KEY

Five, three, six, two, six, four

EXPANSION ACTIVITY: Three numbers

- Have students name three important numbers in their lives (e.g., *number of children, number of years married, number of years in this country, number of brothers*). Have students write the numbers, but not what they refer to.
- Put students in pairs to share the numbers only as their partners guess what it refers to.
- Call on students to say a number to the class. Elicit guesses from the class as to what it means.

3 READ. What is the story about? Circle the correct letter.

- Have students look at the picture, read the title, and the article, or read the article aloud sentence by sentence and have students repeat.
- Have students circle the letter for the main idea.
- Ask comprehension questions: *Who is his wife? What is his job? Is he a good father?*

ANSWER KEY

B

4 MATCH the numbers to the information.

- Go over the directions and the example.
- Have students write the letter to match the information to the number.
- Put students in pairs to compare answers.
- Go over the answers with the class.

ANSWER KEY

1. d; **2.** a; **3.** e; **4.** c; **5.** b

EXPANSION ACTIVITY: Literacy development—sentence strips

- Copy the sentences from the article onto separate strips. Leave enough space between each word for word discrimination. The sentences need to be large enough to be read by all the students.
- Put the sentence strips on the board in the correct order. Read each sentence aloud and have students repeat. You may want to point to each word as you read.
- Take the sentences down and mix them up.
- Have volunteers come to the board and put the sentences in the correct order. Have the other students help.

COMMUNITY CONNECTION: Newspaper articles

- Have students bring in three articles from the newspaper or an online news source. Suggest that they find articles from different sections or on different topics (front page news, sports, business).
- Write examples on the board of different types of numbers that can be found in a newspaper article: for example, price, time, quantity, statistics, date, and so on.
- Have students scan for and circle any numbers they find in each article. Then have students write the type of number that it is.
- Elicit the type of numbers found in different types of articles and write the information on the board.

Writing

- Go over the writing tip in the box. Point out that using time and frequency expressions helps readers to understand our writing better.

1 WRITE a list of activities you do every day.

- Go over the directions.
- Model the activity. Write your activities on the board in random order.
- Have students list their activities.

2 WRITE four activities from your list. Use complete sentences.

- Go over the directions and the example sentences.
- Model the activity. Write sentences about four of your activities, using the chronological connectors.
- Have students complete the sentences about their own activities.
- Put students in pairs to read their sentences.

GRAMMAR NOTE

Point out that commas follow three of the four words: *first, next, last*. No comma is needed after *then*.

❸ WRITE your sentences again on the lines. Use *first, next, then,* and *last*.

- Go over the directions and the example.
- Have students rewrite their sentences.

❹ READ your sentences to a partner.

- Have students work together to practice reading and speaking their schedules.

EXPANSION ACTIVITY: Who is it?

- Have students rewrite the sentences from Activity 4 on a piece of paper.
- Put students in small groups. Collect their papers and redistribute. Have students guess which group member wrote the paragraph.

BIG PICTURE READING EXPANSION ACTIVITY: What's Next?

- Photocopy and distribute Worksheet 16: What's Next?
- Put the transparency for Unit 7 on the OHP or have students look at the Big Picture in their books.
- Have students read the paragraphs and write the name of the person.
- Put students in pairs to compare answers.
- Go over the answers with the class.

WORKSHEET 16 ANSWER KEY

1. Roberto; 2. Miguel; 3. Rosa; 4. Luz; 5. Jose and Mariela

BIG PICTURE WRITING EXPANSION ACTIVITY: Three sentences

- Put the transparency for Unit 7 on the OHP or have students look at the Big Picture in their books.
- Have each student write three sentences about a person in the picture. Remind students to use the simple present tense, adverbs of frequency, and words like *first, next, then,* and *last*.
- Ask volunteers to read sentences to the class.

Career Connection

Plan for continuing education

COMPETENCIES

Understand class schedules

WARM-UP ACTIVITY: Class times

- Put students in pairs to talk about when they could take a different class. Discuss days, evenings, semesters, and time of day.

❶ READ AND LISTEN. Then practice with a partner.

- Direct students' attention to the pictures. Tell students this is the continuation of the story about Isabel. Have students point to Isabel in the photos.
- Play the CD and have students follow along silently.
- Play the CD again. Stop after each line and have students repeat.
- Put students in pairs to take turns reading the roles of Isabel and her friend.
- Ask *What is Isabel doing?*

❷ TALK. Answer the questions.

- Go over the directions.
- Read each question and have students repeat.
- Put students in pairs to ask and answer the questions. Encourage students to use complete sentences.

ANSWER KEY

1. They are looking at a class schedule.
2. Yes, she works on Wednesdays.
3. Yes, there are classes at night (in the evening at 6:00).
4. No, Isabel finishes work at 5 P.M.

❸ WHAT ABOUT YOU? Isabel talks about three different class times. Are they good or bad class times for you? Talk with a partner.

- Go over the directions and the example.
- Put students in pairs to talk about the class times.
- Call on students and ask which class or classes they could take.

ACADEMIC CONNECTION: Class times

- As an out-of-class assignment, have students find out about class times for a specific class at your school, an adult school or program, a community college, or a community center.
- Have students write the class times and choose a time that would work for them.
- Put students in pairs to talk about the class and times.

CHECK YOUR PROGRESS!

- Have students circle the answers.
- Have students check whether each answer is right or wrong.
- Have students total their correct answers and fill in the chart.
- Have students create a learning plan and/or set learning goals.

ANSWER KEY

1. eats; 2. play; 3. clean; 4. always; 5. usually; 6. sometimes; 7. Do; 8. take; 9. Do; 10. play soccer; 11. clean my apartment; 12. cook dinner

Unit Overview

LESSON	OBJECTIVE	STUDENT BOOK	WORKBOOK
1 Grammar and Vocabulary 1	Use count and non-count nouns to talk about food	p. 118	p. 100
2 Grammar Practice Plus	Use container words Ask for and give prices in a grocery store	p. 120	p. 101
3 Listening and Conversation	Ask for and give locations in a store Interpret a food ad	p. 122	p. 102
4 Grammar and Vocabulary 2	Use information questions in the present tense	p. 124	p. 104
5 Grammar Practice Plus	Use *have/want/need* Measure food Interpret a recipe	p. 126	p. 106
6 Apply Your Knowledge	Order from a menu	p. 128	p. 107
7 Reading and Writing	Understand connecting words (*and*, *but*)	p. 130	p. 108
• Career Connection	Make plans at work	p. 132	p. 110
• Check Your Progress	Monitor progress	p. 133	p. 112

Reading/Writing Strategies

• Notice and use connecting words *and* and *but*.

Connection Activities

LESSON	TYPE	SKILL DEVELOPMENT
1	Academic	Identify count and non-count nouns in a dictionary
2	Community	Research prices in a supermarket
3	Community	Interview to gather information
3	Community	Identify and locate sections of supermarket
4	Community	Read food labels
5	Academic	Research and write measurement conversions
6	Community	Read and order from menus
8	Community	Interview to gather information

WORKSHEET #/FOCUS	TITLE	TEACHER'S EDITION
17 Grammar	What Do They Have?	p. 262
18 Speaking	Sentence Strip Match	p. 263
19 Reading	At the Supermarket	p. 264

LESSON 1: Grammar and Vocabulary

OBJECTIVE
Use count and non-count nouns to talk about food

VOCABULARY

an apple	an egg
a banana	fish
bread	milk
broccoli	an onion
a carrot	an orange
cereal	rice
cheese	yogurt
chicken	

GRAMMAR
Count and non-count nouns

COMPETENCIES
Identify common foods and food groups
Simple countable and non-countable nouns

WARM-UP ACTIVITY: Food words

- If possible, bring in food or photos of food.
- Put students in pairs or small groups.
- Give students one minute to list all the kinds of food they know.
- Elicit the number from each group.

🎧 ❶ GRAMMAR PICTURE DICTIONARY. Listen and repeat.

- Have students open their books and look at the pictures. Ask: *What do you see?*
- Say the sentences or play the CD and have students repeat.
- Call on students. Say a number and elicit the food noun.
- Put students in pairs and take turns saying the food words in random order as their partner points to the picture.

EXPANSION ACTIVITY: Name a food

- Call on a student and say a letter (e.g., *a*). Have the student name a word in the Grammar Picture Dictionary that has that letter (e.g., *banana*).
- Continue to call on students and say other letters, eliciting words.

EXPANSION ACTIVITY: Food pyramid

- Bring in or draw a traditional food pyramid (can be found online).
- Put students in pairs to list the words they know for each category.

❷ NOTICE THE GRAMMAR. Look at Activity 1. Circle the nouns with *a* or *an*.

- Go over the directions.
- Have students circle the nouns with *a* or *an*.

ANSWER KEY
an apple, an orange, a banana, an onion, a carrot, an egg

EXPANSION ACTIVITY: Alphabetical order

- Have students write the words in alphabetical order in their notebooks.
- Have volunteers write the words in alphabetical order on the board.

GRAMMAR CHART: Count and Non-count Nouns

- Direct students' attention to the chart or project the transparency or CD.
- Go over the information on the chart. You may want to read the questions and answers, pausing to have students repeat.
- Go over the usage note and the Professor note.

CHART EXPANSION ACTIVITY: Add two

- Have students copy the chart into their notebooks.
- Have students add two nouns to each column.

3 WRITE C for count or N for non-count.

- Go over the directions and the example.
- Have students write C or N next to each noun.
- Put students in pairs to check their answers.
- Go over the answers with the class.

EXPANSION ACTIVITY: Write plurals

- Have students write plurals of all the count nouns in Activity 3.
- Have volunteers write the plurals on the board.

4 CIRCLE the answer.

- Go over the directions and the example.
- Have students circle the correct form of the verb.
- Put students in pairs to compare answers.
- Go over the answers with the class.

EXPANSION ACTIVITY: Name a dairy product

- Model the activity. Say *Name a dairy product.* Elicit an example (*milk*) and say a sentence (*Milk is a dairy product.*).
- Call on students and have them name examples of different food groups. Remind students to use the food noun in a sentence. Make sure students use the correct forms for count and non-count nouns.

5 WHAT ABOUT YOU? Write foods you love, like, and don't like.

- Go over the directions. Make sure students understand what *love*, *like*, and *don't like* mean.
- Copy the chart on the board.

- Model the activity. Write examples of what you love, like and don't like on the chart.
- Have students complete the chart.
- Go over the example conversation.
- Put students in pairs to talk about the information in their charts.

EXPANSION ACTIVITY: Category sort

- Have students stand. Say a food (e.g., *broccoli*). Have students sort themselves by *love*, *like*, and *don't like*. Call on a student in each group to say a sentence (e.g., *I love broccoli.*).
- Continue with other food words.

ACADEMIC CONNECTION: Dictionary work

- Have students look up several count and non-count nouns in their dictionaries and note if the non-count nouns are identified in some way.

LESSON 2: Grammar Practice Plus

OBJECTIVES

Use container words
Ask for and give prices in a grocery store

VOCABULARY

bag	carton
bottle	loaf
box	pound

GRAMMAR

Quantity words with food nouns

COMPETENCIES

Using count/non-count nouns
Identifying food
Using quantity words

WARM-UP ACTIVITY: Realia

- Bring in different food containers.
- With books closed, elicit the words for containers that students know and write them on the board.

1 WRITE the food or drink.

- Go over the directions and the example.
- Have students write the food or drink on the lines to complete the sentences.
- Put students in pairs to compare answers.

LISTEN and repeat. Are your answers correct?

- Play the CD and have students repeat. Have students check their answers.

GRAMMAR NOTES

- Your students may not know how to make plurals for all of the quantity words in Activity 1. Point out that we add *-es* to words ending in *s, sh, ch, x.*
- We also change an *f* to a *v* and add *-es* (loaf—loaves).
- Point out that using containers or other quantity words helps us to talk about non-count nouns.

VOCABULARY/CULTURE NOTE

Point out that *pound* is abbreviated as *lb.*

TCD3, 3

LISTENING SCRIPT AND ANSWER KEY
Lesson 2, Activity 1

Listen and repeat. Are your answers correct?

1. a loaf of bread; **2.** a carton of milk; **3.** a bag of carrots; **4.** a box of cereal; **5.** a bottle of juice; **6.** a pound of fish

EXPANSION ACTIVITY: Beanbag toss

- Call on a student, toss the beanbag, and say a quantity word (e.g., *loaf*). Elicit an appropriate food word (*bread*).
- Continue until everyone has had a chance to participate. For more advanced classes, you may want to have students call on their classmates, taking turns saying words and eliciting opposites.

2 WRITE. Complete the sentences. Use a word in the box.

- Go over the directions and the words in the box, explaining which words are singular and which are plural.

- Go over the example.
- Have students write the words on the lines.
- Put students in pairs to compare answers.
- Go over the answers with the class.

ANSWER KEY

1. loaf; 2. box; 3. bags; 4. pound; 5. cartons;
6. bottle

EXPANSION ACTIVITY: Dictation

- Dictate three sentences using quantity words and food nouns (e.g., *There are two cartons of milk on the table. Do you want a loaf of bread? I eat a pound of cheese every week.*).
- Put students in pairs to compare sentences.
- Have volunteers write the sentences on the board.

---

3 WHAT ABOUT YOU? Make a list of foods and drinks you buy.

- Go over the directions.
- Copy the chart on the board.
- Model the activity. Write something you buy in each category. Tell the class.
- Have students write their lists. If students want to add container or quantity words they know (*jar, package, can*), encourage them to do so.
- Go over the example conversation.
- Put students in pairs to talk about their lists.

4 TALK about the picture.

- Go over the directions.
- Direct students' attention to the Big Picture or put the transparency on the OHP. Point to Pedro and Patricia (the couple with the full shopping cart), and ask what they are doing. Elicit that they are buying oranges.

- Put students in pairs. Have students take turns describing things and activities in the picture.
- Call on students. Point to different characters in the Big Picture and elicit sentences.

BIG PICTURE SPEAKING EXPANSION ACTIVITY: Who Am I?

- Have students look at the Big Picture or put the color overhead transparency for Unit 8 on the OHP.
- Model the activity. Say several sentences about a character in the picture (e.g., *I am with my brother. I am buying oranges.*). Elicit the name (*Patricia*).
- Put students in pairs to practice describing and guessing characters. You may want to put students in small groups and assign each student a character to facilitate this activity.
- Call on students to say their sentences to the class and elicit the name from the other students.

---

5 LISTEN and write the price.

- Go over the directions.
- Remind students that *pound* is abbreviated *lb* and *pounds* is abbreviated *lbs.*
- Have students write the prices as you say the questions or play the CD.
- Put students in pairs to compare answers.
- Say the questions or play the CD again so students can confirm.
- Go over the answers with the class.

LISTENING SCRIPT
Lesson 2, Activity 5

TCD3, 4

Listen and write the price.

1. How much are the bananas?
2. How much are the apples?
3. How much are the onions?
4. How much is the coffee?

ANSWER KEY

1. 3 pounds/$1.00; 2. 5 pounds/$3.00;
3. bag/$2.29; 4. free

BIG PICTURE LISTENING EXPANSION ACTIVITY: Dictation

• Dictate three questions: *How much are the carrots? How much is the chicken? How much are two bottles of orange juice?*

• Have students write the questions and then compare their sentences with a partner.

• Have volunteers write the questions on the board.

COMMUNITY CONNECTION: Your supermarket

• As an out-of-class assignment, have students research the prices of three items at their usual supermarket.

• Put students in pairs to share what they found out.

• Elicit items and prices and write them on the board.

EXPANSION ACTIVITY: Compare prices

• Bring in or have students bring in flyers from their supermarkets. Make sure you have several supermarkets represented.

• Put students in small groups. Have them compare three or more items at different supermarkets.

• Elicit the stores with the best prices for different food items.

6 TALK. Work with a partner. Ask questions about the prices of (the following items.)

• Go over the directions and the sample conversation.

• Read each phrase aloud and have students repeat.

• Put students in pairs to practice asking and answering questions about prices.

LESSON 3: Listening and Conversation

OBJECTIVES
Ask for and give locations in a store
Interpret a food ad

COMPETENCIES
Distinguishing between /i/ and /I/
Talking about prices and location of food in a store

PRONUNCIATION
/i/ vs. /I/

WARM-UP ACTIVITY: Shopping list

- Give students two minutes to write a shopping list for next week. Remind students to use quantity words.
- Put students in pairs to talk about their lists.

PRONUNCIATION: Vowel sounds in *eat* and *it*

A LISTEN and repeat.

- Go over the directions.
- Play the CD and have students repeat.

EXPANSION ACTIVITY: Group words

- Copy the chart below on the board.

/i/	/I/
eat	it

- Have students write the words from Activity A in the correct places in the chart.
- Put students in pairs to compare answers.
- Go over the answers with the class.

ANSWER KEY

/i/	/I/
eat	it
cheese	fish
leave	chips
meat	live
	sit

B LISTEN and circle the word you hear.

- Go over the directions.
- Play the CD and have students circle the words they hear.
- Play the CD again if necessary.
- Go over the answers with the class.

LISTENING SCRIPT AND ANSWER KEY
Lesson 3, Activity B
TCD3, 6

Listen and circle the word you hear.

1. live
2. meat
3. eat
4. cheap
5. sit
6. chick

C TALK with a partner. Say a word in Activity B. Your partner listens and points to the word.

- Go over the directions.
- Model the activity with a more advanced student. Say a word and have the student point to the word you said in the book.
- Put students in pairs to take turns saying and pointing to the word.

EXPANSION ACTIVITY: Point on the board

- Copy the words from Activity B on the board.
- Call a student to the board. Say a word and have the student point to it.
- Continue with other students and other words.
- In a variation, have a student say a word to a classmate who identifies it on the board.

 ❶ **LISTEN** and check. What are the people shopping for?

- Go over the directions.
- Play the CD and have the students check what the people are shopping for in each conversation.
- Go over the answers with the class.

LISTENING SCRIPT
Lesson 3, Activity 1

TCD3, 7

Listen and check. What are people shopping for?

1: *A:* Let's buy apples. They're on sale.
   B: How much are they?
   A: $3.00 a bag.

2: *A:* Let's buy some orange juice. It's on sale.
   B: How much is it?
   A: $2.50 a bottle.

3: *A:* The chicken is on sale.
   B: How much is it?
   A: $1.29 a pound.

4: *A:* Bread is a good price.
   B: How much is it?
   A: $2.15 a loaf.

ANSWER KEY

1. apples; 2. juice; 3. chicken; 4. bread

LISTEN AGAIN and complete the chart.

- Go over the directions.
- Play the CD and have students complete the chart.
- Put students in pairs to compare answers.
- Go over the answers with the class.

ANSWER KEY

Food	Price	Quantity
1. apples	$3.00	a bag
2. juice	$2.50	a bottle
3. chicken	$1.29	a pound
4. bread	$2.15	a loaf

❷ **LISTEN** and read.

- Direct students' attention to the picture. Ask *Who do you see?*
- Play the CD or read the conversation as students follow along silently.
- Play the CD or read the conversation again and have students repeat.
- Ask: *How much are the apples? Where are they?*

❸ **PRACTICE THE CONVERSATION** with a partner.

- Go over the directions.
- Model the activity. Have a more advanced student read B's lines. Model how to substitute a different food and price.
- Put students in pairs to practice the conversation, making the appropriate substitutions.
- Walk around to monitor the activity and provide help as needed.
- Call on students to say the conversation to the class.

4 **WHAT ABOUT YOU?** Walk around the room and talk to your classmates. Complete the chart.

- Copy the chart on the board.
- Go over the directions and the example conversation.
- Model the activity. Ask a student if he or she buys chicken every week. If the answer is *yes*, ask for the student's name and write it on the chart on the board.
- Have students stand and walk around the room to talk to classmates and complete the chart.
- When students are finished, call on students to tell the class about someone on their charts (e.g., *Lena likes broccoli.*).

COMMUNITY CONNECTION: Interview

- As an out-of-class assignment, have students interview a friend, neighbor or coworker, asking the questions in Activity 4, or making up their own food questions.
- Have students write sentences about the answers (*Nick doesn't buy chicken every week.*).
- Put students in pairs to read their sentences.
- Call on students to read their sentences to the class.

COMMUNITY CONNECTION: What aisle?

- As an out-of-class assignment, have students choose three food words. Make sure students understand what an *aisle* is. Point out or elicit that fresh foods are usually found in a section, but not on an aisle.
- Have students go to their supermarkets and write down where each of the three foods can be found (by section, and if possible, by aisle).
- Put students in pairs to share what they found out.

LESSON 4: Grammar and Vocabulary

OBJECTIVE

Use information questions in the present tense

VOCABULARY

French fries
a hamburger
a hot dog
ice cream
pie

salad
sandwiches
soda
soup

GRAMMAR

Information questions (*what, where, when*)

COMPETENCIES

Identify food
Use information questions

WARM-UP ACTIVITY: What restaurant do you like?

- Ask students how often they go out to eat at a restaurant.
- Elicit the names of their favorite restaurants and write them on the board.

🎧 **❶ GRAMMAR PICTURE DICTIONARY.** Listen and repeat.

- Have students look at the picture. Ask *What do you see?*
- Play the CD or say the sentences and have students repeat.
- Say the new words in random order and have the students point to the pictures.

EXPANSION ACTIVITY: Pair work

- Put students in pairs to take turns asking and answering the questions in Activity 1.
- With more advanced students, have students practice asking the questions of each other (e.g., *What do you usually order for lunch?*).
- Call on students and ask questions.

❷ NOTICE THE GRAMMAR. Circle *do* or *does.* Underline the verbs.

- Have students circle *do* and *does* and underline verbs.
- Go over the answers with the class.

ANSWER KEY

1. *A:* What (does) he usually <u>order</u> for lunch?
   B: A hamburger.
2. *A:* What (does) she usually <u>order</u> for lunch?
   B: A hot dog.
3. *A:* What (do) they usually <u>order</u> for lunch?
   B: Sandwiches.
4. *A:* When (does) she usually <u>eat</u> salad?
   B: For dinner.
5. *A:* When (does) he usually <u>eat</u> soup?
   B: At lunch.
6. *A:* When (do) they usually <u>eat</u> French fries?
   B: At dinner.
7. *A:* Where (do) they usually <u>eat</u> ice cream?
   B: At the park.
8. *A:* Where (does) she usually <u>eat</u> pie?
   B: At Joe's Bakery.
9. *A:* Where (does) he usually <u>drink</u> soda?
   B: At the movies.

GRAMMAR CHART: Information Questions with *Where, When, What*

- Go over the information in the chart.
- You may want to read the sample sentences in the chart and have students repeat.
- Make sure students understand the difference between long and short answers. Explain that long answers are sentences and they usually repeat part of the question. They contain a subject, verb, and other information. Short answers only give the information asked for.

CHART EXPANSION ACTIVITY: Long answers

- Have students rewrite three questions from the chart, using *where*, *when* and *what.*
- Have students write long answers to the questions.
- Put students in pairs to take turns asking and answering their questions.

❸ WRITE. Complete the sentences with *do* or *does*. Then match.

- Go over the directions and the example.
- Go over the sentences in the box.
- Have students complete the sentences with *do* or *does,* and then match the questions and answers.
- Put students in pairs to compare answers.
- Go over the answers with the class.

ANSWER KEY

1. b/does; 2. f/does; 3. e/do; 4. c/does; 5. a/do;
6. d/do

EXPANSION ACTIVITY: Pair work

- Put students in pairs to take turns asking and answering the questions in Activity 3.

❹ WHAT ABOUT YOU? Write your answers.

- Go over the directions.
- Have students answer the questions. They can use short answers.
- Put students in pairs to take turns asking and answering the questions.
- Call on students to tell the class about their partners.

EXPANSION ACTIVITY: Category sort

- Tell students that you will ask a question and they should talk to classmates and stand with classmates who have the same answer.
- Have students stand. Ask *Where do you usually eat lunch?* Remind students to repeat the question to their classmates in order to stand with those who have the same answer.
- When students are sorted, have a student from each group say a sentence (*We usually eat at home.*).
- Repeat with other questions from Activity 4. This activity should be fast-paced.

COMMUNITY CONNECTION: Food labels

- Bring in food labels.
- Elicit the type of information found on labels (calories, serving size, grams of fat, protein, sugars) and write it on the board.
- Give each student a label.
- Put students in pairs to compare the information on the two labels. Ask questions: *Which one is lower in calories? Which one has more fat?*

LESSON 5: Grammar Practice Plus

WARM-UP ACTIVITY: Containers

- Bring in the containers/packaging for milk, water, eggs, butter, bread, cheese, broccoli and spices.
- Hold the containers up and review the container word and food word.

❶ WRITE. Complete the sentences with a food or drink.

- Write *eggs, milk* and *water* on the board.
- Go over the directions and the example
- Have students write the missing words on the lines.

 LISTEN and repeat. Are your answers correct?

- Play the CD and have students repeat and correct their answers.

 LISTENING SCRIPT
Lesson 5, Activity 1

TCD3, 10

Listen and repeat. Are your answers correct?

1. They have milk.
2. They need water.
3. They want eggs.

ANSWER KEY

1. milk; 2. water; 3. eggs

EXPANSION ACTIVITY: *Want/have/need* clothes

- Have students list clothing that they have, want, and need.
- Put students in pairs to talk about their lists.
- Call on students and ask what they have, want, or need in clothing.

❷ WRITE. Look at the picture. Write the answers.

- Direct students' attention to the picture and ask questions: *Do they have milk? Do they have fish?*
- Go over the directions and the example.
- Have students write sentences about what the people in the picture have and need.
- Put students in pairs to compare answers.
- Go over the answers with the class.

ANSWER KEY

1. They have milk. They have chicken. They have hot dogs. They have carrots.
2. They need cheese. They need fish. They need soda. They need juice. They need broccoli.

3 WHAT ABOUT YOU? Complete the chart with foods and drinks.

- Go over the directions and the example in the chart.
- Have students complete the chart.
- Put students in pairs to talk about their charts.
- Call on students to tell the class about something in their partner's chart.

EXPANSION ACTIVITY: Index cards

- Give each student three index cards. Have students write *have, want* and *need* on separate cards.
- Have students stand in a circle.
- Name a food, and have students show the appropriate card. For example, if you say *chicken,* students who already have it should show *have,* students who need it should show *need,* and students who want it should show *want.* Point out that there aren't really correct answers.
- Call on a student to say a sentence about a classmate (e.g., *Tam needs chicken.*).
- Continue with other food words.

BIG PICTURE GRAMMAR EXPANSION ACTIVITY: What Do They Have?

- Photocopy and distribute Worksheet 17: What Do They Have?
- Put the color transparency for Unit 8 on the OHP or have students look at the Big Picture in their books.
- Go over the directions.
- Have students complete the worksheet.
- Put students in pairs to compare answers.
- Go over the answers with the class.

WORKSHEET 17 ANSWER KEY (Answers may vary.)

1. At the store; 2. at the store/next to the coffee; 3. coffee; 4. in the bakery; 5. onions; 6. a bag of oranges (six), a loaf of bread, a bag of rice, a box of cereal, a whole salmon fillet, three cartons of milk, a glass bottle of orange juice; 7. Steak, bananas, broccoli, onions, and soda; 8. at the cash register, by the flowers, in the produce section.

MATH: Weights and Measurements

- Go over the information about weights and measurements. If needed, hold up the containers from the warm-up activity.
- Have students write the amounts.
- Go over the answers with the class.

CULTURE/CIVICS NOTE

Point out that these are the measurements used in the United States.

ANSWER KEY

1. 6; 2. 6; 3. 20; 4. 8; 5. 48; 6. 2

4 WRITE. Look at the recipe for Strata. Write the amounts.

- Direct students' attention to the recipe. Point out or elicit that this is a recipe card for strata, an egg dish. Ask questions: *How many eggs are in the recipe? How many pieces of bread?*
- Explain that when we follow a recipe, we look at what we have to see if we have to go out to buy something or buy more of something.
- Go over the directions and the example.
- Have students write the amounts on the line. Make sure students see that they have to figure out how much the recipe requires, how much they already have, and how much more they will need to make the recipe.
- Put students in pairs to compare answers.
- Go over the answers with the class.

ANSWER KEY

1. 2; 2. 2; 3. 4; 4. 1/4; 5. 5; 6. 8

EXPANSION ACTIVITY: Just two eggs?

- Put students in pairs to write how many/how much of each food in Activity 4 they would actually have to buy from the store. For example, they need a loaf of bread, not just eight pieces.
- Elicit the answers and write them on the board.

ANSWER KEY

eggs—$\frac{1}{2}$ dozen or dozen
milk—pint or quart
cheese—four ounces/$\frac{1}{4}$ pound or one package
butter—$\frac{1}{2}$ pound or pound
broccoli—one package/bunch
bread—one loaf

EXPANSION ACTIVITY: Favorite foods

- Put students in small groups to talk about their favorite dish. Have students say the name, the ingredients, and when it is eaten.
- Call on students to tell the class about their own favorite dish or about someone in their group.

ACADEMIC CONNECTION: Conversions

- As an out-of-class assignment, have students use a search engine to find conversions for ounces/pounds and grams/kilograms, and quarts/liters.
- Have students write the ingredients lists for their favorite dish in both forms.

LESSON 6: Apply Your Knowledge

OBJECTIVE
Order from a menu

COMPETENCIES
Order food at a restaurant

WARM-UP ACTIVITY: Restaurants

- Put students in pairs to talk about their favorite restaurants. Elicit the names. Ask students what information they can find on menus.

1 READ. Answer the questions below.

- Go over the directions.
- Direct students' attention to the menu and ask questions: *What is this? Where do you see these? What kind of sandwiches do they have? How much are the French fries?*
- Have students read the menu and answer the questions.
- Go over the answers with the class.

ANSWER KEY
1. Main Street Café; **2.** 1932 Main Street; **3.** 11 A.M.; **4.** four

 2 LISTEN. Look at the menu. Circle the foods the woman orders.

- Go over the directions.
- Play the CD and have the students circle the things the woman orders.
- Go over the answers with the class.

 LISTENING SCRIPT
Lesson 6, Activity 2

TCD3, 11

Listen. Look at the menu. Circle the foods the woman orders.

Male:	Hello. What would you like today?
Female:	Hmm. I'll have a hamburger, please.
Male:	Would you like French fries or chips with that?
Female:	I'll have chips, please.
Male:	Any soup?
Female:	Oh, no thank you. But maybe dessert. . . .
Male:	We have ice cream and pie.
Female:	The ice cream, please.
Male:	And something to drink?
Female:	Yes, a small milk, please.
Male:	Of course. So, that's a hamburger with chips, ice cream, and a small milk.
Female:	Yes, thank you.

ANSWER KEY
Circle: hamburger, chips, ice cream, milk

EXPANSION ACTIVITY: Write questions

- Have students write two questions about the menu. Instruct them to use question words (*what, where, when, how much/many*) for their information questions.
- Put students in pairs to take turns asking and answering the questions.

❸ WRITE. How much is the woman's lunch?

- Have students write the prices of what the woman orders on the lines, and then write the total.
- Put students in pairs to compare answers.
- Go over the answer with the class.

ANSWER KEY

$5.95 + $1.00 + $2.00 + $1.00 = $9.95

❹ LISTEN and read.

- Direct students' attention to the picture. Ask: *Who do you see? Where are they?*
- Have students follow along and repeat as you say the conversation or play the CD.
- Ask comprehension questions: *Who is the server? What does the customer order?*
- Play the CD again and have students repeat.
- Put students in pairs to take turns reading the conversation.

GRAMMAR/VOCABULARY NOTE

Point out that we often use two expressions when ordering in a restaurant: *I'd like* and *I'll have*. They are more polite than saying *I want*.

❺ PRACTICE THE CONVERSATION with a partner.

- Go over the directions and the information.
- Model the activity with a student. Have the students read the server's lines. Substitute the information in Activity 1 (e.g., *I'd like a cheese sandwich with soup.*).
- Put students in pairs. Have students take turns ordering meals using the information in Activity 4.
- Walk around the room to monitor the activity and provide help as needed.
- Have pairs of students say the conversations in front of the class.

❻ TALK with a partner. Order meals from the menu on page 128. Write the things your partner orders.

- Go over the directions.
- Copy the chart on the board.
- Model the activity. Pretend you are a server and a student is the customer. Write the food and drink that the student orders on the board.
- Put students in pairs to practice ordering and taking orders.
- Call on students to tell the class about their partners' order.

COMMUNITY CONNECTION: Menus

- For an out-of-class assignment, have students pick up a menu from a restaurant or get one online.
- Have students bring in their menus.
- Put students in pairs to talk about the food on the menus.
- Have students practice ordering food from the menu with their partners.

LESSON 7: Reading and Writing

OBJECTIVE

Understand connecting words *and, but*

READING TIP

Notice connecting words *and, but*

WRITING TIP

Use *and* to connect sentences with similar ideas, use *but* to connect sentences with different, or contrasting ideas

COMPETENCIES

Use *and* and *but*

WARM-UP ACTIVITY: Colors and groups

- Bring in different fruits and vegetables with a variety of colors: banana, lemon, squash, green beans, broccoli, lime, carrots, orange.
- Hold up two items. Call on a student and ask *Similar or different?* Elicit ideas. If the students says the items are similar because they are yellow, restate the idea using *and* (*The banana and squash are yellow.*). If the student says the items are different because one is a fruit and one is a vegetable, restate with *but* (*The banana is a fruit, but the squash is a vegetable.*).

Reading

① THINK ABOUT IT. What do you usually eat for breakfast?

- Read the question. Elicit answers from students.

② BEFORE YOU READ. Look at the article. Circle the countries.

- Go over the directions.
- Have students look at the title, the photo, and the article and circle the names of countries. Remind students that South America, Asia and Europe are continents, not countries.
- Elicit the names of the countries in the article.

ANSWER KEY

Vietnam, China, India, United States, England, Russia

③ READ. What is the article about? Check the answer.

- Go over the directions.
- Have students read the article and check the answer.
- Elicit that *Breakfast is different in different countries* is the best answer.

ANSWER KEY

Breakfast is different in different countries.

EXPANSION ACTIVITY: Sentence strip match

- Photocopy the Worksheet 18 and cut along the dotted lines. There are 14 strips, so make enough so that all your students can participate.
- Give each student a strip.
- Have students stand and walk around the room, first to find the match that completes their sentences, then to reorder themselves like the article.
- Have students read or recite their sentence fragment to recite the entire article.

❹ CHECK *similar* or *different*.

- Go over the reading tip in the box.
- Have students check *similar* or *different*.
- Put students in pairs to compare ideas.
- Elicit ideas from the students and write the ideas on the board.

ANSWER KEY

1. similar; 2. different; 3. different; 4. similar;
5. different

EXPANSION ACTIVITY: Chart it!

- Copy the chart on the board.
- Go over the example.
- Have students copy the charts in their notebooks.
- Have students complete the charts with the information from the article.
- Put students in pairs to compare charts.
- Have volunteers complete the chart on the board.

COUNTRY	EAT	DRINK
Vietnam	rice and soup	tea
China		
India		
Colombia		
United States		
England		
France		
Russia		

BIG PICTURE READING EXPANSION ACTIVITY: At the Supermarket

- Photocopy and distribute Worksheet 19: At the Supermarket.
- Put the transparency for Unit 8 on the OHP or have students look at the Big Picture in their books.
- Go over the directions.
- Have students read the information on the worksheet and then check similar or different.
- Put students in pairs to share their ideas.
- Go over the answers with the class.

WORKSHEET 19 ANSWER KEY

1. every morning; 2. every week; 3. a sandwich;
4. No, it doesn't. 5. No, it's not. 6. apples, oranges, bananas, and grapes

Writing

- Go over the writing tip in the box.
- Model the tip. Say something you like (*I like coffee.*). Elicit who else likes it (*Min, Tina, and Kay*). Elicit who doesn't like it, but likes something else (*Mika likes tea.*). Say a sentence (*Min, Tina, and Kay like coffee, but Mika likes tea.*).

❶ WRITE. Look at the diagram. Complete the sentences with *and* or *but*.

- Direct students' attention to the diagram. Ask questions: *What does Ming eat for breakfast? What do both Lisa and Ming drink for breakfast?*

- Go over the directions and the example.
- Point out that if the information is similar, we use *and*. If it is different, we can use *but*.
- Have students complete the sentences with *and* or *but*.
- Go over the answers with the class.

ANSWER KEY

1. but; 2. and; 3. but; 4. and

2 TALK to a partner about what you eat for breakfast. Complete the diagram.

- Go over the directions. Remind students to put the things they both eat in the middle section.
- Put students in pairs to talk about what they eat for breakfast.
- Have students complete the diagram.

3 WRITE sentences. Use information from your Venn diagram.

- Go over the directions.
- Have students complete the sentences with information about themselves and their partners. Remind students to use the information from Activity 2.
- Walk around to monitor the activity and provide help as needed.
- Put students in pairs to read their sentences.
- Call on students to read their sentences to the class.

BIG PICTURE WRITING EXPANSION ACTIVITY: Three sentences

- Put the transparency for Unit 8 on the projector or have students look at the Big Picture in their books.
- Have students write three sentences about what the people eat or drink.

Career Connection

<table>
<tr><td>**OBJECTIVE**</td></tr>
<tr><td>Make plans at work</td></tr>
</table>

<table>
<tr><td>**COMPETENCIES**</td></tr>
<tr><td>Get food and drinks for a group</td></tr>
</table>

WARM-UP ACTIVITY: Food for a group
Put students in pairs to talk about when they prepare food for a lot of people. Ask students what they usually prepare if they have to serve a big group.

🎧 **❶ READ AND LISTEN.** Then practice with a partner.

- Direct students' attention to the photos. Tell students this is the continuation of the story about Isabel. Have students point to Isabel in the photos.
- Play the CD and have students follow along silently.
- Play the CD again and have students repeat.
- Put students in pairs to take turns reading the roles of Isabel and her boss.
- Ask *What is the problem?*

❷ WRITE. Work with a partner. How much do you think Isabel needs to get?

- Go over the directions and the example.
- Put students in pairs to talk about what Isabel needs and how much. Have students complete the chart.
- Call on students to share their ideas with the class.

❸ WHAT ABOUT YOU? What food and drinks do you like for a snack?

- Explain or elicit that a snack is a small amount of food that we eat between meals.

- Put students in pairs to talk about what they eat for snacks.
- Elicit ideas from students and write the ideas on the board.

COMMUNITY CONNECTION: Interview

- As an out-of-class assignment, have students ask a friend, neighbor or family member if they have snacks for meetings at work, and what they eat and drink.
- Have students tell the class what they found out.

CHECK YOUR PROGRESS!

- Have students circle the answers.
- Have students check whether each answer is right or wrong.
- Have students total their correct answers and fill in the chart.
- Have students create a learning plan and/or set learning goals.

ANSWER KEY
1. carrot; 2. oranges; 3. Bananas; 4. do; 5. want; 6. do; 7. dessert; 8. coffee; 9. eggs; 10. a bottle; 11. a pound; 12. a carton

Unit Overview

LESSON	OBJECTIVE	STUDENT BOOK	WORKBOOK
1 Grammar and Vocabulary 1	Use *can* to talk about ability	p. 134	p. 114
2 Grammar Practice Plus	Identify job requirements	p. 136	p. 115
3 Listening and Conversation	Pronounce *can* and *can't* Identify job skills	p. 138	p. 116
4 Grammar and Vocabulary 2	Make statements with regular past tense verbs	p. 140	p. 118
5 Grammar Practice Plus	Make statements with irregular past tense verbs	p. 142	p. 119
6 Apply Your Knowledge	Interpret a pay stub Understand job ads Interview for a job	p. 144	p. 120
7 Reading and Writing	Understand and fill out a job application	p. 146	p. 122
• Career Connection	Set employment goals	p. 148	p. 124
• Check Your Progress	Monitor progress	p. 149	p. 126

Reading/Writing Strategies

- Use headings to find information on a form.
- Edit documents and forms.

Connection Activities

LESSON	TYPE	SKILL DEVELOPMENT
1	Academic	Understand skills for academic success
2	Community	Understand work skills
3	Community	Access job lines
4	Community	Understand news reports
5	Academic	Describe educational background
6	Academic	Use the Internet for research
8	Community	Understand job evaluations

WORKSHEET #/FOCUS	TITLE	TEACHER'S EDITION
20 Grammar	Yesterday	p. 265
21 Reading	Application Forms	p. 266
22 Speaking/Listening	Pair Interview	p. 267

LESSON 1: Grammar and Vocabulary

OBJECTIVE

Use *can* to talk about ability

VOCABULARY

drive a forklift	take blood pressure
fix a copier	take measurements
read an X-ray	take patient information
speak French	use a blood pressure cuff
supervise workers	use a scanner

GRAMMAR

Can for ability

COMPETENCIES

Use *can* to express ability and inability (e.g., *I can lift it. I can't lift it.*)

Describe the use of common equipment for home and work

WARM-UP ACTIVITY: What do you know?

- Put the transparency for Unit 9 on the OHP or have students look at the Big Picture in their books.
- Elicit which words students know already.

🎧 ❶ GRAMMAR PICTURE DICTIONARY. Listen and repeat.

- Have students open their books and look at the pictures. Ask *What do you see?* Write all the words the students know on the board.
- Have students look at the pictures and listen while you say the words or play the CD.
- Say the sentences or play the CD again and have students repeat.
- Put students in pairs and take turns saying the questions in random order as their partner points to the picture.

EXPANSION ACTIVITY: *Take/Use/Fix*

- Write the words *take, use* and *fix* on the board.
- Put students in pairs or small groups to list as many things as they can that would follow each verb.
- Elicit ideas and write them on the board. Have students add the collocations to their vocabulary notebooks.

ANSWER KEY (Answers may vary.)

Take	Use	Fix
food orders	a computer	a car
measurements	power tools	a truck
a test	a fax	a forklift
a message	machine	a television
a temperature	a copier	a copier
a picture/photo	a calculator	a computer
a bus/a train	a dictionary	
	a scanner	
	the library	
	the Internet	

❷ NOTICE THE GRAMMAR. Look at Activity 1. Underline *can* or *can't*. Circle the verbs.

- Have students read the sentences and underline *can* or *can't*. Then have students circle the verbs.
- Ask questions: *Does* can *come first or the verb? Do we add an* s *to* can*? Do we add an* s *to the verb?*

ANSWER KEY

1. Ming can take patient information
2. She can take blood pressure.
3. She can't read an X-ray.
4. Radek can measure things.
5. He can supervise workers.
6. He can't drive a forklift.
7. Bernice can speak French.
8. She can use a scanner.
9. She can't fix a copier.

GRAMMAR CHART: *Can* for Ability

- Direct students' attention to the chart or project the transparency or CD.
- Go over the information on the chart, including the usage note and the Professor note. You may want to read the questions and answers, pausing to have students repeat.
- Students will not study all of the uses of *can* (for permission, for possibility, for requests). In this level, they will only focus on *can* for ability/skills.

CHART EXPANSION ACTIVITY: Literacy development

- Distribute index cards to students.
- Have students write the new vocabulary phrases (e.g., take food orders, use a cash register) on separate cards. Have students write *I* on a card, and *can* and *can't* on cards.
- "Dictate" sentences beginning with *I* (e.g., *I can use power tools*). Have students choose the correct cards to make the sentence.
- When students have enough practice finding the correct cards to make your sentences, have students make their own sentences and read them to a partner.

❸ MATCH.

- Go over the directions and the example.
- Have students match the sentences.
- Put students in pairs to check their answers.
- Go over the answers with the class.
- Put students in pairs to practice reading the questions and answers.

ANSWER KEY

1. c; 2. b; 3. a; 4. e; 5. f; 6. d

EXPANSION ACTIVITY: Write questions

- Have students rewrite the sentences in Activity 3 as questions (e.g., *Can Jim check teeth?*).
- Put students in pairs to take turns asking and answering the questions. Tell students to practice both affirmative and negative short answers.
- Walk around the room to monitor the activity and provide help as needed.
- Call on students and ask questions about the information in Activity 3 (*Can Hector supervise people?*). Elicit the appropriate answer.

❹ WHAT ABOUT YOU? Check your answer.

- Read the questions aloud and have students repeat.
- Call on students and ask the first question. Elicit the answers. Tell students to check the answer that is true for them.
- Have students check the answers to the other questions.
- Put students in pairs to take turns asking and answering the questions.
- Call on students and ask the questions.

EXPANSION ACTIVITY: Category sort

- Have students stand. Ask a question (*What language or languages can you speak besides English?*). Have students stand with classmates who have the same answer. Remind students to keep asking the questions until they sort themselves out. Point out that if there are multiple answers, students should stand with classmates who have the same answers.

- Ask other questions (*What can you fix? What office equipment can you use? What can you drive? What sports can you play?*). Keep the activity fast-paced and short.

ACADEMIC CONNECTION: Skills for school

- Put students in pairs to list five skills that are necessary for academic success.

- Elicit ideas and write them on the board (e.g., *can use a dictionary, can read, can write, can use a computer*).

- As an out-of-class extension of the assignment, have students go online and search for "academic skills" or "skills for academic success" and write down one idea.

- Call on students to share their ideas with the class.

LESSON 2: Grammar Practice Plus

OBJECTIVE

Identify job requirements

VOCABULARY

an accountant	a plumber
a calculator	a toilet
an electrician	a truck
a mechanic	wiring

GRAMMAR

Can for ability

COMPETENCIES

Identify common occupations
Identify basic duties of common occupations
Use general work-related vocabulary

WARM-UP ACTIVITY: Ball toss

- Call on a student, toss a ball or beanbag and say *A nurse can* . . . Elicit an appropriate completion (*use a blood pressure cuff, help the doctor*).
- Have the student toss the ball or beanbag to a classmate and begin another sentence with an occupation and *can.*
- Continue until everyone has had a chance to participate or you have exhausted students' knowledge of occupations and skills.

❶ MATCH.

- Go over the directions and the example.
- Have students match the object to the sentence.
- Put students in pairs to compare answers.

LISTEN and repeat. Are your answers correct?

- Play the CD and have students repeat. Have students check their answers.

 LISTENING SCRIPT
Lesson 2, Activity 1
TCD3, 15

Listen and repeat. Are your answers correct?

1. A plumber can fix toilets.
2. An accountant can use a calculator.
3. An electrician can fix wiring.
4. A mechanic can fix trucks.

ANSWER KEY

1. toilets; 2. a calculator; 3. wiring; 4. trucks

EXPANSION ACTIVITY: Spell it

- Give students two minutes to study the new words from Lessons 1 and 2.
- With books closed, call on students and say a word (e.g., *electrician*). Elicit the correct spelling.

❷ WRITE. Complete the chart.

- Go over the directions and the example.
- Have students complete the chart. Point out that there is more than one right answer for each.
- Put students in pairs to read their sentences aloud.
- Call on students to share their ideas with the class.

ANSWER KEY
Answers may vary.

Occupations (People)		Tools and Equipment (Things)
A plumber	can fix	toilets.
A cook	can prepare	meals.
An accountant	can use	a calculator.
A taxi driver	can drive	a taxi.

EXPANSION ACTIVITY: Question practice

- Have students use the information in the chart to write five questions (e.g., *Can a plumber fix toilets? Can a plumber fix trucks?*). Encourage students to write at least two questions that might have a negative answer.
- Walk around to monitor the activity and provide help as needed.
- Elicit questions and write them on the board.
- Put students in pairs to practice asking and answering their questions or the ones on the board.

LITERACY DEVELOPMENT EXPANSION ACTIVITY: Flashcards

- Distribute index cards to students.
- Have students write an occupation on one side of each card (e.g., *electrician*), and a skill on the other (e.g., *fix wiring*).
- Put students in pairs. Have one partner display the occupation and elicit the skill, then switch roles.

❸ WHAT ABOUT YOU? Write three things you can do and three things you can't do.

- Go over the directions.

- Model the activity. Say and write three things you can do and three things you can't do.
- Have students fill in the blanks.
- Put students in pairs to read their sentences.
- Call on students to tell the class one thing they can do and one thing they can't do.

❹ TALK about the picture.

- Go over the directions.
- Direct students' attention to the Big Picture or put the transparency on the OHP. Point to Ana and read the example sentence *Maria is reading an x-ray.*
- Put students in pairs. Have students take turns saying sentences about the picture.
- Call on students. Point to different characters in the Big Picture and elicit sentences.

BIG PICTURE CONVERSATION/ VOCABULARY EXPANSION ACTIVITY: *Yes/no* questions

- Have students look at the Big Picture or put the color overhead transparency for Unit 9 on the OHP.
- Model the activity. Think of a person in the picture. Tell students they must ask *yes/no* questions to find out who you are thinking about. Explain that they must ask five *yes/no* questions (e.g., *Are you female? Can you take phone messages? Can you drive a taxi? Are you a plumber? Can you fix toilets?*) before they can ask a name (e.g., *Are you Ana?*). Also explain that each question must be asked by a different student.
- After students have guessed, have a volunteer come to the front of the class and think of someone in the picture, and answer questions about the person's identity.
- Continue with several more students.

⑤ LISTEN. Complete the sentence. Use *can* or *can't*.

- Go over the directions.
- Have students fill in the blanks as you say the sentences or play the CD.
- Put students in pairs to compare answers.
- Say the sentences or play the CD again so students can confirm.
- Go over the answers with the class.

🎧 **LISTENING SCRIPT**
Lesson 2, Activity 5
TCD3, 16
Listen. Complete the sentences. Use *can* or *can't*.

1. Kathy and Jake can make lunch.
2. Andy can't lift the box.
3. Ana can fix water pipes.
4. Trung can take blood pressure.
5. Greg can't fix the car.
6. Yuri can drive an ambulance.

ANSWER KEY

1. can; 2. can't; 3. can; 4. can; 5. can't; 6. can

EXPANSION ACTIVITY: Dictation

- Have students write the questions from Activity 4 as you read the questions or play the CD. Repeat twice.
- Put students in pairs to compare sentences.
- Have volunteers write the questions on the board.

⑥ LOOK at the sentences above. Write the people's names on the picture.

- Go over the directions.
- Have students refer to the information in Activity 5.

⑦ TALK to a partner. Ask and answer questions.

- Go over the directions and the example.
- Put students in pairs to ask and answer questions about the people's abilities.
- Walk around to monitor the activity and provide help as needed.

COMMUNITY CONNECTION: Interview

- As an out-of-class assignment, have students interview someone they know who has a job. Ask students to find out what job the person does, and what skills or abilities the person uses in the job.
- Put students in pairs to share what they found out.
- Call on students to tell the class about the person interviewed, the job and one thing he or she can do.

LESSON 3: Listening and Conversation

OBJECTIVES

Pronounce *can* and *can't*
Identify job skills

COMPETENCIES

Use *can* and *can't* to talk about job skills

WARM-UP ACTIVITY: Finding jobs

- Put students in pairs or small groups to talk about the different ways people can find out about jobs.
- Elicit ideas and write them on the board.

 **1 LISTEN** and circle the correct letter.

- Direct students' attention to the pictures and elicit the names of the jobs.
- Read the script or play the CD and have students circle the letter.
- Have students compare answers in pairs.
- Go over the answers with the class.

VOCABULARY NOTE

The recordings in Activity 1 may contain words that are unfamiliar to students. It's not important that they understand every word, as they would probably not understand every word of an actual job listing recording. Point out that students should be listening for occupations and skills only.

CULTURE/CIVICS NOTES

- Many cities have job listings that can be accessed by telephone. The listings often give the position, an ID number, and a number to call or website to visit.
- Communities often post jobs on municipal or county websites also.

 LISTENING SCRIPT
Lesson 3, Activity 1
TCD3, 17

Listen and circle the correct letter.

1. Welcome to Jobline. Please listen for available openings. There is an opening for an office assistant, position number A112. This person needs to use a computer and other office equipment.
2. Welcome to Jobline. Please listen for available openings. There are two openings for a salesperson, position number G801. The position requires phone skills in English and Spanish.
3. Welcome to Jobline. Please listen for available openings. There is one opening for a mechanic, position number T99. Applicants must be able to fix cars and trucks.

ANSWER KEY

1. c; **2.** a; **3.** b

LISTEN AGAIN. Write the letter on the line for the skill you hear.

- Play the CD again and have students write the letter next to the number of the conversation.
- Go over the answers with the class.

ANSWER KEY

1. c; **2.** b; **3.** a

EXPANSION ACTIVITY: Write a job listing

- Write a model for a job listing on the board: Welcome to Jobline. Please listen for available openings. There is _____ opening(s) for _____, position number T15. Applicants must be able to _____.

- Write appropriate completions on the line. Point out that a verb begins the last completion.

- Have students write their own job listings using the template.

- Call on students to read their listings to the class.

PRONUNCIATION: *Can* and *Can't*

Ⓐ LISTEN and circle the letter of the sentence you hear.

- Remind students to listen for the difference between *can* and *can't.*

- Play the CD and have students circle the answer.

- Go over the answers with the class.

LISTENING SCRIPT
Lesson 3, Activity A

TCD3, 18

Listen and circle the letter of the sentence you hear.

1. I can cook Japanese food.
2. She can't fix the toilet.
3. You can't drive a bus.

ANSWER KEY

1. A; 2. B; 3. B

Ⓑ TALK with a partner. Read the sentence above.

- Have students practice saying each sentence.

- Point out that *can* is said quickly and is unstressed, while *can't* has a longer vowel sound and is stressed.

- Elicit or point out that we don't always say or hear the final *t* in *can't*—we know it is the negative by the vowel sound and stress.

❷ LISTEN and read.

- Direct students' attention to the picture. Ask questions: *Who do you see? What are they doing?*

- Play the CD or read the conversation as students follow along silently.

- Play the CD or read the conversation again and have students repeat.

- Ask: *What job does he want? What can he do?*

- Put students in pairs to practice the conversation.

❸ PRACTICE THE CONVERSATION with a partner.

- Go over the directions.

- Model the activity. Have a more advanced student read A's lines. Model how to substitute a different job and skill.

- Put students in pairs to practice the conversation, making the appropriate substitutions.

- Walk around to monitor the activity and provide help as needed.

- Call on students to say the conversation to the class.

❹ WHAT ABOUT YOU? Walk around the room and talk to your classmates. Complete the chart.

- Copy the chart on the board.
- Go over the directions and the example conversation.
- Model the activity. Ask a student if he or she can fix electrical problems. If the answer is yes, ask for the student's name and write it on the chart on the board.
- Have students stand and walk around the room to talk to classmates and complete the chart.
- When students are finished, call on students to tell the class about someone on their charts (e.g., *Trung can use a computer.*).

COMMUNITY CONNECTION: Joblines

- As an out-of-class assignment, have students look for job listings in your city or county. The blue pages of the telephone directory may list a phone number for job listings, or students can go online and look at job listings at a city or county website.
- Have students write down the information for three job listings, including the position name, the skills or knowledge needed and the contact information.
- Put students in pairs to share what they learned.
- Call on students to tell the class what they found out.

BIG PICTURE LISTENING EXPANSION ACTIVITY: *Can/can't*

- Have students write the numbers 1–5 on a piece of paper.
- Tell students you will read five sentences. If the sentence says *can,* students should write *yes* next to the number. If the sentence says *can't,* they should write *no.*
- Read the sentences below once. Do not emphasize the words *can* and *can't*—just say them naturally.
- Have students write *yes* or *no* next to the number.
- Go over the answers with the class.
  1. Jake can't cook.
  2. Ana can fix any plumbing problem.
  3. Trung can use a blood pressure cuff.
  4. Andy can't lift the box.
  5. Greg can't fix cars.

ANSWER KEY

1. no; 2. yes; 3. yes; 4. no; 5. no

LESSON 4: Grammar and Vocabulary

OBJECTIVE

Make statements with regular past tense verbs

VOCABULARY

borrow	organize
count	paint
deliver	study
open	clean
order	

GRAMMAR

Past tense of regular verbs

COMPETENCIES

Use simple past tense of common regular verbs

WARM-UP ACTIVITY: Yesterday's activities

- Elicit or point out what *yesterday* means.
- Have students list verbs for the activities they did yesterday.
- Elicit the verbs and write them on the board. Circle the regular verbs in the list.

🎧 ❶ GRAMMAR PICTURE DICTIONARY. Listen and repeat.

- Have students look at the picture. Ask: *Who do you see? What are they doing?*
- Play the CD or say the sentences and have students repeat.
- Say the sentences in random order and have the students point to the pictures.

❷ NOTICE THE GRAMMAR. Look at Activity 1. Underline the verbs. Circle the time expressions.

- Have students underline the verbs and circle the time expressions.
- Go over the answers with the class.

ANSWER KEY

1. My husband underline{studied} business (for four years).
2. We borrowed money from the bank (in March).
3. Painters painted our store (last month).
4. We ordered the clothing (two weeks ago).
5. We cleaned the store (last week).
6. They delivered the clothes (yesterday).
7. I organized the shelves (last night).
8. We opened for business this morning (at 9 A.M.).
9. We closed (at 8 P.M.) and I counted our money!

GRAMMAR CHART: Past Tense Statements with Regular Verbs

- Go over the information in the chart, including the usage note and the Professor note.
- You may want to read the sample sentences in the chart and have students repeat.

CHART EXPANSION ACTIVITY: Time expressions

- Put students in pairs to generate time expressions using the ones in the chart and in Activity 1 as a model.
- Elicit expressions and write them on the board.

3 WRITE. Complete the sentences with the past tense form of the verb.

- Go over the directions and the example.
- Have students complete the sentences with the past tense form of the verb.
- Put students in pairs to compare answers.
- Go over the answers with the class.

ANSWER KEY

1. delivered; 2. studied; 3. ordered; 4. cleaned;
5. used; 6. painted; 7. borrowed; 8. counted

4 WHAT ABOUT YOU? Write three things you did and three things you didn't do last night.

- Go over the directions and the example.
- Model the activity. Copy the chart on the board and write sentences about what you did or didn't do last night.
- Have students write sentences about what they did or didn't do last night.
- Put students in pairs to read their sentences to a partner.
- Call on students to tell the class one thing they did and one thing they didn't do last night.

COMMUNITY CONNECTION: News report

- As an out-of-class assignment, have students watch the news on TV and write down one thing that happened and was reported.
- Call on students to tell the class about something that happened in the news.

LESSON 5: Grammar Practice Plus

OBJECTIVES

Make statements with irregular past tense verbs
Interpret a pay stub

GRAMMAR

Simple past tense of regular and some irregular verbs

MATH

Understand paycheck stubs

COMPETENCIES

Use regular and some irregular verbs to talk about jobs

1 LISTEN AND REPEAT. Then circle the *irregular* past tense verbs.

- Go over the directions and the example.
- Have students read the story and circle the irregular past tense verbs.
- Ask comprehension questions: *Who is in the story? What happened first? When did the girlfriend arrive? What did the man do last night? What happened at the end?*
- Put students in pairs to compare answers.
- Play the CD and have students repeat and check their answers.

ANSWER KEY

Circle: went, made, broke

EXPANSION ACTIVITY: Picture stories

- Point out that Activity 1 tells a story about a man and his girlfriend.
- Have students draw picture stories about an event in their lives.
- Brainstorm past time expressions and write them on the board.
- Put students in pairs to tell their stories. Encourage students to use the past tense and time expressions if possible.
- Call on students to tell the class their stories.
- Optionally, have students write the text to go with their picture stories.

2 WRITE the past tense form of the verb.

- Go over the directions.
- Have students write the correct form of the word in parentheses on the line.
- Put students in pairs to compare answers.
- Go over the answers with the class.

ANSWER KEY

1. worked; 2. visited; 3. didn't come; 4. asked; 5. answered; 6. helped; 7. closed; 8. cleaned; 9. went; 10. made

EXPANSION ACTIVITY: Personalization

- Have students write three sentences about what they did yesterday.
- Put students in pairs to read their sentences.
- Call on students to read their sentences to the class.

BIG PICTURE GRAMMAR EXPANSION ACTIVITY: Yesterday

- Photocopy and distribute Worksheet 20: Yesterday.
- Put the transparency for Unit 9 on the OHP or have students look at the Big Picture in their books.
- Go over the directions and the example.
- Have students complete the worksheet.
- Put students in pairs to compare answers.
- Go over the answers with the class.

1. c; 2. d; 3. a; 4. b

❸ WHAT ABOUT YOU? Complete the sentences. Use the affirmative or negative past tense of the verb.

- Go over the directions and the example.
- Have students complete the sentences.
- Put students in pairs to read their sentences.
- Call on students to read their sentences to the class.

WORKSHEET 20 ANSWER KEY

1. fixed; 2. cooked; 3. didn't work;
4. delivered; 5. used; 6. read; 7. didn't go;
8. didn't drive; 9. didn't fix; 10. talked

ANSWER KEY

Answers will vary.

MATH: Pay Stubs

Read Ken's pay stub for last week. Match.

- Direct students' attention to the pay stub. Make sure they understand that this is the information attached to a paycheck.
- Go over the directions and the example.
- Have students write the letter on the line to complete the sentences.
- Go over the answers with the class.

CULTURE/CIVICS NOTES

- Point out that the pay stub provides important information but should be detached before the check is deposited or cashed. Employees should save their pay stubs.
- Point out that money is deducted from most paychecks: for state and federal taxes, for Social Security, and sometimes for benefits.

ACADEMIC CONNECTION: Educational background

- Point out that we usually have to give our educational background on employment applications and applications for schools and colleges.
- Write headings on the board: *Name of school, When attended, Degree or certificate.*
- Model the activity. Write your information on the board under the appropriate headings.
- Have students list all the schools they have attended and when. If students received a diploma, certificate or degree, help them to write the appropriate information.
- Put students in pairs to talk about their educational background.

LESSON 6: Apply Your Knowledge

OBJECTIVES

Understand job ads
Interview for a job

COMPETENCIES

Reading job ads
Identifying common occupations and job skills
Answering questions
Interpret general work-related vocabulary
Respond to interview questions
Follow procedures to apply for a job

❶ READ the job ads. Circle the abbreviations (*FT, PT, M-F, exper.*).

- Go over the directions.
- Have students circle the abbreviations.
- Go over the answers with the class.

ANSWER KEY

exp., PT, FT, M-W

❷ WRITE the word next to the abbreviation.

- Go over the directions and the example.
- Have students write the full forms next to the abbreviations.
- Go over the answers with the class.

ANSWER KEY

1. full-time; 2. part-time; 3. Monday through Wednesday; 4. experience

❸ WRITE. Look at the job ads again. Complete the chart.

- Go over the directions and the example.
- Have students complete the chart.

- Put students in pairs to compare charts.
- Go over the answers with the class.

ANSWER KEY

Position	Skills	How to apply
Electrician's Assistant	Fix wiring, fix other electrical problems	Call 555-9012
Restaurant Manager	Supervise servers, schedule workers, order food.	Apply in person
Cook	Prepare salads and soups	Apply in person
Office Assistant	Use computer and copier, answer phones	Call 555-6600

❹ LISTEN. What job from Activity 1 is good for each person? Complete the chart.

- Go over the directions.
- Play the CD and have students complete the chart. Repeat if necessary.
- Put students in pairs to compare charts.
- Go over the answers with the class.

LISTENING SCRIPT
Lesson 6, Activity 4

TCD3, 22

Listen. What job from Activity 1 is good for each person? Complete the chart.

1: In my last job, I used the cash register and served customers at a restaurant.

2: In my last job, I used a computer and answered the phone.

3: I can fix anything. I worked at a small company. I fixed electrical problems.

4: I need a job. I can cook all types of food. In my last job, I worked at a hospital. I made salads and cooked meals.

EXPANSION ACTIVITY: Dictation

- Play the CD as many times as necessary. Pause after each item so students can write the sentences.
- Put students in pairs to compare sentences.
- Have volunteers write the sentences on the board.

🎧 **5 LISTEN** and read.

- Direct students' attention to the picture. Ask questions: *Who do you see? Where are they?*
- Have students follow along and repeat as you say the conversation or play the CD.
- Ask comprehension questions: *What was his last job? What did he do?*
- Play the CD again and have students repeat.
- Put students in pairs to take turns reading the two parts.

GRAMMAR NOTE

Students will learn the past tense of *be* in Unit 10. For now, just point out that *was* is the past of *be*.

CULTURE/CIVICS NOTES

- Point out that in job interviews in the United States, applicants usually describe their past work experience, including positions and duties. Interviewers often ask why the applicant left their previous jobs.
- Explain that it is important to be honest in interviews, but that students should also sound professional and responsible. For example, it is better to say *I wanted a part-time job,* than to say *I didn't want to work very hard.*

6 PRACTICE THE CONVERSATION with a partner. Use the past tense.

- Go over the directions and the information.
- Model the activity with a student. Have the student read B's lines. Use the information from 1.
- Put students in pairs. Have students take turns asking and answering questions using the information in Activity 6.
- Walk around the room to monitor the activity and provide help as needed.
- Have pairs of students say the conversations in front of the class.

7 WHAT ABOUT YOU? Talk with a partner. Ask and answer questions about skills and jobs.

- Go over the directions and the example conversation.
- Model the activity with a more advanced student. Have the student ask you questions. Respond with your information.
- Put students in pairs to take turns asking and answering questions about skills and jobs.
- Walk around the room to monitor the activity and provide help as needed.
- Have pairs of students say the conversations in front of the class.

ACADEMIC CONNECTION: Internet research

- For an out-of-class assignment, have students go online and research "interview questions."
- Call on students to tell the class one question that is commonly asked in job interviews.
- Write the questions on the board.

LESSON 7: Reading and Writing

Understand and fill out a job applications

Use headings to find information on a form

Always edit important documents and forms

Complete job applications

Reading

1 THINK ABOUT IT. What can you do to find a job?

- Put students in pairs to answer the question.
- Elicit ideas and write them on the board.

2 BEFORE YOU READ. Look at the application. Match the heading to the definition.

- Go over the tip in the box.
- Go over the directions.
- Have students match the heading to the information.
- Go over the answers with the class.

ANSWER KEY

1. c; 2. b; 3. a

3 READ the application. Answer the questions below.

- Go over the directions and the example.
- Have students read the application and answer the questions.
- Put students in pairs to compare answers.
- Go over the answers with the class.

ANSWER KEY

1. office manager; 2. Monday through Friday; 3. 8–5; 4. can use a computer, can use a scanner, good people skills, can speak Spanish and English; 5. Oakton Dental Group; 6. She ordered office supplies, answered the phone, and made copies.

BIG PICTURE READING EXPANSION ACTIVITY: Application Forms

- Photocopy and distribute Worksheet 21: Application Forms
- Put the transparency for Unit 9 on the OHP or have students look at the Big Picture in their books.
- Go over the directions.
- Have students read the excerpts from job applications and write the character's name after the application.
- Put students in pairs to share their ideas.
- Go over the answers with the class.

WORKSHEET 21 ANSWER KEY

1. Maria; 2. Yuri; 3. Kathy; 4. Ana

Writing

❶ WRITE. Answer the questions.

- Go over the directions.
- Model the activity. Read each question aloud and answer it for yourself.
- Have students answer the questions. If students have difficulty naming the job they would like, ask them to choose a job they might want for a short period of time.
- Put students in pairs to talk about their answers.

❷ WRITE. Complete the job application.

- Go over the directions.
- Have students complete the application for themselves.
- Walk around to monitor the activity and provide help as needed.

❸ EDIT your application.

- Go over the tip in the box.
- Read each question aloud.
- Have students use the questions to edit their applications, checking the box as they finish each item.

BIG PICTURE WRITING EXPANSION ACTIVITY: Abdul and Trung

- Put the transparency for Unit 9 on the OHP or have students look at the Big Picture in their books.
- Have students write one sentence about a skill and one sentence about a job responsibility for Abdul and Trung for a total of four sentences.
- Put students in pairs to read their sentences.
- Ask volunteers to read sentences to the class.

EXPANSION ACTIVITY: Pair Interview

- Photocopy and distribute Worksheet 22: Pair Interview.
- Go over the directions.
- Read each question aloud and have students repeat.
- Put students in pairs to take turns asking and answering the questions to complete the job application for their partners.
- Walk around to monitor the activity and provide help as needed.

Career Connection

OBJECTIVE

Set employment goals

COMPETENCIES

Understand job evaluations

🎧 **1 READ** and listen. Then practice with a partner.

- Direct students' attention to the photos. Tell students this is the continuation of the story about Isabel. Have students point to Isabel in the photos.
- Play the CD and have students follow along silently.
- Play the CD again and have students repeat.
- Put students in pairs to take turns reading the roles of Isabel and her boss Laura.
- Ask *Is Isabel doing a good job?*

CULTURE/CIVICS NOTE

Point out that in job evaluations, it is a good idea to say you will do better in the future if there is something you need to improve.

2 WRITE. Complete the chart.

- Go over the directions and the example.
- Have students complete the chart.
- Go over the answers with the class.

ANSWER KEY

Things Isabel did well	Things Isabel needs to improve
Learned the new computer system Worked hard	spelling

3 WHAT ABOUT YOU? Talk with a partner. Ask and answer the questions.

- Go over the directions.
- Read each question and have students repeat.
- Put students in pairs to ask and answer the questions.
- Call on students to tell the class about something they did well or something they can improve.

COMMUNITY CONNECTION: Job evaluation forms

- As an out-of-class assignment, have students bring in job evaluation forms. They can either pick one up at their workplace or they can go online to download one.
- Put students in pairs to talk about the information on the forms.
- Elicit examples of information on evaluation forms and write them on the board.

CHECK YOUR PROGRESS!

- Have students circle the answers.
- Have students check whether each answer is right or wrong.
- Have students total their correct answers and fill in the chart.
- Have students create a learning plan and/or set learning goals.

ANSWER KEY

1. fix; 2. use; 3. can take; 4. studied; 5. didn't; 6. worked; 7. cars; 8. an electrician; 9. an accountant; 10. painted; 11. cleaned; 12. used

Unit Overview

LESSON	OBJECTIVE	STUDENT BOOK	WORKBOOK
1 Grammar and Vocabulary 1	Use the past tense of *be* to talk about transportation	p. 150	p. 128
2 Grammar Practice Plus	Use past time phrases	p. 152	p. 129
3 Listening and Conversation	Interpret a bus schedule Apologize for being late	p. 154	p. 130
4 Grammar and Vocabulary 2	Ask and answer questions with past tense of *be*	p. 156	p. 132
5 Grammar Practice Plus	Use adjectives Interpret a train schedule	p. 158	p. 133
6 Apply Your Knowledge	Understand advertisements Complete a questionnaire	p. 160	p. 134
7 Reading and Writing	Guess meaning through context	p. 162	p. 136
• Career Connection	Respond to an emergency in the workplace	p. 164	p. 138
• Check Your Progress	Monitor progress	p. 156	p. 140

Reading/Writing Strategies

- Guess the meaning of new words through context.
- Check and edit sentences for subject/verb agreement.

Connection Activities

LESSON	TYPE	SKILL DEVELOPMENT
1	Academic	Create pie charts
2	Community	Research travel options
3	Academic	Research and report on tardiness and absence policies
4	Community	Identify local attractions
5	Community	Calculate travel times
6	Community	Research travel bargains
8	Community	Identify evacuation plans

WORKSHEET #/FOCUS	TITLE	TEACHER'S EDITION
23 Grammar, Literacy	Paul and James	p. 268
24 Grammar	More about Paul's Trip	p. 269
25 Reading	Definitions	p. 270

LESSON 1: Grammar and Vocabulary

OBJECTIVE

Use the past tense of be to talk about
   transportation

VOCABULARY

airplane	platform
airport	ticket counter
baggage claim	train
bus	train station
bus stop	

GRAMMAR

Simple past tense of *be*

COMPETENCIES

Use the past tense of be to communicate about
   past locations, feelings, occupations and time
   references
Identify forms of transportation

WARM-UP ACTIVITY: Unit opener

- Put the transparency for Unit 10 on the
  overhead projector (OHP) or have students look
  at the Big Picture on page 153.
- Elicit words the students know and write them
  on the board.

🎧 ❶ GRAMMAR PICTURE DICTIONARY.
   Listen and repeat.

- Have students open their books and look at the
  pictures. Ask *What do you see?* Write all the
  words the students know on the board.
- Say the sentences or play the CD and have
  students repeat.
- Say sentences or new vocabulary words in
  random order and have students point to the
  pictures.

- Put students in pairs and take turns saying the
  sentences or words in random order as their
  partner points to the picture.

PRONUNCIATION NOTE

Point out that we often link an ending consonant
sound of one word to a beginning vowel sound of
the next (*was on, were at*).

EXPANSION ACTIVITY: What's there?

- Put students in pairs or small groups.
- Give students three minutes to list as many
  things as they can that are at an airport, a
  train station and a bus station.
- After three minutes, ask how many things
  they listed for each place. Elicit ideas and
  write them on the board.

❷ **NOTICE THE GRAMMAR.** Look at Activity 1.
   Underline *was* and *were*.

- Have students read the sentences and
  underline *was* and *were*. Then have students
  circle *isn't* and *aren't*.

ANSWER KEY

1. I <u>was</u> on an airplane.
2. Roger <u>was</u> on a train.
3. Anna <u>was</u> on a bus.
4. Don <u>was</u> at the airport.
5. Mia <u>was</u> at the train station.
6. Helen <u>was</u> at the bus stop.
7. Jack and Tim <u>were</u> at the baggage claim.
8. Hector and Rosa <u>were</u> on the platform.
9. Paula <u>was</u> at the ticket counter.

GRAMMAR CHART: The Simple Past Tense of _Be_

- Direct students' attention to the chart.
- Go over the information on the chart and the usage note. You may want to read the sentences, pausing to have students repeat.

CHART EXPANSION ACTIVITY: Present to past

- Call on students and say a sentence in the present tense (_I am happy._). Elicit the past tense (_I was happy._).

❸ CIRCLE _was_ or _were._

- Go over the directions and the example.
- Have students circle _was_ or _were._
- Put students in pairs to check their answers.
- Go over the answers with the class.
- Put students in pairs to practice reading the questions and answers.

ANSWER KEY

1. was; 2. were; 3. were; 4. were; 5. was; 6. was; 7. were

EXPANSION ACTIVITY: Negative rewrite

- Write the first sentence on the board (_I was at the airport at 10:00 last night._). Then rewrite it in the negative with a different complement (_I wasn't at the train station._).
- Have students rewrite the sentences in Activity 3, following the model on the board.
- Put students in pairs to compare sentences.
- Have volunteers write sentences on the board.

❹ WHAT ABOUT YOU? Complete the sentences. Use _was._

- Model the activity. Tell what you were doing or where you were at each of the times. Review prepositions of location with students if necessary.
- Have students complete the sentences.
- Put students in pairs to read their sentences.
- Call on students to read a sentence to the class.

ACADEMIC CONNECTION: Pie charts

- Have students talk to eight classmates to find out where they were at one of the times in Activity 4.
- Have students create pie charts to illustrate where their eight classmates were. Students can refer to Unit 4 to review pie charts.
- Walk around to monitor the activity and provide help as needed.

LESSON 2: Grammar Practice Plus

OBJECTIVE
Use past time phrases

VOCABULARY	
crowded	noisy
early	on time
empty	quiet
late	

GRAMMAR
Simple past of *be*

COMPETENCIES
Use descriptive adjectives

WARM-UP ACTIVITY: Opposites

- Write *Opposite pairs* on the board.
- Elicit examples from earlier lessons (*messy-neat, tall-short*), and write them on the board.
- Tell students that some of the new words are also opposite pairs.
- Have students look at the new words and guess which ones are opposite pairs.

1 WRITE. Complete the sentences with *was* or *were*.

- Go over the directions and the example.
- Have students write *was* or *were* on the lines to complete the sentences.
- Put students in pairs to compare answers.

LISTEN and repeat. Are your answers correct?

- Play the CD and have students repeat. Have students check their answers.

LISTENING SCRIPT
Lesson 2, Activity 1

TCD3, 26

Listen and repeat. Are your answers correct?

1. Three students were early yesterday.
2. Four students were on time yesterday.
3. One student was late.
4. The classroom was crowded at 11:00.
5. The classroom was empty last night.
6. The students were noisy yesterday.
7. The teacher was quiet this morning.

ANSWER KEY
1. were; **2.** were; **3.** was; **4.** was; **5.** was; **6.** were; **7.** was

EXPANSION ACTIVITY: Beanbag toss

- Call on a student, toss the beanbag, and say a word. Elicit the opposite.
- Continue until everyone has had a chance to participate. For more advanced classes, you may want to have students call on their classmates, taking turns saying words and eliciting opposites.

2 WRITE sentences. Use the negative form of the verb.

- Go over the directions and the example. Make sure students understand that they are to use the negative form of the verb and the adjective that means the opposite.
- Have students write sentences.
- Put students in pairs to compare sentences.
- Go over the answers with the class.

ANSWER KEY

1. It wasn't neat. 2. It wasn't empty. 3. They weren't noisy. 4. It wasn't early./It wasn't late. 5. They weren't quiet.

EXPANSION ACTIVITY: Describe a place

- Model the activity. Describe a place you were yesterday and the people in that place (e.g., *The supermarket was quiet last night. It was empty. There weren't many people in the store.*).
- Have students choose a place and write three sentences.
- Put students in pairs to read their sentences.
- Call on students to read their sentences to the class.

3 WHAT ABOUT YOU? Circle the correct word(s).

- Go over the directions.
- Have students circle the answer.
- Put students in pairs to compare answers.
- Call on students and elicit their answers.

ANSWER KEY

Answers will vary.

4 TALK about the pictures.

- Go over the directions.
- Direct students' attention to the Big Picture and to different frames of the story and elicit sentences.
- Put students in pairs. Have students take turns describing the situation in each picture.

5 LISTEN. Circle *True* or *False*.

- Go over the directions.
- Have students check the boxes for the answer as you say the questions or play the CD.
- Put students in pairs to compare answers.
- Say the questions or play the CD again so students can confirm.
- Go over the answers with the class.

LISTENING SCRIPT
Lesson 2, Activity 5
TCD3, 27

Listen. Circle *True* or *False*.

1. The airport was empty.
2. The flight was noisy.
3. The train was crowded.
4. The street was noisy.

ANSWER KEY

1. False; 2. True; 3. True; 4. True

BIG PICTURE CONVERSATION/ VOCABULARY EXPANSION ACTIVITY: Team challenge

- Divide the class into teams. Have each team write 10 or more true or false sentences about the pictures. Remind students to use the past tense, but they can use any verbs they know.
- Give students two minutes to look at the picture.
- With books closed, call on a student to read a sentence to a member of the opposite team. Elicit if the sentence is true or false. Each incorrect answer earns the sentence-posing team a point.
- Continue to call on different students, alternating teams.

6 WRITE sentences about the pictures. Use *was*, *wasn't*, *were*, or *weren't*.

- Go over the directions and the example.
- Have students write sentences.
- Put students in pairs to compare sentences.
- Go over the answers with the class.

ANSWER KEY

1. The airplane wasn't quiet. **2.** The weather was rainy. **3.** The children were noisy. **4.** The baggage claim area and train were crowded.

BIG PICTURE LISTENING EXPANSION ACTIVITY: Paul and James

- Have students look at the Big Picture or put the color overhead transparency for Unit 10 on the OHP.
- Photocopy and distribute Worksheet 23: Paul and James.
- Read the following story about James. Have students complete the Venn diagram to compare Paul's trip with James's trip.
- Put students in pairs to compare ideas.
- Copy the diagram on the board.
- Have volunteers complete the diagram.
- SCRIPT: *James went to Haiti last week. He called a taxi to take him to the airport. The airport wasn't crowded. The airplane was almost empty. It was a very quiet trip. From the airport in Haiti, James took a bus to his hotel. The bus was very hot and crowded.*

WORKSHEET 23 ANSWER KEY

Paul: took a trip, took a taxi, airport was crowded, plane was crowded, noisy trip, took a train from airport, rainy weather
James: took a trip, took a taxi, airport wasn't crowded, plane was almost empty, quiet trip, took a bus from the airport, hot weather
Both: took a trip, took an taxi, took an airplane

7 TALK. Think about Paul's trip. What happened next? Tell a partner.

- Go over the directions.
- Put students in pairs to talk about what happened next in the story.
- Call on students and elicit ideas.

ACADEMIC NOTE

Predicting is an important academic strategy that students should practice when they are reading.

EXPANSION ACTIVITY: Draw a story

- Have students draw a story about a trip they took in the past.
- Put students in pairs to talk about their picture stories.
- Call on students to tell their stories to the class.

COMMUNITY CONNECTION: The best way to go

- As on out-of-class assignment, have students individually choose a destination they would like to go to.
- Have students research at least two ways they can go to that destination, and find out the following information: the price, the duration of the trip, and the possible times they could go.
- Put students in pairs to share what they found out.
- Call on students to tell the class which way they would go and why.

Unit 10 193

LESSON 3: Listening and Conversation

OBJECTIVES

Interpret a bus schedule
Apologize for being late

COMPETENCIES

Understand a bus schedule
Apologize for lateness

WARM-UP ACTIVITY: Travel problems

- Put students in pairs to talk about problems people have when they travel.
- Elicit ideas and write them on the board.

🎧 **❶ LISTEN** to the phone message. Circle the problem.

- Direct students' attention to the picture. Ask questions: *Who do you see? Where is she? What's wrong?*
- Say the message or play the CD and have students check the problem.
- Have students compare answers in pairs.
- Go over the answers with the class.

 LISTENING SCRIPT
Lesson 3, Activity 1

TCD1, 28

Listen to the phone message. Circle the problem.

> *Beep.* Hi, Patricia, this is Liza. I'm calling from the bus station in Orlando. The weather is terrible. My bus from Atlanta was late, so I didn't get the 1:45 bus to Miami. Now, I'm getting on the 3:15 bus. Can you pick me up at the Miami bus station?

ANSWER KEY

A

LISTEN AGAIN. Look at the bus schedule. Answer the questions.

- Direct students' attention to the schedule. Ask questions: *When does the A train depart? When does it arrive? How long is the trip?*
- Play the CD again and have students answer the questions. Point out that the message will tell students which bus, and the schedule will tell them the other information.
- Go over the answers with the class.

ANSWER KEY

1. C; **2.** $44.50; **3.** 6 hours, 5 minutes; **4.** 9:20

PRONUNCIATION: Interjections

🎧 **Ⓐ LISTEN** and repeat.

- Go over the information in the box about interjections.
- Play the CD or read the interjections and have students repeat.

🎧 **Ⓑ LISTEN** and circle the man's idea.

- Play the CD and have students circle the answer.
- Go over the answers with the class.

LISTENING SCRIPT
Lesson 3, Activity B

TCD3, 30

Listen and circle the man's idea.

1. *A:* Is the train here?
   B: Uh-huh. It's on Platform 2.
2. *A:* Is the bus here?
   B: Unh-uh. The bus comes at 4:00. It's only 3:30.
3. *A:* The meeting started at 9:00.
   B: Uh-oh. We're late.
4. *A:* Is the meeting over?
   B: Uh-huh. It's lunch time.
5.   Oh no! I missed my bus!

ANSWER KEY

1. C; 2. D; 3. A; 4. C; 5. B

 2 LISTEN and read.

- Direct students' attention to the picture. Ask questions: *Who do you see? Where are they?*
- Play the CD or read the conversation as students follow along silently.
- Play the CD or read the conversation again and have students repeat.
- Ask *Why was he late?*

EXPANSION ACTIVITY: Write sentences

- Have students write three sentences or questions that would lead to one of the interjections.
- Have students read a sentence to a classmate. Elicit an answer with an interjection from the classmate.
- Continue until everyone has had a chance to participate.

3 PRACTICE THE CONVERSATION with a partner.

- Go over the directions.
- Model the activity. Have a more advanced student read B's lines. Model how to substitute a different problem. Cue the student to substitute a different missed event.
- Put students in pairs to practice the conversation, making the appropriate substitutions.
- Walk around to monitor the activity and provide help as needed.
- Call on students to say the conversation to the class.

4 WHAT ABOUT YOU? Walk around the room and talk to your classmates. Complete the chart.

- Copy the chart on the board.
- Go over the directions and the example conversation.
- Model the activity. Ask a student if he or she was early to class today. If the answer is yes, ask for the student's name and write it on the chart on the board.
- Have students stand and walk around the room to talk to classmates and complete the chart.
- When students are finished, call on students to tell the class about someone on their charts (e.g., *Paula was on a bus at 8:00 last night.*).

ACADEMIC CONNECTION: Tardiness and absence policies

- Have students write up tardiness and absence policies for your school or classroom. Students can find policies online for some community colleges and adult schools. Otherwise, they can ask you or find out if there are published policies.
- Review the policies with your students. Ask students who work what the policies are at their workplaces.

LESSON 4: Grammar and Vocabulary

OBJECTIVE

Ask and answer questions with past tense of *be*

VOCABULARY

amusement park	interesting
beach	movie
boring	museum
exciting	relaxing
fun	scary
good	stressful

GRAMMAR

Yes/no questions with the past tense of *be*

COMPETENCIES

Describe events and trips

WARM-UP ACTIVITY: What did you do last weekend?

- Write the question on the board.
- Put students in pairs to talk about what they did last weekend. Remind students to use the simple past if possible.
- Call on students and elicit one thing they did last weekend.

🎧 ❶ GRAMMAR PICTURE DICTIONARY. Listen and repeat.

- Have students look at the picture. Ask *Who do you see?*
- Point to each person, say the relationship word and have students repeat.
- Play the CD or say the sentences and have students repeat.
- Say the words in random order and have the students point to the pictures.

EXPANSION ACTIVITY: Read with a partner

- Put students in pairs to take turns reading the questions and answers in Activity 1.

❷ NOTICE THE GRAMMAR. Look at Activity 1. Underline *was*. Circle *wasn't*.

- Have students underline *was* and circle *wasn't*.
- Go over the answers with the class.

ANSWER KEY

1. I went to the beach.
   Was it relaxing?
   No, it wasn't. It was stressful.
2. I went to a movie.
   Was it good?
   Yes, it was. It was exciting!
3. I went to a museum.
   Was it interesting?
   No, it wasn't. It was boring.
4. I went to an amusement park.
   Was it fun?
   Yes, it was. It was scary, too!

EXPANSION ACTIVITY: Follow-up questions

- Model the activity. Ask a student *What did you do last weekend?* When the student responds, ask a follow-up question (e.g., *Was it fun?*).
- Put students in pairs to practice asking follow-up questions.

GRAMMAR CHART: *Yes/No* Questions with the Past Tense of *Be*

- Go over the information in the chart.
- You may want to read the sample sentences in the chart and have students repeat.

CHART EXPANSION ACTIVITY: Pair practice

- Put students in pairs to practice asking and answering the questions in the chart.

3 WRITE. Complete the conversation with *was*, *were*, *wasn't* or *weren't*.

- Go over the directions and the example.
- Have students complete the conversations.
- Put students in pairs to compare answers.
- Go over the answers with the class.
- Have students practice reading the conversations in pairs.

ANSWER KEY

1. Was/wasn't; **2.** Were/were; **3.** Were/was; **4.** Was/wasn't; **5.** Was/wasn't

4 WHAT ABOUT YOU? Answer the questions about you.

- Go over the directions and the example conversation.
- Have students answer the questions.
- Put students in pairs to take turns asking and answering the questions.

COMMUNITY CONNECTION: Attractions

- Put students in small groups.
- For each adjective in Activity 1, have students brainstorm a list of places in your community that might be described by that adjective.
- Have students look up information for each place: location, hours, price.

LESSON 5: Grammar Practice Plus

OBJECTIVES

Use adjectives
Interpret a train schedule

VOCABULARY

beautiful	dirty
clean	fast
dangerous	slow

GRAMMAR

Yes/no questions with the past tense of *be*

MATH

Understand schedules

COMPETENCIES

Interpret transportation schedules

WARM-UP ACTIVITY: Picture prompts

- Bring in pictures of vacation spots from newspapers or magazines.
- Put students in pairs. Give each pair a picture.
- Have students write as many words as they can about the picture in two minutes.
- Elicit ideas from students and write them on the board.

❶ **WRITE.** Complete the sentences with *was* or *were*.

- Go over the directions and example.
- Have students write *was* or *were* on the lines.
- Play the CD and have students repeat and check their answers.
- Go over the answers with the class.

VOCABULARY NOTE

Four of the six new words are part of opposite pairs (*clean-dirty, fast-slow*). If students ask, point out that *safe* is the opposite of *dangerous* (in Lesson 7) and *ugly* is the opposite of *beautiful*.

LISTENING SCRIPT
Lesson 5, Activity 1

TCD3, 33

Listen and repeat. Are your answers correct?

1. The traffic was slow.
2. The roads were dangerous.
3. The mountains were beautiful.
4. The boat was fast.
5. The lake was clean.
6. The hotel was dirty.

ANSWER KEY

1. was; 2. were; 3. were; 4. was; 5. was; 6. was

EXPANSION ACTIVITY: Add to the description

- Have students look at the pictures from the warm-up activity again and add one sentence using a new word.

EXPANSION ACTIVITY: What is fast?

- Put students in pairs or small groups to list as many things as they can that are described by each adjective. Set a time limit of five minutes.
- At the end of five minutes, elicit ideas and write them on the board (e.g., *fast: airplanes, my watch, trains, racecar, horse, my brother Sam, holidays*).

2 **WHAT ABOUT YOU?** Write *Was* or *Were* to complete the questions. Answer the questions about your native country.

- Go over the directions and the example.
- Have students complete the questions.
- Have students answer the questions using full forms about the place they lived when they were children.
- Put students in pairs to ask and answer the questions.
- Ask students questions about their previous homes.

BIG PICTURE GRAMMAR EXPANSION ACTIVITY: More About Paul's Trip

- Photocopy and distribute Worksheet 24: More About Paul's Trip.
- Put the color transparency for Unit 10 on the OHP or have students look at the Big Picture in their books.
- Have students complete the worksheet.
- Put students in pairs to check their answers.
- Go over the answers with the class.
- Put students in pairs to practice asking and answering the questions.

WORKSHEET 24 ANSWER KEY

1. Was/No, the traffic was slow.
2. Were/No, they weren't shy.
3. Was/Yes, it was clean.
4. Were/No, they were wet.
5. Was/No, it wasn't.
6. Was/No, it wasn't.

---

3 **READ** the emails. Underline *was, wasn't, were,* and *weren't.*

- Go over the directions.
- Have students read the emails and underline the past tense forms of *be.*

- Put students in pairs to compare answers.
- Ask comprehension questions: *Who went to the beach? Who is Maria emailing? Where did Dan and Hugo go?*

4 **WRITE** questions about the emails. Use *was* or *were.*

- Go over the directions.
- Have students use the cues to write questions.
- Have volunteers write the questions on the board.
- Put students in pairs to take turns asking and answering the questions.

ANSWER KEY

1. Was Maria's vacation terrible? (No, it wasn't.);
2. Was Dan's vacation boring? (Yes, it was.);
3. Was Maria happy at the beach? (Yes, she was.);
4. Were Dan and Hugo happy to go home? (Yes, they were.); 5. Was Dan sick? (No, he wasn't.)

MATH: Understand Schedules

READ the train schedule. Compute how long each trip takes.

- Go over the directions and the example. Point out or elicit that students must figure out the time interval between the departure time and the arrival time and write it in the last column. For example, the difference between 6:23 and 7:35 A.M. is one hour and twelve minutes (1:12).
- Have students calculate the time for each train and write the information in the last column.
- Put students in pairs to compare answers.
- Go over the answers with the class.

ANSWER KEY

A. 1 hour, 12 minutes; B. 2 hours; C. 1 hour, 5 minutes; D. 1 hour, 17 minutes; E. 1 hour, 12 minutes; F. 1 hour, 22 minutes

CULTURE/CIVICS NOTES

- Public transportation often runs more frequently during rush hours. Encourage students to check rush hour versus off-peak schedules when they are using public transportation.
- In many metropolitan areas, there are multiple forms of public transportation. Students may want to look for express or direct trains if speed is an issue and local trains if they need to ride for shorter distances.

EXPANSION ACTIVITY: Slow to fast

- Put the trains in order from slow to fast.
- Go over the directions and the example. Make sure students understand the slowest train is on the left, the fastest on the right, and the others in order in between.
- Have students write the trains in order on the lines.
- Go over the answers with the class.

ANSWER KEY

Slow to fast: B, F, D, E, A, C

COMMUNITY CONNECTION: Bus or train schedule

- Have students get a bus or train schedule for your city.
- Have students choose two stops on the route, and calculate the time it takes to travel from one to the other.

LESSON 6: Apply Your Knowledge

OBJECTIVES

Understand advertisements
Complete a questionnaire

COMPETENCIES

Fill out forms
Understand ads

WARM-UP ACTIVITY

- Bring in ads for vacation spots around the country and the world. Display the ads and elicit where the place is.
- Ask students what are the best places to vacation in their countries.

❶ READ the ads. Circle the places.

- Go over the directions.
- Have students read the ads and circle the places.
- Go over the answers with the class.

ANSWER KEY

Circle: NC, mountains, Lake Vista Hotel, Brevard, Florida, San Fernandina Beach, Lost Lake, lake

EXPANSION ACTIVITY: Realia

- Have students find and bring in ads for vacation spots or bring in ads for them to see.
- Put students in pairs to talk about if they would want to go to that place, giving reasons.
- Call on students to tell the class about the vacation place and why they would or wouldn't want to go there.

❷ LISTEN. Where did Susan go on vacation? Check the correct ad in Activity 1.

- Play the CD and have students check the box under the ad that is in the conversation.

LISTENING SCRIPT
Lesson 6, Activity 2

TCD3, 34

Listen. Where did Susan go on vacation? Check the correct ad in Activity 1.

A: How was your vacation, Susan?
B: Okay, I guess.
A: Did you go to the mountains?
B: No, I was at the beach in San Fernandina.
A: How was the weather?
B: It was warm and rainy. But the hotel was really nice. My room was large and clean. It was a little noisy, though.
A: How did you get there?
B: By bus. Unfortunately, the bus was really slow and dirty.

ANSWER KEY

San Fernandina

LISTEN AGAIN and complete the form.

- Direct students' attention to the form. Ask: *What kind of form is it? When do people fill out forms like this?*
- Play the CD again and have students complete the form.
- Put students in pairs to compare answers.
- Go over the answers with the class.

ANSWER KEY

Name: _____Susan Miller_____

Tell us what you think . . .

1. How was your vacation?
   ☐ terrible ☐ bad ☑ okay ☐ good ☐ excellent

2. How was your room? (Check all that are true.)
   ☑ large   ☐ small
   ☑ clean   ☐ dirty
   ☐ quiet   ☑ noisy

3. How was the bus trip?
   ☐ fast   ☑ slow   ☐ clean   ☑ dirty

EXPANSION ACTIVITY: Role play

- Put students in pairs to practice playing the roles of Susan and her friend. Remind students to use the form to remember the information.

🎧 **3 LISTEN** and read.

- Direct students' attention to the picture. Ask questions: *Who do you see? Where are they?*
- Have students read and follow along silently as you play the CD.
- Have students follow along and repeat as you say the conversation or play the CD.
- Ask comprehension questions: *How was the vacation? How was the weather? How was the trip?*
- Put students in pairs to take turns reading the parts in the conversation.

4 PRACTICE THE CONVERSATION with a partner.

- Go over the directions and the information.
- Model the activity with a student. Have the students read A's lines. Demonstrate how to substitute the information in item 1.
- Put students in pairs. Have students take turns asking and answering questions about the vacations.

- Walk around the room to monitor the activity and provide help as needed.
- Have pairs of students say the conversations in front of the class.

5 WHAT ABOUT YOU? Complete the questionnaire about your last trip.

- Go over the directions. Point out that the trip doesn't have to be a vacation; it could be a visit or a business trip.
- Have students complete the questionnaire.
- Put students in pairs to talk about their trips.

COMMUNITY CONNECTION: Travel bargains

- Point out that we often look for bargains, or cheap prices, when we are planning at trip. Two popular ways to find bargains are looking at ads in the newspaper and going to online travel services (expedia.com, priceline.com, travelocity.com).
- Put students in pairs to select a destination they might want to go to for a weekend.
- Have students research their trip in the newspaper and online to find out the cost of traveling there (by plane, train, car, or bus) and to stay in a hotel. Have students report the cheapest option they can find.
- Call on students to report to the class.

LESSON 7: Reading and Writing

OBJECTIVE

Guess meaning through context

VOCABULARY

dangerous	rain
destination	shelter
electricity	snow
hurricane	wind

READING TIP

Look at sentences nearby to find the meaning of a new word

WRITING TIP

Check for subject-verb agreement

COMPETENCIES

Respond appropriately to weather emergencies

WARM-UP ACTIVITY

- Write four phrases on the board: *a good trip, a bad trip, a long trip, a fun trip.*
- Put students in pairs to talk about an example of each from their own experience.

Reading

1 THINK ABOUT IT. What are some problems people have on vacations?

- Read the question.
- Put students in pairs or small groups to answer the question.
- Brainstorm weather vocabulary (e.g., *hurricane, tornado, typhoon, monsoon, fire, drought, tsunami*).
- Write student ideas on the board.

2 BEFORE YOU READ. Look at the story and picture. Check the problems.

- Go over the directions.
- Have students check the problems they think will be in the story.
- Elicit ideas from the class.

ANSWER KEY

Too rainy, too windy, too hot

3 READ the story. Write the definitions of *hurricane* and *shelter.*

- Go over the tip in the box.
- Have students read the paragraph, or read the paragraph aloud sentence by sentence and have students repeat.
- Ask comprehension questions: *Where did Anna go? What weather problem did she have? What did they do?*
- Have students write the definitions of the two words.
- Go over the definitions with the class.

ACADEMIC NOTE

Students often become over-reliant on their dictionaries or translators. Point out that it takes a lot of time to look words up and it is not always possible. Elicit or explain the advantages of figuring out the meaning of a new word by looking at nearby sentences, or the context in general (it takes less time, you develop skills, you don't have to stop your reading).

ANSWER KEY

Hurricane: a weather problem, weather that is very windy, rainy and dangerous
Shelter: a safe place, not dangerous

4 WRITE sentences about Anna's vacation.

- Go over the directions.
- Have students write sentences in the chart.
- Put students in pairs to read their sentences aloud.
- Call on student to read their sentences to the class.

Place: Anna went to Florida.
Weather: The weather was hot and sunny. Then there was a hurricane. It rained.
Problems: The roads were dangerous. There was no electricity. There were no trains, buses or airplanes.

EXPANSION ACTIVITY: Literacy development—sentence strips

- Copy the sentences from the paragraph onto separate strips. Leave enough space between each word for word discrimination. The sentences need to be large enough to be read by all the students.
- Put the sentence strips on the board in the correct order. Read each sentence aloud and have students repeat. You may want to point to each word as you read.
- Take the sentences down and mix them up.
- Have volunteers come to the board and put the sentences in the correct order. Have the other students help.
- You may want to photocopy the sentences and cut them into strips so that each student or pair of students has a set to reassemble.

BIG PICTURE READING EXPANSION ACTIVITY: Definitions

- Photocopy and distribute Worksheet 25: Definitions.
- Put the transparency for Unit 10 on the OHP or have students look at the Big Picture in their books.
- Go over the directions. Have students write the definitions for the words in bold.
- Put students in pairs to share their ideas.
- Go over the answers with the class.

WORKSHEET 25 ANSWER KEY

1. a; 2. c; 3. b; 4. a; 5. a

Writing

- Go over the writing tip in the box.

1 EDIT. Read the story. Find three errors with *was/wasn't/were/weren't.* Correct the errors.

- Go over the directions and the example.
- Have students find and correct three more errors.
- Go over the errors with the class.

ANSWER KEY

Last winter, my family went to the mountains. The car ride ~~were~~ was long. At first, the weather ~~were~~ was rainy and cold. We weren't happy. The vacation ~~were~~ was boring. Then it snowed. We ~~was~~ were very excited. After that, the vacation was fun.

2 WRITE five sentences about your trip. Use the simple past tense.

- Go over the directions.
- Write questions on the board: *Where did you go? How was the weather? How did you get there? Was it fun?*
- Have students write sentences. Suggest students use the questions on the board to get ideas.
- Walk around to monitor the activity and provide help as needed.
- Put students in pairs to read their sentences.
- Call on students to read their sentences to the class.

EXPANSION ACTIVITY: Who is it?

- Have students rewrite all their sentences on a separate sheet of paper.
- Collect the papers. Read a paragraph aloud to the class and elicit guesses as to who wrote the paragraph.
- Continue with other papers.
- In a variation, put students in small groups. Collect their papers and redistribute. Have students guess which group member wrote the paragraph.

---

3 EDIT. Work with a partner. Read your partner's sentences. Correct errors in the past tense form.

- Go over the directions.
- Put students in pairs to exchange and edit their sentences.
- Have students correct their own sentences after their partners' edits.

BIG PICTURE WRITING EXPANSION ACTIVITY—Paul's Story

- Put the transparency for Unit 10 on the OHP or have students look at the Big Picture in their books.
- Have each student write the story presented in the Big Picture in sentences. Remind students to use the past tense.
- Put students in pairs to talk about their ideas.
- Ask volunteers to read sentences to the class.

Career Connection

OBJECTIVE

Respond to an emergency in the workplace

COMPETENCIES

What to do during a tornado

WARM-UP ACTIVITY: Weather emergencies

- Bring in pictures of different weather emergencies and natural disasters.
- Elicit the names for each problem and write them on the board.

🎧 **1 READ AND LISTEN.** Then practice with a partner.

- Direct students' attention to the photos. Tell students this is the continuation of the story about Isabel. Have students point to Isabel.
- Play the CD and have students follow along.
- Play the CD again and have students repeat.
- Put students in pairs to take turns reading the roles of Isabel and her coworker.
- Ask *What is the weather emergency?*

2 WRITE. Answer the questions.

- Go over the directions.
- Have students answer the questions.
- Go over the answers with the class.

ANSWER KEY

1. a tornado; 2. went under a desk

3 CHECK. What should you do if there is a tornado?

- Go over the directions.
- Have students check the procedures.
- Go over the answers with the class.

ANSWER KEY

Go to a safe room in the building. Go under a desk. Cover your head.

COMMUNITY CONNECTION: School and work evacuation plan

- Have students find the evacuation routes for your school. These are usually posted in classrooms or on hall walls. If your school doesn't have them, ask for the procedures and go over them with your students.
- Have students find out their evacuation routes/plans at their jobs. Call on students to share the plan with the class.

EXPANSION ACTIVITY: FEMA website

- Have students go to www.fema.gov and look at the topics under *Get Disaster Information.*
- Assign a weather disaster topic and have students print the fact sheets for each.
- Have students share the information.

CHECK YOUR PROGRESS!

- Have students circle the answers.
- Have students check whether each answer is right or wrong.
- Have students total their correct answers and fill in the chart.
- Have students create a learning plan and/or set learning goals.

ANSWER KEY

1. was; 2. wasn't; 3. were; 4. Was; 5. Were; 6. Was; 7. train; 8. bus; 9. late; 10. boring; 11. relaxing; 12. dangerous

UNIT 11 Health Matters

Unit Overview

LESSON	OBJECTIVE	STUDENT BOOK	WORKBOOK
1 Grammar and Vocabulary 1	Use *have* to describe ailments	p. 166	p. 142
2 Grammar Practice Plus	Identify parts of the body Use *have* to describe ailments	p. 168	p. 143
3 Listening and Conversation	Take a phone message Call in sick to work	p. 170	p. 144
4 Grammar and Vocabulary 2	Give advice with *should* Describe remedies	p. 172	p. 146
5 Grammar Practice Plus	Understand medicine labels	p. 174	p. 147
6 Apply Your Knowledge	Understand an appointment card Describe health problems to a doctor	p. 176	p. 148
7 Reading and Writing	Identify healthy habits	p. 178	p. 150
• Career Connection	Demonstrate a positive attitude at work	p. 180	p. 152
• Check Your Progress	Monitoring progress	p. 181	p. 154

Reading/Writing Strategies

- Use pictures to guess meaning of new words.
- Indent the first sentence of a paragraph.

Connection Activities

LESSON	TYPE	SKILL DEVELOPMENT
1	Community	Discuss medical attention
2	Academic	Compare and contrast symptoms
3	Community	Research school sickness policies
4	Community	Interview to gain information
6	Academic	Understand degrees and credentials

WORKSHEET #/FOCUS	TITLE	TEACHER'S EDITION
26 Grammar	What Should They Do?	p. 271
27 Reading	Tips for Airline Travel	p. 272

LESSON 1: Grammar and Vocabulary

OBJECTIVE

Use *have* to describe ailments

VOCABULARY

backache	headache
cold	runny nose
cough	sore throat
earache	stomachache
fever	toothache
flu	

GRAMMAR

Have for health problems

COMPETENCIES

Recognize body parts
Vocabulary for illness/accidents

WARM-UP ACTIVITY: Unit opener

- Put the transparency for Unit 11 on the overhead projector (OHP) or have students look at the Big Picture on page 169.
- Elicit words the students know and write them on the board.

🎧 ❶ GRAMMAR PICTURE DICTIONARY. Listen and repeat.

- Have students open their books and look at the pictures. Ask *What do you see?* Write all the words the students know on the board.
- Say the sentences or play the CD and have students repeat.
- Say the sentences in random order and have students point to the picture.
- Put students in pairs and take turns saying the questions in random order as their partner points to the picture.

❷ **NOTICE THE GRAMMAR.** Look at Activity 1. Circle *have*. Underline *has*.

- Have students read the sentences and circle *have* and underline *has.*
- Ask questions: *What subject pronouns use has? Which ones use have?*

ANSWER KEY

1. She has the flu.
2. They have colds.
3. He has a fever.
4. She has a backache.
5. She has a headache.
6. He has a stomachache.
7. She has a sore throat.
8. He has a cough.
9. They have runny noses.

EXPANSION ACTIVITY: Replace the word

- Give students two minutes to review the sentences.
- Have students close their books.
- Write the sentences on the board but leave out all forms of the verb *have*.
- Elicit the missing words from the students.
- Have students open their books and confirm their answers.

GRAMMAR CHART: *Have* for Health Problems

- Direct students' attention to the chart or project the transparency or CD.
- Go over the information on the chart. You may want to read the questions and answers, pausing to have students repeat.
- Go over the usage and Professor notes.

CHART EXPANSION ACTIVITY: Negative statements

- Have students write a negative statement for each sentence in Activity 1. For example, the first sentence is *She has a cold.* Demonstrate creating a negative statement with another health problem (*She doesn't have the flu.*).
- Put students in pairs to read their sentences.
- Call on students to read negative statements to the class.

3 WRITE. Complete the sentences. Use *have, has, don't have,* or *doesn't have.*

- Go over the directions.
- Have students complete the sentences with *have* or *has.*
- Put students in pairs to check their answers.
- Go over the answers with the class.
- Put students in pairs to practice reading the sentences.

ANSWER KEY

1. have; 2. has; 3. don't have; 4. have; 5. don't have; 6. have; 7. doesn't have; 8. have; 9. has; 10. don't have

EXPANSION ACTIVITY: Question review

- Review how to make *yes/no* questions and short answers in the simple present with *have.*
- Have students write questions about the pictures in Activity 1 (*e.g., 1. Does she have a cold?*). Encourage students to write about different health problems in their questions.
- Have volunteers write the questions on the board.
- Put students in pairs to take turns asking and answering the questions.

4 GAME. Work in a small group. Act out a health problem. Your classmates guess your problem.

- Go over the directions.
- Model the activity. Act out a health problem and elicit what it is.
- Have students act out problems and elicit the name of the problem or illness from the class.

EXPANSION ACTIVITY: Past tense personalization

- Write *last year, last month,* and *last week* on the board.
- Model the activity. Point to each time expression and say a sentence about a health problem you had or didn't have at that time (e.g., *Last year, I had the flu. Last month, I didn't have a cold.*).
- Have students write sentences using each time expression and *had* or *didn't have* with a health problem.
- Put students in pairs to read their sentences.
- Call on students to tell the class about their partner.

COMMUNITY CONNECTION: ER or doctor

- Put students in small groups to discuss when they would go to the emergency room (ER) versus when they would go to the doctor.
- Have students confirm their guesses, using a search engine and "When to go to the ER."
- Elicit if any of the health problems in this lesson warrant a trip to the hospital or ER.

LESSON 2: Grammar Practice Plus

OBJECTIVES

Identify parts of the body
Use *have* to describe ailments

VOCABULARY

arm	head
back	hurt
ear	leg
foot/feet	neck
hand	stomach

GRAMMAR

Hurt for health problems

COMPETENCIES

Recognize body parts
Vocabulary for illness/accidents

WARM-UP ACTIVITY: Body part TPR (Total Physical Response)

- Model the activity. Say a body part and touch it.
- Continue to say body parts and have students touch the body part you say.
- As a variation, touch a body part and elicit the word.

❶ WRITE. Complete the sentences. Use a word in the box.

- Go over the directions and the example.
- Say each word in the box and have students repeat.
- Have students write the body part on the lines to complete the sentences.
- Put students in pairs to compare answers.

🎧 **LISTEN** and repeat. Are your answers correct?

- Play the CD and have students repeat. Have students check their answers.

 LISTENING SCRIPT
Lesson 2, Activity 1

TCD3, 38

Listen and repeat. Are your answers correct?

1. Samira's back hurts.
2. Antonio's head and neck hurt.
3. Eva's stomach hurts.
4. Ramon's ear hurts.
5. Rosa's hands and arms hurt.
6. Joe's legs and feet hurt.

ANSWER KEY

1. back; **2.** neck; **3.** stomach; **4.** ear; **5.** hands; **6.** feet

EXPANSION ACTIVITY: Beanbag toss

- With books closed, call on a student, toss the beanbag, and say something hurts (e.g., *My throat hurts.*). Elicit another way to say the health problem.
- Continue until everyone has had a chance to participate. Students can also call on their classmates, taking turns saying words and eliciting opposites.

LITERACY DEVELOPMENT ACTIVITY: Alphabetical order

- Write body parts on the board (*head, ear, eye, throat, chest, stomach, back, arm, leg, foot, hand, nose*).
- Have students rewrite the list in alphabetical order in their notebooks.

2 WRITE. Complete the email. Use *have*, *has*, *hurt*, or *hurts*.

- Go over the directions.
- Have students write *have, has, hurt,* or *hurts* on the lines.
- Put students in pairs to compare answers.
- Go over the answers with the class.

ANSWER KEY

1. have; 2. hurts; 3. hurts; 4. have; 5. have;
6. hurt

3 TALK about the picture.

- Go over the directions.
- Direct students' attention to the Big Picture or put the transparency on the OHP. Point to the baby and elicit a sentence.
- Put students in pairs. Have students take turns describing people and problems in the picture.
- Call on students. Point to different characters in the Big Picture and elicit sentences.

 4 LISTEN and complete the sentences.

- Go over the directions.
- Have students write the problem as you say the questions or play the CD.
- Put students in pairs to compare answers.
- Say the questions or play the CD again so students can confirm.
- Go over the answers with the class.

LISTENING SCRIPT
Lesson 2, Activity 4
TCD3, 39

Listen and complete the sentences.

1. Elena has a backache.
2. Eliza's ears hurt.
3. Alex has a stomachache.
4. Gloria's nose hurts.
5. Luis has a headache.
6. Ibrahim has a cold.

ANSWER KEY

1. backache; 2. ears; 3. stomachache; 4. nose;
5. headache; 6. cold

5 WRITE the names next to the people in the picture.

- Go over the directions.
- Have students write the names in the boxes. Remind students to look at Activity 4.
- Go over the answers with the class.

BIG PICTURE CONVERSATION/ VOCABULARY EXPANSION ACTIVITY: Who am I?

- Have students look at the Big Picture or put the transparency for Unit 11 on the OHP.
- Model the activity. Say several sentences about a character in the picture (e.g., *I have an earache. I am a baby. My mother is holding me.*). Elicit the name (*Eliza*).
- Put students in pairs or groups to practice describing and guessing characters.
- Call on students to say their sentences to the class and elicit the name from the other students.

6 TALK to a partner. Say how the people feel.

- Go over the directions and the example conversation.
- Say the question and have students repeat.
- Put students in pairs to take turns asking and answering questions about people in the picture.

ACADEMIC CONNECTION: Cold and flu

- Point out that comparing and contrasting is an important academic skill.
- Have students research cold versus flu symptoms.
- Elicit ideas and write them on the board.

LESSON 3: Listening and Conversation

OBJECTIVES

Take a phone message
Call in sick to work

COMPETENCIES

Take messages
Call to explain absence

WARM-UP ACTIVITY: When do you stay home?

- Put students in groups of three. Give each student a number in the group.
- Explain the activity. You will ask a question and students will discuss their answers in their groups. After a few minutes, you will say a number, and the student with that number will report the group's answers to the class.
- Ask questions related to health (*How many days did you miss work last year because of a health problem? How many days did you go to class when you weren't feeling well? What was your biggest health problem last year? Do you have health insurance?*). Call on different numbers to report the group's answers to each question.

 ❶ LISTEN. Complete the sentences. Use the words in the box.

- Go over the directions and the words in the box.
- Say the sentences or play the CD.
- Have students compare answers in pairs.
- Go over the answers with the class.

 LISTENING SCRIPT
Lesson 3, Activity 1

TCD3, 40

Listen. Complete the sentences. Use the words in the box.

1. *A:* Hi, Elga! Are you okay?
   B: Not really. I have a really bad stomachache. My head hurts too. . . . I think I have the flu.
   A: I'm sorry!

2. *A:* Jung, are you okay?
   B: I'm okay . . . my whole family is sick.
   A: I'm sorry to hear that!
   B: Yeah. We all have colds. We all have coughs, and our throats hurt a lot. Our ears hurt, too, and we have headaches.

3. *A:* Richard, what's wrong?
   B: Ooohhh . . . my back really hurts. I was in a car accident last weekend. Oooh. . . My head hurts, too.
   A: Oh no—I'm sorry. Call a doctor!

GRAMMAR NOTE

Elicit or explain the meaning of *really*—that we use it to express degree, that if something *really* hurts, it hurts a lot.

ANSWER KEY

1. the flu; 2. colds; 3. a backache

LISTEN AGAIN. Check the body parts that hurt.

- Play the CD again and have students check the body parts that hurt for each person or people.
- Go over the answers with the class.

Elga: stomach, head; Jung and her family: throat, ears, head; Richard: back, head

🎧 **2 LISTEN** to the conversations. Complete the messages.

- Direct students' attention to the message slips. Ask questions: *What are they? Who is calling in the first message? What date does he call? What's wrong with Patricia? When does Elga call?*
- Go over the directions.
- Play the CD and have students write the appropriate information on the message slips.
- Put students in pairs to compare messages.
- Go over the answers with the class.

🎧 **LISTENING SCRIPT**
Lesson 3, Activity 2

TCD3,
41–43   Listen to the conversations. Complete the messages.

1. *A:* AAA Construction Company.

   B: Mrs. Green? Hi, this is Radek.

   A: Oh hi, Radek! Are you okay?

   B: Not really. I have the flu. I can't come to work today.

   A: Oh, that's too bad!

   B: Can you tell Mr. Howard for me?

   A: Sure.

2. Please leave a message after the tone. {BEEP} Hi, Mr. Brown. This is Patricia. I can't work today. I have a cold and a bad headache. Can Isaac work instead? Thanks. {BEEP. [automated voice: "Monday, September 4, 10:24 A.M."]}

3. *A:* Hi, Maria? This is Audrey. I know it's 9:30 already, but I can't come to work today.

   B: Oh no. Why not?

   A: I have a terrible backache.

   B: Oh, I'm sorry.

   A: I can't even walk.

   B: Oh, how awful.

   A: Can you tell Mrs. Smith?

   A: Yes, sure. Thanks for calling . . . Get better soon!

Message 1—the flu, He can't come to work
Message 2—Time: 10:24 A.M., Date: 9/4.
Message 3—Time: 9:30, backache/walk

EXPANSION ACTIVITY: Expressing sympathy

- Explain that when someone is sick, we usually express sympathy—say something to show we care and we want the person to feel better.
- Play the CD for Activity 2 and have students write the expressions of sympathy they hear.
- Elicit the expressions and write them on the board.

That's too bad, I'm sorry, how awful, get better soon

🎧 **3 LISTEN** and read.

- Direct students' attention to the picture. Ask questions: *Who do you see? What's happening?*
- Play the CD or read the conversation as students follow along silently.
- Play the CD or read the conversation again and have students repeat.
- Ask *What is the problem?*
- Put students in pairs to practice the conversation.

EXPANSION ACTIVITY: Conversation line-up

- Write each word from the conversation on a separate index card. If you have fewer students than words, write more than one word on a card.
- Shuffle the cards, then give a card to each student.
- Have students organize themselves to put the conversation back in order.
- Have students say their words in order to recreate the conversation. Encourage students to read their single words in such a way so that more natural speech is approached.

COMMUNITY CONNECTION: School policies

- Explain that many schools have policies regarding when students can be sent to school. For example, a school might say that a student cannot come to class until they have been fever-free for at least 24 hours.
- As an out-of-class assignment, have students find out the policy for a school in your area. Policies are usually written in parents' handbooks and can also be found online.
- Call on students to share what they found out.

4 PRACTICE THE CONVERSATION with a partner.

- Go over the directions.
- Model the activity. Have a more advanced student read A's lines. Model how to substitute a different name and problems.
- Put students in pairs to practice the conversation, making the appropriate substitutions.
- Walk around to monitor the activity and provide help as needed.
- Call on students to say the conversation to the class.

5 WRITE. You are sick. You can't go to class. You call your teacher. Write the conversation.

- Go over the directions and a sample conversation.
- Have students write a telephone conversation saying why they can't come to class.
- Have students work with a partner to practice their conversation with a partner.

EXPANSION ACTIVITY: Create a policy

- Put students in small groups to create a policy for your classroom regarding sickness and attendance.
- Have the groups share their ideas with the class. Vote on a policy for your class.

LESSON 4: Grammar and Vocabulary

OBJECTIVES

Give advice with *should*
Describe remedies

VOCABULARY

call 911	put on a bandage
drink liquids	rest
get a prescription	see a doctor
put ice on it	use a heating pad

GRAMMAR

Use the modal *should*

COMPETENCIES

Call 911
Give advice
Follow instructions

WARM-UP ACTIVITY: **Chart it**

- Write three headings on the board from left to right: *body part, problem, remedy.*
- Under body part, write *back,* and under problem, write *backache.* Elicit what students do when they have that problem. Write the ideas on the board.
- Put students in pairs to complete the chart for two more body parts and problems.
- Call on students to share their ideas with the class (*I have a backache. I go to bed.*).

🎧 ❶ GRAMMAR PICTURE DICTIONARY. Listen and repeat.

- Have students look at the picture. Ask *What problems do you see?*
- Play the CD or say the sentences and have students repeat.
- Say the sentences in random order and have the students point to the pictures.

EXPANSION ACTIVITY: **Call and response**

- Call on students and say one of the problems in random order (e.g., *They were in a car accident.*). Elicit the advice (e.g., *They should call 911.*).

❷ NOTICE THE GRAMMAR. Look at Activity 1. Underline *should.* Circle the verb.

- Go over the directions.
- Have students underline *should* and circle the verb.
- Go over the answers with the class.

ANSWER KEY

1. Lisa has the flu.
   She should (rest.)
   She should (drink) liquids.
2. Bill's back hurts.
   He should (use) a heating pad.
   He should (get) a prescription for a pain reliever.
3. Isha's fingers hurt.
   She should (put) ice on them.
   She should (put) on a bandage.
4. They were in a car accident.
   She should (call) 911.
   He should (see) a doctor.

GRAMMAR CHART: *Should* for Advice

- Go over the information in the chart, including the usage note.
- You may want to read the sample sentences in the chart and have students repeat.
- Point out that *should* is used like *can.* The form of *should* doesn't change, and it is followed by the base form of the verb.

CHART EXPANSION ACTIVITY: *Should I?*

- Ask the students questions beginning with *Should I: Should I write notes in my notebook? Should I write on the wall?*
- Elicit the appropriate answers.

3 WRITE. Complete the sentences with *should* or *shouldn't.*

- Go over the directions and the example.
- Have students complete the sentences with *should* or *shouldn't.*
- Put students in pairs to compare answers.
- Go over the answers with the class.

ANSWER KEY

1. shouldn't; 2. should; 3. should; 4. should;
5. shouldn't

EXPANSION ACTIVITY: Weather and advice

- Model the activity. Give a weather report (e.g., *Today is very cold and rainy. The temperature is 37 degrees.*). Elicit advice from students regarding clothing and behavior (*You should wear a coat. You should stay inside. You should drink hot liquids.*).
- Put students in pairs to write a weather report for one of the seasons of the year.
- Have students exchange weather reports with another pair and write advice.
- Call on students to read the weather report and advice to the class.

4 WHAT ABOUT YOU? Choose a health problem. Ask a partner for advice. Check your partner's answers.

- Go over the directions.
- Model the activity. Say you have a health problem (e.g., *My stomach hurts.*). Ask the questions.
- Put students in pairs to practice asking for and giving advice for health problems.

EXPANSION ACTIVITY: Vote with your feet

- Write *Yes* on one side of the board and *No* on the other.
- Have a group of students stand.
- Read statements such as the ones below and have students stand in front of the word that indicates their answer. Call on students on each side of the room to say more about their answers.
  I have a stomachache. I should eat food.
  I have a cold. I should stay in bed.
  I have the flu. I should go to the hospital.
  I have a fever. I should use a heating pad.
  I play soccer. My leg hurts. I should stop playing.

COMMUNITY CONNECTION: Interview

- Have students choose a health problem.
- Have students interview three people outside of class to find out what they think people should do for the health problem.
- Call on students to tell the class what they found out.

LESSON 5: Grammar Practice Plus

OBJECTIVE

Understand medicine labels

VOCABULARY

cough medicine	pain reliever
ear drops	throat lozenge

GRAMMAR

Should for advice

MATH

Understanding medicine and time

PRONUNCIATION

Should and *shouldn't*

COMPETENCIES

Read medicine labels
Use over-the-counter medications

WARM-UP ACTIVITY: Realia

- Bring in common medications or the packaging, or ads from magazines.
- Hold each up and elicit its name and what it is used for.
- Write the names students know on the board.

1 MATCH.

- Go over the directions and the example.
- Have students write the medicine on the lines.
- Put students in pairs to compare answers.

LISTEN and repeat. Are your answers correct?

- Play the CD and have students check their answers.
- Go over the answers with the class.

LISTENING SCRIPT
Lesson 5, Activity 1

TCD3, 46

Listen and repeat. Are your answers correct?

1. Mark has a cold.
   He should take cough medicine.
2. Musa has an earache.
   He should use ear drops.
3. Ellen's head hurts.
   She should take a pain reliever.
4. Tina has a sore throat.
   She should take a throat lozenge.

ANSWER KEY

1. b; 2. d; 3. a; 4. c

PRONUNCIATION: *Should* and *Shouldn't*

A LISTEN and repeat.

- Go over the directions.
- Play the CD and have students repeat.

B LISTEN. Circle *should* or *shouldn't*.

- Go over the directions and the example.
- Play the CD and have students circle the word they hear.
- Put students in pairs to compare answers.
- Go over the answers with the class.

LISTENING SCRIPT
Lesson 5, Activity B
TCD3, 48
Listen. Circle *should* or *shouldn't*.

1. Marco shouldn't call 911.
2. Henry should take cough medicine.
3. Sara should stay in bed.
4. Gloria should use ear drops.

ANSWER KEY

1. shouldn't; 2. should; 3. should; 4. should

C TALK. Read the sentences to a partner.

• Go over the directions.
• Put students in pairs to take turns reading the sentences.
• Walk around to monitor the activity and correct pronunciation if necessary.

2 WRITE the words in the chart.

• Read each word in the box and have students repeat.
• Go over the directions and the examples.
• Have students write the words in the correct columns in the chart.
• Put students in pairs to compare answers.
• Go over the answers with the class.

ANSWER KEY

PROBLEM	REMEDY
flu	sleep
cough	throat lozenge
sore throat	pain reliever
backache	rest
headache	drink liquids
cold	ear drops
stomachache	cough medicine
fever	bandage
	heating pad
	ice

3 WRITE advice for each person. Use remedies from the chart in Activity 2.

• Go over the directions.
• Direct students' attention to the first picture. Ask *What's the problem?*
• Read the first line of conversation 1. Elicit advice and have students write the advice on the lines.
• Have students write advice for each situation.
• Put students in pairs to compare ideas. Then have students practice the conversations with their partners.
• Call on students and elicit their advice for each situation.

EXPANSION ACTIVITY: Research

• Have students choose a health problem and then go online to research appropriate remedies. You may want to have them search for the problem and remedy.
• Put students in groups to talk about what they found out.
• Go over common health problems and elicit the remedies students researched.

BIG PICTURE GRAMMAR EXPANSION ACTIVITY: What Should They Do?

• Photocopy and distribute Worksheet 26: What Should They Do?
• Put the color transparency for Unit 11 on the OHP or have students look at the Big Picture in their books.
• Go over the directions.
• Have students complete the worksheet.
• Put students in pairs to compare answers.
• Go over the answers with the class.

WORKSHEET 26 ANSWER KEY

1. You should put a pillow behind your back.
2. You shouldn't eat all the food. 3. You should
put ice on it. 4. You should use ear drops or drink
something. 5. You should take cold medicine.

MATH: Medicine Labels

- Go over the directions.
- Direct students' attention to the label. Ask questions: *What kind of medicine is this? What is it for? How many should you take? How often can you take the medicine? Can young children take the medicine?*
- Have students answer the other questions.
- Go over the answers with the class.

ANSWER KEY

1. 6 P.M.; 2. no; 3. two; 4. no

CULTURE/CIVICS NOTE

Point out that aspirin is a pain reliever that is not safe for children to take.

LESSON 6: Apply Your Knowledge

OBJECTIVES

Understand an appointment card
Describe health problems to a doctor

VOCABULARY

appointment	group number
customer service	patient
family practice	policy number
fill prescription	

COMPETENCIES

Make and keep doctor's appointments
Understand medical forms

WARM-UP ACTIVITY: What to bring

- Put students in pairs to write down everything they need to bring when they go to the doctor's office.
- Elicit ideas and write them on the board (e.g., money, insurance card, medical forms if the first time, dictionary/translator).

❶ READ the appointment card and insurance card. Circle (the items):

- Go over the directions. Make sure students see that they are to circle four things.
- Have students read the cards and circle the information.
- Ask questions: *What is the patient's name? What is the date and time? What is the doctor's name? What is the policy number? What is the group number?*

ANSWER KEY

Circle: **1.** 1:45 P.M.; **2.** Carlos Rodriguez;
3. 108407; **4.** ATL1948

 ❷ LISTEN to the conversation. Complete the sentences.

- Go over the directions.
- Play the CD and have students complete the sentences.
- Put students in pairs to compare answers.
- Go over the answers with the class.

LISTENING SCRIPT
Lesson 6, Activity 2
TCD3, 49

Listen to the conversation. Complete the sentences.

A: Centerville Family Practice. Can I help you?

B: Hi, I need to make an appointment.

A: Are you a new patient?

B: Yes, I am.

A: Okay. There is an appointment on Friday, July 28th with Dr. Lopez.

B: Great. What time?

A: 1:45 P.M.

B: Okay.

A: What is your name?

B: Carlos Rodriguez.

A: And your phone number?

B: 973-1265.

A: What is your insurance?

B: Excellent Health Insurance. The policy number is 108407.

A: What is the reason for your visit?

B: I have a stomachache and a fever.

A: Okay. For the appointment, you should bring your insurance card. You should arrive 15 minutes early.

B: Okay. Thank you!

A: You're welcome. See you on Friday.

ANSWER KEY

1. Friday, July 28; **2.** 973-1265; **3.** a stomachache and a fever

---

EXPANSION ACTIVITY: Make an appointment

- Write the script on the board, leaving blanks for name, phone number, insurance information and symptoms.
- Put students in pairs to practice making doctors' appointments, substituting appropriate information for themselves.
- Have volunteers perform their conversations in front of the class.

---

❸ WRITE. Complete the Patient Information Form. Use the information in Activities 1 and 2.

- Go over the directions.
- Direct students' attention to the form. Ask questions: *What is his address? What is his date of birth? What city does he live in? Who is his employer?*
- Have students complete the patient information form.
- Go over the answers with the class.

ANSWER KEY

CENTERVILLE FAMILY PRACTICE

Name: *Carlos Rodriguez*   Date of Birth: *7/5/62*

Address: *4972 Brown Street*
Street

Centerville   *New York*   *14029*
City   State   Zip

Telephone: *973-1265*   *977-9241*
Home   Work

Insurance: *Excellent Health Insurance*

Policy Number: *108407*   New Patient: (Yes) No

Doctor's Name: *Dr. Lopez*

Reason for Visit: *Stomachache and fever*

🎧 ❹ LISTEN and read.

- Direct students' attention to the picture. Ask questions: *Who do you see? Where are they? What are they doing?*
- Have students follow along silently as you play the CD.
- Play the CD again and have students repeat.
- Ask comprehension questions: *Who is the patient? Why is he at the doctor's office? What is the problem? What is the advice?*
- Put students in pairs to take turns reading the parts of the patient and the person at the doctor's office.

❺ PRACTICE THE CONVERSATION with a partner.

- Model the activity with a student. Have the students read A's lines. Substitute the information in Activity 1 (*I have a cough.*).
- Put students in pairs. Have students practice the conversation, using the information in Activity 4. Monitor as needed.
- Have pairs of students say the conversations in front of the class.

❻ WHAT ABOUT YOU? Tell a partner about a health problem you or a family member has. Your partner gives advice.

- Go over the directions.
- Put students in pairs to practice saying symptoms and problems and giving advice.

ACADEMIC CONNECTION: Understanding degrees and credentials

- Assign students to research the degrees or training necessary for one of the following medical careers: Medical Technician, Certified Nursing Assistant (CNA), Licensed Practical Nurse (LPN), Registered Nurse (RN), and a Family Practitioner (MD).
- Put students in small groups to share what they found out.

LESSON 7: Reading and Writing

OBJECTIVE

Identify healthy habits

VOCABULARY

exercise	junk food
floss	relax
healthy	

READING TIP

Before you read, look at the pictures. Use the pictures to guess the meaning of new words.

WRITING TIP

A paragraph is a group of sentences about the same idea. Indent the first sentence of each paragraph.

COMPETENCIES

Read a health article

WARM-UP ACTIVITY: Habits

- Write *healthy habits* and *unhealthy habits* on the board.
- Elicit examples of each.

Reading

❶ THINK ABOUT IT. What do you do to be healthy?

- Read the question. Elicit answers from students.

❷ BEFORE YOU READ. Look at the pictures. What words can you say about each picture?

- Go over the tip in the box.
- Go over the directions.

- Have students list verbs to match the pictures.
- Put students in pairs to talk about their ideas.
- Elicit ideas from the class.

❸ READ the article. What is it about? Circle the answer.

- Have students read the paragraph, or read the paragraph aloud sentence by sentence and have students repeat.
- Have students circle what it is about.
- Go over the answer.
- Ask comprehension questions: *How many keys to good health does the article list? What should you eat? What shouldn't you eat? What else should you do? Should you drink a lot of water?*

ANSWER KEY

c

❹ MATCH the word with the definition.

- Go over the directions and the definitions.
- Have students write the letter of the definition next to the new word.
- Put students in pairs to compare ideas.
- Go over the answers with the class.

ANSWER KEY

1. d; 2. c; 3. a; 4. b

EXPANSION ACTIVITY: Literacy development—sentence strips

- Copy the sentences from the paragraph onto separate strips. Leave enough space between each word for word discrimination. The sentences need to be large enough to be read by all the students.
- Put the sentence strips on the board in the correct order. Read each sentence aloud and have students repeat. You may want to point to each word as you read.
- Take the sentences down and mix them up.
- Have volunteers come to the board and put the sentences in the correct order. Have the other students help.
- You may want to photocopy the sentences and cut them into strips so that each student or pair of students has a set to reassemble.

5 WRITE the five keys to good health.

- Go over the directions.
- Have students write the five keys.
- Put students in pairs to compare answers.
- Go over the answers with the class.

ANSWER KEY

1. Eat right; **2.** Brush and floss your teeth;
3. Exercise; **4.** Drink lots of water; **5.** Relax

EXPANSION ACTIVITY: Add two ideas

- Have students write two more suggestions for good health.
- Put students in pairs to share their ideas.
- Elicit ideas and write them on the board.

BIG PICTURE READING EXPANSION ACTIVITY: Tips for Airline Travel

- Photocopy and distribute Worksheet 27: Tips for Airline Travel
- Put the transparency for Unit 11 on the OHP or have students look at the Big Picture on page 169.
- Go over the directions.
- Have students answer the questions.
- Put students in pairs to share their ideas.
- Go over the answers with the class.

WORKSHEET 27 ANSWER KEY

1. c; **2.** d; **3.** e; **4.** b; **5.** a

Writing

- Go over the writing tip in the box.

1 READ. Look at the paragraph below. Underline the first sentence. Circle the space before the first word.

- Go over the directions. Make sure students understand what a paragraph is.
- Have students notice and circle the space, or indentation, that begins the paragraph.
- Walk around the room to make sure students have circled the space correctly.

2 READ the paragraph. Underline the things Mike should do for good health.

- Go over the directions.
- Have student read the paragraph and underline the things Mike should do.
- Put students in pairs to compare what they underlined.
- Elicit the things Mike should do.

ANSWER KEY

For good health, I should do many things. I should eat vegetables and fruit every day, and I shouldn't eat potato chips. I should drink water. I shouldn't drink coffee and soda. I should floss my teeth. I should eat healthy food and exercise. Then I can have a healthy life.

❸ WHAT ABOUT YOU? What should you do for good health? Write four sentences.

- Go over the directions.
- Model the activity. Tell the class four things you should do.
- Have students write four things they should do to improve their health.
- Call on students to share their ideas with the class.

EXPANSION ACTIVITY: Venn diagrams

- Draw a Venn diagram with two overlapping circles on the board.
- Model the activity. Use the information about your health and about Mike's to complete the diagram. As you fill in the outer edges, say *different.* As you add details to the overlapping area, say *similar.*
- Have students complete the Venn diagrams about themselves and Mike. Encourage students to use the information in Activity 3 and to add information as needed.
- Put students in pairs to share their information.

❹ WRITE your sentences from Activity 3 in a paragraph.

- Go over the directions.
- Have students write their sentences as a paragraph. Remind students to indent and use *should* and *shouldn't.*
- Put students in pairs to read their paragraphs.
- Call on students to read their paragraphs to the class.

BIG PICTURE WRITING EXPANSION ACTIVITY: Advice

- Put the transparency for Unit 11 on the OHP or have students look at the Big Picture in their books.
- Have each student choose a character or assign each student a character from the Big Picture.
- Have students write two pieces of advice for their character. Remind students to use *should* and *shouldn't.*
- Ask volunteers to read sentences to the class.

Career Connection

OBJECTIVE

Demonstrate a positive attitude at work

WARM-UP ACTIVITY: Roles

- Model the activity. Write several of your roles on the board (e.g., *parent, teacher, friend*). Tell the class who helps with each of those roles when you are sick (*My husband takes care of the children, My supervisor gets a substitute teacher.*).
- Have students list some of their roles.
- Put students in pairs or small groups to talk about the people who help them when they are sick.

1 READ AND LISTEN. Then practice with a partner.

- Direct students' attention to the photos. Tell students this is the continuation of the story about Isabel. Have students point to Isabel in the photos.
- Play the CD and have students follow along silently.
- Play the CD again and have students repeat.
- Put students in pairs to take turns reading the roles of Isabel and her coworker.
- Ask *What is the problem?*

2 WRITE. Answer the questions.

- Go over the directions and the example.
- Have students answer the questions.
- Put students in pairs to compare answers.
- Go over the answers with the class.

ANSWER KEY

1. She has the flu. 2. She helped others.
3. She should go back to school.

3 WHAT ABOUT YOU? Think of a time you helped someone or did a good job. What did you do? What did the person think?

- Model the activity. Tell the class about a time you helped someone.
- Put students in pairs to talk about a time they did a good job or helped someone.
- Call on students to tell the class about their partner.

CHECK YOUR PROGRESS!

- Have students circle the answers.
- Have students check whether each answer is right or wrong.
- Have students total their correct answers and fill in the chart.
- Have students create a learning plan and/or set learning goals.

ANSWER KEY

1. have; 2. has; 3. have; 4. head; 5. back;
6. stomachs; 7. should take; 8. Should she use; 9. should not take; 10. cough medicine;
11. put ice on it; 12. see a doctor

Unit Overview

LESSON	OBJECTIVE	STUDENT BOOK	WORKBOOK
1 Grammar and Vocabulary 1	Use *going* to talk about future plans	p. 182	p. 156
2 Grammar Practice Plus	Use object pronouns Interpret a calendar	p. 184	p. 157
3 Listening and Conversation	Interpret a timeline Ask for help	p. 186	p. 158
4 Grammar and Vocabulary 2	Identify furniture and appliances	p. 188	p. 160
5 Grammar Practice Plus	Identify rooms of a house Communicate with a landlord	p. 190	p. 161
6 Apply Your Knowledge	Interpret housing ads Add and subtract numbers	p. 192	p. 162
7 Reading and Writing	Predict the content of a text from the title	p. 194	p. 164
• Career Connection	Set personal, education, or career goals	p. 196	p. 166
• Check Your Progress	Monitor progress	p. 197	p. 168

Reading/Writing Strategies

- Predict the content by reading the title.
- Use examples in writing.

Connection Activities

LESSON	TYPE	SKILL DEVELOPMENT
1	Community	Research community events
2	Academic	Make a study plan
3	Academic	Use school calendars
4	Academic	Ask questions and research information
6	Community	Find movie listings
7	Academic	Find self-help resources in a bookstore
8	Community	Identify career path and courses available

WORKSHEET #/FOCUS	TITLE	TEACHER'S EDITION
28 Grammar	Are They Going To Get Married?	p. 273
29 Reading	Planning a Wedding	p. 274

LESSON 1: Grammar and Vocabulary

OBJECTIVE

Use *going* to talk about future plans

VOCABULARY

ask for a raise	pay a bill
finish school	rent an apartment
get married	sell a car
go on a honeymoon	sell a house
have a baby	start a new job
move to a new city	

GRAMMAR

Future with *going to*

COMPETENCIES

Talk about the future

WARM-UP ACTIVITY: Unit opener

- Put the transparency for Unit 12 on the overhead projector (OHP) or have students look at the Big Picture on page 185.
- Elicit words the students know and write them on the board.

🎧 **❶ GRAMMAR PICTURE DICTIONARY.** Listen and repeat.

- Have students open their books and look at the pictures. Ask *What do you see?* Write all the words the students know on the board.
- Say the sentences or play the CD and have students repeat.
- Say the sentences in random order and have students point to the picture.
- Put students in pairs and take turns saying the questions in random order as their partner points to the picture.

EXPANSION ACTIVITY: *Yes/no* statements

- Direct students' attention to the pictures and sentences in Activity 1.
- Say statements about Activity 1 (e.g., *Beth is going to have a baby.*). Elicit *yes* or *no* from the class.
- If the class says *no,* restate your sentence in the negative (*Beth isn't going to have a baby.*).
- For greater challenge, call on students and say a statement. Have the student say *yes* or *no,* and change all *no* statements to the positive.

❷ NOTICE THE GRAMMAR. Look at Activity 1. Underline *is/are going to*. Circle the verb.

- Have students read the sentences and underline *is/are going to* and circle the verbs.
- Ask questions: *What subjects pronouns use is going to? What form of the verb follows going to?*

ANSWER KEY

1. Tim is going to start a new job.
2. Beth is going to ask for a raise.
3. Julia is going to have a baby.
4. Jane is going to finish school.
5. Jane and Scott are going to get married.
6. They are going to go on a honeymoon.
7. Peter is going to sell his house.
8. He is going to move to a new city.
9. He is going to rent an apartment.

GRAMMAR CHART: Future With *Be Going To*

- Direct students' attention to the chart or project the transparency or CD.
- Go over the information on the chart and the usage notes. You may want to read the sentences, pausing to have students repeat.
- It may be helpful to review contractions of the verb *be* with students.
- Note that students will not learn about using *will* to talk about the future in this book. If students ask, explain that in this unit they are going to focus on *going to* for the future. The distinction between the two ways to talk about the future is a little too difficult at this level.

CHART EXPANSION ACTIVITY: Contractions

- Have students write a negative statement for each subject pronoun, using contractions.
- Put students in pairs to read their sentences.
- Call on students to read negative statements to the class.

❸ WRITE. Complete the sentences with the correct form of *be going to* + verb.

- Go over the directions.
- Have students complete the sentences with *be going to* + verb.
- Put students in pairs to check their answers.
- Go over the answers with the class.
- Put students in pairs to practice reading the questions and answers.

ANSWER KEY

1. is going to move; **2.** are going to finish; **3.** are not going to rent; **4.** are going to visit; **5.** is not going to sell; **6.** am going to ask; **7.** are going to eat; **8.** is going to watch

EXPANSION ACTIVITY: Rewrite

- Have students rewrite the sentences using contractions.
- Have volunteers write the sentences on the board.

❹ WHAT ABOUT YOU? Complete the sentences about you. Use *be going to.*

- Go over the directions.
- Model the activity. Tell the class what you are going to do.
- Have students complete the sentences.
- Put students in pairs to read their sentences.
- Call on students to tell the class about their partner's plans.

GRAMMAR/VOCABULARY NOTE

- Make sure students understand the meaning of *next.*
- Point out that we often say *this* to talk about a future event that is very close in time (e.g., *This weekend, I'm going to study.*), and *next* for the one after that (*Next weekend, I'm going to have fun.*).

EXPANSION ACTIVITY: Venn diagrams

- Put students in pairs to talk about what they are going to do this weekend.
- Have students make Venn diagrams to show the things that both of them are going to do, and the things that only one of them is going to do.
- Call on students to tell the class about their Venn diagrams.

COMMUNITY CONNECTION: Community events

- Have students look in a newspaper or an online news source to find out three events that are happening later in the month.
- Call on students to tell the class about the events they found out about.
- Write the events on the board.

LESSON 2: Grammar Practice Plus

OBJECTIVES

Use object pronouns
Interpret a calendar

VOCABULARY

her	them
him	us
it	you
me	

GRAMMAR

Object pronouns

COMPETENCIES

Use object pronouns

WARM-UP ACTIVITY: Beanbag toss

- Call on a student, toss a beanbag and say an object pronoun (e.g., *me*). Elicit the subject pronoun (e.g., *I*). Point out that these may be new words for students, but they may have heard the words before.
- Continue playing until everyone has had a chance to participate.

GRAMMAR CHART: Object Pronouns

- Direct students' attention to the chart or project the transparency or CD.
- Go over the information on the chart. You may want to read the sentences, pausing to have students repeat.
- Object pronouns can follow, or be the object of, verbs and prepositions. When they are the object of the preposition *to,* they can move in front of the object of the verb (*She gave the book to him, She gave him the book.*).

CHART EXPANSION ACTIVITY: Reversals

- Model the activity. Write *I like her*. Then write its reversal: *She likes me.*
- Put students in pairs to take turns saying sentences with *like* and different subject and object pronouns. Their partners will say the reversal.
- Call on students and say a sentence using *like.* Elicit the reversal.

❶ WRITE. Look at Julie's calendar. Correct the sentences. Use object pronouns.

- Direct students' attention to the calendar and ask questions: *What month is it? What date is the first Sunday? When is Julie going to finish class?*
- Go over the directions and the example.
- Have students rewrite the sentences using correct dates and object pronouns.
- Put students in pairs to compare answers.
- Go over the answers with the class.

ANSWER KEY

1. Julie is going to finish it on May 14. **2.** Their friends are going to help them move on May 24. **3.** Julie is going to marry him on May 17. **4.** Julie is going to call her on May 12.

❷ TALK about the picture.

- Go over the directions and the example.
- Put students in pairs to talk about the picture.
- Call on students and ask questions: *Where is Leyla? What is Ella doing? How's the weather?*

BIG PICTURE CONVERSATION/ VOCABULARY EXPANSION ACTIVITY: Create conversations

- Put students in pairs. Assign each pair one of these character pairs: John and Mary, Ben and Julie, Ella and Jacob; Joe and Thomas.

- Have students create conversations between their two characters.

- Have students perform their conversations in front of the class. Elicit the names of the two characters.

❸ MATCH.

- Go over the directions and the example.

- Have students write the letter on the line to complete the sentences.

- Go over the answers with the class.

ANSWER KEY

1. c; **2.** e; **3.** d; **4.** b; **5.** a

❹ TALK with a partner. What is going to happen next? Use your own ideas.

- Go over the directions.

- Put students in pairs to talk about what is going to happen next. Remind students to use the future with *be going to.*

- Call on students to share their ideas with the class.

ACADEMIC CONNECTION: Make a study plan

- Write three questions on the board: *How are you going to learn more vocabulary? How are you going to practice speaking English? How are you going to improve your reading skills in English?*

- Have students write at least one sentence to answer the questions. Remind students to be specific (e.g., *I am going to write three new words each day in my vocabulary notebook.*) and to use *be going to.*

- Put students in pairs to talk about their plans.

- Call on students to share their ideas with the class.

LESSON 3: Listening and Conversation

OBJECTIVES

Interpret a timeline
Ask for help

PRONUNCIATION

going to (gonna)

COMPETENCIES

Talk about plans

WARM-UP ACTIVITY: What are you gonna do tonight?

- Model the activity. Tell the class what you are going to do tonight. Use the reduction *gonna* in your sentences. You don't need to explain the reduction now.
- Put students in pairs to talk about their plans.
- Call on students to tell the class about something they are going to do. Restate the sentences using the reduction.

PRONUNCIATION: *Going To (Gonna)*

LISTEN for the pronunciation of *going to.*

- Go over the information about *gonna* and the directions. Point out that you used *gonna* in the warm-up activity.
- Say the sentences or play the CD.

EXPANSION ACTIVITY: Dictation

- Tell students you are going to dictate three sentences using *gonna.* They should write the full form, *going to.*
- Dictate sentences: *I'm gonna move next month; He's gonna sell his car next week; They're gonna get married next year.*
- Have volunteers write the sentences on the board.

1 LISTEN and number the pictures.

- Direct students' attention to the pictures. Ask questions: *What do you see? Who do you see?*
- Go over the directions.
- Play the CD and have students number the pictures in the order in which they occur in the script.
- Put students in pairs to compare answers.
- Go over the answers with the class.

LISTENING SCRIPT
Lesson 3, Activity 1

TCD3, 54

Listen and number the pictures.

A: Good news, Mark.

B: What?

A: James and Linda are going to get married.

B: Really? That's great. When?

A: Next month.

B: Wow! So . . . what are they going to do after the wedding?

A: Well, first, they're going to go to California for their honeymoon. Then they are going to move.

B: Oh really?

A: Yeah. After they move, Linda's going to start a new job.

B: Huh. What's James going to do?

A: He's going to sell his car to save money. This fall, he's going to go back to school.

B: That's great.

ANSWER KEY

A. 4; B. 3; C. 6; D. 1; E. 5; F. 2

EXPANSION ACTIVITY: Write the story

- Have students use the pictures in order to retell the story (*First, Linda is going to start a new job. Then, Linda and James are going to move.*). Have students write a sentence for each picture.
- Put students in pairs to read their sentences.
- Have volunteers write the sentences on the board.

❺ WHAT ABOUT YOU? Write about your plans for the next six months.

- Copy the chart on the board.
- Go over the directions and the examples.
- Model the activity. Write sentences about you on the chart.
- Have students complete the charts.
- Put students in pairs to read their sentences.
- When students are finished, call on students to tell the class about their partner (e.g., *Marie is going to start a new job.*).

❷ TALK. Tell a partner about James' and Linda's plans.

- Put students into pairs.
- Have students take turns talking about what James and Linda are going to do.

🎧 **❸ LISTEN** and read.

- Direct students' attention to the picture. Ask questions: *Who do you see? What's happening?*
- Play the CD or read the conversation as students follow along silently.
- Play the CD or read the conversation again and have students repeat.
- Ask *What are they going to do on Saturday?*
- Put students in pairs to practice the conversation.

❹ PRACTICE THE CONVERSATION with a partner.

- Model the activity. Have a more advanced student read A's lines. Model how to substitute a different activity.
- Put students in pairs to practice the conversation, making the appropriate substitutions. Monitor as needed.
- Call on students to say the conversation to the class.

ACADEMIC CONNECTION: School calendars

- Have students look at the school calendar for your school or for their children's school. Remind students they can often find these online if they don't have one.
- Have students write three sentences about the calendar using *be going to* (e.g., *They are not going to have classes on November 10.*).
- Put students in pairs to read their sentences.

LESSON 4: Grammar and Vocabulary

OBJECTIVE

Identify furniture and appliances

VOCABULARY

bed	microwave
cable television	phone company
dishwasher	refrigerator
dresser	sofa
Internet access	

GRAMMAR

Yes/no questions with *be going to*

COMPETENCIES

Talk about furniture and appliances for home, utilities

WARM-UP ACTIVITY: Moving day

- With books closed, put students in pairs or small groups to brainstorm things people need to do before they move.
- Elicit ideas and write them on the board.

🎧 **❶ GRAMMAR PICTURE DICTIONARY.** Listen and repeat.

- Have students look at the pictures. Ask *What do you see?*
- Play the CD or say the sentences and have students repeat.
- Ask the questions in random order and have the students say the answers.

EXPANSION ACTIVITY: Pair practice

- Put students in pairs to practice the conversations.

❷ NOTICE THE GRAMMAR. Look at Activity 1. Circle *am, is,* or *are.* Underline the subject.

- Go over the directions.
- Have students circle *am, is* and *are.* Have students underline the subject.
- Go over the answers with the class.

ANSWER KEY

1. A: Are you going to call the phone company today?
   B: Yes, I am.
2. A: Are you going to order cable television?
   B: Yes, we are.
3. A: Are you going to order Internet access?
   B: No, we're not.
4. A: Are you going to buy a new sofa?
   B: No, we like this one!
5. A: Is James going to fix this bed?
   B: Yes, he is.
6. A: Are you going to paint this dresser?
   B: Yes, we are.
7. A: Is the landlord going to buy a new refrigerator?
   B: No, he's going to fix the old one.
8. A: Is your landlord going to fix the dishwasher?
   B: No, he's going to call a plumber.
9. A: Is James going to put in the new microwave?
   B: No, he isn't. I am.

GRAMMAR CHART: Questions With *Be Going To*

- Go over the information in the chart.
- You may want to read the sample sentences in the chart and have students repeat.

CHART EXPANSION ACTIVITY: Forms of *be*

- Cover the first column. Elicit the appropriate form of *be* to complete the questions.

3 MATCH the questions with the answers.

- Go over the directions and the example.
- Have students write the letters on the lines to match the questions and answers.
- Put students in pairs to compare answers.
- Go over the answers with the class.
- Put students in pairs to practice asking and answering the questions in Activity 3.

ANSWER KEY

1. b; 2. c; 3. d; 4. e; 5. a

EXPANSION ACTIVITY: Magazine photos

- Bring in photos of different rooms from magazines or have students bring them in.
- Put students in pairs. Give each pair a photo.
- Have students write sentences to describe the room first. You may need to review prepositions of place and the structure *There is/are.*
- Then have students write three sentences using *be going to* to talk about changes they would make to the room (*I'm going to buy a chair. I'm going to move the sofa by the window. We're going to paint the walls.*).
- Call on students to tell the class about the room and the things they're going to do to it.

4 WHAT ABOUT YOU? Walk around the room and talk to your classmates. Complete the chart.

- Go over the directions and the example conversation.
- Have students stand and walk around the room to complete the chart. Remind students to write a classmate's name only if he or she answers *yes.*
- Call on students to tell you about someone in the chart.

ACADEMIC CONNECTION: Ask questions

- Have students write three questions about future activities at your school or in your program. (e.g., *When is the class going to end? When are we going to take tests? When are we going to start the next level?*).
- Have students write where they think they can get the answers (e.g., *the teacher, the program office, the school website*).
- Have students find out the answers to their questions.
- Call on students to tell the class what they found out.

LESSON 5: Grammar Practice Plus

OBJECTIVES

Identify rooms of a house
Communicate with a landlord

VOCABULARY

bathroom	living room
bedroom	kitchen
cabinet	stair
carpenter	toilet
dining room	

COMPETENCIES

Identify rooms in a house
Understand common household problems

WARM-UP ACTIVITY: Who works on a house?

- Put students in pairs to list common problems people have in a house or apartment.
- Have students list who could help with each problem. Remind students that Unit 9 lists some of those jobs.
- Elicit ideas of problems and people who could help and write them on the board.

🎧 **❶ LISTEN** and repeat.

- Direct students' attention to the pictures and elicit the words they know.
- Go over the directions.
- Play the CD and have students repeat.

EXPANSION ACTIVITY: Write sentences

- Have students write three sentences to describe the things they see in the picture in Activity 1.
- Put students in pairs to read their sentences.
- Call on students to read their sentences.

❷ WRITE. Put the words in order to make questions.

- Go over the directions.
- Elicit how to write the first question.
- Have students write the questions.
- Put students in pairs to compare questions.
- Go over the questions with the class.

GRAMMAR NOTE

Students may be unfamiliar with where to put some of the phrases in the sentences. Tell students that the places should go at the end of the question.

ANSWER KEY

1. Is a plumber going to fix the toilet? **2.** Are carpenters going to fix the stairs? **3.** Are carpenters going to fix the cabinets in the living room? **4.** Is the landlord going to fix the window in the bedroom? **5.** Is the landlord going to paint the walls in the dining room?

🎧 **❸ LISTEN** to Linda's conversation with her landlord. Check *yes* or *no* above.

- Go over the directions.
- Play the CD and have students check the answers to the questions.
- Go over the answers with the class.

LISTENING SCRIPT
Lesson 5, Activity 3

TCD3, 58

Listen to Linda's conversation with her landlord. Check *yes* or *no* above.

A: Hi, Mr. Smith? This is Linda Herrera.

B: Oh hi, Linda. How can I help you?

A: Well, I'm calling about some problems in our apartment.

B: Um. . . . Can you tell me again what the problems are?

A: Well, the toilet is broken.

B: Oh, I'm going to fix the toilet.

A: Oh, good. And the stairs aren't safe.

B: Okay. Well, the carpenters are going to fix the stairs.

A: All right. And what about the cabinets in the living room?

B: Oh . . . right. The carpenters can fix those, too.

A: Okay. Thanks. Oh, and can you fix the window in the bedroom?

B: Oh, yes, yes . . .

A: By the way, we're going to paint the dining room white. Is that okay?

B: Yes, sure.

A: Okay. Thanks again. See you tomorrow?

B: Um. . . . Yes. . . . Tomorrow.

ANSWER KEY

1. no; 2. yes; 3. yes; 4. yes; 5. no

BIG PICTURE GRAMMAR EXPANSION ACTIVITY: Are They Going To Get Married?

- Photocopy and distribute Worksheet 28: Are They Going to Get Married?
- Put the color transparency for Unit 12 on the OHP or have students look at the Big Picture in their books.
- Go over the directions.
- Have students complete the worksheet. You may want to help complete the first question.
- Put students in pairs to compare answers.
- Go over the answers with the class.

WORKSHEET 28 ANSWER KEY

1. Are/Yes, they are. 2. Is/Yes, she is. 3. Is/Yes, he is. 4. Are/No, they aren't. 5. Is/No, she isn't. 6. Is/No, he isn't. 7. Are/Yes, they are.

4 WRITE. Complete the chart. Use the words in the box.

- Go over the directions and the words in the box.
- Have students complete the chart.
- Go over the answers with the class.

ANSWER KEY

Our House Plans

Room	Jobs for James	Jobs for Linda	Jobs for James and Linda
dining room	fix the <u>table</u> and chairs	fix the window	paint the <u>walls</u>
living room	clean the <u>sofa</u>	call the <u>cable TV</u> company	fix the <u>cabinets</u>
kitchen	fix the refrigerator	buy a <u>dishwasher</u>	clean the microwave
bedroom	fix the <u>bed</u>	vacuum the <u>carpet</u>	paint the <u>dresser</u>

5 TALK with a partner. Look at the chart in Activity 4. Use the words below. Ask and answer questions about James and Linda.

- Go over the directions and the example conversation.
- Put students in pairs to take turns asking and answering questions using the prompts.
- Call on students and ask questions.

ANSWER KEY

1. Are James and Linda going to paint the walls in the dining room? Yes, they are.
2. Is Linda going to buy a refrigerator? No, she isn't.
3. Is James going to clean the sofa? Yes, he is.
4. Are James and Linda going to paint the walls in the living room? No, they aren't.
5. Is Linda going to vacuum the carpet? Yes, she is.
6. Is James going to call the cable TV company? No, he isn't.

EXPANSION ACTIVITY: Do it yourself

- Ask students to look at James and Linda's house plans.
- Have students list the items they personally can (are able to) do.
- Put students in pairs to talk about their own skills in the home.

6 WHAT ABOUT YOU? Write your plans for this week. Ask your classmates if they are going to do the same things.

- Model the activity. Write your plans on the board. Encourage students to list things they need to do around the house, as well as other things they need to do.
- Have students write their lists.
- Put students in pairs or small groups to compare lists.
- Call on students to tell the class about something on their to-do lists.

LESSON 6: Apply Your Knowledge

OBJECTIVES

Interpret housing ads
Add and subtract numbers

COMPETENCIE

Understand housing ads
Inquire about rentals
Talk about household maintenance

MATH/NUMERACY

Add and subtract

WARM-UP ACTIVITY: **Describe your house**

- Have students list characteristics of their home (number of bedrooms, bathrooms, other rooms). Encourage students to also list the things they like about their homes (yard, big windows, sunny kitchen).
- Put students in pairs to talk about their homes.

❶ READ the ads. In each ad, underline one thing you like.

- Go over the directions.
- Have students read the ads and underline things they like.
- Elicit ideas from the class.

EXPANSION ACTIVITY: **Real ads**

- Bring in ads for houses or apartments from the newspaper
- Put students in small groups to talk about the information in the ad.
- Have students work individually to write ads for their homes using the information from the warm-up activity.

❷ LISTEN to the conversation. Circle the ad for the place that Paula is going to rent.

- Go over the directions.
- Play the CD and have students circle the ad.
- Elicit the answer.

LISTENING SCRIPT
Lesson 6, Activity 2

TCD3, 59

Listen to the conversation. Circle the ad for the place that Paula is going to rent.

B: Hi, Paula! How are you?

A: Fine. I'm looking for a new place to live.

B: Great. Is there anything good?

A: Well, I think I'm going to rent a little house. It has three bedrooms and two bathrooms.

B: Wow!

A: Yes, it's exciting, but it has a lot of problems. . . .

B: Oh no! Like what?

A: Well, the kitchen cabinets are very old, and I don't like the paint color. And the dishwasher doesn't work.

B: Oh, that's too bad.

A: It's okay. The carpet isn't clean either, but I'm going to call someone to clean it. It's going to be very nice soon.

B: Good luck.

A: Thanks.

ANSWER KEY

House for Rent

LISTEN AGAIN. Check the things with problems.

- Go over the directions.
- Play the CD again and have students check the items.
- Go over the answers with the class.

ANSWER KEY

Check: kitchen cabinets, paint, dishwasher, carpet

ANSWER KEY

1. $350; 2. $2,350; 3. $950; 4. $1,350

EXPANSION ACTIVITY: Virtual tours

- Have students go online and search for virtual tours for houses or homes. Point out that they will have to enter certain information such as the city or zip code where they want to look, as well as the price range.
- Have students find a house they like and take a virtual tour.
- Have students tell the class about the house/home they toured.

MATH REVIEW: Add and Subtract

- Go over the directions.
- Direct students' attention to the estimate. Ask questions: *How much is the estimate to paint the cabinets? How much to fix the stairs?*
- Have students answer the questions.
- Put students in pairs to compare answers.
- Go over the answers with the class.

CULTURE/CIVICS NOTE

- Point out that a handyman is a person who does small household repair jobs.
- In the United States, customers often get estimates from more than one company in order to compare prices.
- Most communities have contact information for the Better Business Bureau in the telephone directory. This is a good place to find out if a company is reliable.

🎧 ❸ LISTEN and read.

- Direct students' attention to the picture. Ask questions: *Who do you see? Where are they? What are they doing?*
- Have students follow along silently as you play the CD.
- Play the CD again and have students repeat.
- Ask comprehension questions: *What are they talking about? What are they going to do tomorrow?*
- Put students in pairs to take turns reading the conversation.

❹ PRACTICE THE CONVERSATION with a partner.

- Go over the directions and the information.
- Model the activity with a student. Have the students read B's lines. Substitute the information in Activity 1 (*I'm going to study at the library.*). Cue the student to answer *Fix the toilet.*
- Put students in pairs. Have students practice the conversation, using the information in Activity 4.
- Walk around the room to monitor the activity and provide help as needed.
- Have pairs of students say the conversations in front of the class.

CULTURE/CIVICS NOTE

- Point out that in the United States, it is common to give a reason when you refuse an invitation.
- We refuse invitations politely using expressions such as *I'm sorry I can't* or *I wish I could.*

5 TALK. Invite your partner to do something this weekend.

• Go over the directions and the example conversation.

• Put students in pairs to practice inviting and declining invitations.

• Have students perform their conversations in front of the class.

COMMUNITY CONNECTION: What's at the movies?

• As an out-of-class assignment, have students find a movie schedule for this weekend. Point out that they can find one in the newspaper or online.

• Have students write the name of one movie they want to see, three different times they could go, and the location.

• Elicit the information from students.

• Put students in pairs to practice inviting each other to specific movies.

LESSON 7: Reading and Writing

OBJECTIVE

Interpret the content of a text from the title

READING TIP

Before you read, look at the title to find out the topic

WRITING TIP

Use examples in writing

COMPETENCIES

Set goals

WARM-UP ACTIVITY: One thing to change

- Put students in pairs to talk about a thing in their life that is not really good right now. Point out that it doesn't have to be a big problem, just something they are not happy about.
- Elicit ideas from the class.

Reading

❶ THINK ABOUT IT. What part of your life do you want to change?

- Read the question. Have students check one or more boxes.
- Elicit answers from students.

❷ BEFORE YOU READ. Look at the title. What is the article about?

- Go over the tip in the box.
- Go over the directions.
- Have students check the topic.
- Put students in pairs to talk about their ideas.
- Elicit the answer from the class.

ACADEMIC NOTE

Remind students that pre-reading strategies help students prepare for the topic by reminding them of what they already know, and by helping them start to predict what they are going to read about. This helps them understand and remember information better.

ANSWER KEY

There are easy ways to change something.

❸ READ. Underline the three steps to change.

- Have students read the paragraph, or read the paragraph aloud sentence by sentence and have students repeat.
- Have students underline the three steps.
- Elicit the sentences they underlined.
- Ask comprehension questions: *How can you describe the problem? What are some things you can brainstorm, or list? How is Luke going to get a new job?*

ANSWER KEY

First, write about the problem. Next, think of ways to fix the problem. Last, start to change.

EXPANSION ACTIVITY: Literacy development—sentence strips

- Copy the sentences from the paragraphs onto separate strips. Leave enough space between each word for word discrimination. The sentences need to be large enough to be read by all the students.
- Put the sentence strips on the board in the correct order, one paragraph at a time. Read each sentence aloud and have students repeat. You may want to point to each word as you read.
- Take the sentences down and mix them up.
- Have volunteers come to the board and put the sentences in the correct order. Have the other students help.
- You may want to photocopy the sentences and cut them into strips so that each student or pair of students has a set to reassemble.

BIG PICTURE READING EXPANSION ACTIVITY: Planning a Wedding

- Photocopy and distribute Worksheet 29: Planning a Wedding
- Put the transparency for Unit 12 on the OHP or have students look at the Big Picture on page 185.
- Go over the directions.
- Have students answer the questions.
- Put students in pairs to share their ideas.
- Go over the answers with the class.

WORKSHEET 29 ANSWER KEY

A. 1. so you don't have problems; 2. no; 3. food, flowers, music
B. There are children, the photographer dropped things, there is a dog

4 WRITE. Look at the article. What are the three steps to change something in your life?

- Go over the directions.
- Have students write the three steps using *First*, *Next*, and *Last*.
- Put students in pairs to compare answers.
- Go over the answers with the class.

ANSWER KEY

1. First, write about the problem. 2. Next, think of ways to fix the problem. 3. Last, start to change.

ACADEMIC CONNECTION: Self-help sections

- Explain that many books and articles suggest ways people can help themselves to solve problems (self-help).
- As an out-of-class assignment, have students go to a bookstore and list five sections they see there.
- Ask students to find the self-help section and write the titles of three books they find there.
- Call on students to tell the class the sections and the titles they found.

Writing

- Go over the writing tip in the box.

1 WRITE. What are your plans? Complete the chart.

- Go over the directions.
- Have students choose something they want to do and write it on the line.
- Have students brainstorm ideas and list them in the chart.
- Put students in pairs to talk about their ideas.

2 WRITE sentences about your plans.

- Go over the directions and the example.
- Point out that we say *to + verb* to talk about our purpose for doing something (e.g., *to improve my English*).
- Have students follow the example sentence and the information in Activity 1 to write sentences.
- Put students in pairs to read their sentences.
- Have volunteers write sentences on the board.

3 WRITE your sentences as a paragraph.

- Go over the directions.
- Review the way to write a paragraph (e.g., indent, write one sentence after another, write on one topic). Point out that when students are writing a paragraph, they shouldn't begin each sentence in the same way (e.g., *to improve my English . . .*).
- Have students write their sentences as a paragraph.
- Collect the paragraphs and provide feedback.

EXPANSION ACTIVITY: Make a brochure

- Put students who wrote on similar topics in small groups.
- Have the groups collaborate to write a tip sheet or brochure on their topics.
- Have the groups present their ideas to the class.

BIG PICTURE WRITING EXPANSION ACTIVITY: Ideal wedding

- Put the transparency for Unit 12 on the projector or have students look at page 185 in their books.
- Have students write about an ideal or perfect wedding. If they aren't married, they can plan one for themselves. If they are, they can plan a wedding for one of their children or a friend or relative.
- Put students in small groups to share their ideas.
- Ask volunteers to read sentences to the class.

Career Connection

OBJECTIVE

Set personal, education or career goals

WARM-UP ACTIVITY: Next week

- Put students in pairs to talk about something they are going to do next week, next month and next year.
- Call on students to tell the class about their partners.

🎧 **❶ READ AND LISTEN.** Then practice with a partner.

- Direct students' attention to the photos. Tell students this is the continuation of the story about Isabel. Have students point to Isabel in the photos.
- Play the CD and have students follow along silently.
- Play the CD again and have students repeat.
- Put students in pairs to take turns reading the roles of Isabel and her boss.

❷ TALK. Answer the questions.

- Go over the directions and the example.
- Have students answer the questions.
- Put students in pairs to compare answers.
- Go over the answers with the class.

ANSWER KEY

1. a class about medicine and prescriptions;
2. next month; 3. happy

❸ WHAT ABOUT YOU? Make a list of your plans for your future.

- Model the activity. Tell the class about your plans.

- Have students list their plans.
- Put students in pairs to talk about a time their plans.
- Call on students to tell the class about their partner's plans.

COMMUNITY CONNECTION: Career training and goals

- Have students research the training needed for one career/job they are interested in. They can look at ads in the newspaper or online to find out required training. They can also look at community college catalogs to find out what courses lead to what degrees.
- Have students write down one course needed or helpful for one career path.
- Call on students to tell the class what they found out.

CHECK YOUR PROGRESS!

- Have students circle the answers.
- Have students check whether each answer is right or wrong.
- Have students total their correct answers and fill in the chart.
- Have students create a learning plan and/or set learning goals.

ANSWER KEY

1. aren't going to; 2. is going to; 3. is not going to; 4. ask for a raise; 5. sell; 6. move to a new city; 7. Are; 8. Am; 9. Is; 10. bathroom; 11. dining room; 12. dresser

Name: _____

Date: _____

Using Singular and Plural Nouns

DIRECTIONS: Look at the Big Picture in Lesson 5. Write the number and the correct form of the noun in parentheses.

1. _____ (construction worker)

2. _____ (nurse)

3. _____ (police officer)

4. _____ (server)

5. _____ (cook)

6. _____ (taxi driver)

7. _____ (man)

8. _____ (woman)

9. _____ (child)

10. _____ (person)

Name: _____   Date: _____

Letters

DIRECTIONS: Look at the Big Picture in Lesson 5. Read the letters. Write the name of the character on the line.

1.

Dear Ms. Smith,

    I am a student in your ESL class. My name is _____. I am from Russia. In Russia, I am a dentist, but here in the United States, I am a taxi driver and a student. I am single. It's nice to meet you.

    Thank you for teaching the class.

2.

Dear Ms. Smith,

    I am a student in your ESL class. My name is _____. I am from Mexico. In Mexico, I am an actor, but here in the United States, I am a server and a student. I am single. It's nice to meet you.

    Thank you for teaching the class.

3.

Dear Ms. Smith,

    I am a student in your ESL class. My name is _____. I am from Vietnam. In Vietnam, I am a doctor, but here in the United States, I am a nurse and a student. I am married and have three children. It's nice to meet you.

    Thank you for teaching the class.

Name: _____   **Date:** _____

Adjectives

DIRECTIONS: Look at the Big Picture on page 25. Circle the correct adjective.

1. Carl is **tall / short**.

2. Berta is **tall / short**.

3. Carl and Berta are **young / old**.

4. Chin is **young / old**.

5. Gabby is **pretty / not pretty**.

6. Leo is **thin / heavy**.

7. Sam is **hardworking / lazy**.

Possessive Forms

DIRECTIONS: Look at the Big Picture on page 25. Write the possessive form of the noun.

1. Sam is _____ brother.

2. Berta is _____ sister. They are both Oscar's children.

3. Bob is _____ husband.

4. Pam is _____ wife.

5. Sam and Gabby are _____ grandchildren.

Name: _____

Date: _____

Berta and Carl

DIRECTIONS: Look at the Big Picture on page 25. Read the story. Complete the diagram with adjectives from both the story and the picture.

Berta and Carl are Oscar's children. Carl is very serious about soccer. He isn't very serious about school. Carl is funny at school. Berta is serious all the time. Berta is shy and Carl is outgoing. Both Berta and Carl are messy.

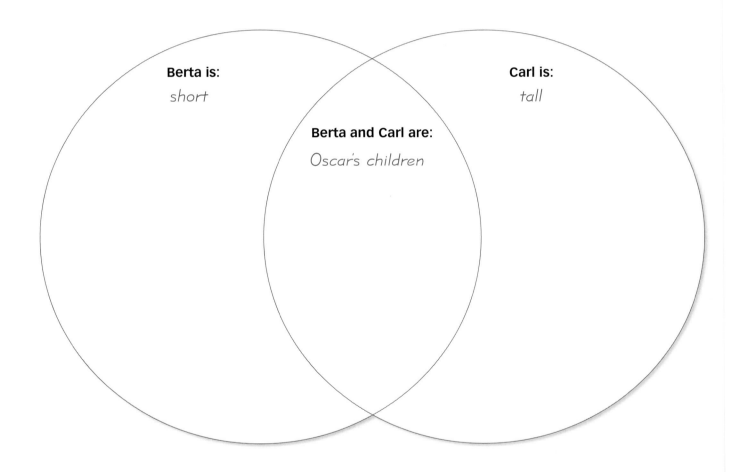

Berta is:
short

Carl is:
tall

Berta and Carl are:
Oscar's children

Name: _____ **Date:** _____

In the Classroom

DIRECTIONS: Look at the Big Picture for Unit 3. Answer the questions.

1. Are there any phones in the classroom?

   _____

2. Is there a clock in the classroom?

   _____

3. Are there any copiers in the classroom?

   _____

4. Is there a map in the classroom?

   _____

5. How many teachers are there in the classroom?

   _____

6. How many bags are there?

   _____

7. How many men are there?

   _____

8. How many women are there?

   _____

Name: _____   **Date:** _____

Icons

DIRECTIONS: Work with a partner. Talk about what the pictures mean. Write the words.

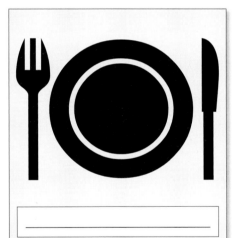

Name: _____   **Date:** _____

Our Classroom/Our School

A **DIRECTIONS:** Look at the Big Picture for Unit 3 and write the numbers on the lines.

> Our school is very small. There are only three classrooms. Every classroom is
> the same. There are _____ students in each classroom. There are
> _____ desks in each classroom. There is _____
> teacher in each classroom. There is _____ clock in each classroom. The
> restrooms are in the lobby. The vending machines and the water fountains are in the hall.
> There isn't a snack bar. There isn't a library. There is a small room that has books and CDs.
> In our classroom, there are students from many countries.

B **DIRECTIONS:** Answer with complete sentences. Use capital letters and periods.

1. How many classrooms are there in the school?

   _____

2. How many students are there in the school?

   _____

3. How many teachers are there?

   _____

4. Is there a snack bar?

   _____

5. Are there restrooms?

   _____

6. Where are the vending machines?

   _____

Name: _____   Date: _____

Making Conversation

DIRECTIONS: Photocopy and cut along dotted lines. Make conversations.

Hi! How's the weather in	Rio de Janeiro?
It's	hot.
It's	85.
How's the weather in	Seattle?
It's	cold and rainy
It's	49.
Mexico City	75
warm and sunny	warm
70	30
cold and snowy	Bogotá
Washington	London
cloudy	40
warm and windy	65
Chicago	Atlanta

Name: _____   **Date:** _____

It's with Time and Weather

DIRECTIONS: Look at the Big Picture on page 57. Answer the questions.

Top Left picture: (Hong)

1. What is the date? _____

2. What is the season? _____

3. How is the weather? _____

4. What city is it? _____

Top Right picture: (Carlos)

5. What is the date? _____

6. What is the season? _____

7. How is the weather? _____

8. What city is it? _____

Bottom Left picture: (Eduardo)

9. What is the date? _____

10. What is the season? _____

11. How is the weather? _____

12. What city is it? _____

Bottom Right picture: (Elizabeth)

13. What is the date? _____

14. What is the season? _____

15. How is the weather? _____

16. What city is it? _____

Name: _____

Date: _____

Emails

DIRECTIONS: Look at the Big Picture on page 57. Read the emails. Circle the words for seasons and weather. Write the name of the person.

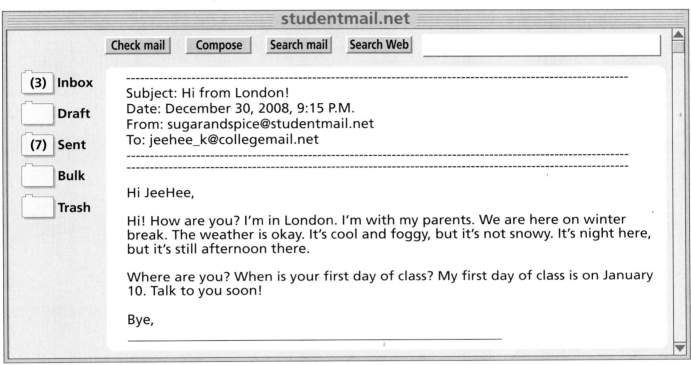

studentmail.net

Check mail   Compose   Search mail   Search Web

(3) Inbox
Draft
(7) Sent
Bulk
Trash

Subject: Hi from London!
Date: December 30, 2008, 9:15 P.M.
From: sugarandspice@studentmail.net
To: jeehee_k@collegemail.net

Hi JeeHee,

Hi! How are you? I'm in London. I'm with my parents. We are here on winter break. The weather is okay. It's cool and foggy, but it's not snowy. It's night here, but it's still afternoon there.

Where are you? When is your first day of class? My first day of class is on January 10. Talk to you soon!

Bye,

_____

studentmail.net

Check mail   Compose   Search mail   Search Web

(1) Inbox
(2) Draft
(6) Sent
Bulk
Trash

Subject: Hi from Bogotá!
Date: December 31, 2008, 11 A.M.
From: erlatino@studentmail.net
To: jeehee_k@collegemail.net

Hi JeeHee,

Hi! How are you? I'm great. I'm home in Colombia with my family. The weather is great! It's warm and humid. It's also sunny. I'm happy it's summer here. It's too cold in the United States in the winter.

Where are you? Are you in the U.S.? Are you on break too?
See you soon!

Bye,

_____

Name: _____   **Date:** _____

Where Is It?

DIRECTIONS: Look at the Big Picture for Unit 5. Write directions from one place to the other.

1. The hospital to the school

    A. Turn _____.

    B. _____ one block.

    C. The school is _____.

2. The gas station to the apartment building

    A. _____ the street.

    B. Turn _____.

    C. The apartment building is _____.

3. The school to the hotel

    A. _____.

    B. _____.

    C. _____.

    D. _____.

Name: _____   **Date:** _____

Places in the Community

DIRECTIONS: Look at the Big Picture for Unit 5. Read the sentences for the brochure for this city. Check ☑ yes or no.

1. The police station is on _____, across from the fire station.

   ☐ Yes   ☐ No

2. The bank is also on _____ Street, between the fire station and the supermarket.

   ☐ Yes   ☐ No

3. Many important community places are on _____ Street, including a post office, movie theater and bank. Figaro's restaurant is a great place to eat.

   ☐ Yes   ☐ No

4. The Park Hotel is across the street from the school.

   ☐ Yes   ☐ No

5. The school is next to the movie theater.

   ☐ Yes   ☐ No

Name: _____   **Date:** _____

What Are They Doing?

DIRECTIONS: Look at the Big Picture for Unit 6. Match the answers to the question.

_____ 1. What is Marta doing?

_____ 2. What is Brad doing?

_____ 3. What is Clara doing?

_____ 4. What is Ali doing?

_____ 5. What are Lydia and her children doing?

a. He is reading a magazine.

b. He is trying on pants.

c. She is looking at black skirts.

d. They are waiting for the elevator.

e. She is buying shoes.

ANSWER the questions.

6. Lydia has a baby in her arms. What is she doing?

_____

7. Brad's friend is Lara. What is she doing?

_____

8. Elena is at the counter. What is she doing?

_____

Name: _____   Date: _____

Match the Quotes

DIRECTIONS: Look at the Big Picture for Unit 6. Read the quotes below and write the name.

1. The children's shoes are on the second floor. _____*Lydia*_____

2. Can I help you with those skirts? _____

3. I like these red pants! _____

4. I'm tired. _____

5. The shoe colors are great. I really like the white ones. _____

6. These black skirts are a good price. _____

WRITE the sentences as quotes.

1. *Lydia says, "The children's shoes are on the second floor."*

2. _____

3. _____

4. _____

5. _____

6. _____

Name: _____   **Date:** _____

Yes/No Questions

DIRECTIONS: Look at the Big Picture for Unit 7 and answer the questions.

1. Does Miguel brush his teeth at 9 A.M. on Saturday morning?

   _____

2. Does Rosa watch TV at 9 A.M. on Saturday morning?

   _____

3. Do Luz and Roberto go to work at 8 A.M. on Saturdays?

   _____

4. Do Jose and Mariela play soccer at 9 A.M. on Saturday?

   _____

5. Does Luz take a shower on Saturday morning?

   _____

6. Does Roberto cook breakfast?

   _____

7. Do Miguel and Rosa get up at 10 A.M. on Saturday mornings?

   _____

8. Does Mariela look at books?

   _____

Name: _____   **Date:** _____

What's Next?

DIRECTIONS: Read the information about Saturday schedules and look at the Big Picture. Write the name of the person.

1. _____ usually gets up at 7:00 on Saturday morning. Next, he goes for a walk and reads the newspaper. Then at 8:30, he cooks breakfast. After breakfast, he cleans the kitchen. Last, he takes a shower.

2. _____ never gets up before 8:30 He usually goes to bed late on Friday night. First, he takes a shower. Then he gets dressed and brushes his teeth. He is very handsome.

3. First, _____ gets up at 8:00 on Saturdays. Next, she takes a shower. Then, she tries on clothes. She takes 45 minutes to get dressed.

4. First, _____ gets up at 7:30. Next, she goes for a run. Then at 9:00, she takes a shower. After her shower, she eats breakfast.

5. _____ and _____ get up around 6:30. Everyone else is still sleeping. First, they play with their toys. Next, they watch television. Then they read books until breakfast.

Name: _____ **Date:** _____

What Do They Have?

DIRECTIONS: Look at the Big Picture on page 121. Answer the questions.

1. Where are the people?

   _____

2. Alex is filling up a cup. Where is he?

   _____

3. What is Alex drinking?

   _____

4. Where is the bread?

   _____

5. What does the store need? (something the store doesn't have)

   _____

6. Pedro and Patricia are pushing a full cart. What do they have in their shopping cart?

   _____

7. What do they need?

   _____

8. Where are the people who work at the supermarket?

   _____

Name: _____ **Date:** _____

Sentence Strip Match

DIRECTIONS: Photocopy and cut along the lines. Give strips to students.

Most people	eat breakfast.
People in different countries eat	different kinds of food for breakfast.
For example, people in Vietnam and China often eat	rice and soup for breakfast.
In India, rice, eggs, and vegetables are popular,	but people in South America usually eat something small, such as a piece of bread.
In the United States and England, people often eat cereal with milk,	but people in Russia sometimes eat cereal with cheese.
People all over the world drink	tea or coffee for breakfast.
Tea is more popular in Asia, but coffee	is more popular in the United States and in Europe.

Name: _____   **Date:** _____

At the Supermarket

DIRECTIONS: Look at the Big Picture on page 121. Pedro and Patricia are pushing a full shopping cart, and Alex is getting coffee. Read the information below. Answer the questions.

> Pedro and Patricia usually shop at *Fresh and Friendly Supermarket*. It's not a big store, but it has fresh food. They like the bread from the bakery. The store makes the bread every morning. They like the fish too. It is very good. The store sells a lot of fruit and vegetables, but it doesn't sell a lot of food in boxes. Patricia loves the fresh fruit—apples, oranges, bananas and grapes.
>
> Pedro and Patricia go to *Fresh and Friendly* every week, but Alex doesn't go to *Fresh and Friendly* often. He goes there sometimes to buy a sandwich. *Fresh and Friendly* sells sandwiches in the meat and cheese section. The sandwiches are very big and they are very good.

1. When does *Fresh and Friendly Supermarket* make bread?

   _____

2. How often do Pedro and Patricia shop at *Fresh and Friendly*?

   _____

3. What does Alex eat from *Fresh and Friendly*? What does he drink?

   _____

4. Does the store sell a lot of food in boxes?

   _____

5. Is the store big?

   _____

6. What fruit does *Fresh and Friendly* sell?

   _____

Name: _____   **Date:** _____

Yesterday

DIRECTIONS: Look at the Big Picture. Write the past tense form of the word in parentheses. Use negatives if necessary.

1. Ana _____ *fixed* _____ (fix) the water pipe.

2. Jake _____ (cook) food at the hospital.

3. Pedro _____ (work).

4. A man _____ (deliver) boxes to the hospital.

5. Trung _____ (use) a blood pressure cuff.

6. Maria _____ (read) the X-ray.

7. Kathy _____ (go) to the store.

8. Yuri _____ (drive) a taxi.

9. Greg _____ (fix) a car.

10. Abdul _____ (talk) to a patient in his office.

Name: _____ **Date:** _____

Application Forms

DIRECTIONS: Look at the Big Picture on page 137. Read the sections from the application forms. Write the name of the character on the line next to the number.

1. _____ *Maria* _____

Skills: *can take temperature, blood pressure, and other vital signs*	
WORK EXPERIENCE	
Present or last position: *nurse*	
Employer: *Carmel Family Health*	
Responsibilities: *I helped the doctor with patients. I talked to patients to get medical history. I recorded information in files.*	

2. _____

Skills: *can read maps, drive well*	
WORK EXPERIENCE	
Present or last position: *ambulance driver*	
Employer: *A-1 Ambulance Service*	
Responsibilities: *I drove all over town, worked 60 hours a week, worked well with customers, followed directions.*	

3. _____

Skills: *prepare foods, salads, desserts, speak English and Spanish*	
WORK EXPERIENCE	
Present or last position: *cook*	
Employer: *The Hot Tamale*	
Responsibilities: *I helped the chef. I made the salads and appetizers. I made the desserts.*	

4. _____

Skills: *can fix all plumbing—toilets, showers, water pipes*	
WORK EXPERIENCE	
Present or last position: *Plumber*	
Employer: *self*	
Responsibilities: *I fixed plumbing, ordered supplies, billed customers.*	

Name: _____ Date: _____

Pair Interview

DIRECTIONS: Work with a partner. Ask the questions below and complete the form.

1. What is your name?
2. What position do you want?
3. What is your address?
4. What hours can you work?
5. What are your skills?
6. What was your last job?
7. Who was your employer?
8. What did you do?

Name:	Position wanted:						
Address:	**Hours available:**						
	S	M	T	W	Th	F	S

Skills:

WORK EXPERIENCE

Present or last position:

Employer:

Responsibilities: (e.g., I ordered supplies)

Name: _____ **Date:** _____

Paul and James

DIRECTIONS: Look at the Big Picture for Unit 10 and list the details about Paul's trip. Then listen to your teacher tell you more about James' trip. Complete the Venn diagram.

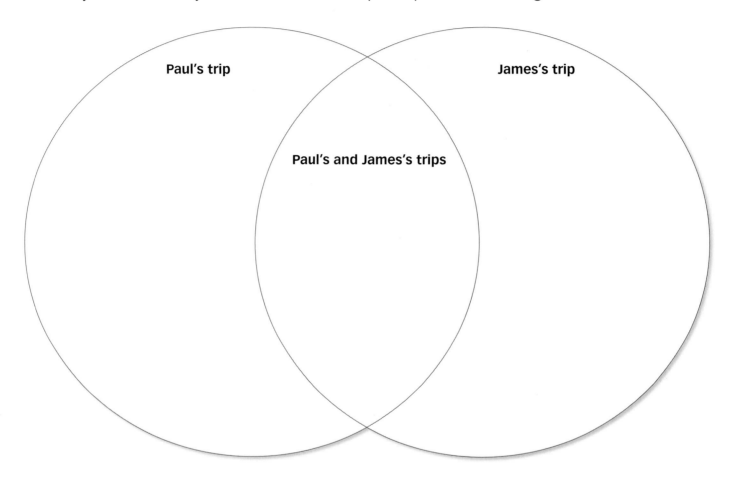

Paul's trip

James's trip

Paul's and James's trips

Name: _____ **Date:** _____

More About Paul's Trip

DIRECTIONS: Look at the Big Picture for Unit 10. Write *Was* or *Were* to complete the questions. Answer the questions. Use short answers.

1. _____ the traffic fast on the way to the airport?

   _____

2. _____ the people at the baggage claim shy?

   _____

3. _____ the airport clean?

   _____

4. _____ the people on the train dry?

   _____

5. _____ the street dangerous late at night?

   _____

6. _____ the city crowded?

   _____

Name: _____   **Date:** _____

Definitions

DIRECTIONS: Look at the pictures on page 153. Read the sentences. Circle the meaning of the bold-faced word.

1. The traffic on the way to the airport was very **congested**.

   a. crowded   **b.** fast   **c.** fun

2. When Paul arrived at the end of his trip, the streets were **deserted**.

   a. crowded   **b.** noisy   **c.** empty of people

3. It rained a lot. The people on the train were **soaked**.

   a. dry   **b.** wet   **c.** boring

4. Paul's trip was not **enjoyable**.

   a. fun   **b.** stressful   **c.** interesting

5. The **passengers** on the plane weren't happy.

   a. people   **c.** chairs   **d.** windows

Name: _____   Date: _____

What Should They Do?

DIRECTIONS: Look at the Big Picture for Unit 11 on page 169. Next to each name, give advice using one of the ideas in the box and *should* or *shouldn't*.

eat all the food	put ice on it	put a pillow behind your back	use ear drops or drink something	take cold medicine

1. Elena

_____

2. Alex

_____

3. Gloria

_____

4. Eliza

_____

5. Ibrahim

_____

6. (Your idea):

_____

Name: _____   **Date:** _____

Tips for Airline Travel

DIRECTIONS: Look at the Big Picture for Unit 11 on page 169. Read the tips. Match the problem to the remedy.

Do you travel a lot by plane? Do you wish your trip could be more comfortable? Are you tired of a sore back, stiffness and having no energy? Follow the tips below and your trip will be much more fun.

- Drink water. Don't drink alcohol. People get dehydrated when they fly, and this can make them get sick. You don't get dehydrated if you drink a lot of water.

- Bring chewing gum. Sometimes your ears can hurt, especially when the plane is going up or down. Chewing gum, eating, and drinking can relieve pressure in your ears.

- Use a pillow. The seats on an airplane don't fit everyone equally. Use a pillow behind your lower back so you don't get a backache.

- Listen to music. Use earphones to block out noise and help you relax.

- Stretch. You should try to stretch or walk around the airplane if possible. This helps blood flow to your legs.

Problem	Remedy
1. My ears hurt. _____	a. You should listen to music.
2. My back hurts. _____	b. You should drink some water.
3. My legs hurt. _____	c. You should chew gum.
4. My mouth is dry. _____	d. You should put a pillow behind your lower back.
5. It's stressful. _____	e. You should walk around.

Name: _____   **Date:** _____

Are They Going To Get Married?

DIRECTIONS: Look at the Big Picture on page 185. Write *Is* or *Are* to complete the questions. Then answer the questions with a complete sentence.

1. Are Ben and Julie going to get married today?

   Answer: _____

2. _____ Mary going to help John?

   Answer: _____

3. _____ Joe going to take a picture?

   Answer: _____

4. _____ Jacob and Sara going to eat some cake?

   Answer: _____

5. _____ Ella going to play soccer in five minutes?

   Answer: _____

6. _____ Thomas going to drive the car?

   Answer: _____

7. _____ the people going to eat something after the wedding?

   Answer: _____

Name: _____   Date: _____

Planning a Wedding

A **DIRECTIONS:** Read the article below and answer the questions.

> So, you're going to get married. For most people, their wedding day is a very big event in their lives. You want it to be perfect. There are many things that can go wrong on your big day. Follow the tips below to make sure your wedding is problem-free.
>
> - *Talk to your soon-to-be husband or wife. Make sure you agree on the important things (for example, how many people to invite).*
>
> - *Decide if the wedding is going to be formal. Don't invite young children to a formal wedding—it will be boring for them.*
>
> - *Think about the details. What kind of food do you want? Is it easy to serve? Are you going to have music? What kind of music? Are you going to have flowers? What flowers do you want?*
>
> - *Choose professionals to do the important jobs. Make sure the people who are doing important jobs (taking pictures, preparing food, playing music) are professional and well-trained.*
>
> - *Plan for problems. Maybe you want a wedding outdoors. What are you going to do if it rains?*

1. Why is it important to plan for a wedding?

   _____

2. Should you invite children to all weddings?

   _____

3. What are some wedding details you should think about?

   _____

B **LOOK** at the Big Picture for Unit 12 on page 185. List three things in the article that are problems at this wedding.

_____

_____

_____

Pre-Unit

Pages 2–3

1
1. C
2. F
3. M
4. I
5. T
6. A
7. R
8. W
9. S
10. U

2
1. HI
2. IS
3. MY
4. DO
5. UP
6. TO
7. HE
8. IT
9. YOU
10. THE

3
1. Brenda
2. Maria
3. Lee
4. Peter
5. Betty
6. Kendra
7. Stan
8. Tim
9. Susan
10. Craig

4
1. David
2. Anna
3. Julia
4. Hector
5. Sonia
6. Raul
7. Hiro
8. Tomas
9. Cindy
10. Eliot

5
1. 3
2. 4
3. 7
4. 19
5. 11
6. 14
7. 16
8. 20
9. 80
10. 70
11. 15
12. 8
13. 50
14. 30

6
1. 4239
2. 941
3. 2653
4. 8249
5. 7256
6. 3108
7. 9524
8. 1657
9. 9203
10. 2106
11. 75238
12. 96028
13. 45391
14. 97284

7
25 32 (48) (54) 33 57
(72) 85 (12) 94 77 (35)
82 (63) 66 23 (56) (81)
98 (26) 39 40 14 (30)
46 (78) 93 45 (17) 91

Page 4

1
1. Open your book.
2. Read.
3. Stand up.
4. Turn to page 15.
5. Listen.
6. Take out your pen.
7. Write your name.
8. Raise your hand.
9. Sit down.

2
1. up
2. down
3. pen
4. name
5. book
6. page
7. hand

Page 5

1
1. c
2. f
3. b
4. a
5. d
6. e

2

NOUNS	VERBS	ADJECTIVES
a book	talk	tall
a school	study	happy
a pen	write	red

3
1. We
2. He
3. They
4. You
5. She
6. You
7. I
8. You
9. They
10. We

Unit 1

Page 6

1
1. e
2. g
3. a
4. b
5. c
6. h
7. d
8. f

2 Answers will vary.

3
1. is
2. am
3. is
4. are
5. are
6. are
7. are
8. is

Page 7

1
1. am not
2. is not (isn't)
3. am not
4. is not (isn't)
5. are not (aren't)
6. are not (aren't)

2
1. address
2. first name
3. city
4. single
5. telephone number
6. zip code

Page 8

1
1. 50
2. 19
3. 13
4. 16 Main Street
5. 80 Center Road
6. 1820 Park Street
7. 555-1217
8. 555-4019

2
1. 117
2. 230
3. 814
4. 1890
5. 1519
6. 3016

3
1. my name's
2. I'm
3. Hi
4. from
5. student
6. to meet you
7. It's nice

Page 9

3 Answers will vary.

Page 10

1
1. a salesclerk
2. a police officer
3. a nurse
4. an office assistant
5. a construction worker
6. a housekeeper

2
1. a server
2. cooks
3. a doctor
4. actors
5. a teacher
6. firefighters
7. students
8. a housekeeper

3
1. children
2. child
3. men
4. man
5. woman
6. women
7. people
8. person

Page 11

1
1. student
2. people
3. teacher
4. woman
5. taxi drivers
6. nurses
7. women
8. people

2
1. students
2. men
3. woman
4. children
5. child
6. people
7. person

3 teacher

Page 13

3
1. no
2. yes
3. yes
4. no
5. yes
6. no
7. yes
8. no

4 Answers will vary.

Page 14

2
1. yes
2. no
3. yes
4. no
5. yes
6. no

3 Answers will vary.

Page 15

4 Answers will vary.
5 Answers will vary.

Page 16

3
1. B
2. A
3. I
4. E
5. F

Page 17

3
1. ~~Scan~~ Copy
2. ~~computer~~ copy machine
3. ~~Open~~ Close
4. ~~telephone number~~ number of copies
5. ~~Stop~~ Start
6. ~~copy machine~~ copy

A tdaysun@myschool.com
bmarcos@myschool.com

B hchavez@myschool.com
cpeng@myschool.com
msingh@myschool.com
kklein@myschool.com
Answers will vary; students should write their own first initial, last name, and @myschool.com.

Pages 18–19
1. A
2. B
3. C
4. A
5. D
6. C
7. B
8. A
9. D
10. B
11. C
12. D
13. C
14. A
15. C
16. B
17. A
18. A
19. B
20. D

Unit 2

Page 20

1
1. c
2. e
3. h
4. g
5. a
6. d
7. f
8. b

2
1. I am
2. he is
3. she isn't
4. they aren't
5. I'm not
6. he isn't
7. they are
8. she is

3 Answers will vary.

Page 21

1
1. Is Sally neat? No, she isn't. She's messy.
2. Is Daniel lazy? No, he isn't. He's hardworking.
3. Are Sam and Maria old? No, they aren't. They're young.
4. Are Mr. and Mrs. Anderson serious? No, they aren't. They're funny.

2
1. young
2. hardworking
3. outgoing
4. a cook
5. heavy
6. shy
7. funny
8. an actor

Page 22

1 3, 5, 1, 4, 2

2
1. No, she isn't.
2. Yes, she is.
3. Yes, she is.
4. No, she isn't.
5. Yes, she is.
6. Yes, she is.
7. No, she isn't.
8. No, she isn't.

3
A
1. Is he
2. Is she
3. Is she
4. Is he
5. Is she
6. Is he
7. Is she
8. Is he

B
1. No, he isn't.
2. No, she isn't.
3. Yes, she is.
4. Yes, he is.
5. No, she isn't.
6. No, he isn't.
7. Yes, she is.
8. Yes, he is.

Page 23

2
1. short, medium height, tall
2. thin, average weight, heavy
3. messy, not very neat, neat
4. young, middle aged, old
5. lazy, not very lazy, hardworking

Page 24

1
1. father
2. sister
3. grandmother
4. mother
5. husband
6. brother
7. grandfather
8. children

2
1. Claire and Tonio's
2. Oscar and Lilia's
3. Tonio's
4. Tonio's
5. Claire and Tonio's
6. Miguel and Julia's

3
1. His
2. Our
3. Her
4. your
5. Their
6. My
7. Your

Page 25

4
A
1. 33 lb.
2. 44 lb.
3. 132 lb.
4. 66 lb.

B
1. thin
2. thin
3. heavy
4. average weight

5
1. cousin
2. grandfather
3. aunt
4. brother
5. uncle
6. sister

Page 26

1 Kevin Milano, Nancy Milano, Nick Milano, Dr. Saleem Aziz

2
1. Kevin Milano
2. Kevin's mother
3. (904) 555-3298
4. (904) 555-8822
5. Kevin's grandfather
6. (904) 555-4176
7. Kevin's mother
8. Kevin's grandfather
9. Kevin's doctor
10. Answers will vary. Penicillin is a medicine (antibiotic) used to fight disease and infection.

Page 27

3
1. d
2. f
3. e
4. c
5. a
6. b

4 Answers will vary.

Page 28

1
1. d
2. e
3. b
4. f
5. a
6. c

2 Circled words: Fire, Police, Ambulance, Poison, Hospital

3
1. emergency
2. fire
3. address
4. wife
5. truck

Page 29

4
1. the hospital
2. a fire
3. poison
4. an ambulance
5. the doctor
6. 555-0924
7. 555-2365
8. 911

5
1. doctor
2. hospital
3. fire truck
4. EMT
5. ambulance
6. doctor

6 Answers will vary.

Pages 30

2
1. no
2. yes
3. no
4. yes
5. yes
6. no
7. yes
8. yes

3 Answers will vary.

Page 31

A
1. Don't use
2. Don't use
3. Don't use
4. Use
5. Don't use
6. Don't use
7. Don't use

4 TO: Dr. Vasquez; From: Hector Garcia; Phone: 508-555-1742; Message: Please call.

Pages 32–33

1. C
2. D
3. D
4. B
5. D
6. B
7. C
8. C
9. D
10. C
11. A
12. B
13. C
14. D
15. A
16. C
17. D
18. C
19. A
20. D

Unit 3

Page 34

1 desks, computer, chairs, cell phone, table, pencils, books, board

2 (Order of sentences may vary.)
1. There are 3 desks.
2. There is 1 computer.
3. There are 5 chairs.
4. There is 1/a cell phone.
5. There is 1/a table.
6. There are 5 pencils.
7. There are 3 books.
8. There is 1/a board.

3
1. Yes, there are.
2. No, there isn't.
3. No, there aren't.
4. Yes, there is.
5. Yes, there are.
6. No, there isn't.

Page 35

1 Answers will vary.

2
```
R E T U P M O C I T
E N E L B A T H O C
K K C A P K C A B A
R U G I C G L I O M
A M A F L O O R A E
M I R O O D C P R O
B O O K S U K E D R
C L O S E T A N E I
A E N O T E B O O K
```

Page 36

1
1. Is there
2. Are there
3. Is there
4. Is there
5. Are there
6. Are there

2 4, 1, 3, 10, 5, 2, 8, 7, 6, 11, 9

3
1. Yes, (the library is in a school).
2. (It's) Washington School Library.
3. No, the questions are about videos and books on tape.
4. (There are) hundreds of videos.
5. (There are) more than 500 books on tape.
6. (There are) 200 books on tape that are in Spanish.

Page 37

1
1. Excuse me
2. a question
3. any computers
4. there are
5. 24
6. thanks
7. No problem

2 Answers will vary.

Page 38

1
1. on
2. at
3. at
4. in
5. on
6. at
7. on
8. in

2
1. first floor
2. second floor
3. first floor
4. first floor
5. second floor
6. first floor
7. second floor
8. first floor

Page 39

1
1. e
2. g
3. b
4. h
5. a
6. c
7. d
8. f

2 Answers may vary.
1. vending machine, water fountain, or telephone
2. restrooms, computers, or classrooms
3. restrooms, computers, or classrooms
4. vending machine, water fountain, or telephone
5. vending machine, water fountain, or telephone
6. restrooms, computers, or classrooms
7. classrooms, restrooms, or computers
8. Answers will vary.

3
1. notebook
2. restroom
3. snack bar
4. trash can
5. vending machine
6. water fountain
7. computer lab
8. public telephone
9. security office
10. information desk
11. children
12. backpack

Page 40

1 Redding Middle School
Dear Parent/Guardian,

You are invited to Open House night at our school on Wednesday, September 23, from 7:00 P.M. to 9:00 P.M. We have a new computer lab and many new classrooms. Our teachers are here to help you.

There are school maps in the office on the first floor. In the library on the second floor there are snacks and coffee. Your son's teacher, Mr. Garvin, is in Room 214. There are 20 new computers in the computer lab on the first floor. Come and see them!

Please call 555-2300 for more information.

2
1. no
2. no
3. no
4. yes
5. yes
6. no
7. yes
8. no
9. yes
10. no

Page 41

3
1. A
2. E
3. C
4. G
5. H
6. B
7. D
8. I
9. on the second floor
10. on the first floor

4 Answers will vary.

Page 42

1
1. No, it isn't. It's on the second floor.
2. Yes, it is.
3. They're on the second floor.
4. It's on the second floor.
5. No, it isn't. It's on the third floor.
6. The supply room is on the fourth floor.
7. They're on the second floor.
8. It's on the first floor.
9. Yes, it is.
10. No, it isn't.

2

1st floor	2nd floor	3rd floor	4th floor
Information desk	Computer lab	F. Carter	Supply Room
Snack bar	M. Halle	Meeting Room	
	Restrooms	A. Martin	
	Vending Machines	T. Nguyen	

Page 43

4 Answers will vary.

Page 44

2
1. no
2. yes
3. yes
4. yes
5. no
6. yes

3 Sample answers:

There isn't...

a telephone, a copier, a printer, paper, a table, a trash can, a bookshelf...

There aren't....

pens, pencils, windows, lamps, books, notebooks...

Page 45

A 6, 3, 1, 2, 5, 4

B GHaines, (student name), Mr. Haines, desk, clocks, trash cans, (student name)

Pages 46–47

1. B
2. D
3. A
4. C
5. C
6. B
7. C
8. C
9. A
10. B
11. D
12. B
13. C
14. A
15. B
16. D
17. B
18. A
19. C
20. C

Unit 4

Page 48

1
1. d
2. e
3. f
4. c
5. b
6. a

2
1. it's cloudy
2. it's snowy
3. it's windy
4. It's cool
5. It's sunny
6. It's hot
7. it's cold
8. it's warm
9. It's rainy

Page 49

1
1. January
2. cold/snowy
3. snowy/cold
4. cool
5. Summer
6. hot

2

A
1. February
2. October
3. March
4. May
5. April
6. November
7. August
8. January
9. July
10. December
11. June
12. September

B
1. January
2. February
3. March
4. April
5. May
6. June
7. July
8. August
9. September
10. October
11. November
12. December

Page 50

1
1. rainy, warm; 75°
2. cool, windy; 45°
3. dry, sunny; 64°
4. hot, humid; 92°

2
1. rainy
2. warm
3. 75
4. San Diego
5. hot
6. humid

3
1. 41°F; cold
2. 10°C; cool
3. 20°C; warm
4. 86°F; hot
5. 38°C; hot
6. 59°F; cool
7. 32°F; cold
8. –17°C; cold
9. 24°C; warm
10. 98°F; hot

Page 51

2 Answers will vary.
3 Answers will vary.

Page 52

1
1. e
2. f
3. a
4. b
5. d
6. c

2
1. It's at 8:00.
2. It's at 4:30.
3. It's in July.
4. It's in the evening.
5. It's at 10:45.
6. It's at 2:15.
7. They're at 8:00 and 9:00.
8. They're in December and July.

3
1. on
2. in
3. on
4. at
5. on
6. on
7. at
8. in

Page 53

1
1. sixth
2. eight
3. twentieth
4. fourth
5. thirty
6. seventeen
7. twenty-fifth
8. ninth

2
1. Halloween
2. New Year's Day
3. Valentine's Day
4. Independence Day
5. Thanksgiving
6. Labor Day

Page 54

1
1. tornado
2. flood
3. blizzard
4. hurricane

2 Students should circle icons for blizzards, hurricane, tornado, and flood.

Page 55

3
1. There are two blizzards.
2. The blizzards are in Denver and Buffalo.
3. No, there isn't.
4. There's a flood in St. Louis.
5. There's a tornado in Dallas.
6. No, there isn't.
7. There's a hurricane in Miami.
8. Answers will vary.

4
1. windy
2. hurricane
3. windows
4. weather
5. school
6. home

5 Answers will vary.

Page 56

1
1. f
2. e
3. h
4. g
5. a
6. c
7. b
8. d

2 Circle: 8/25, 8/26, 8/27, 8/28, 8/29

Underlined: sunny, winds, cloudy, rain, rain, clearing, cloudy, sun; 85°, 76°, 72°, 78°, 83°

3
1. August
2. hot
3. cloudy
4. rainy
5. afternoon
6. morning

Page 57

4 Answers will vary.
5 Answers will vary.

Page 58

1
1. Sun
2. Mon
3. Tues
4. Wed
5. Thurs
6. Fri
7. Sat

2
1. It's on November 14th. (It's on Thursday.)
2. It's at 2:45.
3. It's on November 11th. (It's on Monday.)
4. At 11:30.
5. On Saturday at 10:00. (on the 16th)

Page 59

3
1. 1/1
2. 7/4
3. 9/4
4. 11/11
5. 11/23
6. 12/25
   Veteran's Day

A 4, 1, 3, 2, 5

B
1. 11/16
2. "Mom"
3. "all-day"
4. "Repeat"
5. "every year"

Pages 60–61

1. C
2. B
3. C
4. A
5. C
6. D
7. C
8. B
9. A
10. B
11. C
12. B
13. A
14. D
15. C
16. A
17. A
18. D
19. B
20. C

Unit 5

Page 62

1
1. apartment building
2. bank
3. drugstore
4. gas station
5. supermarket
6. library
7. post office
8. hospital

2
1. no
2. no
3. no
4. yes
5. yes
6. no
7. no
8. yes

Page 63

1
1. across from
2. next to
3. between
4. across from
5. next to
6. in front of

2
1. It's next to
2. It's next to
3. It's between
4. It's across from
5. It's across from
6. It's between

3
1. restaurant
2. supermarket
3. hospital
4. police station
5. hotel
6. fire station

4 apartment

Page 64

1
1. C
2. B
3. D
4. A

2
1. Where's the supermarket?
2. It's next to the post office.
3. It's across from the supermarket.
4. Where is the community center?

3
1. Where is the community center?
2. It's across from the supermarket.
3. Where's the supermarket?
4. It's next to the post office.

Page 65

1
1. d
2. b
3. c
4. a

2
1. Excuse me
2. Where's the
3. next to the bank
4. not right
5. Thank you
6. No problem

3
1. yes
2. no
3. no
4. yes

Page 66

1
1. Make
2. Go
3. Stop
4. Start
5. Turn
6. Cross

2
1. Start on Elm Street.
2. Turn left on Maple Street.
3. Go straight on Maple Street.
4. Cross 1st Avenue.
5. Make a U-turn.
6. Stop in front of the apartment building.

3
1. Don't park
2. Don't turn left
3. Don't make a U-turn
4. Don't turn right
5. Don't go the wrong way on
6. Don't go

Page 67

1
1. right
2. left
3. straight
4. Cross
5. U-turn
6. next to

2 stop; go; cross; enter; park; U-turn; straight; turn left; turn right

Page 68

1
1. the room
2. Go straight
3. right
4. the stairs
5. the door
6. the building

2 Students should number directions on map as follows:
1. Go out of the room.
2. Go straight down the hall.
3. Turn right.
4. Go down the stairs.
5. Go to the Emergency Exit and open the door.
6. Go away from the building.

3
1. b
2. d
3. a
4. c

Page 69

4
1. schools
2. emergency
3. directions
4. building
5. exits
6. alarm

5 Answers will vary.

Page 70

1
1. driving
2. Department of Motor Vehicles
3. 3
4. driving test
5. written test
6. eye test

2
1. e
2. g
3. f
4. h
5. b
6. d
7. a
8. c

Page 71

3
1. c
2. b
3. e
4. d
5. f
6. h

4 Answers will vary.
5 Answers will vary.

Page 72

2
1. in the morning, in the afternoon, in the evening
2. Mon., Tues., Wed., Thurs., Fri., Sat., Sun.
3. 2
4. nursing and health care
5. on the computer
6. How to Enroll

Page 73

3
1.
2. ✓
3.
4. ✓
5. ✓
6. ✓
7.
8.

1. B
2. A
3. E
4. G
5. C
6. F

4 Answers will vary.

Pages 74–75

1. D
2. B
3. C
4. B
5. D
6. A
7. C
8. B
9. D
10. B
11. D
12. D
13. C
14. B
15. B
16. A
17. C
18. B
19. D
20. A

Unit 6

Page 76

1
1. is
2. are
3. are
4. am
5. is
6. are
7. is
8. are

2
1. are talking
2. are working
3. are waiting
4. is carrying
5. am trying
6. are helping

3
1. isn't working
2. aren't shopping
3. am not talking
4. isn't looking
5. aren't waiting
6. aren't carrying

4
1. John is wearing a yellow shirt.
2. Hector is looking for a black hat.
3. Hana is trying on white shoes.
4. I'm buying red shorts.
5. They aren't wearing blue pants.
6. The salesclerk is helping the customers.

Page 77

1
1. Lei is wearing a skirt, shirt, and shoes. She's working in a restaurant.
2. Rachid is wearing a jacket, pants, and a shirt. He's looking/shopping for shoes.
3. Alan is wearing shorts, shoes, and a hat. He's talking on a cell phone.
4. Rita is wearing a dress, hat, and shoes. She's going to the bank.

2 Colors: red, black, brown, green, orange, white, yellow, blue

Clothing: shirt, pants, dress, shorts, shoes, jacket, skirt, hat

Verbs: look for, work, talk, help, carry, wait, shop, buy

Page 78

1
1. c
2. a
3. e
4. f
5. b
6. d

2
1. large, white
2. small, yellow
3. large, blue
4. medium, brown
5. small, black
6. medium, blue

3
1. aren't
2. is
3. are
4. aren't
5. isn't
6. are

Page 79

1 Answers will vary.

2
1. it's different
2. It's OK
3. the blue dress
4. I'm buying
5. great on you

Page 80

1
1. $1.25
2. $.55
3. $.75
4. $2.75
5. $7.15
6. $30.25

2
1. is   It's
2. are   They're
3. are   They're
4. is   It's
5. is   It's
6. are   They're

3
1. This
2. These
3. Those
4. Those
5. This
6. That

Page 81

1
1. This/That
2. These/Those
3. These/Those
4. This/That
5. These/Those
6. This/That
7. These/Those
8. This/That

2
1. September 23, 2009
2. $35.88
3. Glove's Dept. Store
4. Emil La Plante

3
1. $8.40
2. $21.85
3. $66.25
4. $15.10
5. $32.50
6. $29.11

Page 82

1
1. debit card
2. cash
3. check
4. credit card

2
1. a, b, c or d
2. a, c or d
3. a
4. c

Page 83

3
1. Are you
2. cash
3. credit card
4. checks
5. driver's license
6. bag
7. Thanks

4
1. no
2. yes
3. yes
4. no
5. no
6. yes

5 Answers will vary.

Page 84

1 Answers will vary.

2
1. white shirt
2. on sale
3. small
4. dirty
5. It's
6. How much is it?
7. cheap

Page 85

3
1. She's looking for a new white shirt.
2. It's too small.
3. It's too dirty.
4. It's cheap.
5. It's $9.98.
6. Yes, she does.

4
1. The shirt is cheap.
2. The dress is out of style.
3. The jacket is clean.
4. The hat is old.

5
1. It isn't expensive.
2. It isn't in style.
3. It isn't dirty.
4. It isn't new.

6 Answers will vary.

Page 86

1 debit card, cash, checks, credit card

2
1. The check is to ABC Day Care.
2. The check is for $100.00.
3. The date is March 28, 2009.
4. Isabel is signing the check.

3

Isabel Thompson
523 West Street, Apt. 17
My Town, FL 34759
Date: (current date)   325
Pay to the Order of Milford Realty Company $ $650.00
Six hundred and fifty dollars and 0/100   dollars
People's Bank
Isabel Thompson
⑆012345⑈ ⑈123456543⑈ ⑈234567

Page 87

B
1. E
2. D
3. A
4. F
5. C
6. B

Pages 88–89

1. D
2. C
3. D
4. B
5. C
6. C
7. C
8. A
9. B
10. A
11. D
12. B
13. D
14. C
15. A
16. B
17. A
18. D
19. B
20. A

Unit 7

Page 90

1
1. e
2. c
3. a
4. f
5. b
6. d

2
1. do
2. work
3. goes
4. cook
5. eat
6. doesn't
7. don't
8. don't

3
1. work, don't work
2. reads, doesn't read
3. does, doesn't do
4. eat, don't eat
5. take, don't take
6. goes, doesn't go

Page 91

1
1. always
2. sometimes
3. usually
4. often
5. never

2
1. always
2. never
3. usually
4. usually
5. often
6. never
7. sometimes
8. often

Page 92

1
1. c
2. a
3. b
4. e
5. f
6. d

2
1. doing
2. going
3. evening
4. often
5. go
6. get up

3 Answers will vary.

Page 93

2 1. e
2. a
3. d
4. b
5. c
6. f

3 Answers will vary.

Page 94

1 1. Do
2. Does
3. Do
4. Do
5. Does
6. Does
7. Do
8. Do

2 1. f
2. e
3. b
4. d
5. a
6. c

3 1. he does
2. he/she doesn't
3. we do
4. they do
5. Yes, I do. or No, I don't.
6. Yes, I do. or No, I don't.

Page 95

1 1. do, play
2. do, play
3. Do, play
4. play
5. do, eat
6. don't, eat
7. Does, play
8. doesn't, works
9. Do, eat
10. eat, eat
11. Do, watch
12. don't, read
13. do, works, play

2 1. she
2. she
3. he
4. he
5. he
6. she

Page 96

1 1. c
2. e
3. d
4. a
5. b
6. f

2 1. assignments
2. usually
3. Does
4. doesn't
5. answers
6. after school
7. extra help
8. on time

Page 97

3 1. no
2. yes
3. no
4. yes
5. yes
6. no

4 Answers will vary.

5 Answers will vary.

Page 98

1 1. 9:35
2. 9:50
3. 10:10
4. 10:20
5. 10:45

2 1. The first bus leaves Main Street at 7:15.
2. The bus is at the hospital at 7:35.
3. The first bus arrives at Central Square at 8:00.
4. Ana arrives at Community College at 8:35.
5. John leaves Main Street at 8:00.
6. Oscar arrives at Central Square at 10:45.

Page 99

3 1. 9:15
2. 35 minutes
3. Park Place
4. hospital

4 1. d
2. e
3. b
4. a
5. c

5 Answers will vary.

Page 100

1 circle: 8:52, 8:57, 9:00, 8:58, 8:55

underline: 4:52, 5:02, 4:30, 4:31, 4:29

2 1. no
2. yes
3. no
4. yes
5. yes
6. no

3 1. b
2. b
3. c

Page 101

A 1. d
2. a
3. e
4. b
5. c
6. F

Pages 102–103

1. B
2. D
3. B
4. D
5. A
6. B
7. C
8. B
9. D
10. B
11. A
12. A
13. B
14. B
15. C
16. A
17. B
18. A
19. D
20. C

Unit 8

Page 104

1
1. H
2. E
3. K
4. D
5. B
6. C
7. A
8. I
9. L
10. G
11. J
12. F

2
1. an
2. a
3. —
4. —
5. an
6. —
7. an
8. —
9. a
10. —
11. —
12. —

3
1. are
2. is
3. are
4. are
5. is
6. is
7. is
8. are

Page 105

1
1. d
2. e
3. a
4. b
5. f
6. c

2
1. pounds
2. bag
3. loaf
4. boxes
5. carton
6. bottle

3
1. loaf
2. yogurt
3. pound
4. rice
5. carrot
   fruit

Page 106

1
1. buy
2. on sale
3. How much
4. a pound
5. Where
6. aisle

2
1. g
2. b
3. h
4. f
5. c
6. a
7. d
8. e

3
1. it
2. seat
3. cheap
4. bit
5. meat
6. chick
7. feet
8. pick

Page 107

2
1. like
2. please *or* thanks
3. would
4. broccoli *or* carrots
5. want
6. thanks *or* thank you
7. get
8. please *or* thank you

3 Answers will vary.

Page 108

1
1. $2.00
2. $3.75
3. $2.50
4. $3.75
5. $1.75
6. $1.50
7. $1.75
8. $4.25
9. $3.25

2
1. e
2. d
3. a
4. c
5. f
6. b

3
1. Where does
2. What do
3. When do
4. Where does
5. What do
6. When does

Page 109

1
1. need
2. kitchen
3. have
4. have
5. need
6. quart
7. pound
8. dozen
9. have
10. quarts

2
1. 1/2
2. 2
3. 1/2
4. 16
5. 2
6. 4
7. 1
8. 16, 1

Page 110

1

grains
6 oz.

vegetables
2 1/2 cups

fruit
1 1/2 cups

meat and other
proteins 5 1/2 oz.

milk (dairy products)
3 cups

oils

2

Grains	Vegetables	Fruit	Milk (Dairy Products)	Meats and Beans	Other
bread	broccoli	apple	milk	chicken	pie
cereal	carrot	banana	cheese	egg	soda
rice	onion	orange	yogurt	fish	(French fries)
	(French fries)		(ice cream)	hamburger	(ice cream)
	salad			hot dog	

3
1. Yes, she does.
2. He can eat bananas and apples.
3. meats and beans
4. Fruit is not in the soup.
5. She can eat chicken, (eggs,) hamburger, or hot dogs.
6. He needs to drink milk.

Page 111

4
1. vegetables
2. grain
3. meat
4. milk
5. Fruit

5 Answers will vary.

Page 112

1
1. f
2. d
3. g
4. b
5. a
6. h
7. c
8. e

2
1. 1/4 cup, 4 oz.
2. 3.9 oz., 1/2 cup, 2 cups (2 c.)
3. 2 oz., 1/4 cup, One Pound, 16 oz., 8 cups, 5 qts., 1 tbs., 2 tbs.
4. 10 3/4 oz., 1/2 cup

Page 113

3
1. No. It weighs 4 ounces.
2. You need 2 cups.
3. One pound makes 8 cups.
4. No. You use water.

4
1. 4
2. 2
3. 2
4. 4

5 Answers will vary.

Page 114

1
1. morning
2. breakfast
3. quarts
4. boxes
5. coffee
6. fruit

2 Drinks: tea, coffee, orange juice, milk

Food: fruit, yogurt, bread, cereal, jam, cream cheese, sugar

Other: bowls, spoons, knives, plates

Page 115

A
1. c
2. e
3. d
4. a
5. b

B 3, 1, 4, 2, 5

Pages 116–117
1. C
2. B
3. A
4. B
5. D
6. C
7. B
8. B
9. A
10. D
11. C
12. B
13. A
14. B
15. C
16. C
17. D
18. D
19. D
20. A

Unit 9

Page 118

1
1. server
2. salesclerk
3. cook
4. construction worker
5. office assistant
6. taxi driver

2
1. can
2. can
3. can't
4. can
5. can't
6. can
7. can
8. can't

3
1. e
2. h
3. b
4. g
5. c
6. d
7. a
8. f

Page 119

1
1. cabinets
2. power tools
3. carpenter
4. toilet
5. plumber
6. water pipes
7. electrician
8. wires
9. trucks
10. mechanic

2
1. server, food orders (f)
2. plumber, water pipes (c)
3. receptionist, fax machine (d)
4. carpenter, power tools (b)
5. mechanic, trucks (a)
6. electrician, wires (e)

Page 120

1
1. can't
2. can
3. can
4. can't
5. can
6. can
7. can't
8. can't

2 3, 5, 1, 6, 4, 2

3 Answers will vary.

Page 121

1
1. drive, drive
2. use, use

2
1. Nice to meet you
2. I like to use
3. but I can speak
4. I'd like to learn

Page 122

1
1. e
2. g
3. f
4. b
5. d
6. a
7. h
8. c

2
1. visited
2. cleaned
3. studied
4. helped
5. prepared
6. arrived
7. ordered
8. closed

3
1. didn't paint
2. didn't work
3. didn't help
4. didn't wash
5. didn't borrow
6. didn't use
7. didn't study
8. didn't order

Page 123

1
1. went
2. received
3. broke
4. arrived
5. opened
6. came
7. made
8. went
9. started
10. rained
11. went
12. watched

2
1. I made a pie./I didn't make a pie.
2. I received a package./I didn't receive a package.
3. I went to a restaurant./I didn't go to a restaurant.
4. I came to school late./I didn't come to school late.
5. I went to the bank./I didn't go to the bank.
6. I broke a window./I didn't break a window.

3
1. no
2. yes
3. no
4. no
5. yes

Page 124

1 A: Carpenter: use power tools, make door and window frames.

B: Receptionist: use office equipment (computer, fax, copier)

C: Painter: drive a truck

D: Electrician: fix wires, lights, fuse boxes; install switches and outlets

2
1. Monday, Tuesday, Wednesday, Thursday, Friday
2. From 8:00.
3. In the morning.
4. 20 hours per week.
5. In the summer.
6. It's full time.

3 1. C
2. A
3. D
4. B

Page 125

4 Answers will vary.
5 Answers will vary.

Page 126

1 1. I'd like to apply for
2. an ad
3. What skills
4. I can fix
5. Did you study
6. fill out this application

2 1. He wants a job as an electrician.
2. He saw the ad in the newspaper.
3. Yes, he does.
4. He can fix electrical problems and fix wires in houses.
5. He studied electrical engineering.
6. He gives Stan an application to fill out.

3 1. d
2. f
3. e
4. b
5. a
6. c

Page 127

4 Answers will vary.
5 Answers will vary.
6 Answers will vary.

Page 128

1 Circled: check your reports for spelling; learn something new

2 1. No, she doesn't.
2. She checked two.
3. She cleans her tools and work area, and she answers phones politely.
4. She checked two.
5. She needs to check reports for spelling and to learn something new.
6. She can use "Spell Check" on her computer and ask co-workers for help. She can look online and on the company bulletin board to find job training classes, and she can ask co-workers about job training classes.

Page 129

3 Answers will vary.
A 1. A
2. E
3. D
4. B
5. C

Pages 130–131

1. C
2. D
3. C
4. D
5. B
6. C
7. D
8. B
9. C
10. A
11. A
12. C
13. A
14. B
15. D
16. C
17. B
18. B
19. A
20. B

Unit 10

Page 132

1 1. H
2. E
3. A
4. D
5. C
6. G
7. F
8. I
9. B

2 1. weren't
2. were
3. was
4. weren't
5. were
6. were
7. wasn't
8. weren't
9. weren't
10. were

Page 133

1 1. was early
2. was late
3. was early
4. were on time
5. were late
6. was on time

2 1. claim
2. noisy
3. crowded
4. platform
5. stop
6. early
7. counter
   airport

3 Possible answers:
1. early, on time, late
2. early, on time, late
3. bus, train, airplane
4. quiet, crowded, noisy
5. bus, train, airplane
6. bus, train, airplane
7. bus, train, airplane

Page 134

1
1. There's a problem.
2. There's a problem.
3. I'm upset.
4. Yes
5. No
6. No

2
1. I'm late
2. the bus
3. You missed
4. important customer
5. I'm so sorry
6. call next time

3
1. C
2. H
3. F
4. B
5. A
6. D
7. E
8. G

Page 135

1
1. A. No problem. I can take your phone calls.

   B. Well, please call next time. You missed some important phone calls.

2
1. I'm really sorry
2. 30 minutes late
3. late for work
4. What time
5. No problem
6. take your phone calls

3
1. ✓
2.
3. ✓
4.
5. ✓
6.

Page 136

1
1. mountains
2. beach
3. movies
4. amusement park
5. lake
6. museum

2
1. went to the beach
2. went to the mountains
3. went to the museum
4. went to the amusement park
5. went to the lake
6. went to the movies

3
1. c
2. d
3. a
4. e
5. b

Page 137

1
1. Was; was
2. Were; weren't
3. Was; was
4. Was; wasn't
5. Was; wasn't
6. Were; were
7. Were; wasn't
8. Were; weren't

2
A. 4:30
B. 4:45
C. 4:30
D. 4:05
E. 7:15
F. 4:15

3
1. Bus A
2. Bus D
3. Bus E
4. Bus C
5. Bus F
6. Bus A

Page 138

1
1. pass
2. exact change
3. ticket
4. token

2
1. exact change
2. pass
3. tokens
4. ticket

Page 139

3
1. this bus go
2. it doesn't
3. Bus 57
4. this bus stop
5. it's an express
6. local bus
7. the fare
8. exact change

4
1. no
2. no
3. yes
4. no
5. no
6. yes

5 Answers will vary.

Page 140

1
1. red
2. green
3. blue
4. Washington
5. red
6. Clark/Lake

Page 141

2
1. Where
2. the subway
3. the red line
4. the blue line
5. the last stop
6. the airport
7. on time
8. What time

3
1. She's going to Colorado on vacation.
2. It's on the blue line.
3. She changes at Washington.
4. It leaves at 7:30.

4
1. Harrison
2. red line
3. Washington, blue line
4. Medical Center

Page 142

1
1. c
2. e
3. d
4. a
5. b

2
1. traffic
2. highway
3. alternate route
4. to avoid

Page 143

3
1. D
2. C
3. E
4. A
5. F
6. H
7. G
8. B

4
1. Open
2. Get directions
3. address
4. Enter
5. Check
6. Find
7. map

5 Answers will vary.

Pages 144–145
1. A
2. B
3. D
4. C
5. C
6. A
7. D
8. A
9. C
10. A
11. D
12. B
13. D
14. A
15. B
16. C
17. A
18. C
19. D
20. B

Unit 11

Page 146

1
1. d
2. e
3. f
4. c
5. a
6. b

2
1. have
2. has
3. have
4. have
5. don't have
6. doesn't have
7. doesn't have
8. don't have

Page 147

1 Students should fill out the diagram with the correct body parts. Any answers are acceptable for 1–8.

4
1. my ears hurt
2. his feet hurt
3. her head hurts
4. his stomach hurts
5. his back hurts
6. my throat hurts
7. toothache
8. flu, fever
9. hands
10. cold, nose

Page 148

1
1. d
2. f
3. e
4. b
5. c
6. a

2
1. I'm sick
2. come to work
3. What's wrong
4. My stomach
5. a fever
6. That's too bad
7. a lot of people
8. get well soon

3
1. c
2. b
3. a
4. d

Page 149

2
1. yes
2. no
3. no
4. no
5. yes
6. yes

3 Answers will vary

Page 150

1
1. f
2. h
3. a
4. e
5. d
6. g
7. b
8. c

2
1. should
2. should
3. shouldn't
4. shouldn't
5. should
6. should
7. shouldn't
8. should, shouldn't
9. shouldn't, should

3
1. shouldn't
2. shouldn't
3. should
4. should
5. should
6. shouldn't

Page 151

1
1. shouldn't
2. shouldn't
3. should
4. should
5. Should
6. should
7. should

2
1. 3:00 P.M.
2. Yes, he should.
3. She should take more at 4:00 P.M.
4. No, he shouldn't.

Page 152

1
1. e
2. d
3. f
4. c
5. b
6. a

2 1. I help you
2. my daughter
3. a rash
4. the doctor
5. daughter's name
6. her birthdate
7. her temperature
8. an opening
9. Is that OK?

Page 153

3 Answers will vary.
4 Answers will vary.
5 Answers will vary.

Page 154

1 1. C
2. B
3. D
4. A

2 1. Tom cut his hand with a knife.
2. A pot of hot water fell on his leg.
3. Raul hit his head.
4. Jill fell off her bicycle.

3
A 1. should
2. clean
3. should put
4. can use
5. can't use
6. Take

Page 155

B 1. emergency room
2. Don't use
3. should
4. don't move
5. should

4

For burns, you need...	For a broken bone, you need...
cool water	sling or crutches
soap	ice
dry bandage	bandage
antibiotic ointment	pain reliever
pain reliever	x-rays and emergency room treatment

5 Answers will vary.

Page 156

2 1. d
2. a
3. e
4. f
5. b
6. c

3
A 1. no
2. no
3. yes
4. no
5. no
6. yes
7. no
8. yes

Page 157

A Answers will vary.

Pages 158–159

1. D
2. B
3. B
4. A
5. A
6. C
7. A
8. B
9. C
10. C
11. B
12. D
13. C
14. A
15. B
16. B
17. B
18. C
19. D
20. C

Unit 12

Page 160

1 1. is going to
2. are going to
3. is going to
4. are going to
5. is going to
6. am going to

2 1. ask for a raise
2. move to a new city
3. rent an apartment
4. start my new job
5. finish school

3 1. I am going to ask for a raise.
2. You aren't going to finish school this year.
3. We are going to move to a new city.
4. My parents aren't going to sell their house.
5. David is going to buy a new computer.
6. She isn't going to look for a new job.

Page 161

1 1. it
2. you
3. her
4. them, it
5. it, us
6. her

2 1. are going to go
2. them
3. is going to meet
4. him
5. them
6. are going to go
7. am going to bring
8. her

3 1. house
2. married
3. finish
4. raise
5. start
   a. honeymoon
   b. move
   c. apartment
   d. raise
   e. job

1. b
2. a
3. e
4. c
5. d

Page 162

1
1. going to; f
2. gonna; g
3. gonna; e
4. going to ; d
5. going to; a
6. gonna; b
7. gonna; h
8. going to; c

2
1. c
2. e
3. f
4. d
5. a
6. b

3 4, 3, 1, 6, 2, 5

Page 163

1
1. what are you going to
2. I'm going to
3. You're going to
4. It's my favorite
5. What time
6. Are you going to

2 Answers will vary.

Page 164

1
1. get Internet access
2. get cable television
3. call the phone company
4. fix the bed
5. fix the dishwasher
6. get a new microwave
7. buy a new refrigerator
8. vacuum the carpet

2
1. Yes, she is.
2. No, she's not.
3. Yes, he is.
4. No, he's not.
5. Yes, they are.
6. No, they're not.
7. No, she's not.
8. Yes, they are.

Page 165

1
1. Is, going to; she is
2. Is, going to; he/she isn't
3. Are, going to; they are
4. Are, going to; I'm not or We're not
5. Are, going to; we're not
6. Is, going to; he is

2 Answers will vary.

3
1. the garage
2. the living room
3. the bathroom
4. the kitchen
5. the bedroom
6. the yard

Page 166

1
1. refrigerator
2. vacuum cleaner
3. microwave oven
4. toaster
5. washer
6. dryer
7. stove
8. iron

2
1. I'm calling
2. the electricity
3. your name and address
4. your account number
5. with the wires
6. What time

Page 167

3 Students should circle the words from the box.

4
1. no
2. no
3. no
4. yes
5. no

5 Answers will vary.

Page 168

2
1. She's looking for a washer.
2. The energy-efficient model is going to save money on Flora's electric bill.
3. The energy-efficient model costs more in the store.
4. The guarantee is for 6 months.
5. The warranty is for 12 months.
6. The instructions are in the owner's manual.

Page 169

3 Answers will vary.
4 Answers will vary.

Page 170

1
1. You're going to
2. are you going to
3. I'm going to
4. it's going
5. I can buy
6. I should take

2
1. Yes, she is.
2. No, she isn't. Isabel is.
3. No, it doesn't. It pays more.
4. No, she doesn't.
5. She's going to buy a dryer.
6. No, she isn't.
7. She's planning to take some classes.

Page 171

3 Answers will vary.
4
1. It's East Bank.
2. No, she isn't.
3. She's paying the electric bill.
4. Her account number is 12972411.
5. No, she doesn't.
6. The phone number is (800) 555-7700.
7. She should click "Submit."

Page 172-173

1. D
2. C
3. C
4. B
5. A
6. B
7. D
8. A
9. A
10. C
11. D
12. B
13. A
14. C
15. B
16. B
17. C
18. A
19. B
20. C

Pre-Unit

**Pre-Unit, Letters and Numbers
Activity 1**
1. C
2. F
3. M
4. I
5. T
6. A
7. R
8. W
9. S
10. U

**Pre-Unit, Letters and Numbers
Activity 2**
1. H, I
2. I, S
3. M, Y
4. D, O
5. U, P
6. T, O
7. H, E
8. I, T
9. Y, O, U
10. T, H, E

**Pre-Unit, Letters and Numbers
Activity 3**
1. My name's Brenda. That's B-R-E-N-D-A.
2. I'm Maria. M-A-R-I-A.
3. Hello. I'm Lee. That's L-E-E.
4. My name is Peter. P-E-T-E-R.
5. I'm Betty. B-E-T-T-Y.
6. My name's Kendra. That's K-E-N-D-R-A.
7. Hi. Stan's my name. That's S-T-A-N.
8. I'm Tim. That's T-I-M.
9. I'm Susan. That's S-U-S-A-N.
10. Hello. My name is Craig. That's C-R-A-I-G.

**Pre-Unit, Letters and Numbers
Activity 4**
1. I'm David. D-A-V-I-D.
2. My name's Anna. A-N-N-A.
3. I'm Julia. That's J-U-L-I-A.
4. My name's Hector. H-E-C-T-O-R.
5. I'm Sonia. S-O-N-I-A.
6. My name's Raul. R-A-U-L.
7. I'm Hiro. H-I-R-O.

8. My name's Tomas. That's T-O-M-A-S.
9. Hi. My name's Cindy. That's C-I-N-D-Y.
10. I'm Eliot. That's E-L-I-O-T.

**Pre-Unit, Letters and Numbers
Activity 5**
1. 3
2. 4
3. 7
4. 19
5. 11
6. 14
7. 16
8. 20
9. 80
10. 70
11. 15
12. 8
13. 50
14. 30

**Pre-Unit, Letters and Numbers
Activity 6**
1. 4, 2, 3, 9
2. 9, 4, 1
3. 2, 6, 5, 3
4. 8, 2, 4, 9
5. 7, 2, 5, 6
6. 3, 1, 0, 8
7. 9, 5, 2, 4
8. 1, 6, 5, 7
9. 9, 2, 0, 3
10. 2, 1, 0, 6
11. 7, 5, 2, 3, 8
12. 9, 6, 0, 2, 8
13. 4, 5, 3, 9, 1
14. 9, 7, 2, 8, 4

**Pre-Unit, Letters and Numbers
Activity 7**
48, 48
26, 26
30, 30
72, 72
17, 17
35, 35
56, 56
12, 12
81, 81
63, 63
78, 78
54, 54

Pre-Unit, Grammar: Parts of Speech
Activity 3

1. We study English.
2. He is tall.
3. They walk to school.
4. You read books.
5. She is happy.
6. You listen to the teacher.
7. I write my name.
8. You talk at school.
9. They sit down.
10. We stand up.

Unit 1

Unit 1, Lesson 3
Activity 1

1. 50
2. 19
3. 13
4. 16 Main Street
5. My address is 80 Center Road.
6. The address is 1820 Park Street.
7. My telephone number is 555-1217.
8. The number is 555-4019.

Unit 1, Lesson 3
Activity 2

1. My address is 117 Bayview Street.
2. Stefan's address is 230 Lowell Avenue.
3. The address is 814 Woods Avenue.
4. The telephone number is 555-1890.
5. Please call 555-1519.
6. Maria's phone number is 555-3016.

Unit 1, Culture and Communication—Greetings, Activity 2

Cecelia: Good morning, Mr. Nelson.
Mr. Nelson: Hello, Cecelia. It's nice to see you.
Cecelia: How are you doing today?
Mr. Nelson: I'm OK, and you?
Cecelia: I'm fine, thanks. Well, I've got to run. Take care.
Mr. Nelson: OK. See you later.

Unit 1, Practice Test
1

Number 1. Listen to the speakers. What is the man's first name?
Male: Hi, I'm José Paez. I'm from Colombia.
Female: Hi, José. My name's Eva.

2

Number 2. Listen to the speaker. Choose the best response.
Female: Hi, I'm Laura.
Male: Hi, Laura. I'm Tran. It's nice to meet you.

3

Number 3. Listen to the speakers. Then answer the questions.
Female: What's your first and last name?
Male: Nick Clark.
Female: What's your address?
Male: 50 East Street.
Female: What's your occupation?
Male: I'm a construction worker.

Unit 2

Unit 2, Lesson 3
Activity 3

1. *A:* Is he from India?   *B:* No, he isn't.
2. *A:* Is she a nurse?   *B:* No, she isn't.
3. *A:* Is she tall and hardworking? *B:* Yes, she is.
4. *A:* Is he serious?   *B:* Yes, he is.
5. *A:* Is she neat?   *B:* No, she isn't.
6. *A:* Is he young?   *B:* No, he isn't.
7. *A:* Is she pretty?   *B:* Yes, she is.
8. *A:* Is he short?   *B:* Yes, he is.

Unit 2, Culture and Communication—Describe People, Activity 1

A: I'm short. I'm not tall.
B: You're not short. You're medium height.

A: I'm too heavy.
B: No, you're not heavy. You're average weight.

A: You're so thin!
B: Well, I'm average weight, too.

A: Are you messy?
B: No, I'm not. I'm not very neat, but I'm hardworking.

A: I'm hardworking, too. And I'm outgoing.
B: I'm not. I'm shy.

A: You're funny!
B: No, I'm serious!

Unit 2, Practice Test
1

Number 1. Listen to the speaker. Who is a nurse?
Male: Is that Emma?
Female: No, that's the Dr. Abel. Emma's a nurse. She's the tall and thin one.

2
Number 2. Listen to the speaker. Choose the best response.
Male: Is she short and thin?

3
Number 3. Listen to the speakers. Then answer the questions.
Male: Hi. Is Mary there?
Female: No, I'm sorry. She isn't. Can I take a message?
Male: Sure. This is her brother, John. My number is 555-5384.
Female: Did you say 555-5384?
Male: Yes, that's right. Thanks.

Unit 3

Unit 3, Lesson 5
1. **note**book
2. **rest**room
3. **snack** bar
4. **trash** can
5. **ven**ding machine
6. **wa**ter fountain
7. com**put**er lab
8. public **tele**phone
9. se**cur**ity office
10. infor**ma**tion desk
11. **chil**dren
12. **back**pack

Unit 3, Practice Test
1
Number 1. Listen to the speaker. Choose the best response.
Male: Is there a library in the school?
Female: Yes, there is. It's on the second floor.

2
Number 1. Listen to the speaker. Choose the best response.
Male: How many computers are in the library?

3
Number 3. Listen to the speakers. Then answer the questions.
Female: Excuse me, where's the snack bar?
Male: It's in the Williams Building.
Female: In the Williams Building?
Male: Yes, on the first floor.
Female: Are there restrooms there, too?
Male: Yes, there are.
Female: Thanks.

Unit 4

Unit 4, Lesson 3
Activity 1
1. Now, it's time for the weather. In Atlanta today, it is rainy. It's warm with a temperature of 75 degrees.
2. Over in Detroit, it's a cool and windy day. It's 45 degrees in the city.
3. In Salt Lake City, it's a beautiful day. It's dry and sunny. It's 64 degrees out there.
4. Finally, in San Diego, it's hot and humid. It's 92 degrees.

**Unit 4, Culture and Communication—
Talk about the Weather, Activity 1**
Carmen: Hi, Stan.
Stan: Hi, Carmen. How are you?
Carmen: Fine. And you?
Stan: OK.
[nervous pause/laughter as they try to think of something to say next.]
Carmen: It's really cold today.
Stan: You're right. And it's windy, too. It's terrible weather today.

Unit 4, Lesson 5
Activity 4
1. There's a party on the sixth of June.
2. There are eight birthdays this month.
3. Is your birthday on the twentieth?
4. July fourth is Independence Day.
5. There are thirty students in the snack bar.
6. Seventeen people are in class today.
7. The twenty-fifth is my birthday.
8. Today is the ninth.

Unit 4, Practice Test
1
Number 1. Listen to the speaker. Choose the best response.
Female: How's the weather in Chicago?
Male: It's windy and cold. It's 25 degrees. How is it in Atlanta?

2
Number 2. Listen to the speaker. Choose the best response.
Male: It's really hot today.

3
Number 3. Listen to the speakers. Then answer the questions.
Female: Excuse me, when's Valentine's Day?
Male: It's in February.
Female: Are there classes on Valentine's Day?

Male: Yes, there are. There's also a party at 8:00 in the evening after class.
Female: Oh, that's nice.

Unit 5

Unit 5, Lesson 3
Activity 1
1. *A:* Where's the supermarket?
   B: It's behind the police station.
2. *A:* Where's the supermarket?
   B: It's between the library and the post office.
3. *A:* Where's the supermarket?
   B: It's across from the movie theater.
4. *A:* Where's the supermarket?
   B: It's next to the library.

Unit 5, Lesson 5
Activity 1
1. Go right on Maple Street.
2. Turn left at the corner.
3. Go straight on First Street.
4. Cross the street.
5. Make a U-turn.
6. Park next to the library.

Unit 5, Practice Test
1
Number 1. Listen to the speaker. Where does the woman want to go?
Female: Excuse me, where's the Windsor Hotel?
Male: It's between the library and the supermarket. It's on Center Street.

2
Number 2. Listen to the speaker. Choose the best response.
Male: The post office is between the movie theater and the police station. It's on Green Street.

3
Number 3. Listen to the speakers. Then answer the questions.
Female: Excuse me, how do I get to the movie theater?
Male: Walk straight two blocks. Then turn left on Oak Street. It's between the drugstore and the supermarket.
Female: How far is it?
Male: About three blocks.
Female: Thank you.

Unit 6

Unit 6, Lesson 3
Activity 2
1. I'm looking for a large white shirt.
2. Rita is buying a small yellow hat.
3. Are there any blue jackets? I'm looking for a large one.
4. They're shopping for some brown pants. They need medium.
5. You're buying a black dress? What size—small?
6. Nick is looking for some blue shorts. His size is medium.

Unit 6, Listening and Conversation
Activity 3
1. We aren't shopping for books.
2. Nina is looking for some green shorts.
3. The customers are waiting in line for the salesclerk.
4. You aren't buying that purple hat.
5. Ivan isn't carrying the bags.
6. Nina and I are working here.

Unit 6, Practice Test
1
Number 1. Listen to the speaker. What does the customer want?
Female: I'm looking for some blue pants.
Male: OK. The blue and black pants are next to the shoes.

2
Number 2. Listen to the speaker. Choose the best response.
Male: What size?

3
Number 3. Listen to the speakers. Then answer the questions.
Male: Can I help you?
Female: Yes, I'm looking for some pants.
Male: What color?
Female: Blue.
Male: And what size?
Female: Medium.
Male: They're over here.

Unit 7

Unit 7, Culture and Communication
Activity 1
Al: I always eat breakfast. What about you?
Amare: Not me. I'm never hungry in the morning.
Al: I often read the newspaper. What about you?
Amare: Me, too. I always read about events around the world.
Al: I usually cook dinner. What about you?
Amare: No way. I never cook. My brother is a cook.
Al: I always go to bed early. What about you?
Amare: I never do. I do my homework, and then I read.
Al: I usually sleep eight hours a night. What about you?
Amare: I don't. But I always get up and exercise in the morning.
Al: Really? I never do. I hate exercise.

Unit 7, Lesson 5
Activity 5
1. Does she eat dinner at 6:00?
2. Does she drive to work or take the bus?
3. Does he come home at 8:00?
4. Does he work on Fridays?
5. Does he leave work at 7:00?
6. Does she take a class at night?

Unit 7, Practice Test
1
Number 1. Listen to the speakers. Then answer the question.
Male: What are you doing, Maria?
Female: I'm cleaning the apartment. My mother always comes for dinner on Thursday.

2
Number 1. Listen to the speaker. Choose the best response.
Male: What time do you usually arrive at work?

3
Number 3. Listen to the speakers. Then answer the questions.
Male: Do you drive to work, Pam?
Female: Yes, I do.
Male: What time do you usually leave work in the afternoon?
Female: At 4:30. Do you need a ride home, Bill?
Male: Yes, I do. My car isn't working. It's at the gas station.
Female: No problem. I'll meet you at 4:30.

Unit 8

Unit 8, Lesson 3
Activity 3
1. it
2. seat
3. cheap
4. bit
5. meat
6. chick
7. feet
8. pick

Unit 8, Culture and Communication
Activity 1
A: Would you like something to drink?
B: Yes, please.

A: Do you want some juice?
B: No, thank you.

Unit 8, Practice Test
1
Number 1. Listen to the speaker. Choose the best response.
Are they on sale?

2
Number 2. Listen to the speaker. Choose the best response.
Where are they?

3
Number 3. Listen to the speakers. Then answer the questions.
Male: Hi, Margot.
Female: Oh, hello, David.
Male: Tell me, when do we have lunch here?
Female: Usually at 12:00. Do you want to eat with us?
Male: Sure. Where do you eat?
Female: Sometimes in the restaurant.
Male: Is there anything good there?
Female: Soup, salad, and sandwiches. I like the vegetable soup. It's great.
Male: Sounds good.

Unit 9

Unit 9, Lesson 3
Activity 1
1. Eva can't fix the wires.
2. She can use power tools.
3. Marcos can drive a truck.
4. He can't drive a forklift.
5. We can use a computer.
6. We can prepare Chinese food.
7. My brothers can't work at night.
8. They can't work Saturdays.

Unit 9, Culture and Communication
Activity 1
1. *A:* Can you drive a truck?
   B: Yes, I can. I love to drive trucks.

2. *A:* Can you use a computer?
   B: No, I can't, but I learn quickly. And I can use other machines.

Unit 9, Practice Test
1
Number 1. Listen to the speaker. Choose the best response.
What kind of job are you looking for?

2
Number 2. Listen to the speaker. Choose the best response.
Can you take food orders?

3
Number 3. Listen to the speakers. Then answer the questions.
Male: I'm looking for a job.
Female: What was your last job?
Male: I was an electrician.
Female: I see. What did you do?
Male: I fixed wires and electrical problems.
Female: Did you study to be an electrician in school?
Male: No, I didn't. I worked with my father.

Unit 10

Unit 10, Lesson 3
Activity 1
1. **Uh**-oh. We missed the train.
2. There's the bus! **Uh**-oh. We're too late.
3. Oh, **no**. I can't find my ticket.
4. *A:* Are you going away on vacation?
   B: Uh-**huh**.
5. *A:* Was Sheila at work today?
   B: **Unh**-uh.
6. *A:* Did you buy the tickets yet?
   B: **Unh**-uh.

Unit 10, Culture and Communication
Activity 1
1. *Female:* I'm sorry. The bus was 30 minutes late! I'm late for work.
   Male 1: No problem. I can take your phone calls.

2. *Male 2:* Oops! Sorry. I missed the bus.
   Male 1: Well, please call next time. You missed some important phone calls.

Unit 10, Practice Test
1
Number 1. Listen to the speaker. Choose the best response.
Where were you last week?

2
Number 2. Listen to the speaker. Choose the best response.
You missed an important phone call this morning.

3
Number 3. Listen to the speakers. Then answer the questions.
Male: Hi, Margot.
Female: Oh, hello, David.
Male: Where were you last week?
Female: I went to the lake for vacation.
Male: Was it fun?
Female: Yes. The lake was beautiful and clean. But the water was really cold.
Male: Where did you stay?
Female: In a hotel. It was clean, but it was crowded.

Unit 11

Unit 11, Lesson 3
Activity 3

1. Hi. This is Kevin. I can't come to work today. I have a sore throat and a fever.
2. Hi. This is Alicia. I feel really terrible today. My head hurts and I have a bad cough.
3. Hi. This is Anh-Li. I'm sick. I have the flu and I can't work today.
4. This is Tung. I'm at home and can't come to work today. I have an earache and a fever.

Unit 11, Culture and Communication
Activity 1

Monica: Sara, are you all right?
Sara: Hi, Monica. No, not really.
Monica: What's the problem?
Sara: I have a runny nose and a fever. Do you think I have the flu?
Monica: Maybe. Talk to the boss. You should leave early and go home to rest.
Sara: That's a good idea.
Monica: I hope you feel better.
Sara: Thanks. Me, too.

Unit 11, Lesson 4
Activity 3

1. You have a backache? You **shouldn't** put ice on it.
2. Does he have the flu? Glen **shouldn't** go to work.
3. Do their hands hurt? They **should** put ice on them.
4. Does Nancy still have a high fever? She **should** see a doctor.
5. Does your brother's ear hurt? He **should** use some ear drops.
6. Our stomachs hurt. We **shouldn't** eat hot food.

Unit 11, Practice Test

1
Number 1. Listen to the speaker. Choose the best response.
Are you OK?

2
Number 2. Listen to the speaker. Choose the best response.
What's wrong?

3
Number 3. Listen to the speakers. Then answer the questions.
Female: Hello, Mr. Ruiz. How are you today?
Male: I'm not feeling well at all, Dr. Michaels.
Female: I see. What's the problem?
Male: Well, I have a sore throat. It hurts a lot.
Female: Is there anything else?
Male: Yes, I have a fever, too.
Female: You probably have a bad cold. You should rest and drink plenty of juice and other liquids.
Male: Okay. Thank you.

Unit 12

Unit 12, Lesson 3
Activity 1

1. I'm going to work tonight.
2. I'm not gonna watch TV.
3. Eva's gonna prepare some Chinese food.
4. She isn't going to make pizza.
5. My brothers are going to move to Seattle.
6. They aren't gonna sell the house.
7. Are you gonna ask for a raise?
8. Are you going to look for a new job?

Unit 12, Practice Test

1
Number 1. Listen to the speaker. Choose the best response.
What are you doing this weekend?

2
Number 2. Listen to the speaker. Choose the best response.
Can you help me wash my car?

3
Number 3. Listen to the speakers. Then answer the questions.
Male: I'm going to look for a car tomorrow. Do you want to come?
Female: Sorry, I can't tomorrow. I promised my parents that I'm going to work on my apartment.
Male: Really? What are you going to do?
Female: Fix the doors.
Male: OK. Maybe some other time?
Female: Sure. Thanks.

Name: _____ **Date:** _____

🎧 **LISTENING:** Listen to the conversation. Then choose the correct answer for each sentence.
TCD4, 2

1. What's the woman's name?
   A. Oak Street
   B. Mary Server
   C. Mary Cooper
   D. Full Name

2. What is her occupation?
   A. student
   B. teacher
   C. cook
   D. server

3. What is her address?
   A. 10 Oak Street
   B. 12 Pine Street
   C. 20 Oak Street
   D. 20 Pine Street

LISTEN to the sentences. Choose the best response.

4.
   A. What's your name?
   B. Hi, Ann. I'm Maria. Nice to meet you too.
   C. I'm a student.
   D. My address is 324 South Street.

5.
   A. 1516 Main Street
   B. Mark Tucker
   C. 703-555-9901
   D. 52218

GRAMMAR: Choose the correct word to complete each sentence.

6. I _____ from the United States.
   A. am
   B. is
   C. are
   D. a

7. Marco and Paul _____ cooks.
   A. am
   B. is
   C. are
   D. a

8. _____ is a student.
   A. I
   B. You
   C. We
   D. She

9. _____ are from New York.
   A. I
   B. He
   C. It
   D. They

10. _____ am single.
    A. I
    B. You
    C. He
    D. We

11. _____ are married.
    A. We
    B. He
    C. She
    D. I

12. My address _____ 1400 South Main Street.
    A. am
    B. are
    C. is
    D. not

13. Pedro and I are _____.
    A. a cook
    B. server
    C. construction workers
    D. man

14. Henry is _____.
    A. dentist
    B. doctors
    C. children
    D. a salesclerk

15. You and Elva are _____.
    A. teachers
    B. woman
    C. a student
    D. child

Name: _____   **Date:** _____

READING: Look at the envelope. Choose the correct answer.

Lena Parker
3572 Trade St.
San Diego, CA 92101

Ivan Taylor
123 South Street
Miami, FL 33101

16. What is Lena's zip code?

   A. 3572   C. 123

   B. 92101   D. 33101

17. Ivan is his first name. His last name is _____.

   A. Parker   C. Taylor

   B. Lena   D. Miami

18. My name is Ivan. My address is _____.

   A. 3572 Trade Street   C. 123 South Street

   B. Florida   D. 33101

19. Lena's city is _____.

   A. Trade   C. California

   B. San Diego   D. Parker

20. Ivan's state is _____.

   A. Florida   C. Taylor

   B. California   D. Parker

VOCABULARY: Choose the best word to complete the sentence.

21. I'm not single. I'm _____.

   A. a student   C. married

   B. a teacher   D. female

22. My _____ is 555-4671.

   A. address   C. phone number

   B. zip code   D. email address

23. Your _____ is 55902.

   A. address   C. telephone number

   B. zip code   D. email address

24. Ten people in my class are women. Nine are _____.

   A. female   C. men

   B. cook   D. child

25. I am from _____.

   A. married   C. Somalia

   B. student   D. Habiba

Name: _____   **Date:** _____

🎧 **LISTENING:** Listen to the conversation. Then choose the correct answer for each sentence.

1. What is the phone number?
   A. 585-8225   C. 525-8255
   B. 555-5825   D. 555-8825

2. What's the man's name?
   A. Anna   C. Alex
   B. Bob   D. Bart

3. Who is he?
   A. a brother   C. a cousin
   B. a sister   D. a father

LISTEN to the sentences. Choose the best response.

4.
   A. This is my brother.   C. No, I'm not. He's over there.
   B. I'm at school.   D. My last name is Ruiz.

5.
   A. Her name is Marta.   C. She is shy.
   B. No, she isn't. She's short.   D. She is my mother.

GRAMMAR: Choose the correct word to complete each sentence.

6. _____ you shy?
   A. Am   C. Are
   B. Is   D. Isn't

7. _____ he your brother?
   A. Are   C. Is
   B. Aren't   D. Am

8. _____ I your student?
   A. Are   C. Is
   B. Aren't   D. Am

9. Is _____ a doctor?
   A. I   C. you
   B. he   D. they

10. Are _____ a cook?
    A. I   C. he
    B. you   D. we

11. I am Mark's sister. He is _____ brother.
    A. your   C. their
    B. his   D. my

12. Lisa is married. _____ husband is Yuri.
    A. His   C. Their
    B. Her   D. Our

13. Are you a grandmother? What are the names of _____ grandchildren?
    A. my   C. your
    B. our   D. her

14. This is my friend Ann. _____ last name is Parker.
    A. Ann   C. Ann's
    B. Anns   D. Anns'

15. Robert and Victor are _____.
    A. brothers   C. childrens
    B. brother's   D. childs

Name: _____ **Date:** _____

READING: Read and answer the questions.

> My name is Olga. My brother's name is Ivan. I am a student and a nurse. I am short and heavy. I am also a little shy. I am serious. Ivan is different. He isn't a student. He is a construction worker. He is tall and thin. He is outgoing. He is funny. Ivan and I are both messy.

16. Is Ivan Olga's father?
  A. Yes, he is.   B. No, he isn't

17. Is Olga tall?
  A. Yes, she is.   B. No, she isn't.

18. Is Ivan funny?
  A. Yes, he is.   B. No, he isn't.

19. Is Olga a nurse?
  A. Yes, she is.   B. No, she isn't.

20. Are Ivan and Olga neat?
  A. Yes, they are.   B. No, they aren't.

VOCABULARY: Choose the best word to complete the sentence.

21. I am married. My _____ name is Carl.
  A. mother's   C. cousin's
  B. sister's   D. husband's

22. Your mother's brother is your _____.
  A. aunt   C. cousin
  B. uncle   D. father

23. His mother's daughter is his _____.
  A. sister   C. aunt
  B. cousin   D. brother

24. They are not outgoing. They are _____.
  A. old   C. lazy
  B. messy   D. shy

25. Laura is not lazy. She is _____.
  A. outgoing   C. pretty
  B. hardworking   D. shy

Name: _____   **Date:** _____

🎧 **LISTENING:** Listen to the conversation. Then choose the correct answer for each sentence.
TCD4, 4

1. The _____ is in the Bryant Center.
   A. library   C. information desk
   B. snack bar   D. computer lab

2. It's on the _____ floor.
   A. first   C. third
   B. second   D. fourth

3. It's in room _____.
   A. 205   C. 405
   B. 302   D. 125

LISTEN to the sentences. Choose the best response.

4.
   A. 500   C. Yes, there are.
   B. the vending machines D. It's on the first floor.

5.
   A. 25   C. They're on the second floor.
   B. chairs   D. in room 205

GRAMMAR: Choose the correct answer to complete each sentence.

6. There _____ 10 classrooms.
   A. is   C. isn't
   B. are   D. am

7. There _____ any pencils.
   A. isn't   C. aren't
   B. is   D. are

8. There _____ a water fountain in the hall.
   A. is   C. aren't
   B. are   D. am not

9. _____ there windows in the classroom?
   A. Am   C. Be
   B. Is   D. Are

10. Are there vending machines in the snack bar?
    A. Yes, there is.   C. Yes, there are.
    B. No, there isn't. D. No, there aren't.

11. The stairs are _____ the lobby.
    A. at   C. on
    B. in   D. to

12. The school is _____ 521 South Street.
    A. at   C. on
    B. in   D. to

13. The restrooms are _____ the third floor.
    A. at   C. on
    B. in   D. to

14. The library is _____ the Grant Building.
    A. at   C. on
    B. in   D. to

15. Tina is _____ work.
    A. at   C. on
    B. in   D. to

Name: _____ **Date:** _____

READING: Read and choose the best answer.

- Home
- Register
- Classes
- About Us
- Career

Winter Valley School

There are more than 150 classes at Winter Valley School, including classes in English as a Second Language, computers, and math. There are 10,000 students at Winter Valley School, from 30 different countries. Classes are offered at three locations: Center City, North Campus, and West Campus. There is a snack bar, bookstore, computer lab, and library at each location.

16. At Winter Valley Adult School, there are classes in ESL, _____, and math.

    A. reading   C. computers

    B. writing   D. Spanish

17. There are students from _____ countries.

    A. 30   C. 10,000

    B. 150   D. 3

18. The locations are _____, North Campus, and West Campus.

    A. Center Campus   C. North City

    B. Center City   D. Winter Campus

19. At West Campus, there is a snack bar, bookstore, _____, and library.

    A. security office   C. computer lab

    B. information desk   D. elevator

20. There are _____ students at the school.

    A. 30   C. 3

    B. 150   D. 10,000

VOCABULARY: Choose the best word to complete the sentence.

21. There are three _____ in my bag.

    A. elevators   C. pencils

    B. computers   D. vending machines

22. The elevator is in the _____.

    A. vending machine   C. water fountain

    B. lobby   D. backpack

23. There are 30 _____ in the library.

    A. restrooms   C. snack bars

    B. computers   D. vending machines

24. There is a _____ on the teacher's desk.

    A. water fountain   C. marker

    B. security office   D. table

25. There is a men's _____ in the hall.

    A. computer   C. vending machine

    B. restroom   D. elevator

Name: _____   **Date:** _____

🎧 **LISTENING:** Listen to the conversation. Then choose the correct answer for each sentence.

1. The weather in London is _____.
   A. cool   C. humid
   B. hot   D. sunny

2. The temperature is _____ degrees.
   A. 40   C. 80
   B. 50   D. 90

3. The weather in New York is _____.
   A. cold   C. warm
   B. cool   D. hot

LISTEN to the sentences. Choose the best response.

4.
   A. On Sept. 4   C. 55 degrees
   B. at 2:00   D. It's cool and rainy.

5.
   A. It's hot and sunny.   C. 9:30
   B. It's winter.   D. May 4

GRAMMAR: Answer the questions.

6. What time is it?
   A. It's in May.   C. It's foggy.
   B. It's 2:05.   D. It's on April 1.

7. When is your birthday?
   A. It's in June. C. It's sunny.
   B. It's 3:15.   D. It's in the morning.

8. When are your classes?
   A. It's in November.   C. They're rainy.
   B. They're at 9:00   D. It's at 9:30.
      and 11:30.

9. When is the test?
   A. It's in August.   C. It's rainy.
   B. It's on June 5.   D. It's clear.

10. How is the weather?
    A. It's in May.   C. It's hot.
    B. It's 2:00.   D. It's my birthday.

11. My birthday is _____ June 23.
    A. at   C. on
    B. in   D. to

12. The test is _____ 1:00.
    A. at   C. on
    B. in   D. to

13. His birthday is _____ December.
    A. at   C. on
    B. in   D. to

14. It's cool _____ the morning.
    A. at   C. on
    B. in   D. to

15. It's hot _____ the summer.
    A. at   C. on
    B. in   D. to

Name: _____   **Date:** _____

READING: Read and choose the best answer.

Important School Year Dates				
Days with NO CLASSES in gray				
Registration	August 20–24	Exams	December 13–16
First Day of Class	August 27	Winter Break	December 16–January 3
Labor Day	September 3	New Year's Day	January 1
New Student Meeting	September 7 (1:00)	First Day of Class	January 4
Teacher Workday	October 14	Valentine's Day Party	February 14
Halloween Party	October 31	Spring Break	March 3–10
Thanksgiving	November 22	Last Day of Class	May 23
Last Day of Class	December 15	Exams	May 24–26

16. When is the first day of class?
    A. It's on August 20.   C. It's in September.
    B. It's on August 27.   D. It's a 9 A.M.

17. What time is the new student meeting?
    A. At 1:00   C. On 9/7
    B. In September   D. In the morning

18. When is spring break?
    A. May 24-26   C. December 16-January 3
    B. December 13-16   D. March 3-10

19. When is Thanksgiving?
    A. November 22   C. October 31
    B. September 3   D. January 1

20. When are there classes?
    A. On September 3   C. On August 22
    B. On October 14   D. On September 5

VOCABULARY: Choose the best answer to complete the sentence.

21. It's not clear. It's _____.
    A. sunny   C. cloudy
    B. cold   D. hot

22. It's not cold. It's _____.
    A. hot   C. snowy
    B. rainy   D. foggy

23. It's winter. It's _____.
    A. hot and humid   C. cold and snowy
    B. warm and sunny   D. sunny and windy

24. Independence Day is in _____.
    A. February   C. September
    B. July   D. December

25. It's hot and humid in the _____.
    A. winter   C. spring
    B. fall   D. summer

Name: _____   **Date:** _____

🎧 **LISTENING:** Listen to the conversation. Then choose the correct answer for each sentence.
TCD4, 6

1. Where is he going?

   A. the library   C. the community center

   B. the police station   D. the school

2. How far is it?

   A. one block   C. three blocks

   B. two blocks   D. four blocks

3. How does he get there?

   A. Turn right on   C. Go straight on
      Main Street.   Main Street.

   B. Turn left on   D. Start on Main Street.
      Main Street.

LISTEN to the sentences. Choose the best response.

4.

   A. It's next to the   C. Yes, it is.
      gas station.

   B. Turn left.   D. Park behind it.

5.

   A. It's four blocks away.   C. No, it is next to the
                                   school.

   B. Yes, it is open from   D. Make a U-turn.
      9:00 to 8:00

GRAMMAR: Choose the best answer.

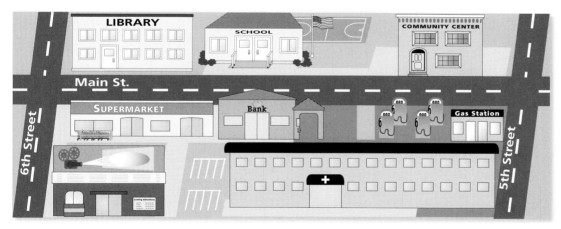

6. The supermarket is in front of the movie theater.
   The bank is _____ the supermarket.

   A. between   C. behind

   B. next to   D. across from

7. The school is _____ the library and the
   community center.

   A. between   C. in

   B. next to   D. at

8. The community center is _____ the gas station.

   A. between   C. behind

   B. next to   D. across from

9. The hospital is _____ the movie theater.

   A. between   C. behind

   B. next to   D. across from

10. The bank is _____ the supermarket and the gas
    station.

   A. between   C. behind

   B. next to   D. across from

11. The gas station is _____ the hospital.

   A. between   C. across from

   B. in front of   D. on

Name: _____   **Date:** _____

12. You are at the library. To get to the community center:
   A. Turn left.
   B. Turn right.
   C. Walk two blocks.
   D. Stop in front of the school.

13. You are at the gas station. To get to the community center:
   A. Turn right on 5th Street.
   B. Turn left on Main Street.
   C. Cross Main Street.
   D. Turn right on 6th Street.

14. You are at the movie theater. To get to the library:
   A. Turn right on 6th Street.
   B. Turn left on 6th Street.
   C. Cross 6th Street.
   D. Turn right on Main Street.

15. You are at the bank. To get to the hospital:
   A. Turn left on Main Street. Walk two blocks.
   B. Turn right on Main Street. Turn right on 5th Street.
   C. Turn left on 5th Street. Turn right on Main Street.
   D. Turn right on 6th Street. Turn left on Main Street.

READING: Read and choose the best answer.

Welcome To Madison!
There are many government services in Madison.

Community Center
The Community Center is on Main Street. It is next to the hospital. It is open from 9 a.m. to 8 p.m. There are English classes in the morning and at night. Call 555-9248 for more information.

MADISON TOWN HALL

Police Station
The police station is on Main Street. Call 911 for emergency help. Call 555-9103 for questions.

POLICE

Fire Station
The fire station is next to the police station on Main Street. There are two fire trucks.

Madison City Hospital
The hospital is across from the fire station and police station. The emergency room is open 24 hours.

PHONE DIRECTORY
Police Station
555-9103

Fire Station
555-7823

Community Center
555-9248

Hospital
555-6534

POLICE STATION		FIRE STATION
MAIN STREET		
COMMUNITY CENTER		HOSPITAL

Name: _____   **Date:** _____

16. Where is the police station?
    A. It's next to the fire station.
    B. It's on 5th street.
    C. It's next to the hospital.
    D. It's between the community center and the fire station.

17. What is the telephone number for the Community Center?
    A. 555-9103
    B. 555-7823
    C. 555-9248
    D. 555-6534

18. Where are the English classes?
    A. at the fire station
    B. at the police station
    C. at the library
    D. at the community center

19. What is the number for emergency help?
    A. 911
    B. 555-7823
    C. 555-9248
    D. 555-6534

20. When is the community center open?
    A. in the morning
    B. from 9 A.M. to 8 P.M.
    C. at night
    D. 24 hours

VOCABULARY: Choose the best word to complete the sentence.

21. There are doctors at the _____.
    A. gas station
    B. supermarket
    C. library
    D. hospital

22. There are servers at a _____.
    A. restaurant
    B. gas station
    C. hospital
    D. post office

23. There are books at a _____.
    A. gas station
    B. restaurant
    C. library
    D. bank

24. There are envelopes at a _____.
    A. restaurant
    B. post office
    C. gas station
    D. hospital

25. There are police officers at the _____.
    A. bank
    B. school
    C. library
    D. police station

Name: _____   **Date:** _____

🎧 **LISTENING:** Listen to the conversation. Then choose the correct answer for each sentence.
TCD4, 7

1. What is she looking for?
   - **A.** pants
   - **C.** a skirt
   - **B.** a shirt
   - **D.** shorts

2. What color is she looking for?
   - **A.** blue
   - **C.** yellow
   - **B.** black
   - **D.** brown

3. What size?
   - **A.** small
   - **C.** large
   - **B.** medium
   - **D.** extra large

LISTENING: Listen to the sentences. Choose the best response.

4.
   - **A.** Yes, I'm looking for a green shirt.
   - **C.** They're on sale.
   - **B.** Gray pants
   - **D.** $19.99.

5.
   - **A.** Small, medium and large.
   - **C.** Yes, they are.
   - **B.** A small, please.
   - **D.** $24.95.

GRAMMAR: Choose the best answer.

6. Bima is _____ for shoes.
   - **A.** look
   - **C.** looking
   - **B.** looks
   - **D.** is looking

7. Ursula and Ben _____ shirts.
   - **A.** is trying on
   - **C.** am trying on
   - **B.** are trying on
   - **D.** trying on

8. I _____ a hat.
   - **A.** am buying
   - **C.** are buying
   - **B.** buying
   - **D.** is buying

9. You are _____ my dress.
   - **A.** wear
   - **C.** wearing
   - **B.** wears
   - **D.** are wearing

10. We _____ today.
   - **A.** isn't
   - **C.** isn't working
   - **B.** aren't
   - **D.** aren't working

11. She _____ customers.
   - **A.** not helping
   - **C.** isn't helping
   - **B.** don't help
   - **D.** is helping not

12. Look at this dress. How much _____?
   - **A.** are they
   - **C.** is it
   - **B.** they are
   - **D.** it is

13. The pants are on sale. How much _____?
   - **A.** are they
   - **C.** is it
   - **B.** they are
   - **D.** it is

14. How much _____ the shoes?
   - **A.** are
   - **C.** aren't
   - **B.** is
   - **D.** isn't

15. How much _____ that shirt?
   - **A.** are
   - **C.** aren't
   - **B.** is
   - **D.** isn't

Name: _____ **Date:** _____

READING: Read and choose the best answer.

16. How much are the children's shirts?
    A. $15   **C.** $22
    B. $7   **D.** $35

17. How much are the jackets?
    A. $15   **C.** $22
    B. $7   **D.** $35

18. It is $12. What am I buying?
    A. pants   **C.** a hat
    B. shorts   **D.** a dress

19. These are $15. What are they?
    A. pants   **C.** shoes
    B. shorts   **D.** skirts

20. These are $19. What are they?
    A. pants   **C.** shoes
    B. shorts   **D.** skirts

VOCABULARY: Choose the best answer.

21. She is wearing pants. She isn't wearing _____.
    A. shoes   **C.** socks
    B. a shirt   **D.** a dress

22. Jack is wearing shorts. He isn't wearing _____.
    A. pants   **C.** shoes
    B. a shirt   **D.** a hat

23. The salesclerk is _____ the customer.
    A. trying on   **C.** helping
    B. buying   **D.** carrying

24. My parents are _____ in line.
    A. waiting   **C.** trying on
    B. buying   **D.** shopping

25. There is one dime and three quarters. There is _____.
    A. 10 cents   **C.** 55 cents
    B. 25 cents   **D.** 85 cents

Name: _____   Date: _____

🎧 **LISTENING:** Listen to the conversation. Then choose the correct answer for each sentence.
TCD8

1. Registration is _____.
   A. Tuesday morning   C. Thursday morning
   B. Tuesday afternoon   D. Thursday night

2. She _____ at that time.
   A. sleeps   C. walks
   B. works   D. cooks

3. He asks about _____.
   A. Bima   C. Sam
   B. Jon   D. James

LISTEN to the sentences. Choose the best response.

4.
   A. at 7:00   C. at home
   B. He gets up at 7:00. D. morning

5.
   A. Yes, she does.   C. Yes, I do.
   B. No, he doesn't.   D. No, we don't.

GRAMMAR: Choose the best answer.

6. I _____ at 8 A.M.
   A. get dressed   B. gets dressed

7. She _____ at 7:15.
   A. eat dinner   B. eats dinner

8. You _____ at 10:00.
   A. go to bed   B. goes to bed

9. It _____ at 11:00.
   A. arrive   B. arrives

10. Jack _____ at 6:30.
    A. brush his teeth   B. brushes his teeth

11. We _____ do homework in the morning.
    A. don't   B. doesn't

12. They _____ read in the evening.
    A. don't   B. doesn't

13. _____ she _____ lunch at 12:00?
    A. Eats/do   C. Do/eat
    B. Does/eat   D. Do/eats

14. _____ you _____ to work every day?
    A. Do/drive   C. Does/drive
    B. Do/drives   D. Does/drives

15. _____ Mike and Rick _____ the bus?
    A. Do/rides   C. Does/ride
    B. Do/ride   D. Does/rides

READING: Read and choose the best answer.

> Lidia works very hard. She works at two jobs. On Monday, Wednesday, and Friday, she cooks at a restaurant. She arrives at 6:00 in the morning. She leaves at 6:00 in the evening. On Tuesday, Thursday and Saturday, Lidia works in a doctor's office. She answers the phone. She arrives at 9:00 and leaves at 5:00. On Tuesday and Thursday evening, Lidia takes classes from 7:00 to 10:00.

Name: _____ **Date:** _____

16. When does Lidia arrive at work on Wednesday?

    A. At 9:00   **C.** At 5:00

    B. At 6:00   **D.** At 7:00

17. How many jobs does Lidia have?

    A. one   **C.** three

    B. two   **D.** four

18. When does Lidia take classes?

    A. On Monday, Wednesday and Friday

    C. On Monday and Wednesday

    B. On Tuesday, Thursday and Saturday

    D. On Tuesday and Thursday

19. How many hours does Lidia work on Saturday?

    A. 8   **C.** 3

    B. 12   **D.** 6

20. How many hours a week does Lidia work at the restaurant?

    A. 12   **C.** 36

    B. 24   **D.** 50

VOCABULARY: Choose the best word to complete the sentence.

21. I get up at 7:00 every day. I _____ get up at 7:00.

    A. never   **C.** often

    B. sometimes   **D.** always

22. We go to the store two days a week. We _____ go to the store.

    A. always   **C.** usually

    B. sometimes   **D.** never

23. I don't eat breakfast. I _____ have cereal in the morning.

    A. always   **C.** usually

    B. sometimes   **D.** never

24. I go to school on Monday and Wednesday. On Monday I drive. On Wednesday, I _____.

    A. take a class   **C.** ride the bus

    B. play soccer   **D.** don't study

25. Jen _____ in the morning. Then she goes to work.

    A. cooks breakfast   **C.** goes to bed

    B. cooks dinner   **D.** comes home

Name: _____   **Date:** _____

🎧 **LISTENING:** Listen to the conversation. Then choose the correct answer for each sentence.
TCD4, 9

1. What is he ordering to eat?

   A. A chicken sandwich   **C.** Soup

   B. A cheeseburger   **D.** A hamburger

2. What does he want to drink?

   A. a small soda   **C.** a large soda

   B. a small milk   **D.** a large milk

3. What side order is he getting?

   A. French fries   **C.** chips

   B. a salad   **D.** soup

LISTEN to the sentences. Choose the best response.

4.

   A. No, thank you.   **C.** A chicken sandwich.

   B. Small, please.   **D.** $2.50.

5.

   A. For breakfast   **C.** $4.05 a box

   B. every day   **D.** in Aisle 4

GRAMMAR: Choose the best answer.

6. Milk _____ a dairy product.

   A. is   **B.** are

7. Bananas _____ a type of fruit.

   A. is   **B.** are

8. A loaf of bread _____ $2.35.

   A. is   **B.** are

9. Onions _____ a good price today.

   A. is   **B.** are

10. A pound of chicken _____ $1.29.

    A. is   **B.** are

11. Where do you eat lunch?

    A. at 12:00   **C.** a sandwich

    B. at home   **D.** in two hours

12. When does he usually shop?

    A. on Saturdays   **C.** chicken and fish

    B. at Best Food   **D.** John

13. What _____ they usually cook for breakfast?

    A. do   **C.** are

    B. does   **D.** is

14. Where _____ I get fruit?

    A. do   **C.** are

    B. does   **D.** am

15. What do we _____ for dinner?

    A. want   **C.** wanting

    B. wants   **D.** are wanting

Name: _____   **Date:** _____

READING: Read and choose the best answer.

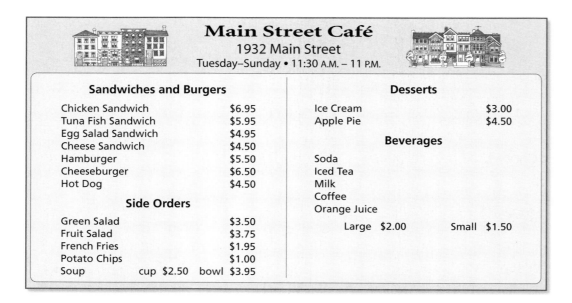

Main Street Café
1932 Main Street
Tuesday–Sunday • 11:30 A.M. – 11 P.M.

Sandwiches and Burgers

Chicken Sandwich	$6.95
Tuna Fish Sandwich	$5.95
Egg Salad Sandwich	$4.95
Cheese Sandwich	$4.50
Hamburger	$5.50
Cheeseburger	$6.50
Hot Dog	$4.50

Side Orders

Green Salad	$3.50
Fruit Salad	$3.75
French Fries	$1.95
Potato Chips	$1.00
Soup	cup $2.50 bowl $3.95

Desserts

Ice Cream	$3.00
Apple Pie	$4.50

Beverages

Soda
Iced Tea
Milk
Coffee
Orange Juice

Large $2.00   Small $1.50

16. When does the restaurant open?
   A. At 11:00 A.M.   **C.** At 11:00 P.M.
   B. At 11:30 A.M.   **D.** At 11:30 P.M.

17. How many desserts are there?
   A. one   **C.** three
   B. two   **D.** four

18. How much is a hamburger and chips?
   A. $5.50   **C.** $7.50
   B. $7.45   **D.** $6.50

19. How much is a bowl of soup and a large soda?
   A. $4.50   **C.** $5.50
   B. $5.95   **D.** $4.00

20. How many beverages are there?
   A. 3   **C.** 5
   B. 4   **D.** 6

VOCABULARY: Choose the best word to complete the sentence.

21. Do you drink _____ for breakfast?
   A. fish   **C.** juice
   B. oranges   **D.** bread

22. I eat _____ every day.
   A. rice   **C.** soda
   B. pound   **D.** bottle

23. We need milk— one _____ or two?
   A. bag   **C.** pound
   B. carton   **D.** box

24. _____ are vegetables.
   A. carrots   **C.** ice cream
   B. bananas   **D.** eggs

25. They need two _____ of chicken.
   A. loaves   **C.** pounds
   B. boxes   **D.** bottles

Name: _____   Date: _____

🎧 **LISTENING:** Listen to the conversation. Then choose the correct answer for each sentence.

1. What job does she want?
   A. an office assistant   C. an office manager
   B. a computer   D. a copier
      programmer

2. What can she do?
   A. supervise other   C. fix a copier
      workers
   B. use a computer   D. fix a computer
      and a scanner

3. What is one thing she can't do?
   A. supervise other   C. fix a copier
      workers
   B. use a computer   D. fix a computer
      and a scanner

LISTEN to the sentences. Choose the best response.

4.
   A. I was a cook.   C. ordered supplies
   B. fix a copier   D. I can't speak Chinese.

5.
   A. a dentist   C. at the supermarket
   B. I can fix trucks.   D. supervised other
                               workers

GRAMMAR: Choose the best answer.

6. She _____ _____ a computer.
   A. can/use   C. cans/use
   B. can/uses   D. can/using

7. They _____ _____ English.
   A. can/speaks   C. speaks/can
   B. can't/speak   D. can/speaking

8. _____ you _____ the TV?
   A. Fix/can   C. Can/fix
   B. Can/fixed   D. Can't/fixing

9. _____ he _____?
   A. Can/swim   C. Can/swims
   B. Swim/can   D. Can't/swims

10. I _____ school supplies yesterday.
    A. order   C. did ordered
    B. ordering   D. ordered

11. They _____ to work at 9:00 last night.
    A. went   C. did go
    B. go   D. are going

12. Luis _____ for two hours last week.
    A. studies   C. study
    B. is studying   D. studied

13. Mary and I _____ the house for five hours last Saturday.
    A. clean   C. cleaned
    B. cleans   D. cleaner

14. Teresa and Lila _____ their homework last night.
    A. don't finish   C. can't finish
    B. doesn't finish   D. didn't finish

15. You _____ me yesterday.
    A. don't call   C. did not called
    B. didn't call   D. not called

Name: _____   **Date:** _____

READING: Read and choose the best answer.

Job Application	
Name: Pedro Martinez	**Position wanted:** Construction supervisor
Address: 1913 South Pine Street Oakton, IL	**Hours available:**

S	M	T	W	R	F	S
	8-5	8-5	8-5	8-5	8-5	

Skills: can use tools, can drive a forklift, can speak Spanish and English

WORK EXPERIENCE

Present or last position: construction worker

Employer: McAdams construction

Responsibilities: I helped build new houses, checked supply orders, and worked with other people.

16. What job does Pedro want?
   A. construction supervisor
   B. construction worker
   C. McAdams Construction
   D. employer

17. How many days does he want to work?
   A. one
   B. two
   C. four
   D. five

18. What can he do?
   A. drive a forklift
   B. take measurements
   C. fix toilets
   D. speak Chinese

19. What did he do in his last job?
   A. delivered building supplies
   B. checked supply orders
   C. cleaned buildings
   D. fixed forklifts

20. When does Pedro want to start work?
   A. at 7:00
   B. at 8:00
   C. at 9:00
   D. at 5:00

VOCABULARY: Choose the best word to complete the sentence.

21. I can fix a water fountain. I am _____.
   A. an electrician
   B. an accountant
   C. a mechanic
   D. a plumber

22. Ellen can fix trucks. She is _____.
   A. an electrician
   B. an accountant
   C. a mechanic
   D. a plumber

23. You are a nurse? Can you _____?
   A. fix wiring
   B. use a calculator
   C. take my temperature
   D. cook dinner

24. The store _____ at 10:00 It closed at 8:00.
   A. delivered
   B. ordered
   C. opened
   D. finished

25. We _____ money from the bank. Now we can buy a new house.
   A. ordered
   B. borrowed
   C. painted
   D. made

Name: _____   **Date:** _____

🎧 **LISTENING:** Listen to the conversation. Then choose the correct answer for each sentence.

1. Where did he go?
   - **A.** the beach
   - **B.** the mountains
   - **C.** the lake
   - **D.** an amusement park

2. How was the weather?
   - **A.** sunny and hot
   - **B.** cool and cloudy
   - **C.** sunny and cool
   - **D.** warm and sunny

3. How did he get there?
   - **A.** by car
   - **B.** by bus
   - **C.** by train
   - **D.** by plane

LISTEN to the sentences. Choose the best response.

4.
   - **A.** warm and sunny
   - **B.** You missed a meeting.
   - **C.** I'm sorry. The train was slow.
   - **D.** You were on the bus.

5.
   - **A.** Please call next time.
   - **B.** It was great.
   - **C.** We were in Mexico.
   - **D.** How was it?

GRAMMAR: Choose the best answer.

6. I _____ sick last week. I didn't come to school.
   - **A.** was
   - **B.** wasn't
   - **C.** weren't
   - **D.** were

7. We _____ late today. The bus was slow.
   - **A.** was
   - **B.** wasn't
   - **C.** weren't
   - **D.** were

8. Matt and Cindy _____ funny at the party last night. They laughed a lot.
   - **A.** was
   - **B.** wasn't
   - **C.** weren't
   - **D.** were

9. Susan _____ at work last night. She stayed home.
   - **A.** was
   - **B.** wasn't
   - **C.** weren't
   - **D.** were

10. You _____ back on time. You were late.
   - **A.** was
   - **B.** wasn't
   - **C.** weren't
   - **D.** were

11. _____ Greg on time yesterday?
   - **A.** Was
   - **B.** Were

12. _____ they at the movies last night?
   - **A.** Was
   - **B.** Were

13. Were you in school yesterday? Yes, I _____.
   - **A.** was
   - **B.** wasn't
   - **C.** were
   - **D.** weren't

14. Was Lisa late to work? No, she _____.
   - **A.** was
   - **B.** wasn't
   - **C.** were
   - **D.** weren't

15. Were you in Mexico last year? No, we _____.
   - **A.** was
   - **B.** wasn't
   - **C.** were
   - **D.** weren't

Name: _____   **Date:** _____

READING: Read and choose the best answer.

16. This ad is for the beach.

   A. A   C. C

   B. B

17. This ad is for the lake.

   A. A   C. C

   B. B

18. This ad is for a place in Brevard.

   A. A   C. C

   B. B

19. Call (800) 555-7722.

   A. A   C. C

   B. B

20. Some rooms are $89 a night.

   A. A   C. C

   B. B

VOCABULARY: Choose the best word to complete the sentence.

21. The school was closed yesterday. It was _____.

   A. empty   C. early

   B. crowded   D. slow

22. My car isn't slow. It's _____.

   A. crowded   C. fast

   B. early   D. pretty

23. I don't like tests. They are very _____.

   A. relaxing   C. fun

   B. stressful   D. interesting

24. We went to the beach on a vacation. It was _____.

   A. late   C. scary

   B. stressful   D. relaxing

25. The train is coming. Let's wait on the _____.

   A. platform   C. counter

   B. baggage claim   D. airport

Name: _____   **Date:** _____

🎧 **LISTENING:** Listen to the conversation. Then choose the correct answer for each sentence.

1. Where is he calling?
   A. school
   B. work
   C. home
   D. the doctor's office

2. What does he have?
   A. a fever and a sore throat
   B. a sore throat and a cold
   C. a sore back and a fever
   D. a sore throat and an earache

3. What should he do?
   A. go to the hospital
   B. exercise
   C. put ice on it
   D. stay in bed

LISTEN to the sentences. Choose the best response.

4.
   A. You should take a pain reliever.
   B. You should take cough medicine.
   C. You should use ear drops.
   D. You should drink liquids.

5.
   A. You should take a pain reliever.
   B. You should put ice on it.
   C. You should drink liquids.
   D. You should use ear drops.

GRAMMAR: Choose the best answer.

6. Her back _____.
   A. has
   B. have
   C. hurt
   D. hurts

7. I _____ an earache.
   A. has
   B. have
   C. hurt
   D. hurts

8. Peter _____ a cough.
   A. has
   B. have
   C. hurt
   D. hurts

9. Your head _____.
   A. has
   B. have
   C. hurt
   D. hurts

10. She _____ sick.
    A. is
    B. are
    C. has
    D. have

11. We _____ the doctor's office.
    A. should
    B. should call
    C. should to call
    D. should calls

12. I'm sick. I should _____ to work.
    A. not go
    B. should go
    C. not going
    D. not went

13. _____ she _____ a lot of food?
    A. Eat/should
    B. Should/eat
    C. Should/eats
    D. Eats/should

14. I have a fever. Should I use cough medicine?
    A. Yes, you should.
    B. No, they shouldn't.
    C. No, you shouldn't.
    D. Yes, we should.

15. Tina has a sore throat. Should she take a throat lozenge?
    A. Yes, I should.
    B. Yes, she should.
    C. No, you shouldn't.
    D. No, they shouldn't.

Name: _____   **Date:** _____

READING: Read and choose the best answer.

```
                    Patient Information Form
        CENTERVILLE FAMILY PRACTICE
                      3587 Main Street
                         565-9834
  Name:   Rodriguez, Alberto      Date of Birth:   7/5/69
  Address:         4972 Brown Street
                          Street
            Centerville,         New York      14029
               City              State       Zip Code
  Telephone:      973-1265          977-9241
                    Home              Work

  Insurance:   Excellent Health Insurance
  Policy Number:    108407      New Patient:   Yes   (No)
  Doctor's Name:   Robert Scott
  Reason for Visit:    sick
  Symptoms:   fever, aches, sore throat
```

16. What is the patient's name?

    A. Robert Scott   C. Rodriguez Albert

    B. Robert Smith   D. Alberto Rodriguez

17. Where does he live?

    A. 3587 Main Street   C. Centerville, NJ

    B. 4972 Brown Street   D. Centerville Family
                                Practice

18. What is the doctor's name?

    A. Robert Scott   C. Rodriguez Albert

    B. Robert Smith   D. Alberto Rodriguez

19. What is the problem?

    A. He has a backache.   C. He has a fever and
                                a sore throat.

    B. His head hurts.   D. His stomach hurts.

20. Which sentence is true?

    A. He has insurance.   C. He is an accountant.

    B. He doesn't have   D. He had an accident
       insurance.   at work.

VOCABULARY: Choose the best word to complete the sentence.

21. He has _____.

    A. an earache

    B. a headache

    C. a stomachache

    D. a backache

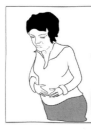

22. She has _____.

    A. an earache

    B. a headache

    C. a stomachache

    D. a backache

23. She has _____.

    A. a cold

    B. the flu

    C. a sore throat

    D. a runny nose

24. His _____ hurts.

    A. back

    B. stomach

    C. arm

    D. head

25. Her _____ hurts.

    A. neck

    B. back

    C. head

    D. leg

Name: _____   **Date:** _____

🎧 **LISTENING:** Listen to the conversations. Then choose the correct answer for each sentence.

1. What is the woman going to do?
   - A. work on the house
   - B. paint the kitchen
   - C. fix the door
   - D. go to the beach

2. She is asking him to _____.
   - A. paint the living room
   - B. fix her bathroom
   - C. go with her
   - D. go to the movies

3. What is the man NOT going to do?
   - A. paint the living room
   - B. go with her
   - C. fix the bathroom door
   - D. work on the house

LISTEN to the questions. Choose the best response.

4.
   - A. She's going to paint the kitchen.
   - B. They're going to visit some friends.
   - C. I'm going to study for a test.
   - D. You're going to go out to eat.

5.
   - A. No, we're not.
   - B. Yes, she is.
   - C. No, they're not.
   - D. Yes, he is.

GRAMMAR: Choose the best answer.

6. Jack needs my book. I'm going to give it to _____ today.
   - A. me
   - B. it
   - C. them
   - D. him

7. The kitchen needs new paint. We're going to paint _____ on Saturday.
   - A. you
   - B. him
   - C. it
   - D. us

8. The cabinets don't work. I need to fix _____.
   - A. it
   - B. them
   - C. me
   - D. us

9. We should talk to the landlord. Can you call _____?
   - A. him
   - B. you
   - C. it
   - D. me

10. Maria is going to the movies. I want to go with _____.
   - A. her
   - B. me
   - C. them
   - D. it

11. Tomorrow, I _____ buy a new refrigerator.
   - A. going to
   - B. am going to
   - C. am going
   - D. am going to buy

12. They _____ class on Friday.
   - A. going to finish
   - B. are going
   - C. are going to finish
   - D. not going to finish

13. _____ she _____ work tomorrow?
   - A. Are/going
   - B. Is/going
   - C. Does/going to
   - D. Is/going to

14. _____ we _____ James and Linda?
   - A. Are/going to help
   - B. Are/going to
   - C. Are going/help
   - D. Are/not going

15. Is it going to rain tomorrow?
   - A. Yes, I am.
   - B. Yes, it is.
   - C. No, we aren't.
   - D. No, he isn't.

Name: _____   **Date:** _____

READING: Read Linda's calendar and choose the best answer.

Sunday	Monday	Tuesday	Wednesday	Thursday	Friday	Saturday
11th Family party	12th Call landlord (Ms. Smith)	13th	14th Finish Class	15th	16th	17th Get married!
18th Honeymoon	19th	20th	21st	22nd	23rd	24th Jim's friends help us move

MAY

16. What is Linda going to do on May 12?
   A. Go to a family party.   C. Finish class.
   B. Call the landlord.   D. Get married.

17. When are Linda and James going to be on their honeymoon?
   A. 5/16-5/23   C. 5/18-5/22
   B. May 18th - May 24th   D. May 11-May 24

18. When are they going to move?
   A. 5/14   C. 5/23
   B. 5/16   D. 5/24

19. What are they going to do on May 17th?
   A. Go on their honeymoon   C. Pack
   B. Get married   D. Move

20. On what day is Linda going to finish class?
   A. Monday   C. Wednesday
   B. Tuesday   D. Friday

VOCABULARY: Choose the best word to complete the sentence.

21. The toilet is not working. There's water on the floor in the _____.
   A. living room   C. bedroom
   B. kitchen   D. bathroom

22. Henry has a new car. He is going to _____ his old car.
   A. buy   C. rent
   B. sell   D. borrow

23. Grace has a new job in Miami. She is going to _____ to Miami next month.
   A. move   C. sell
   B. finish   D. work

24. Laura is sleeping in the _____.
   A. dining room   C. bedroom
   B. kitchen   D. bathroom

25. We have a new _____ in the bedroom.
   A. dresser   C. refrigerator
   B. microwave   D. dishwasher

Unit 1

1. C; 2. D; 3. C; 4. B; 5. A; 6. A; 7. C; 8. D; 9. D;
10. A; 11. A; 12. C; 13. C; 14. D; 15. A; 16. D; B
17. C; 18. C; 19. B; 20. A; 21. C; 22. C; 23. B;
24. C; 25. C

Unit 2

1. D; 2. B; 3. C; 4. C; 5. B; 6. C; 7. C; 8. D; 9. B;
10. B; 11. D; 12. B; 13. C; 14. C; 15. A; 16. B;
17. B; 18. A; 19. A; 20. B; 21. D; 22. B; 23. A;
24. D; 25. B

Unit 3

1. D; 2. B; 3. A; 4. D; 5. A; 6. B; 7. C; 8. A; 9. D;
10. C; 11. B; 12. A; 13. C; 14. B; 15 A; 16. C;
17. B; 18. B; 19. C; 20. D; 21. C; 22. B; 23. B;
24. C; 25. B

Unit 4

1. A; 2. B; 3. D; 4. A; 5. C; 6. B; 7. A; 8. B; 9. B;
10. C; 11. C; 12. A; 13. B; 14. B; 15. B; 16. B;
17. A; 18. D; 19. A; 20. D; 21. C; 22. A; 23. C;
24. B; 25. D

Unit 5

1. C; 2. C; 3. B; 4. A; 5. C; 6. B; 7. A; 8. D; 9. B;
10. A; 11. B; 12. A; 13. C; 14. A; 15. B; 16. A;
17. C; 18. D; 19. A; 20. B; 21. D; 22. A; 23. C;
24. B; 25. D

Unit 6

1. C; 2. A; 3. A; 4. A; 5. D; 6. C; 7. B; 8. A; 9. C;
10. D; 11. C; 12. C; 13. A; 14. A; 15. B; 16. B;
17. C; 18. C; 19. D; 20. B; 21. D; 22. A; 23. C;
24. A; 25. D

Unit 7

1. C; 2. B; 3. D; 4. A; 5. B; 6. A; 7. B; 8. A; 9. B;
10. B; 11. A; 12. A; 13. B; 14. A; 15. B; 16. B;
17. B; 18. D; 19. A; 20. C; 21. D; 22. B; 23. D;
24. C; 25. A

Unit 8

1. D; 2. D; 3. B; 4. B; 5. D; 6. A; 7. B; 8. A; 9. B;
10. A; 11. B; 12. A; 13. A; 14. A; 15. A; 16. B;
17. B; 18. D; 19. B; 20. C; 21. C; 22. A; 23. B;
24. A; 25. C

Unit 9

1. C; 2. B; 3. C; 4. A; 5. D; 6. A; 7. B; 8. C; 9. A;
10. D; 11. A; 12. D; 13. C; 14. D; 15. B; 16. A;
17. D; 18. A; 19. B; 20. B; 21. D; 22. C; 23. C;
24. C; 25. B

Unit 10

1. C; 2. D; 3. B; 4. C; 5. A; 6. A; 7. D; 8. D; 9. B;
10. C; 11. A; 12. B; 13. A; 14. B; 15. D; 16. B;
17. C; 18. A; 19. C; 20. A; 21. A; 22. C; 23. B;
24. D; 25. A

Unit 11

1. B; 2. A; 3. D; 4. A; 5. C; 6. D; 7. B; 8. A; 9. D;
10. A; 11. B; 12. A; 13. B; 14. C; 15. B; 16. D;
17. B; 18. A; 19. C; 20. A; 21. D; 22. C; 23. C;
24. D; 25. A

Unit 12

1. D; 2. C; 3. B; 4. C; 5. A; 6. D; 7. C; 8. B; 9. A;
10. A; 11. B; 12. C; 13. D; 14. A; 15. B; 16. B;
17. C; 18. D; 19. B; 20. C; 21. D; 22. B; 23. A;
24. C; 25. A

Unit 1

LISTENING: Listen to the conversation. Then choose the correct answer for each sentence.

Male:	What's your full name?
Female:	Mary Cooper.
Male:	What's your address?
Female:	20 Oak Street.
Male:	What's your occupation?
Female:	I'm a server.

1. What's the woman's name?
2. What is her occupation?
3. What is her address?

LISTEN to the sentences. Choose the best response.

4. Hi. My name's Ann. It's nice to meet you.
5. What's your address?

Unit 2

LISTENING: Listen to the conversation. Then choose the correct answer for each sentence.

Male voice:	Hi. Is Anna there?
Female voice:	No, I'm sorry. She's not. Can I take a message?
Male:	Sure. This is her cousin Bob. My number is 555-8825.
Female:	555-8825?
Male:	That's right. Thanks.

1. What is the phone number?
2. What's the man's name?
3. Who is he?

LISTEN to the sentences. Choose the best response.

4. Excuse me, are you Alex?
5. Is your sister tall?

Unit 3

LISTENING: Listen to the conversation. Then choose the correct answer for each sentence.

Male voice:	Excuse me. Where's the computer lab?
Female voice:	It's in the Bryant Center.
Male	In the Bryant Center?
Female:	Yes. On the second floor. In room 205.
Male:	Thanks.

1. The _____ is in the Bryant Center.
2. It's on the _____ floor.
3. It's in room _____.

LISTEN to the sentences. Choose the best response.

4. Where's the snack bar?
5. How many desks are there?

Unit 4

LISTENING: Listen to the conversation. Then choose the correct answer for each sentence.

Male:	How's the weather in London?
Female:	It's cool. It's 50 degrees. How's the weather in New York?
Male:	It's hot and humid. It's 90 degrees.

1. The weather in London is _____.
2. The temperature is _____ degrees.
3. The weather in New York is _____.

LISTEN to the sentences. Choose the best response.

4. Excuse me. When is Labor Day?
5. What time is it?

Unit 5

LISTENING: Listen to the conversation. Then choose the correct answer for each sentence.

Male: Excuse me. How do I get to the Community Center?

Female: Turn left on Main Street. It's next to the police station.

Male: How far is it?

Female: About three blocks.

Male: Thanks.

1. Where is he going?

2. How far is it?

3. How does he get there?

LISTEN to the sentences. Choose the best response.

4. Excuse me. Where's the bank?

5. Is the Community Center on South Street?

Unit 6

LISTENING: Listen to the conversation. Then choose the correct answer for each sentence.

A: Hello. Can I help you?

B: Yes, I'm looking for a skirt.

A: What color?

B: Blue.

A: What size?

B: Small.

A: Okay. The blue skirts are over there.

B: Thank you!

1. What is she looking for?

2. What color is she looking for?

3. What size?

LISTEN to the sentences. Choose the best response.

4. Hello. Welcome to Clothes Corner. Can I help you?

5. How much are these black pants?

Unit 7

LISTENING: Listen to the conversation. Then choose the correct answer for each sentence.

Male: What's wrong?

Female: Registration for classes is on Thursday morning. I work on Thursday mornings.

Male: What about James? Could he work for you?

Female: Good idea.

1. Registration is _____.

2. She _____ at that time.

3. He asks about _____.

LISTEN to the sentences. Choose the best response.

4. When do you usually get up?

5. Does he work every day?

Unit 8

LISTENING: Listen to the conversation. Then choose the correct answer for each sentence.

Female: Hi. My name is Marina. What would you like today?

Male: I'd like a hamburger and a salad, please.

Female: Do you want French fries with that?

Male: No, thank you.

Female: And to drink?

Male: I'll have milk.

Female: What size?

Male: A large.

1. What is he ordering to eat?

2. What does he want to drink?

3. What side order is he getting?

LISTEN to the sentences. Choose the best response.

4. What size drink do you want?

5. Where is the cereal?

Unit 9

LISTENING: Listen to the conversation. Then choose the correct answer for each sentence.

Male: What job are you looking for?

Female: A job as an office manager.

Male: Can you use a computer?

Female: Yes. I can use a scanner, too.

Male: Can you fix a copier?

Female: No, I can't.

Male: Too bad.

1. What job does she want?
2. What can she do?
3. What is one thing she can't do?

LISTEN to the sentences. Choose the best response.

4. What was your last job?
5. What did you do in your last job?

Unit 10

LISTENING: Listen to the conversation. Then choose the correct answer for each sentence.

Female: How was your vacation?

Male: Wonderful! It was sunny and warm.

Female: Where did you go?

Male: To the lake.

Female: How did you get there?

Male: By bus. It was fast and clean.

1. Where did he go?
2. How was the weather?
3. How did he get there?

LISTEN to the sentences. Choose the best response.

4. You're late. What happened?
5. I'm really sorry I wasn't here.

Unit 11

LISTENING: Listen to the conversation. Then choose the correct answer for each sentence.

Female: Hello?

Male: Hi, this is Tony. I'm sick. I can't come to work today.

Female: What's wrong?

Male: I have a sore throat and a fever.

Female: That's too bad. You should stay in bed.

Male: Good idea.

1. Where is he calling?
2. What does he have?
3. What should he do?

LISTEN to the sentences. Choose the best response.

4. I have a backache.
5. I have a cold.

Unit 12

LISTENING: Listen to the conversation. Then choose the correct answer for each sentence.

Female: I'm going to the beach tomorrow. Do you want to come?

Male: Sorry, I can't. I'm going to work on the house.

Female: Really? What are you going to do?

Male: Paint the living room and fix the bathroom door.

Female: Okay. Maybe next time?

Male: Sure. Thanks.

1. What is the woman going to do?
2. She is asking him to _____.
3. What is the man NOT going to do?

LISTEN to the questions. Choose the best response.

4. What are you going to do this weekend?
5. Are you going to meet us at the movies?